Psallite

Sacred Song for Liturgy and Life

Cantor / Choir Edition

Music by
The Collegeville Composers Group

LITURGICAL PRESS
Collegeville, Minnesota

www.litpress.org
800.858.5450

ACKNOWLEDGMENTS

Imprimatur: ✠ Most Reverend John F. Kinney, Diocese of Saint Cloud in Minnesota, May 29, 2007.

Music from *Psallite: Sacred Song for Liturgy and Life,* © 2005, 2006, 2007, 2008 by The Collegeville Composers Group (Carol Browning, Catherine Christmas, Cyprian Consiglio, O.S.B. Cam., Paul F. Ford, Ph.D., Paul Inwood). Published and administered by Liturgical Press, Collegeville, Minnesota 56321. All rights reserved.

The Psalm texts from The Grail (England), © 1963, 1986, 1993, 2000, The Grail. The Canticle texts from the Grail (England), © 1967, The Grail. All rights reserved. Licensed for *Psallite* and reprinted by permission of GIA Publications, Inc., 7404 South Mason Avenue, Chicago, IL 60638, North American agent for The Grail. *Imprimatur:* ✠ Most Reverend William Keeler, President, National Conference of Catholic Bishops, September 12, 1993.

The Canticle texts from the New Revised Standard Version (NRSV) Bible, © 1989, Division of Christian Education of the National Council of the Churches of Christ in the United States of America. All rights reserved. Used with permission. *Imprimatur:* ✠ Most Reverend Daniel E. Pilarczyk, President, National Conference of Catholic Bishops, September 12, 1991.

The cover design is by James Rhoades; photograph by Rob Fiocca, Botanica Images.

ISBN: 978-0-8146-3088-4

Contents

About This Edition

Welcome to this cantor/choir edition of the *Psallite* collection for Sundays, solemnities, and major feast days!

Within these pages you will find all the vocal and choral lines for every *Psallite* title in the complete three-year Lectionary cycle. (Music directors and accompanists on keyboard or guitar will continue to need the full accompaniment editions for each of the three years.)

In order to make the music as accessible as possible to cantors and choir members, the psalm and canticle texts have been interlined with the music throughout. With a few of the superimposed verse tones, we have written out new approximate metrical equivalents to assist the singer; in most cases, however, we have retained conventional reciting notes, where the text is chanted to natural speech rhythms.

With the pointing of the psalms and canticles, we have taken the opportunity to correct some minor errors and to clarify a few instances that were not completely clear. For the antiphons, we have also taken the opportunity to introduce a small number of vocal descants that are not present in the original accompaniment editions. In these cases, therefore, the present edition is more up-to-date than the originals. In the Performance Notes we have also noted one or two errors in the current US Lectionary.

Pages vi–viii contain some general introductory notes for the *Psallite* collection, but some extra points here may be helpful for singers:

(a) When chanting superimposed verses over an antiphon, it is always a good idea to establish the antiphon firmly by singing it through several times with the assembly before adding the verses.

(b) When chanting superimposed verses over an antiphon, it is not always necessary to sing the antiphon text under the verses. Sometimes this will work well; sometimes it may prove better to hum the antiphon or vocalize quietly to a neutral vowel under the verses. Both possibilities are demonstrated on the recordings *Where Two or Three Are Gathered* (Year A), *Walk in My Ways* (Year B), and *We Will Follow You, Lord* (Year C).

(c) For reciting notes in superimposed tones, it has generally not proved feasible to indicate graphically the exact positioning of words and syllables, particularly "pick-up" words and syllables linking one psalm line to another. Singers are encouraged to use their common sense and their feeling for natural speech rhythms. Avoid a stilted chanting of the texts. Once again, the recordings are helpful for demonstration purposes. See also under (h) below.

(d) For the Song for the Word, which may act as the Responsorial Psalm for the day, the Lectionary selections of verses are always listed in the Performance Notes at the end of each song. Frequently additional verses are provided; normally this will be because the same item is used elsewhere as a Song for the Week or a Song for the Table, but on particular occasions musicians might decide to include an additional verse or two in the Song for the Word.

(e) When more than one option is provided for an antiphon, or where an antiphon has more than one text, these have been numbered I and II, with clear indications when to use each option. Similarly, options for psalm and canticle verses are lettered A, B, etc.

(f) The Performance Notes also provide other useful information and should always be consulted beforehand.

(g) New SATB harmonizations have been provided for many antiphons and verses, but these do not always have to be used; as in the original editions, all antiphons and verses will work with a single voice or unison voices. The harmonizations have been designed to fit with the existing keyboard accompaniments, but they also work for *a cappella* singing, which is actually the foundation of the entire project.

On some occasions it may be preferable to sing some low bass notes an octave higher. Similarly, low alto parts can be taken by tenors, and high tenor parts can be taken by altos. Descants can also be sung by equal voices, and generally the indications for voices are not sacrosanct! The vocal harmonies can also be played by instruments when singers are not available. Users should feel free to adapt the settings to the resources available, while not forgetting that this music has been designed to be "essentially vocal."

(h) Despite the presence of many SATB harmonizations for the verses, choirs should beware! It is always much easier to comprehend chanted text when sung by a single voice (cantor) than when sung by an SATB choir—and it is the text that is of paramount importance. When using SATB voices to chant psalm verses, therefore, good choral blend (best achieved by eliminating vibrato in the voices) and especially good choral synchronization will be essential. It is better to use a simpler rendition than to obscure the text. So, for example, if there are a number of verses to be sung, consider having one or more solo cantors taking most of them, reserving SATB harmonies for one or two. (This would also have the advantage of saving on rehearsal time!) The psalm or canticle text itself will often suggest the best treatment.

At number 296 in the back of this book, you will find a Liturgical Use Index. This index will assist you in determining the detailed usage of each title, both as regards the liturgical day and the intended point during the Eucharist. However, most of the titles can be used for other occasions, as part of a general parish (or school/seminary/monastery) repertoire. This edition also includes comprehensive topical and liturgical indices, as well as complete biblical indices of antiphons and psalms/canticles, for the entire three-year cycle.

We are delighted that Liturgical Press is able to offer this cantor/choir edition as an invaluable resource in making the *Psallite* project even more user-friendly.

The Collegeville Composers Group
May 2008

INTRODUCTORY NOTES

A new collection of liturgical songs inspired by the antiphons and psalms of the *Roman Missal*, *Psallite: Sacred Song for Liturgy and Life* includes music for each Sunday, Solemnity, and major feast day of the liturgical year.

For each liturgy, *Psallite* provides biblically based options for the entrance/opening song (the SONG FOR THE WEEK/DAY); the response song during the Liturgy of the Word (the SONG FOR THE WORD); and the song during the Communion procession (the SONG FOR THE TABLE). This collection contains a wealth of biblically based liturgical songs. While the music in this collection suggests specific Sundays or celebrations for its use, they have various, repeatable uses throughout the liturgical year.

The name *Psallite* (SAH-lee-tay) comes from the Latin version of Psalm 47:8, *psallite sapienter*, "sing praise with all your skill."

Psallite's music connects liturgy and life, church and home. The SONG FOR THE WEEK may be your theme tune for the entire week. The SONG FOR THE WORD may echo in your mind and keep the Word alive in your heart all day. The SONG FOR THE TABLE may be the one that you sing around your own dining table. All this is achieved by means of memorable music that will transform your life. Once this music gets under your skin, there's no turning back.

The **SONG FOR THE WEEK** opens the celebration, intensifies the unity of the assembly, leads their thoughts to the mystery of the liturgical season or festivity, and accompanies the procession of the presider and ministers. Another option is to use the SONG FOR THE WEEK at the end of the liturgy (with the addition of a doxology) to send forth the assembly into the world.

The **SONG FOR THE WORD**, an entirely new repertory of short, memorable antiphons, serves as the golden thread of the Liturgy of the Word.

The **SONG FOR THE TABLE**, which is the heart of *Psallite,* takes its texts and themes from the Liturgy of the Word, especially from the gospel of the day, transformed into processional music. People will now experience that the promises God made in his Word are fulfilled in the body and blood of Christ.

Psallite's music provides flexibility and allows leaders of music ministry to adapt the music for their assemblies. On the one hand, *Psallite* was designed for those parishes with the most limited musical resources: one well-trained cantor, no accompanist, but an assembly eager to sing the Mass. On the other hand, satisfying vocal, keyboard, and guitar arrangements will win the hearts of the most accomplished choirs and instrumentalists. Many of the descants not marked for a specific voice part may be sung in the alto/tenor range as well as the soprano range.

The style of music is eclectic—with influences ranging from chant to Afro-Caribbean to folk song but in all cases essentially vocal. The cantor calls to the assembly and the assembly responds. And every word they sing is biblically based.

The verse tones of *Psallite* can be used with any translation of the psalms, especially any Grail-based translation. Because *Psallite* models the use of moderately inclusive, horizontally inclusive language, it employs the 1993 Grail revision sponsored by the United States Conference of Catholic Bishops with the *imprimatur* of then-Bishop now Cardinal William H. Keeler, who was president at that time. The biblical canticles are mostly taken from the New Revised Standard Version, with some original translations for good measure.

Singing the antiphons and psalms of *Psallite* restores psalm-singing as our primary prayer language. Singing this kind of music helps our assemblies find their voices so that we all can sing the Mass, not just sing at Mass. Singing the same antiphons that our sisters and brothers sang at least a thousand years ago, and in some cases nearly two thousand years ago, connects us spiritually to the great communion of saints, a procession in which we are only the most recent walkers. Singing the various styles of music in *Psallite* will also help break down the cultural barriers that keep us from being "one body, one spirit, in Christ."

ABOUT THE COMPOSERS

The Collegeville Composers Group, a team of international musicians working collaboratively to create the collection, composed the music of *Psallite*. The composers group includes:

Carol Browning, the Director of Liturgy and Music at Saint Mary Magdalen Catholic Community in Camarillo, California and a music minister for almost twenty years. A member of the Religious Society of Friends (Quakers), Carol is a liturgical composer and an independently published inspirational songwriter.

Catherine Christmas, an accomplished organist and former cathedral director of music, currently working as Pastoral Coordinator for a group of parishes based in Winchester, England, and studying for a Master's in Pastoral Liturgy at Heythrop College, University of London.

Cyprian Consiglio, O.S.B. Cam., a musician, composer, author, and teacher who is a monk of the Camaldolese Congregation. He spends about half his time at home, writing and composing, and the other half of his time on the road, performing and teaching.

Paul F. Ford, Ph.D., a professor of systematic theology and liturgy, Saint John's Seminary, Camarillo, California. He is the author of *By Flowing Waters: Chant for the Liturgy,* published by Liturgical Press.

Paul Inwood, the Director of Liturgy and Director of Music for the Diocese of Portsmouth, England. He is an internationally known liturgist, composer, organist, choir director, and clinician. His liturgical music appears in numerous hymnals worldwide.

ADDITIONAL RESOURCES

Psallite: Sacred Song for Liturgy and Life

Published in three volumes, these editions include the full accompaniment and cantor/schola verses for all Sundays, Solemnities and major feast days of the liturgical cycle. Plastic coil binding, 8½" x 10⅞", over 320 pp.

Individual volumes: 1–4 copies, $24.95 each; 5 or more copies, $19.95* net each; please inquire for bulk purchases.

  978-0-8146-3064-8 Year A
  978-0-8146-3059-4 Year B
  978-0-8146-3065-5 Year C

Complete three-volume set (Years ABC): 1–4 sets, $59.95 per set; 5 or more sets, $49.95* net per set; please inquire for bulk purchases.

  978-0-8146-3060-0 Years ABC

Psallite Cantor/Choir Edition

This edition contains cantor/schola descants and harmonies for all Sundays and solemnities of the liturgical year and includes liturgical and Scriptural indices for various uses and planning. Titles are placed in alphabetical order. Single volume contains all titles in the *Psallite* collection.

  978-0-8146-3088-4

Kivar, 488 pp., 7 x 10, 1–4 copies $24.95; 5–9 copies $19.95 net; 10 or more copies $16.95* net

Psallite Antiphons on CD-ROM

Easy-to-use graphic files of all *Psallite* assembly antiphons (Years ABC) that can be used to select and insert music into desktop publishing documents, PowerPoint presentations, or other custom worship aids and programs. The parish or institution must purchase an annual reprint license in order to legally reproduce the antiphons.

  978-0-8146-7961-6 $39.95 CD-ROM
  978-0-8146-3061-7 $35.00 Annual license

Where Two or Three Are Gathered

A collection of twenty-six titles taken from *Psallite: Sacred Song for Liturgy and Life (Year A).* Titles include: Now Is the Hour • Be Patient, Beloved • Let the King of Glory Come In • Jesus, Mighty Lord, Come Save Us • Clothed in Christ, One in Christ (Rite of Baptism) • Clothed in Christ, One in Christ • Give Us Living Water • Give Thanks to the Lord, Alleluia • At Your Word Our Hearts Are Burning • I Am the Way: Follow Me • Here I Am • Light of the World • In God Alone Is My Soul at Rest • Keep These Words in Your Heart and Soul • Love Is My Desire • The Mercy of God Is for All • Everlasting Is Your Love • All Things Are from the Lord • Where Two or Three Are Gathered • Lord, You Are Close • Remember, Lord • All That Is True • I Shall Dwell in the House of the Lord • The Word of God at Work in Us • Come, All You Good and Faithful Servants • A River Flows

The music collection includes full accompaniment for cantor, schola, keyboard, and guitar plus reprintable antiphon graphics for assembly use. A CD recording of the collection is also available.

> Music collection: 978-0-8146-3077-8 • $11.95; 5 or more copies $9.95* each
> CD recording: 978-0-8146-7965-4 • $16.95

Walk in My Ways

A collection of twenty-seven titles taken from *Psallite: Sacred Song for Liturgy and Life (Year B)*. Titles include: To You, O Lord, I Lift My Soul • Rejoice in the Lord, Again, Rejoice • We Receive from Your Fullness • Here Is My Servant, Here Is My Son • Give, Your Father Sees • Those Who Love Me, I Will Deliver • My Shepherd Is the Lord • There Is Mercy in the Lord • This Is My Body • Send Out Your Spirit • Christ, Our Pasch • Live on In My Love • I Will See You Again • Walk in My Ways • *Venite, adoremus* • God Heals the Broken • Lead Me, Guide Me • Here in Your Presence • All You Nations • Don't Be Afraid • Those Who Do Justice • Let the Word Make a Home in Your Heart • I Loved Wisdom More than Health or Beauty • Courage! Get Up! • My Plans for You Are Peace • Rejoice in the Lord on This Feast of the Saints • May God Grant Us Joy of Heart

The music collection includes full accompaniment for cantor, schola, keyboard, and guitar plus reprintable antiphon graphics for assembly use. A CD recording of the collection is also available.

> Music collection: 978-0-8146-3058-7 • $11.95; 5 or more copies $9.95* each
> CD recording: 978-0-8146-7960-9 • $16.95

We Will Follow You, Lord

A collection of twenty-eight titles taken from *Psallite: Sacred Song for Liturgy and Life (Year C)*. Titles include: The Days Are Coming, Surely Coming • My Soul Rejoices in God • God's Love Is Revealed to Us • Not on Bread Alone Are We Nourished • You Are My Hiding-Place, O Lord • Lord, Cleanse My Heart, Make Me New • People of God, Flock of the Lord • A New Commandment • Joyfully You Will Draw Water • All Who Labor, Come to Me • This Day Is Holy to the Lord Our God • Love Bears All Things • Cast Out into the Deep • Forgive, and You Will Be Forgiven • Speak Your Word, O Lord, and We Shall Be Healed • For You My Soul Is Thirsting, O God, My God • We Will Follow You, Lord • Listen: I Stand at the Door and Knock • Do Not Store Up Earthly Treasures • From the East and West, from the North and South • In Every Age, O Lord, You Have Been Our Refuge • I Am Your Savior, My People • Seek the Lord! Long for the Lord! • Take Hold of Eternal Life • Worthy Is the Lamb Who Was Slain • Let Us Go Rejoicing to the House of the Lord • I Will Praise You, I Will Thank You • I Will Dwell with You, My House a House of Prayer

The music collection includes full accompaniment for cantor, schola, keyboard, and guitar plus reprintable antiphon graphics for assembly use. A CD recording of the collection is also available.

> Music collection: 978-0-8146-3075-4 • $11.95; 5 or more copies $9.95* each
> CD recording: 978-0-8146-7964-7 • $16.95

To order or for further information contact:

Liturgical Press • www.litpress.org • 800.858.5450

*Asterisk indicates discount price available only on "no-returns" basis.

Antiphon ♩ = 69

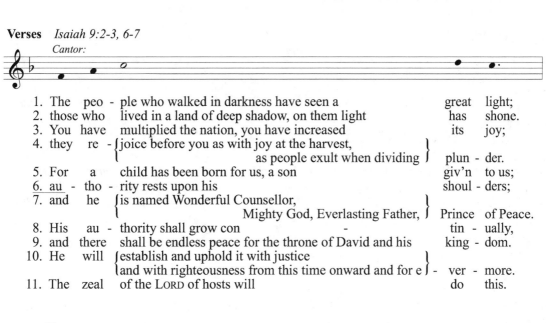

A light will shine on us this day: the Lord is born for us.

Verses *Isaiah 9:2-3, 6-7*

Cantor:

1. The peo - ple who walked in darkness have seen a   great   light;
2. those who   lived in a land of deep shadow, on them light   has   shone.
3. You have   multiplied the nation, you have increased   its   joy;
4. they re - {joice before you as with joy at the harvest,
                     as people exult when dividing }   plun - der.
5. For a   child has been born for us, a son   giv'n   to us;
6. au - tho - rity rests upon his   shoul - ders;
7. and he {is named Wonderful Counsellor,
                     Mighty God, Everlasting Father, } Prince of Peace.
8. His au - thority shall grow con -   tin - ually,
9. and there   shall be endless peace for the throne of David and his   king - dom.
10. He will {establish and uphold it with justice
               and with righteousness from this time onward and for e } - ver - more.
11. The zeal   of the Lᴏʀᴅ of hosts will   do   this.

All:

The Lord is born for us.

A New Commandment I Give to You

Antiphon / Melody ♩ = 72

A new com-mand-ment I give to you, that you

Verses (*Option A) (Superimposed)   *cf. Matthew 20:21, 24; John 13:5, 8, 15, 14, 35, 34; 1 Corinthians 13:13*

A
1. Christ heard the Twelve dis-put-ing a-bout the high-est seat; he
2. I set you an ex-am-ple of what you ought to do, since
3. I give a new com-mand-ment to those I choose and send: that

Verses (*Option B) (Superimposed)   *cf. Revelation 21:2-4, 6; John 13:34; 1 Corinthians 13:13*

B
1. I saw the ho-ly ci-ty, the new Je-ru-sa-lem
2. And God will wipe their tears, and death will be no more,
3. I give a new com-mand-ment to those I choose and send: that

love one an-o-ther as I have loved you. A

A
1. took a bowl of wa-ter, and knelt to wash their feet. He
2. I, your Lord and Mas-ter, have wash'd your feet for you. By
3. you should love each o-ther as I have, to the end. So

B
1. com-ing down from hea-ven as love-ly as a bride. I
2. cry-ing, pain and mourn-ing, these things have passed a-way.
3. you should love each o-ther as I have, to the end. So

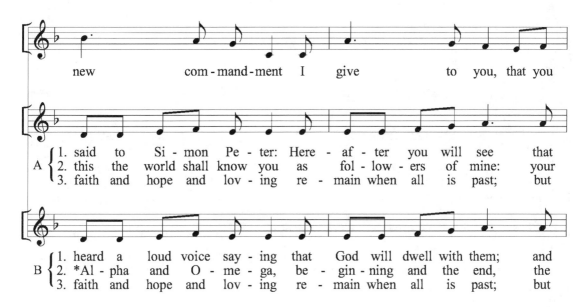

new   com - mand - ment   I   give   to   you, that you

A {
1. said   to   Si - mon Pe - ter: Here - af - ter you   will   see   that
2. this   the   world shall know you as   fol - low - ers of   mine: your
3. faith   and   hope and   lov - ing   re - main when all   is   past;   but

B {
1. heard   a   loud voice say - ing   that   God will dwell with them;   and
2. *Al - pha   and   O - me - ga,   be - gin - ning and   the   end,   the
3. faith   and   hope and   lov - ing   re - main when all   is   past;   but

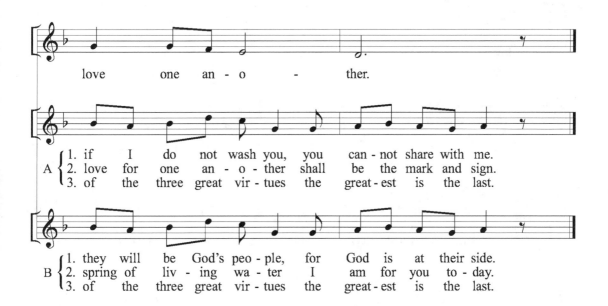

love   one   an - o -   ther.

A {
1. if   I   do   not wash you,   you   can - not share with me.
2. love   for   one   an - o - ther shall   be   the mark and sign.
3. of   the three great vir - tues the   great - est   is   the last.

B {
1. they   will be   God's peo - ple,   for   God   is   at   their side.
2. spring of   liv - ing wa - ter   I   am   for you   to - day.
3. of   the three great vir - tues the   great - est   is   the last.

Performance Notes

Option A verses are used on Holy Thursday of the Easter Triduum. Option B verses are used on the solemnity of the Sacred Heart, Year A, and the Fifth Sunday of Easter, Year C.

In verse 2 of the Option B verses, if you are used to pronouncing "Omega" with the stress on the first and not the second syllable – you should sing "Omega and Alpha."

3

A River Flows

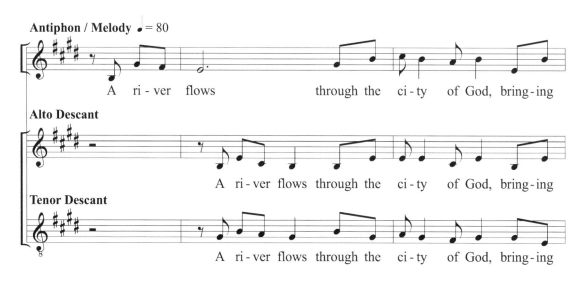

Antiphon / Melody ♩ = 80

A ri-ver flows through the ci-ty of God, bring-ing

Alto Descant

A ri-ver flows through the ci-ty of God, bring-ing

Tenor Descant

A ri-ver flows through the ci-ty of God, bring-ing

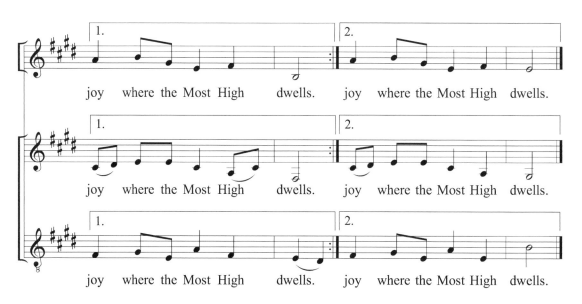

1. joy where the Most High dwells.
2. joy where the Most High dwells.

1. joy where the Most High dwells.
2. joy where the Most High dwells.

1. joy where the Most High dwells.
2. joy where the Most High dwells.

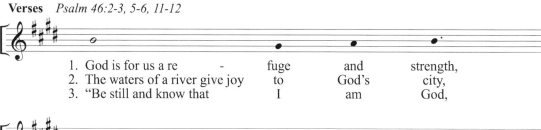

Verses *Psalm 46:2-3, 5-6, 11-12*

1. God is for us a re - fuge and strength,
2. The waters of a river give joy to God's city,
3. "Be still and know that I am God,

1. a helper close at hand, in time of dis - tress,
2. the holy place where the Most High dwells.
3. supreme among the nations, supreme on the earth!"

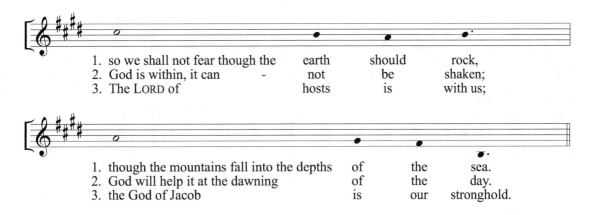

1. so we shall not fear though the earth should rock,
2. God is within, it can - not be shaken;
3. The LORD of hosts is with us;

1. though the mountains fall into the depths of the sea.
2. God will help it at the dawning of the day.
3. the God of Jacob is our stronghold.

A Woman Clothed with the Sun

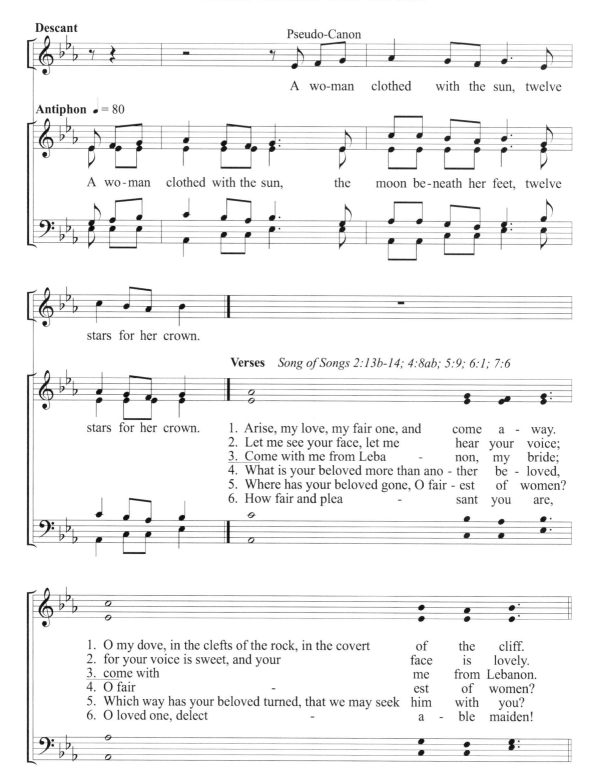

Descant

Pseudo-Canon

A wo-man clothed with the sun, twelve

Antiphon ♩ = 80

A wo-man clothed with the sun, the moon be-neath her feet, twelve

stars for her crown.

Verses *Song of Songs 2:13b-14; 4:8ab; 5:9; 6:1; 7:6*

stars for her crown.

1. Arise, my love, my fair one, and come a - way.
2. Let me see your face, let me hear your voice;
3. Come with me from Leba - non, my bride;
4. What is your beloved more than ano - ther be - loved,
5. Where has your beloved gone, O fair - est of women?
6. How fair and plea - sant you are,

1. O my dove, in the clefts of the rock, in the covert of the cliff.
2. for your voice is sweet, and your face is lovely.
3. come with me from Lebanon.
4. O fair - est of women?
5. Which way has your beloved turned, that we may seek him with you?
6. O loved one, delect - a - ble maiden!

Verses *Psalm 122*

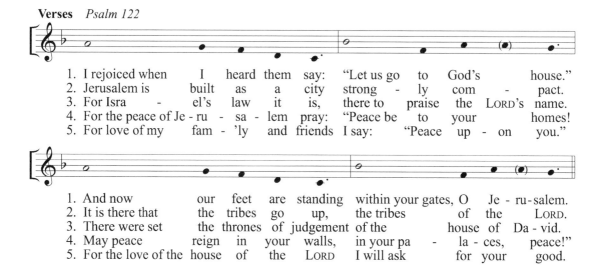

1. I rejoiced when I heard them say: "Let us go to God's house."
2. Jerusalem is built as a city strong - ly com - pact.
3. For Isra - el's law it is, there to praise the LORD's name.
4. For the peace of Je - ru - sa - lem pray: "Peace be to your homes!
5. For love of my fam - 'ly and friends I say: "Peace up - on you."

1. And now our feet are standing within your gates, O Je - ru-salem.
2. It is there that the tribes go up, the tribes of the LORD.
3. There were set the thrones of judgement of the house of Da - vid.
4. May peace reign in your walls, in your pa - la - ces, peace!"
5. For the love of the house of the LORD I will ask for your good.

Performance Notes

The antiphon may be sung as suggested with the cantor leading and the assembly responding to each phrase. Another option is to divide the assembly into two groups, with one group leading and the other responding (women in one group, men in the other or right side of the church in one group, left side in the other).

The antiphon melody is the old English folk melody "O Waly, Waly."

Antiphon ♩ = ca. 120

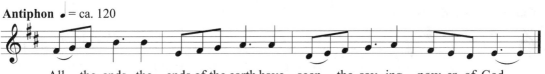

All the ends, the ends of the earth have seen the sav-ing pow-er of God.

Verses *Psalm 98*

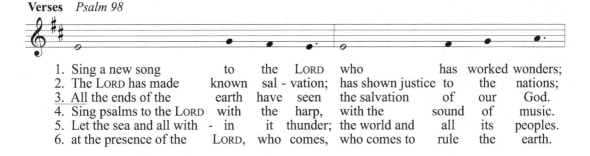

1. Sing a new song to the LORD who has worked wonders;
2. The LORD has made known sal - vation; has shown justice to the nations;
3. All the ends of the earth have seen the salvation of our God.
4. Sing psalms to the LORD with the harp, with the sound of music.
5. Let the sea and all with - in it thunder; the world and all its peoples.
6. at the presence of the LORD, who comes, who comes to rule the earth.

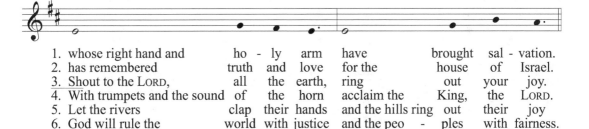

1. whose right hand and ho - ly arm have brought sal - vation.
2. has remembered truth and love for the house of Israel.
3. Shout to the LORD, all the earth, ring out your joy.
4. With trumpets and the sound of the horn acclaim the King, the LORD.
5. Let the rivers clap their hands and the hills ring out their joy
6. God will rule the world with justice and the peo - ples with fairness.

Performance Notes

Verses 1–4 are the Lectionary selections for Christmas.
Verses 1–3 are the Lectionary selections for the Sixth Sunday of Easter, Year B, and the Twenty-eighth Sunday in Ordinary Time, Year C.
The antiphon may be sung twice through each time.

All Things Are from the Lord

Verses   *Psalm 104:1-2a, 13-15, 27-28, 29b-34*

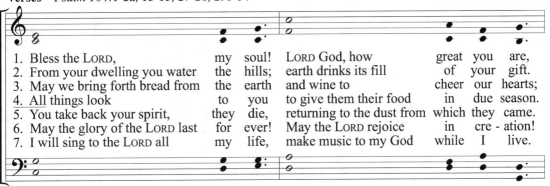

1. Bless the LORD, my soul! LORD God, how great you are,
2. From your dwelling you water the hills; earth drinks its fill of your gift.
3. May we bring forth bread from the earth and wine to cheer our hearts;
4. All things look to you to give them their food in due season.
5. You take back your spirit, they die, returning to the dust from which they came.
6. May the glory of the LORD last for ever! May the LORD rejoice in cre - ation!
7. I will sing to the LORD all my life, make music to my God while I live.

1. clothed in majesty and glory, wrapped in light as in a robe!
2. You make the grass grow for the cattle and the plants to serve our needs.
3. oil to make our fac - es shine and bread to strength - en our hearts.
4. You give it, they gather it up; you open your hand, they have their fill.
5. You send forth your spirit, they are cre - ated; and you renew the face of the earth.
6. God looks on the earth and it trembles; {at God's touch,
   the mountains} send forth smoke.
7. May my thoughts be pleasing to God. I find my joy in the LORD.

All Who Labor, Come to Me

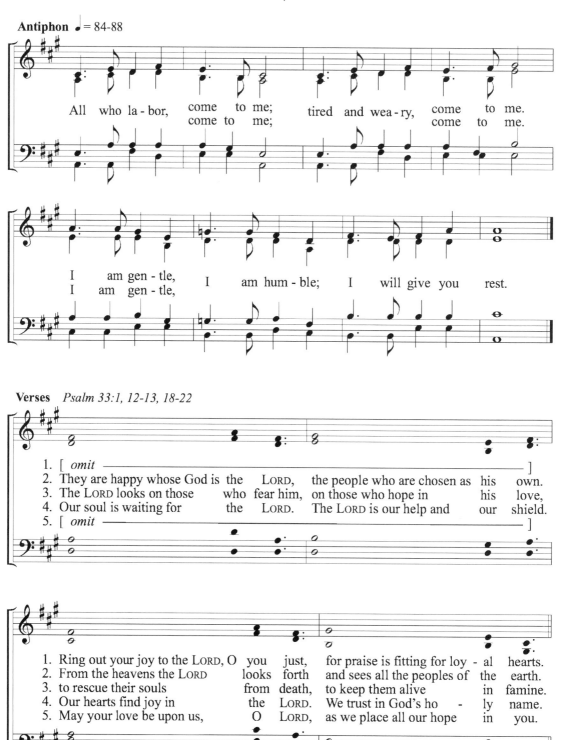

Antiphon ♩ = 84-88

All who la-bor, come to me;
come to me;
tired and wea-ry, come to me.
come to me.

I am gen-tle, I am hum-ble; I will give you rest.
I am gen-tle,

Verses *Psalm 33:1, 12-13, 18-22*

1. [*omit* —————————————————————————]
2. They are happy whose God is the LORD, the people who are chosen as his own.
3. The LORD looks on those who fear him, on those who hope in his love,
4. Our soul is waiting for the LORD. The LORD is our help and our shield.
5. [*omit* —————————————————————————]

1. Ring out your joy to the LORD, O you just, for praise is fitting for loy - al hearts.
2. From the heavens the LORD looks forth and sees all the peoples of the earth.
3. to rescue their souls from death, to keep them alive in famine.
4. Our hearts find joy in the LORD. We trust in God's ho - ly name.
5. May your love be upon us, O LORD, as we place all our hope in you.

Antiphon ♩ = 138-144

All you na - tions, all you peo - ples, clap your hands, O

clap your hands. Shout to God with cries of glad - ness:

clap your hands, O clap your hands.

Verses *Psalm 47*

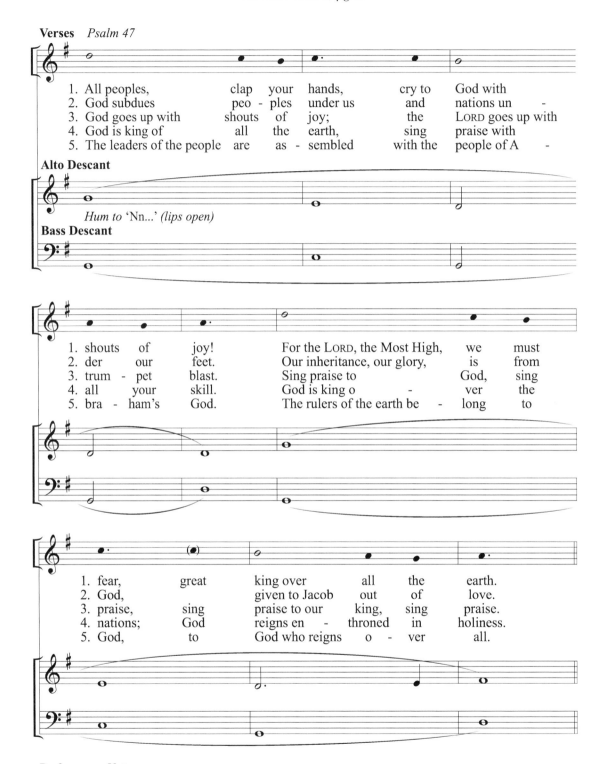

1. All peoples, clap your hands, cry to God with
2. God subdues peo - ples under us and nations un -
3. God goes up with shouts of joy; the LORD goes up with
4. God is king of all the earth, sing praise with
5. The leaders of the people are as - sembled with the people of A -

Alto Descant

Hum to 'Nn...' (lips open)

Bass Descant

1. shouts of joy! For the LORD, the Most High, we must
2. der our feet. Our inheritance, our glory, is from
3. trum - pet blast. Sing praise to God, sing
4. all your skill. God is king o - ver the
5. bra - ham's God. The rulers of the earth be - long to

1. fear, great king over all the earth.
2. God, given to Jacob out of love.
3. praise, sing praise to our king, sing praise.
4. nations; God reigns en - throned in holiness.
5. God, to God who reigns o - ver all.

Performance Notes

The verses should be sung in approximately the same tempo as the antiphon.
Light percussion instruments may easily be added to the antiphon.

1. My heart and my soul ring out their joy to God, the liv-ing God.
2. she lays her young by your altars, LORD of hosts, my king and my God.
3. They are happy, whose strength is in you, in whose hearts are the roads to Zion.
4. They walk with ever - grow-ing strength, they will see the God of gods in Zion.
5. Turn your eyes, O God, our shield, look on the face of your a - nointed.
6. The threshold of the house of God I prefer to the dwellings of the wicked.
7. The LORD will not refuse a - ny good to those who walk with-out blame.
8. LORD, God of hosts, happy are those who trust in you!

Alleluia, Alleluia, Alleluia!

Antiphon ♩. = ca. 60

Al - le - lu - ia, al - le - lu - ia, al - le - lu - ia!

Verses (*Option A) *Psalm 118:1-2, 16-17, 22-23*

A
1. Give thanks to the LORD, the LORD is good, whose
2. The LORD's right hand, tri - umph-ant and strong, the
3. The stone which the build - ers re - ject - ed and scorned is

Verses (*Option B) *Psalm 118:2-4, 13-15, 22-23*

B
1. Child - ren of Is - rael and Aa - ron, say, "God's
2. Though thrust down and fall - ing, God came to my aid. My
3. The stone which the build - ers re - ject - ed and scorn'd is

A
1. love has no end, whose love has no end. Let all the
2. LORD's right hand has raised me up. I shall not
3. now the key, the cor - ner-stone. This is the

B
1. love has no end, God's love has no end." All those who
2. sa - vior gives cou-rage and strength to my soul. Loud shouts of
3. now the key, the cor - ner-stone. This is the

A
1. child-ren of Is - ra - el say: "God's love has no end."
2. die, no, I shall live, tell - ing God's deeds.
3. work of the LORD our God, great in our eyes.

B
1. fear the LORD, now let them say: "God's love has no end."
2. vic - to - ry joy-ful - ly fill the tents of the just.
3. work of the LORD our God, great in our eyes.

Performance Notes

Option A verses are used at the Easter Vigil. Option B verses are used on the Second Sunday of Easter in Years B and C.

Alleluia, Send Out Your Spirit

Antiphon ♩ = 132

Al - le-lu - ia, send out your Spi-rit: you will re-new the face of the earth.

Verses *Psalm 104:1ab, 24ac, 29b-31, 34*

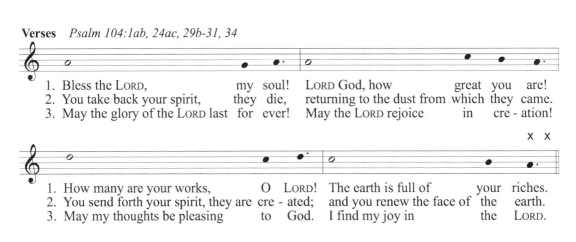

1. Bless the LORD, my soul! LORD God, how great you are!
2. You take back your spirit, they die, returning to the dust from which they came.
3. May the glory of the LORD last for ever! May the LORD rejoice in cre - ation!

1. How many are your works, O LORD! The earth is full of your riches.
2. You send forth your spirit, they are cre - ated; and you renew the face of the earth.
3. May my thoughts be pleasing to God. I find my joy in the LORD.

Performance Notes

Percussion or handclaps may be added, as indicated by X's, both during the antiphon and at the end of the psalm verses to lead back into the antiphon.

The antiphon should be repeated every time it is sung.

The entire piece may be transposed down a whole step.

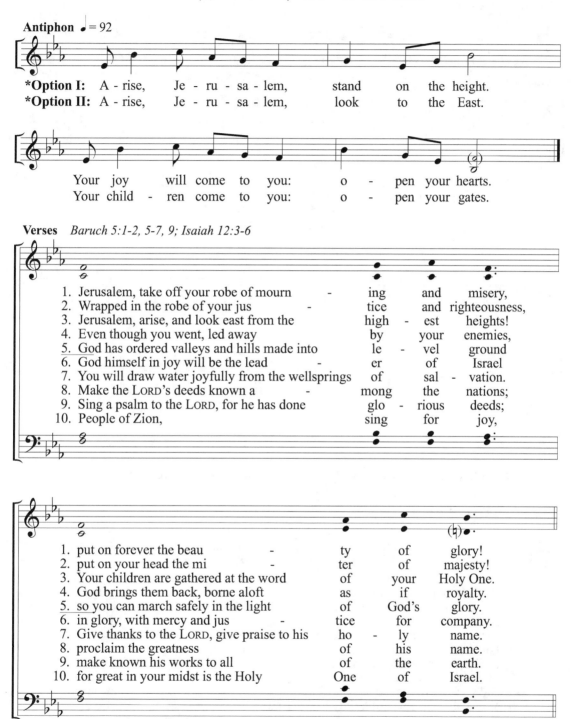

Antiphon ♩ = 92

*Option I: A - rise, Je - ru - sa - lem, stand on the height.
*Option II: A - rise, Je - ru - sa - lem, look to the East.

Your joy will come to you: o - pen your hearts.
Your child - ren come to you: o - pen your gates.

Verses *Baruch 5:1-2, 5-7, 9; Isaiah 12:3-6*

1. Jerusalem, take off your robe of mourn - ing and misery,
2. Wrapped in the robe of your jus - tice and righteousness,
3. Jerusalem, arise, and look east from the high - est heights!
4. Even though you went, led away by your enemies,
5. God has ordered valleys and hills made into le - vel ground
6. God himself in joy will be the lead - er of Israel
7. You will draw water joyfully from the wellsprings of sal - vation.
8. Make the LORD's deeds known a - mong the nations;
9. Sing a psalm to the LORD, for he has done glo - rious deeds;
10. People of Zion, sing for joy,

1. put on forever the beau - ty of glory!
2. put on your head the mi - ter of majesty!
3. Your children are gathered at the word of your Holy One.
4. God brings them back, borne aloft as if royalty.
5. so you can march safely in the light of God's glory.
6. in glory, with mercy and jus - tice for company.
7. Give thanks to the LORD, give praise to his ho - ly name.
8. proclaim the greatness of his name.
9. make known his works to all of the earth.
10. for great in your midst is the Holy One of Israel.

Option I antiphon is used on the Second Sunday of Advent, Years A and C.
Option II antiphon is used on Epiphany.

14   As a Bridegroom Rejoices

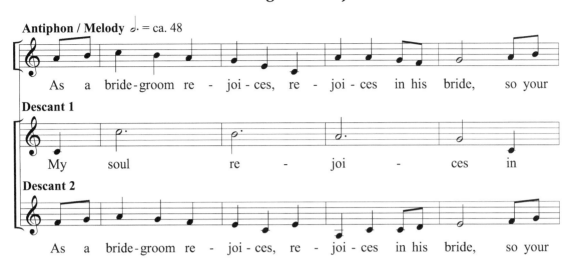

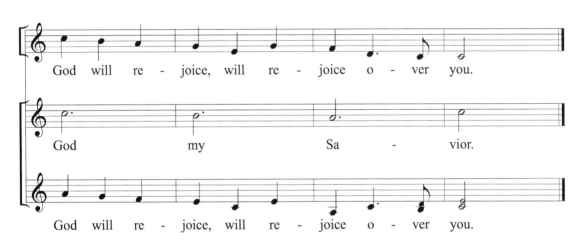

Verses *Isaiah 61:10–62:5*

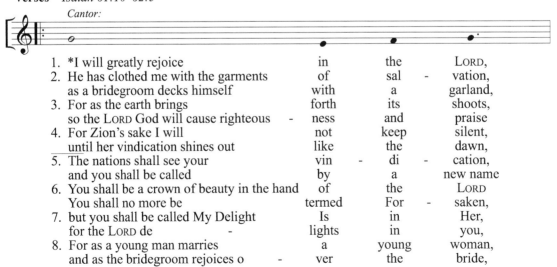

1. *I will greatly rejoice in the LORD,
2. He has clothed me with the garments of sal - vation,
   as a bridegroom decks himself with a garland,
3. For as the earth brings forth its shoots,
   so the LORD God will cause righteous - ness and praise
4. For Zion's sake I will not keep silent,
   until her vindication shines out like the dawn,
5. The nations shall see your vin - di - cation,
   and you shall be called by a new name
6. You shall be a crown of beauty in the hand of the LORD
   You shall no more be termed For - saken,
7. but you shall be called My Delight Is in Her,
   for the LORD de - lights in you,
8. For as a young man marries a young woman,
   and as the bridegroom rejoices o - ver the bride,

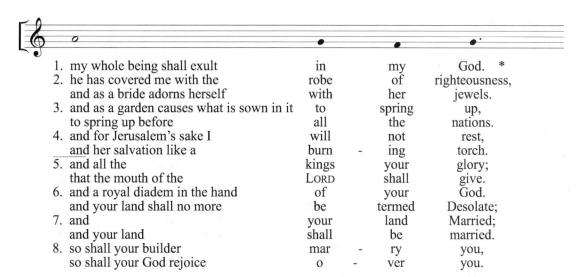

1. my whole being shall exult in my God. *
2. he has covered me with the robe of righteousness,
   and as a bride adorns herself with her jewels.
3. and as a garden causes what is sown in it to spring up,
   to spring up before all the nations.
4. and for Jerusalem's sake I will not rest,
   and her salvation like a burn - ing torch.
5. and all the kings your glory;
   that the mouth of the LORD shall give.
6. and a royal diadem in the hand of your God.
   and your land shall no more be termed Desolate;
7. and your land Married;
   and your land shall be married.
8. so shall your builder mar - ry you,
   so shall your God rejoice o - ver you.

And your God will re - joice, will re - joice o - ver you.

And your God will re - joice, will re - joice o - ver you.

Performance Notes

Omit the tone repeat on this verse only.

As One Body in Your Spirit

Antiphon ♩. = 84

1 (A)   (B)   2 (C)   (D)

As one bo - dy in your Spi - rit, we ful - fill your Word.

Verses *Psalm 33:2-21*

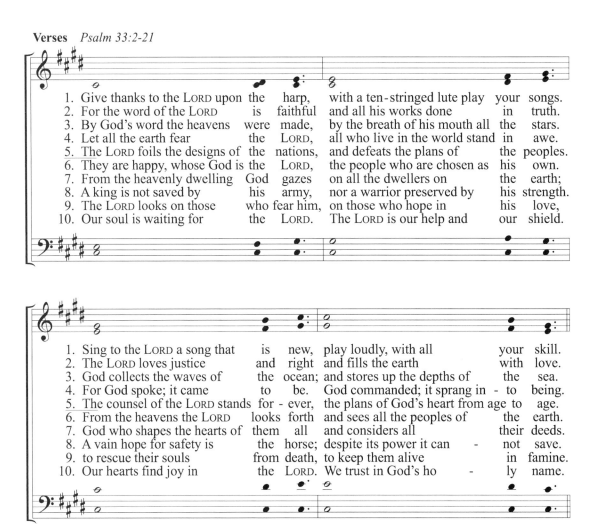

1. Give thanks to the LORD upon the harp, with a ten-stringed lute play your songs.
2. For the word of the LORD is faithful and all his works done in truth.
3. By God's word the heavens were made, by the breath of his mouth all the stars.
4. Let all the earth fear the LORD, all who live in the world stand in awe.
5. The LORD foils the designs of the nations, and defeats the plans of the peoples.
6. They are happy, whose God is the LORD, the people who are chosen as his own.
7. From the heavenly dwelling God gazes on all the dwellers on the earth;
8. A king is not saved by his army, nor a warrior preserved by his strength.
9. The LORD looks on those who fear him, on those who hope in his love,
10. Our soul is waiting for the LORD. The LORD is our help and our shield.

1. Sing to the LORD a song that is new, play loudly, with all your skill.
2. The LORD loves justice and right and fills the earth with love.
3. God collects the waves of the ocean; and stores up the depths of the sea.
4. For God spoke; it came to be. God commanded; it sprang in - to being.
5. The counsel of the LORD stands for - ever, the plans of God's heart from age to age.
6. From the heavens the LORD looks forth and sees all the peoples of the earth.
7. God who shapes the hearts of them all and considers all their deeds.
8. A vain hope for safety is the horse; despite its power it can - not save.
9. to rescue their souls from death, to keep them alive in famine.
10. Our hearts find joy in the LORD. We trust in God's ho - ly name.

Performance Notes

The antiphon may be sung as a 2-part round (1 and 2) or 4-part round (A, B, C, D).

Verses (Superimposed)   *Wisdom 16:20; Psalms 78:23-25, 27, 29; 23:5-6; 145:15-16*

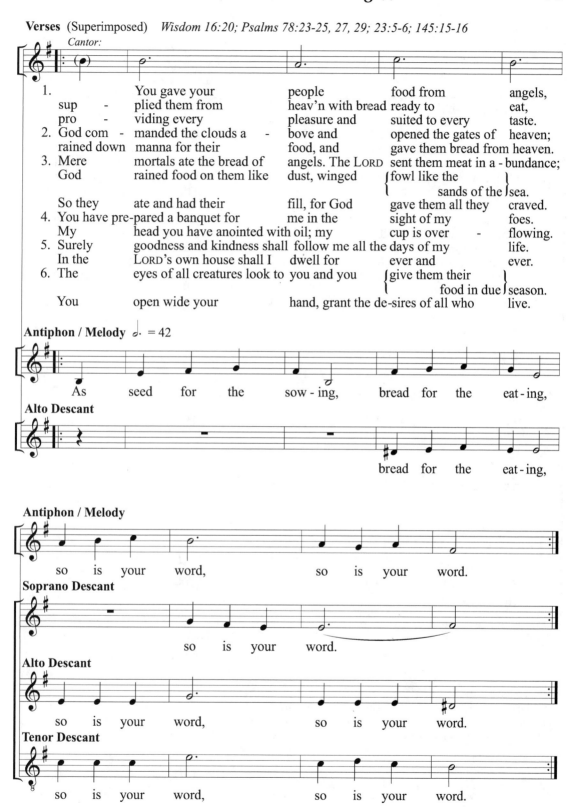

Cantor:

1. You gave your people food from angels,
   sup - plied them from heav'n with bread ready to eat,
   pro - viding every pleasure and suited to every taste.
2. God com - manded the clouds a - bove and opened the gates of heaven;
   rained down manna for their food, and gave them bread from heaven.
3. Mere mortals ate the bread of angels. The LORD sent them meat in a - bundance;
   God rained food on them like dust, winged { fowl like the
   sands of the } sea.

   So they ate and had their fill, for God gave them all they craved.
4. You have pre-pared a banquet for me in the sight of my foes.
   My head you have anointed with oil; my cup is over - flowing.
5. Surely goodness and kindness shall follow me all the days of my life.
   In the LORD's own house shall I dwell for ever and ever.
6. The eyes of all creatures look to you and you { give them their
   food in due } season.

   You open wide your hand, grant the de-sires of all who live.

Antiphon / Melody ♩. = 42

As seed for the sow - ing, bread for the eat - ing,

Alto Descant

bread for the eat - ing,

Antiphon / Melody

so is your word, so is your word.

Soprano Descant

so is your word.

Alto Descant

so is your word, so is your word.

Tenor Descant

so is your word, so is your word.

Verses (Independent) *Wisdom 16:20; Psalms 78:23-25, 27, 29; 23:5-6; 145:15-16*

1. You gave your people food from angels,
   supplied them from heav'n with bread ready to eat,
   providing every pleasure and suited to every taste.
2. God commanded the clouds a - bove and opened the gates of heaven;
   rained down manna for their food, and gave them bread from heaven.
3. Mere mortals ate the bread of angels. The LORD sent them meat in a - bundance;
   God rained food on them like dust, winged fowl like the sands of the sea.
   So they ate and had their fill, for God gave them all they craved.
4. You have prepared a banquet for me in the sight of my foes.
   My head you have anointed with oil; my cup is over - flowing.
5. Surely goodness and kindness shall follow me all the days of my life.
   In the LORD's own house shall I dwell for ever and ever.
6. The eyes of all creatures look to you and you give them their food in due season.
   You open wide your hand, grant the de-sires of all who live.

All / Melody:

so is your word, so is your word.

Soprano Descant:

so is your word.

Alto Descant:

so is your word, so is your word.

Tenor Descant:

so is your word, so is your word.

Performance Notes

The verses may be superimposed as shown on the previous page (with the text sung metrically or free), while the other parts vocalize to "oo" or hum over the first half, responding with "so is your word, so is your word;" or the verses may be sung separately (using the same tone, as shown on this page).

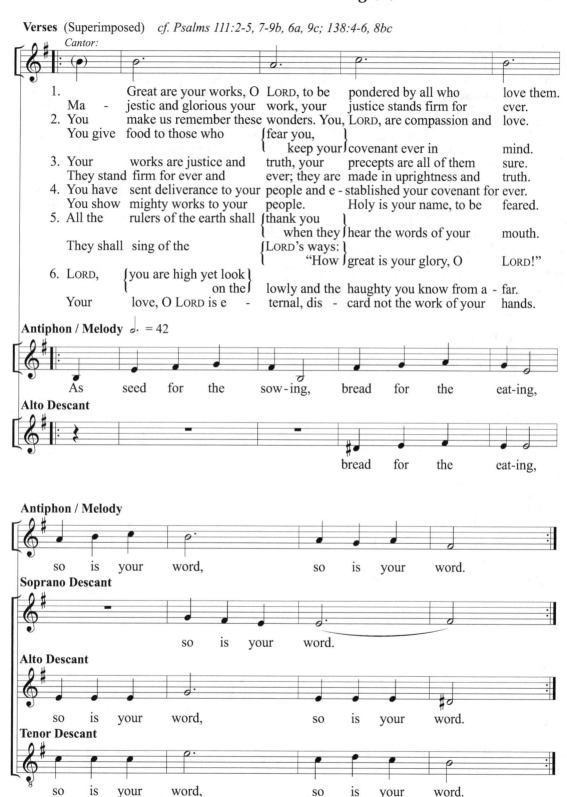

Verses (Superimposed)   *cf. Psalms 111:2-5, 7-9b, 6a, 9c; 138:4-6, 8bc*

Cantor:

1.   Great are your works, O LORD, to be   pondered by all who   love them.
    Ma - jestic and glorious your   work, your   justice stands firm for   ever.
2. You   make us remember these wonders. You, LORD, are compassion and love.
    You give food to those who   {fear you,
                          keep your} covenant ever in   mind.
3. Your   works are justice and   truth, your   precepts are all of them   sure.
    They stand firm for ever and   ever; they are made in uprightness and truth.
4. You have   sent deliverance to your people and e - stablished your covenant for ever.
    You show mighty works to your   people.   Holy is your name, to be   feared.
5. All the   rulers of the earth shall {thank you
                         when they} hear the words of your   mouth.
    They shall sing of the   {LORD's ways:
                        "How {great is your glory, O   LORD!"
6. LORD,   {you are high yet look
                    on the} lowly and the haughty you know from a - far.
    Your   love, O LORD is e - ternal, dis - card not the work of your   hands.

Antiphon / Melody ♩. = 42

As seed for the sow-ing, bread for the eat-ing,

Alto Descant

bread for the eat-ing,

Antiphon / Melody

so is your word, so is your word.

Soprano Descant

so is your word.

Alto Descant

so is your word, so is your word.

Tenor Descant

so is your word, so is your word.

Verses (Independent)   *cf. Psalms 111:2-5, 7-9b, 6a, 9c; 138:4-6, 8bc*

Cantor / Choir:

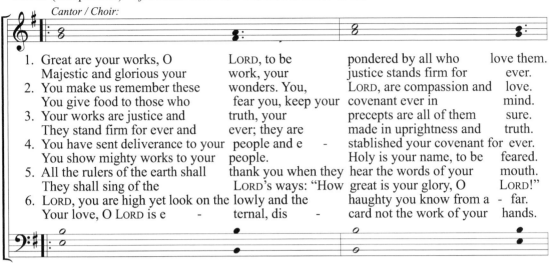

1. Great are your works, O LORD, to be pondered by all who love them.
   Majestic and glorious your work, your justice stands firm for ever.
2. You make us remember these wonders. You, LORD, are compassion and love.
   You give food to those who fear you, keep your covenant ever in mind.
3. Your works are justice and truth, your precepts are all of them sure.
   They stand firm for ever and ever; they are made in uprightness and truth.
4. You have sent deliverance to your people and established your covenant for ever.
   You show mighty works to your people. Holy is your name, to be feared.
5. All the rulers of the earth shall thank you when they hear the words of your mouth.
   They shall sing of the LORD's ways: "How great is your glory, O LORD!"
6. LORD, you are high yet look on the lowly and the haughty you know from afar.
   Your love, O LORD is eternal, discard not the work of your hands.

All / Melody:

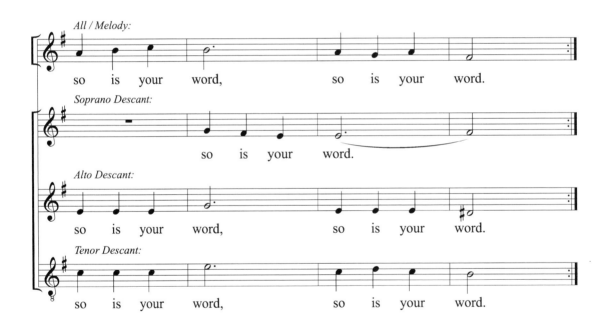

so   is   your   word,   so   is   your   word.

Soprano Descant:

so   is   your   word.

Alto Descant:

so   is   your   word,   so   is   your   word.

Tenor Descant:

so   is   your   word,   so   is   your   word.

Performance Notes

The verses may be superimposed as shown on the previous page (with the text sung metrically or free), while the other parts vocalize to "oo" or hum over the first half, responding with "so is your word, so is your word;" or the verses may be sung separately (using the same tone, as shown on this page).

Antiphon / Melody ♩ = 69

Ask and re-ceive; seek, you will find; give all you have for the king-dom.

Descant

Ask, re-ceive, seek and find; give all you have for the king-dom.

Verses *Psalms 73:1-2, 25-26, 28; 33:12-15, 18-21*

1. How good is God to Israel, to those who are pure of heart.
2. What else have I in heaven but you? Apart from you I want nothing on earth.
3. To be near God is my happiness. I have made the LORD God my refuge.
4. They are happy, whose God is the LORD, the people who are chosen as his own.
5. From the heavenly dwelling God gazes on all the dwellers on the earth;
6. The LORD looks on those who fear him, on those who hope in his love,
7. Our soul is waiting for the LORD. The LORD is our help and our shield.

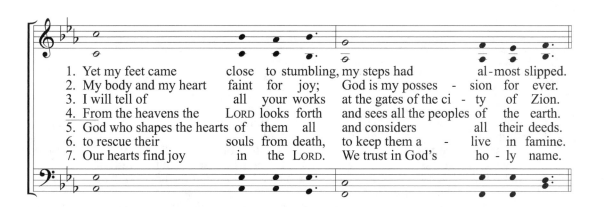

1. Yet my feet came close to stumbling, my steps had al-most slipped.
2. My body and my heart faint for joy; God is my posses - sion for ever.
3. I will tell of all your works at the gates of the ci - ty of Zion.
4. From the heavens the LORD looks forth and sees all the peoples of the earth.
5. God who shapes the hearts of them all and considers all their deeds.
6. to rescue their souls from death, to keep them a - live in famine.
7. Our hearts find joy in the LORD. We trust in God's ho - ly name.

Ask and Receive (II)

Antiphon / Melody ♩ = 69

Ask and re-ceive; seek, you will find; knock and the door will be o-pen'd.

Descant

Come and seek me: knock and the door will be o-pen'd.

Verses (*Option A)   *Psalms 133; 134; 135:1-4, 13-14*

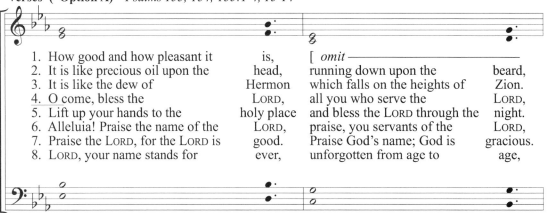

1. How good and how pleasant it is, [*omit* ——————
2. It is like precious oil upon the head, running down upon the beard,
3. It is like the dew of Hermon which falls on the heights of Zion.
4. O come, bless the LORD, all you who serve the LORD,
5. Lift up your hands to the holy place and bless the LORD through the night.
6. Alleluia! Praise the name of the LORD, praise, you servants of the LORD,
7. Praise the LORD, for the LORD is good. Praise God's name; God is gracious.
8. LORD, your name stands for ever, unforgotten from age to age,

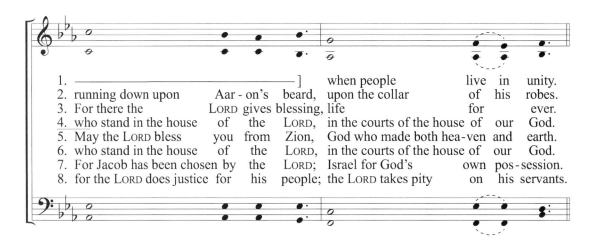

1. ———————————————] when people live in unity.
2. running down upon Aar-on's beard, upon the collar of his robes.
3. For there the LORD gives blessing, life for ever.
4. who stand in the house of the LORD, in the courts of the house of our God.
5. May the LORD bless you from Zion, God who made both hea-ven and earth.
6. who stand in the house of the LORD, in the courts of the house of our God.
7. For Jacob has been chosen by the LORD; Israel for God's own pos-session.
8. for the LORD does justice for his people; the LORD takes pity on his servants.

Verses (*Option B)   *Psalms 73:1-2, 25-26, 28; 33:12-15, 18-21*

1. How good is God to Israel, to those who are pure of heart.
2. What else have I in heaven but you? Apart from you I want nothing on earth.
3. To be near God is my happiness. I have made the LORD God my refuge.
4. They are happy, whose God is the LORD, the people who are chosen as his own.
5. From the heavenly dwelling God gazes on all the dwellers on the earth;
6. The LORD looks on those who fear him, on those who hope in his love,
7. Our soul is waiting for the LORD. The LORD is our help and our shield.

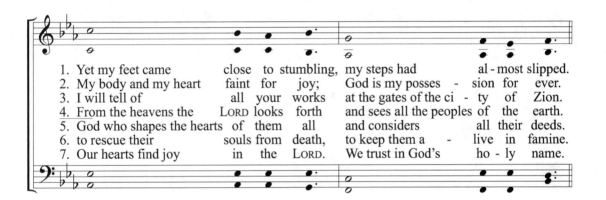

1. Yet my feet came close to stumbling, my steps had al - most slipped.
2. My body and my heart faint for joy; God is my posses - sion for ever.
3. I will tell of all your works at the gates of the ci - ty of Zion.
4. From the heavens the LORD looks forth and sees all the peoples of the earth.
5. God who shapes the hearts of them all and considers all their deeds.
6. to rescue their souls from death, to keep them a - live in famine.
7. Our hearts find joy in the LORD. We trust in God's ho - ly name.

Performance Notes

*Option A verses are used for the Dedication of the Lateran Basilica and Option B verses for the Seventeenth Sunday in Ordinary Time, Year C.

At Your Word Our Hearts Are Burning

Antiphon ♩ = ca. 76 *(or performed in chant style, unaccompanied, ♩ = ca. 80)*

At your word our hearts are burn-ing, Je-sus, ri-sen from the dead.

At this ta-ble, may we know you in the break-ing of the bread.

Verses *Revelation 4:11; 5:9-10, 12b-d, 13b-d; 4:8c*

1. You are worthy, our Lord and God, to receive glory and ho-nor and power,
2. You are worthy to take the scroll and to o - pen its seals,

1. for you crea - ted all things, and by your will
2. for you were slaughtered and by your blood you ran -
3. you have made them to be a kingdom and priests serv -
4. Worthy is the Lamb that was slaughtered to receive power and wealth and wis-
5. To the one seated on the throne and to the Lamb be blessing and honor and glo -
6. Holy, ho - ly, holy, the Lord God

1. they ex - isted and were cre - ated.
2. somed for God saints from every tribe and language and peo-ple and nation;
3. ing our God, and they will reign on earth.
4. dom and might and honor and glo - ry and blessing.
5. ry and might for e - ver and ever.
6. the Al - mighty, who was and is and is to come.

Be Patient, Beloved

Verses (Superimposed)   *Psalm 85:9, 8, 10-14; Isaiah 35:1-7b, 8a-d, 10a-c, 10e*

1. I will hear what the LORD has to say, a
2. Let us see, O LORD, your mercy and
3. Mercy and faithfulness have met;
4. The LORD will make us prosper and our

5. The wilderness and the dry land shall be glad, the
6. The glory of Lebanon shall be given to it, the
7. Strengthen the weak hands, make
8. Here is your God.

9. Then the eyes of the blind shall be opened, and the
10. For waters shall break forth in the wilderness, and
11. A highway shall be there, and
12. The ransomed of the LORD shall re - turn, and

Antiphon ♩ = 66

Be pa - tient, be - lo - ved, for the

1. voice that speaks of peace, peace for his people and
2. give us your saving help. Sal - vation is near for the
3. justice and peace have em - braced. Faithfulness shall spring from the
4. earth shall yield its fruit. Justice shall march in the

5. desert shall rejoice and blossom; like the crocus it shall blossom a -
6. majesty of Carmel and Sharon. They shall see the glory of the
7. firm the feeble knees. Say to those who are of a fearful
8. He will come with vengeance, with terrible

9. ears of the deaf un - stopped; then the lame shall leap like a
10. streams in the desert; the burning sand shall become a
11. it shall be called the Holy Way; the unclean shall not
12. come to Zion with singing; everlasting joy shall be upon their

Lord; be

com - ing of the Lord; be pa - tient, be -

Lord; be

1. friends and those who turn to God in their hearts.
2. God-fearing, and his glory will dwell in our land.
3. earth and justice look down from heaven.
4. forefront, and peace shall follow the way.

5. bundantly, and re - joice with joy and singing.
6. LORD, the majesty of our God.
7. heart, "Be strong, do not fear!
8. recompense. He will come and save you."

9. deer, and the tongue of the speechless sing for joy.
10. pool, and the thirsty ground springs of water.
11. travel on it, but it shall be for God's people.
12. heads, and sorrow and sighing shall flee a - way.

lo - ved: the Lord is close at hand.

Be Strong, Our God Has Come to Save Us

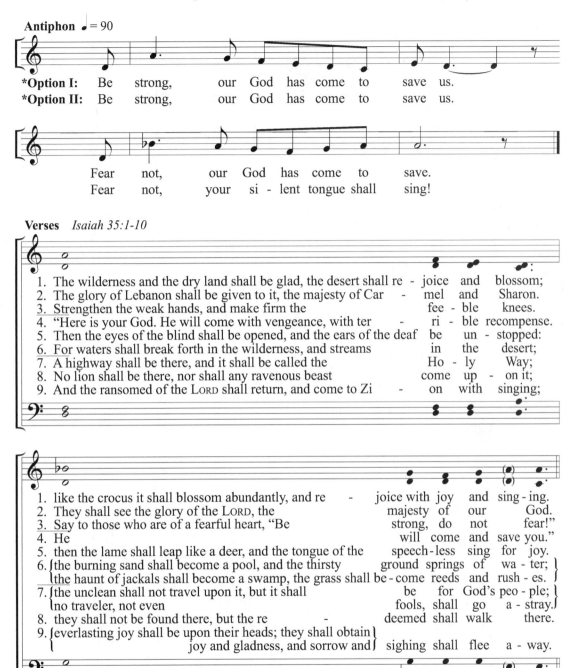

Antiphon ♩ = 90

*Option I: Be strong, our God has come to save us.
*Option II: Be strong, our God has come to save us.

Fear not, our God has come to save.
Fear not, your si - lent tongue shall sing!

Verses *Isaiah 35:1-10*

1. The wilderness and the dry land shall be glad, the desert shall re - joice and blossom;
2. The glory of Lebanon shall be given to it, the majesty of Car - mel and Sharon.
3. Strengthen the weak hands, and make firm the fee - ble knees.
4. "Here is your God. He will come with vengeance, with ter - ri - ble recompense.
5. Then the eyes of the blind shall be opened, and the ears of the deaf be un - stopped:
6. For waters shall break forth in the wilderness, and streams in the desert;
7. A highway shall be there, and it shall be called the Ho - ly Way;
8. No lion shall be there, nor shall any ravenous beast come up - on it;
9. And the ransomed of the LORD shall return, and come to Zi - on with singing;

1. like the crocus it shall blossom abundantly, and re - joice with joy and sing - ing.
2. They shall see the glory of the LORD, the majesty of our God.
3. Say to those who are of a fearful heart, "Be strong, do not fear!"
4. He will come and save you."
5. then the lame shall leap like a deer, and the tongue of the speech - less sing for joy.
6. {the burning sand shall become a pool, and the thirsty ground springs of wa - ter;
   {the haunt of jackals shall become a swamp, the grass shall be - come reeds and rush - es.
7. {the unclean shall not travel upon it, but it shall be for God's peo - ple;
   {no traveler, not even fools, shall go a - stray.
8. they shall not be found there, but the re - deemed shall walk there.
9. {everlasting joy shall be upon their heads; they shall obtain
   { joy and gladness, and sorrow and} sighing shall flee a - way.

Option I antiphon is used on the Third Sunday of Advent, Years B and C. Option II antiphon is used on the Twenty-third Sunday in Ordinary Time, Year B.

23 **Because You Are Filled with the Spirit**

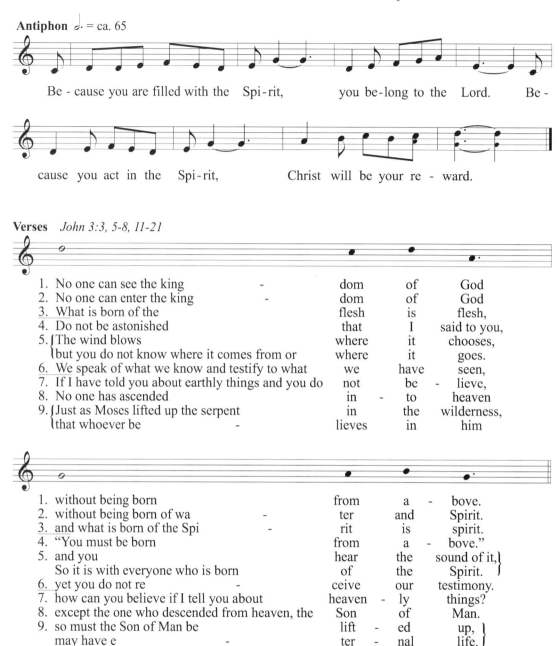

Antiphon ♩. = ca. 65

Be - cause you are filled with the Spi-rit, you be-long to the Lord. Be -

cause you act in the Spi-rit, Christ will be your re - ward.

Verses *John 3:3, 5-8, 11-21*

1. No one can see the king - dom of God
2. No one can enter the king - dom of God
3. What is born of the flesh is flesh,
4. Do not be astonished that I said to you,
5. ⎰ The wind blows where it chooses,
   ⎱ but you do not know where it comes from or where it goes.
6. We speak of what we know and testify to what we have seen,
7. If I have told you about earthly things and you do not be - lieve,
8. No one has ascended in - to heaven
9. ⎰ Just as Moses lifted up the serpent in the wilderness,
   ⎱ that whoever be - lieves in him

1. without being born from a - bove.
2. without being born of wa - ter and Spirit.
3. and what is born of the Spi - rit is spirit.
4. "You must be born from a - bove."
5. and you hear the sound of it, ⎱
   So it is with everyone who is born of the Spirit. ⎰
6. yet you do not re - ceive our testimony.
7. how can you believe if I tell you about heaven - ly things?
8. except the one who descended from heaven, the Son of Man.
9. so must the Son of Man be lift - ed up, ⎱
   may have e - ter - nal life. ⎰

Verses (continued)

10. ⎰God so   loved   the   world
    ⎱so that everyone who be   -   lieves   in   him
11. God did not send the Son into the world to con   -   demn   the   world,
12. Those who believe in him are   not   con   -   demned;
13. ⎰And this   is   the   judgement,
    ⎱and people loved darkness ra   -   ther   than   light
14. For all who do evil hate the light and do not come   to   the   light,
15. But those who do what is true come   to   the   light,

10. that he gave his   on   -   ly   Son,⎱
    may not perish but may have e   -   ter   -   nal   life.⎰
11. but in order that the world might be   saved   through   him.
12. ⎰but those who do not believe are condemned already, ⎱
    ⎱because they have not believed in the name of the only⎰   Son   of   God.
13. that the light has come in   -   to   the   world,⎱
    because their   deeds   were   evil. ⎰
14. so that their deeds may not   be   ex   -   posed.
15. so that it may be clearly seen that their deeds have been   done   in   God.

Performance Notes

At the end of the antiphon, if the main melody is found to be too high, sing the cue-size notes instead.

Behold, the Bridegroom Is Here (I)

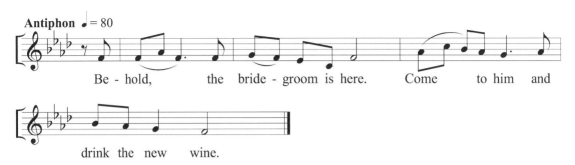

Antiphon ♩ = 80

Be - hold, the bride - groom is here. Come to him and

drink the new wine.

Verses *Hosea 2:14, 15b, 19-20; Ezekiel 36:8-11abcd, 26-28*

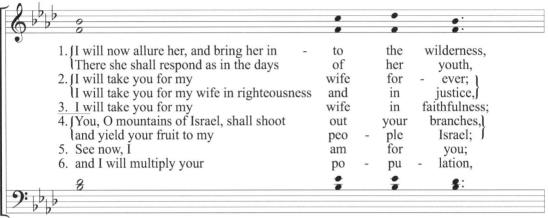

1. {I will now allure her, and bring her in - to the wilderness,
   {There she shall respond as in the days of her youth,
2. {I will take you for my wife for - ever;
   {I will take you for my wife in righteousness and in justice,
3. I will take you for my wife in faithfulness;
4. {You, O mountains of Israel, shall shoot out your branches,
   {and yield your fruit to my peo - ple Israel;
5. See now, I am for you;
6. and I will multiply your po - pu - lation,

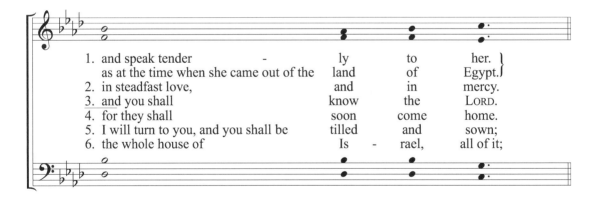

1. and speak tender - ly to her. }
   as at the time when she came out of the land of Egypt.
2. in steadfast love, and in mercy.
3. and you shall know the LORD.
4. for they shall soon come home.
5. I will turn to you, and you shall be tilled and sown;
6. the whole house of Is - rael, all of it;

Verses (continued)

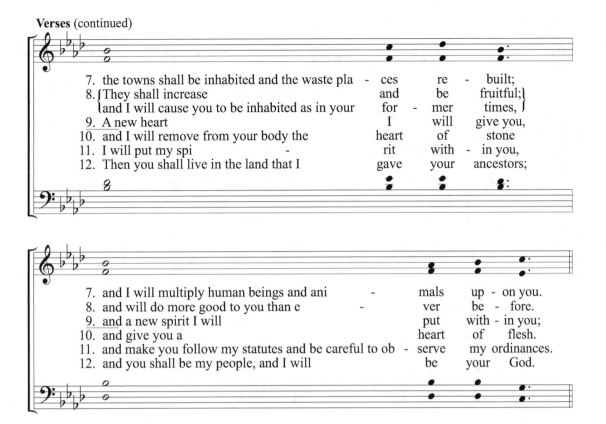

7. the towns shall be inhabited and the waste pla - ces re - built;
8. {They shall increase and be fruitful;}
{and I will cause you to be inhabited as in your for - mer times,}
9. A new heart I will give you,
10. and I will remove from your body the heart of stone
11. I will put my spi - rit with - in you,
12. Then you shall live in the land that I gave your ancestors;

7. and I will multiply human beings and ani - mals up - on you.
8. and will do more good to you than e - ver be - fore.
9. and a new spirit I will put with - in you;
10. and give you a heart of flesh.
11. and make you follow my statutes and be careful to ob - serve my ordinances.
12. and you shall be my people, and I will be your God.

Behold, the Bridegroom Is Here (II)

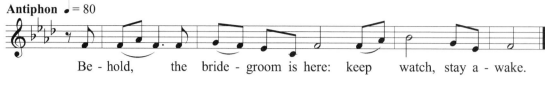

Antiphon ♩ = 80

Be - hold, the bride - groom is here: keep watch, stay a - wake.

Verses *Psalm 37:1, 3-5, 7ab, 8, 11, 18, 27, 29a, 31b, 34abc, 39a, 40*

Cantor: All:

1. Do not fret because of   the   wicked: keep   watch, stay a - wake.
2. Do not envy those who   do   evil:
3. Trust in the LORD and   do   good:
4. Live in the land and be   se - cure:

5. If you find your delight in   the   LORD:
6. The LORD will grant your heart's   de - sire:
7. Commit your life to   the   LORD:
8. Be confident, and God   will   act:

9. Be still before the LORD and wait   in   patience:
10. Do not fret at those   who   prosper:
11. Calm your anger and forget   your   rage:
12. Do not fret, it only leads   to   evil:

13. The humble shall own   the   land:
14. The humble shall enjoy the fullness   of   peace:
15. God protects the lives of   the   upright:
16. The heritage of the upright will last   for   ever:

17. Turn away from evil and   do   good:
18. You shall have a home   for   ever:
19. The just shall inherit   the   land:
20. The steps of the just shall be saved   from stumbling:

21. Wait for the LORD, keep to   God's   way:
22. It is God who will free you from   the   wicked:
23. God will raise you up to possess   the   land:
24. The salvation of the just comes from   the   LORD:

25. The LORD helps the just and   de - livers them:
26. The refuge of the just is   in   God:

Performance Notes

Since the psalm verses are fairly short, it is recommended that the antiphon only be sung after every fourth verse.

27   Bless the Lord, My Soul

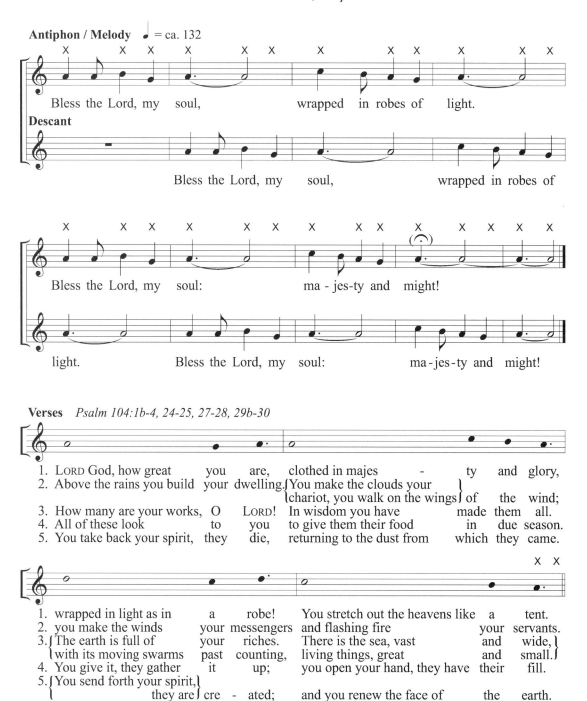

Antiphon / Melody ♩ = ca. 132

Bless the Lord, my soul, wrapped in robes of light.

Descant

Bless the Lord, my soul, wrapped in robes of

Bless the Lord, my soul: ma - jes-ty and might!

light. Bless the Lord, my soul: ma - jes-ty and might!

Verses   *Psalm 104:1b-4, 24-25, 27-28, 29b-30*

1. Lord God, how great you are, clothed in majes - ty and glory,
2. Above the rains you build your dwelling. {You make the clouds your chariot, you walk on the wings} of the wind;
3. How many are your works, O Lord! In wisdom you have made them all.
4. All of these look to you to give them their food in due season.
5. You take back your spirit, they die, returning to the dust from which they came.

1. wrapped in light as in a robe! You stretch out the heavens like a tent.
2. you make the winds your messengers and flashing fire your servants.
3. {The earth is full of your riches. There is the sea, vast and wide,} {with its moving swarms past counting, living things, great and small.}
4. You give it, they gather it up; you open your hand, they have their fill.
5. {You send forth your spirit, they are} cre - ated; and you renew the face of the earth.

Performance Notes

Percussion or handclaps may be added, as indicated by the X's, both during the antiphon and at the end of the psalm verses to lead back into the antiphon.

End the antiphon at the fermata when the descant is not used.

Blessed Are You, Lord

Antiphon ♩ = 84-88

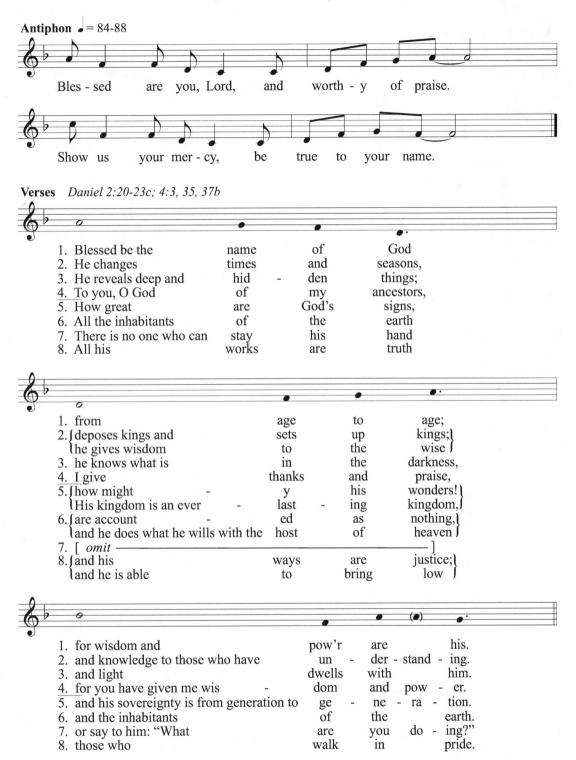

Bles - sed are you, Lord, and worth - y of praise.

Show us your mer - cy, be true to your name.

Verses *Daniel 2:20-23c; 4:3, 35, 37b*

1. Blessed be the name of God
2. He changes times and seasons,
3. He reveals deep and hid - den things;
4. To you, O God of my ancestors,
5. How great are God's signs,
6. All the inhabitants of the earth
7. There is no one who can stay his hand
8. All his works are truth

1. from age to age;
2. { deposes kings and sets up kings; } { he gives wisdom to the wise }
3. he knows what is in the darkness,
4. I give thanks and praise,
5. { how might - y his wonders! } { His kingdom is an ever - last - ing kingdom, }
6. { are account - ed as nothing, } { and he does what he wills with the host of heaven }
7. [*omit*]
8. { and his ways are justice; } { and he is able to bring low }

1. for wisdom and pow'r are his.
2. and knowledge to those who have un - der - stand - ing.
3. and light dwells with him.
4. for you have given me wis - dom and pow - er.
5. and his sovereignty is from generation to ge - ne - ra - tion.
6. and the inhabitants of the earth.
7. or say to him: "What are you do - ing?"
8. those who walk in pride.

Blest Are the Poor in Spirit

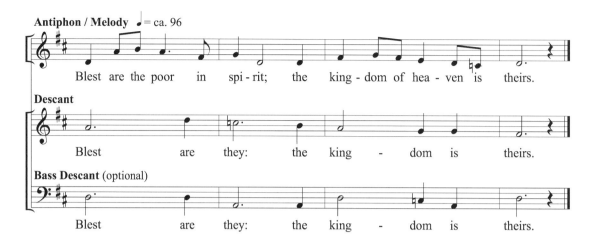

Antiphon / Melody ♩ = ca. 96

Blest are the poor in spi - rit; the king - dom of hea - ven is theirs.

Descant

Blest are they: the king - dom is theirs.

Bass Descant (optional)

Blest are they: the king - dom is theirs.

Verses (*Option A)   *Cf. Psalm 1:1-3; Matthew 5:4-10; Psalm 15:2-5*

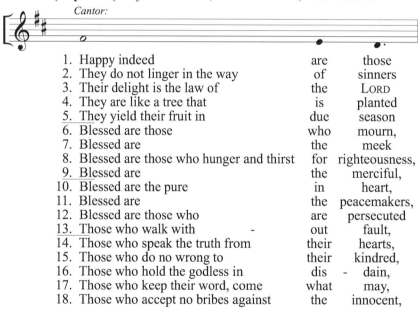

Cantor:

1. Happy indeed	are	those
2. They do not linger in the way	of	sinners
3. Their delight is the law of	the	LORD
4. They are like a tree that	is	planted
5. They yield their fruit in	due	season
6. Blessed are those	who	mourn,
7. Blessed are	the	meek
8. Blessed are those who hunger and thirst	for	righteousness,
9. Blessed are	the	merciful,
10. Blessed are the pure	in	heart,
11. Blessed are	the	peacemakers,
12. Blessed are those who	are	persecuted
13. Those who walk with -	out	fault,
14. Those who speak the truth from	their	hearts,
15. Those who do no wrong to	their	kindred,
16. Those who hold the godless in	dis -	dain,
17. Those who keep their word, come	what	may,
18. Those who accept no bribes against	the	innocent,

Performance Notes

*Option A verses are the Song for the Table on the Fourth Sunday in Ordinary Time, Year A, and Option B verses 6–11 are used as the Song for the Word on the same day.

1. who follow not the counsel	of	the	wicked;
2. nor sit in the compa -	ny	of	scorners;
3. and they ponder God's law	day	and	night;
4. beside the	flow -	ing	waters;
5. {and their leaves shall	ne -	ver	fade; }
{and all that they	do	shall	prosper.}
6. for they	will	be	comforted.
7. for they will inhe -	rit	the	earth.
8. for they	will	be	filled.
9. for they will	re -	ceive	mercy.
10. for they	will	see	God.
11. for they will be called child -	ren	of	God.
12. for right -	eous -	ness'	sake.
13. those who	act	with	justice;
14. and do not slander	with	their	tongue;
15. who cast no slur	on	their	neighbors;
16. and honor those who	fear	the	LORD;
17. who take no interest	on	a	loan;
18. they will stand	firm	for	ever.

All / Melody:

The king - dom of hea - ven is theirs.

Descant:

The king - dom is theirs.

Bass Descant:

The king - dom is theirs.

Verses (*Option B)   *Psalm 146:2-10b*

1. I will praise the LORD	all	my	days,
2. Put no trust	in	the	powerful,
3. Take their breath, they re -	turn	to	clay
4. They are happy who are helped by Ja -	cob's	God,	
5. the LORD who alone made	heav'n	and	earth,
6. It is the LORD who keeps	faith	for	ever,
7. It is God who gives bread	to	the	hungry,
8. the LORD who gives sight	to	the	blind,
9. the LORD, who pro -	tects	the	stranger
10. It is the LORD who	loves	the	just
11. The LORD will	reign	for	ever,

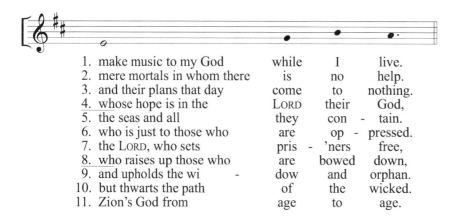

1. make music to my God while I live.
2. mere mortals in whom there is no help.
3. and their plans that day come to nothing.
4. whose hope is in the LORD their God,
5. the seas and all they con - tain.
6. who is just to those who are op - pressed.
7. the LORD, who sets pris - 'ners free,
8. who raises up those who are bowed down,
9. and upholds the wi - dow and orphan.
10. but thwarts the path of the wicked.
11. Zion's God from age to age.

30 Blest Are You Who Weep

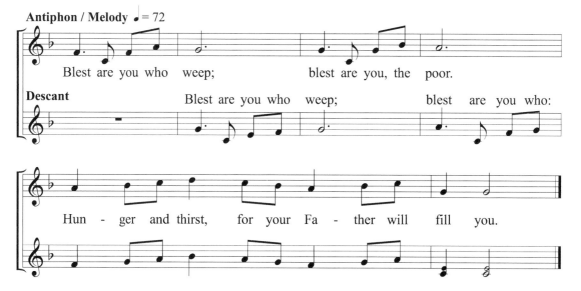

Blest are you who weep; blest are you, the poor.
Blest are you who weep; blest are you who:
Hun - ger and thirst, for your Fa - ther will fill you.

Verses *Matthew 5:3-10; Psalm 103:3-4, 8, 10-12, 17-18*

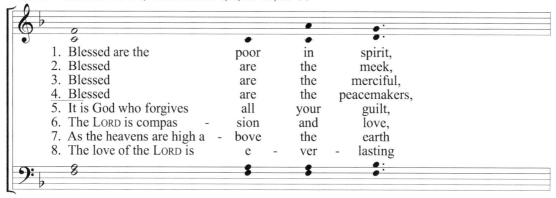

1. Blessed are the poor in spirit,
2. Blessed are the meek,
3. Blessed are the merciful,
4. Blessed are the peacemakers,
5. It is God who forgives all your guilt,
6. The LORD is compas - sion and love,
7. As the heavens are high a - bove the earth
8. The love of the LORD is e - ver - lasting

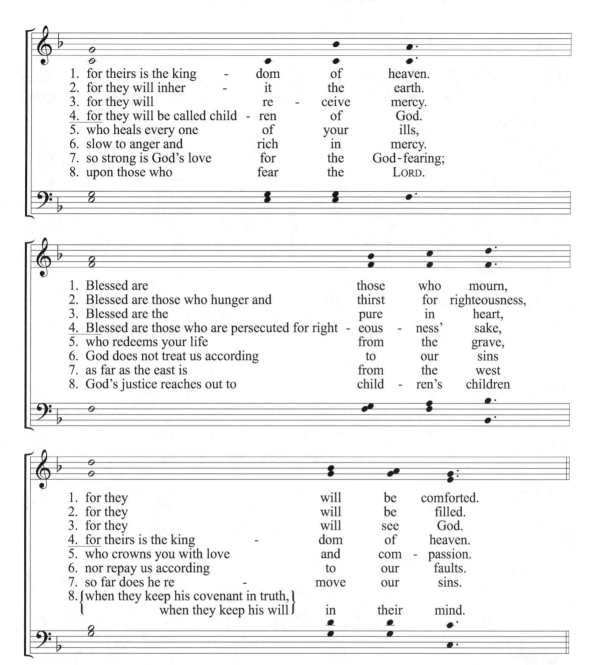

1. for theirs is the king - dom of heaven.
2. for they will inher - it the earth.
3. for they will re - ceive mercy.
4. for they will be called child - ren of God.
5. who heals every one of your ills,
6. slow to anger and rich in mercy.
7. so strong is God's love for the God-fearing;
8. upon those who fear the LORD.

1. Blessed are those who mourn,
2. Blessed are those who hunger and thirst for righteousness,
3. Blessed are the pure in heart,
4. Blessed are those who are persecuted for right - eous - ness' sake,
5. who redeems your life from the grave,
6. God does not treat us according to our sins
7. as far as the east is from the west
8. God's justice reaches out to child - ren's children

1. for they will be comforted.
2. for they will be filled.
3. for they will see God.
4. for theirs is the king - dom of heaven.
5. who crowns you with love and com - passion.
6. nor repay us according to our faults.
7. so far does he re - move our sins.
8. { when they keep his covenant in truth,
     when they keep his will } in their mind.

Cast Out into the Deep

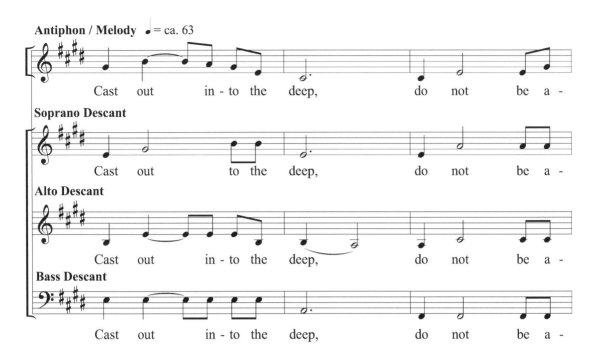

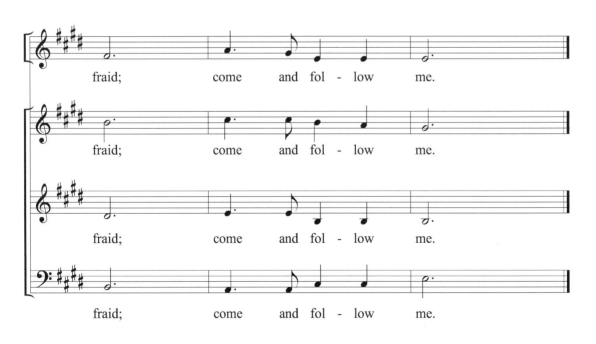

Verses *Psalm 107:23-26, 28-31*

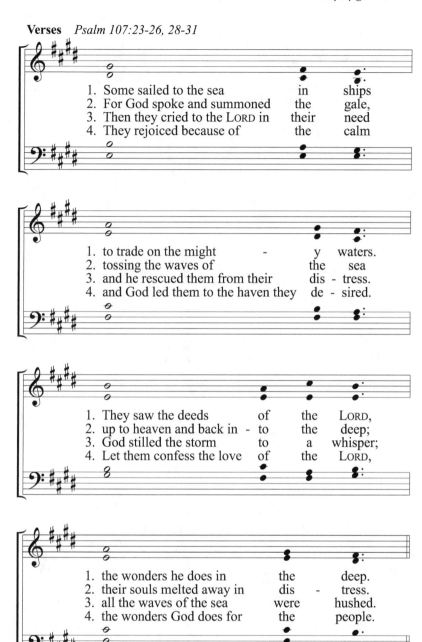

1. Some sailed to the sea in ships
2. For God spoke and summoned the gale,
3. Then they cried to the LORD in their need
4. They rejoiced because of the calm

1. to trade on the might - y waters.
2. tossing the waves of the sea
3. and he rescued them from their dis - tress.
4. and God led them to the haven they de - sired.

1. They saw the deeds of the LORD,
2. up to heaven and back in - to the deep;
3. God stilled the storm to a whisper;
4. Let them confess the love of the LORD,

1. the wonders he does in the deep.
2. their souls melted away in dis - tress.
3. all the waves of the sea were hushed.
4. the wonders God does for the people.

Performance Notes
In the antiphon, the alternation between measures of 4/4 and 3/4 is intentional.

Change Your Heart and Mind

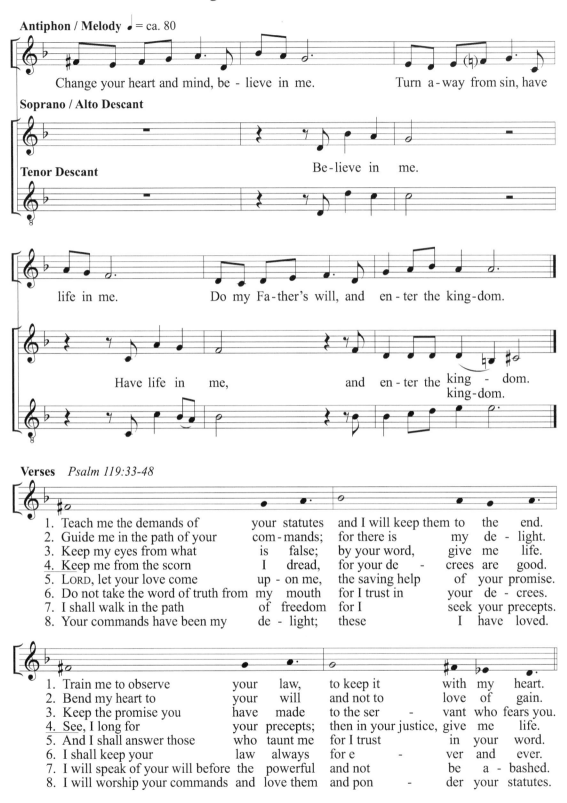

Antiphon / Melody ♩ = ca. 80

Change your heart and mind, be - lieve in me. Turn a - way from sin, have

Soprano / Alto Descant

Be - lieve in me.

Tenor Descant

life in me. Do my Fa - ther's will, and en - ter the king-dom.

Have life in me, and en - ter the king - dom.
king-dom.

Verses *Psalm 119:33-48*

1. Teach me the demands of your statutes and I will keep them to the end.
2. Guide me in the path of your com-mands; for there is my de - light.
3. Keep my eyes from what is false; by your word, give me life.
4. Keep me from the scorn I dread, for your de - crees are good.
5. LORD, let your love come up - on me, the saving help of your promise.
6. Do not take the word of truth from my mouth for I trust in your de - crees.
7. I shall walk in the path of freedom for I seek your precepts.
8. Your commands have been my de - light; these I have loved.

1. Train me to observe your law, to keep it with my heart.
2. Bend my heart to your will and not to love of gain.
3. Keep the promise you have made to the ser - vant who fears you.
4. See, I long for your precepts; then in your justice, give me life.
5. And I shall answer those who taunt me for I trust in your word.
6. I shall keep your law always for e - ver and ever.
7. I will speak of your will before the powerful and not be a - bashed.
8. I will worship your commands and love them and pon - der your statutes.

Antiphon ♩. = 54-56

Cho - sen in Christ, bless'd in Christ, sent by

Christ in praise of God's glo - ry.

Verses *Ephesians 1:3-14, 18-23*

1. Blessed be the God and Father of our Lord — Je - sus Christ,
2. He destined us for adoption as his children through — Je - sus Christ,
3. In him we have redemption — through his blood,
4. With all wisdom and insight he has made known to us the mystery of his will,
5. In Christ we have also obtained — an in - heritance,
6. {In him you also, when you had heard the word of truth, the gospel of your salvation, and} had be-lieved in him,
7. {With the eyes of your heart enlightened, may you know what is the hope to which} he has called you,
8. God put this power to — work in Christ
9. And he has put all things un - der his feet

1. who has blessed us in Christ with every spiritual blessing in the heav'n - ly places,
2. according to the good pleasure of his will,
3. the forgiveness of our trespasses,
4. according to his good pleasure that he set forth in Christ,
5. {having been destined according to the purpose of him who accomplishes all things according to his coun} - sel and will,
6. were marked with the seal of the promised Ho - ly Spirit;
7. what are the riches of his glorious inheritance a - mong the saints,
8. {when he raised him from the dead and seated him at his right hand in the} heav'n - ly places,
9. and has made him the head over all things for the Church,

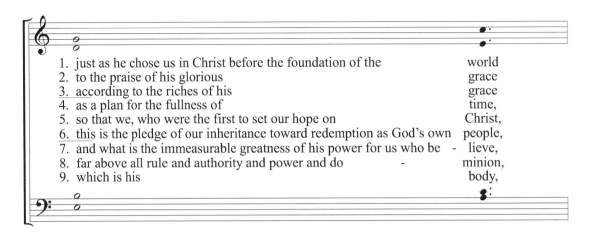

1. just as he chose us in Christ before the foundation of the   world
2. to the praise of his glorious   grace
3. according to the riches of his   grace
4. as a plan for the fullness of   time,
5. so that we, who were the first to set our hope on   Christ,
6. this is the pledge of our inheritance toward redemption as God's own   people,
7. and what is the immeasurable greatness of his power for us who be - lieve,
8. far above all rule and authority and power and do   -   minion,
9. which is his   body,

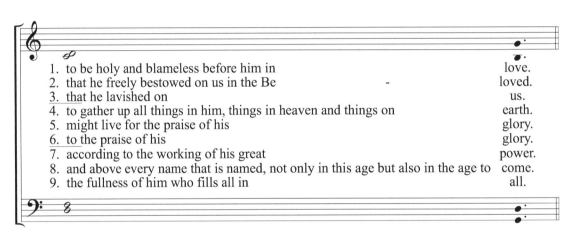

1. to be holy and blameless before him in   love.
2. that he freely bestowed on us in the Be - loved.
3. that he lavished on   us.
4. to gather up all things in him, things in heaven and things on   earth.
5. might live for the praise of his   glory.
6. to the praise of his   glory.
7. according to the working of his great   power.
8. and above every name that is named, not only in this age but also in the age to   come.
9. the fullness of him who fills all in   all.

Antiphon ♩. = 65

Christ is the light, light of the na-tions, glo-ry of Is-ra-el, glo-ry for all.

Verses (*Option A) *Luke 2:29-32*

Cantor / Choir:

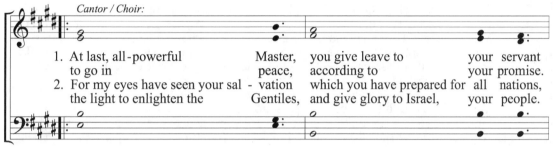

1. At last, all-powerful Master, you give leave to your servant
   to go in peace, according to your promise.
2. For my eyes have seen your sal - vation which you have prepared for all nations,
   the light to enlighten the Gentiles, and give glory to Israel, your people.

All:

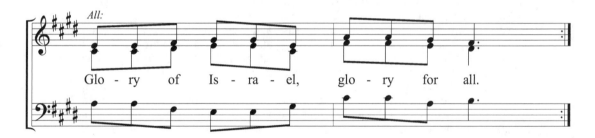

Glo - ry of Is - ra - el, glo - ry for all.

Verses (*Option B) *Psalm 122*

Cantor / Choir:

1. I rejoiced when I heard them say: "Let us go to God's house."
   And now our feet are standing within your gates, O Je - rusalem.
2. Jerusalem is built as a city strongly com - pact.
   It is there that the tribes go up, the tribes of the LORD.
3. For Israel's law it is, there to praise the LORD's name.
   There were set the thrones of judgement of the house of David.
4. For the peace of Jerusalem pray: "Peace be to your homes!
   May peace reign in your walls, in your pala - ces, peace!"
5. For love of my family and friends I say: "Peace up - on you."
   For love of the house of the LORD I will ask for your good.

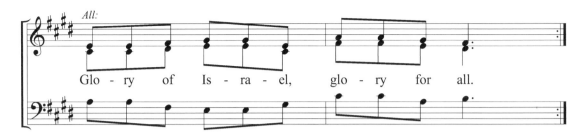

Glo - ry of Is - ra - el, glo - ry for all.

Verses (*Option C) *Psalm 145*

Cantor / Choir:

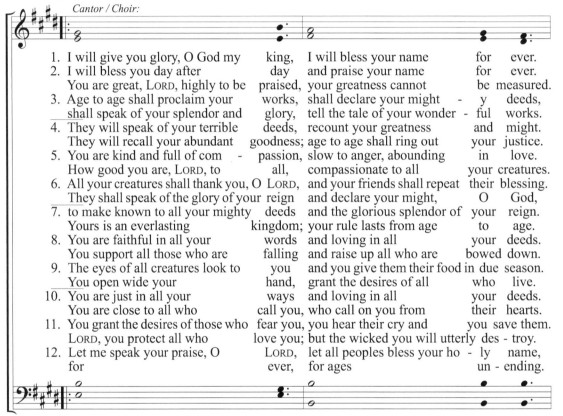

1. I will give you glory, O God my king, I will bless your name for ever.
2. I will bless you day after day and praise your name for ever.
   You are great, LORD, highly to be praised, your greatness cannot be measured.
3. Age to age shall proclaim your works, shall declare your might - y deeds,
   ___ shall speak of your splendor and glory, tell the tale of your wonder - ful works.
4. They will speak of your terrible deeds, recount your greatness and might.
   They will recall your abundant goodness; age to age shall ring out your justice.
5. You are kind and full of com - passion, slow to anger, abounding in love.
   How good you are, LORD, to all, compassionate to all your creatures.
6. All your creatures shall thank you, O LORD, and your friends shall repeat their blessing.
   ___ They shall speak of the glory of your reign and declare your might, O God,
7. to make known to all your mighty deeds and the glorious splendor of your reign.
   Yours is an everlasting kingdom; your rule lasts from age to age.
8. You are faithful in all your words and loving in all your deeds.
   You support all those who are falling and raise up all who are bowed down.
9. The eyes of all creatures look to you and you give them their food in due season.
   ___ You open wide your hand, grant the desires of all who live.
10. You are just in all your ways and loving in all your deeds.
    You are close to all who call you, who call on you from their hearts.
11. You grant the desires of those who fear you, you hear their cry and you save them.
    LORD, you protect all who love you; but the wicked you will utterly des - troy.
12. Let me speak your praise, O LORD, let all peoples bless your ho - ly name,
    for ever, for ages un - ending.

Glo - ry of Is - ra - el, glo - ry for all.

Performance Notes

*On the Presentation of the Lord, Option A verses are used duing the Gathering and Kindling of Candles; Option B verses during the Entrance Procession with Candles; Option C verses as the Song for the Table.
For Option C verses, omit the verse tone repeat on the first verse.

Antiphon / Melody ♩ = ca. 152

Christ laid down his life for us; so we should do for each o - ther.

Descant

so we should do for each o - ther.

Verses *1 Peter 2:21-24; Philippians 2:6-11*

1. To this you have been called,
2. He committed no sin,
3. When he suffered,
4. He himself bore our sins
5. Christ Jesus, though he was in the form of God,
6. And being found in hu - man form,
7. ⎰Therefore God also highly ex - alt - ed him
   ⎱and every tongue con - fess

1. because Christ suf - fered for you,
2. and no deceit was found in his mouth.
3. he did not threaten;
4. in his body on the cross,
5. did not regard equality with God as something to be ex - ploited,
6. he hum - bled him - self
7. and gave him the name that is above e - v'ry name
   that Jesus Christ is Lord,

1. leaving you an ex - ample,
2. When he was a - bused,
3. but he entrusted him - self
4. so that, free from sins, we might live for righteousness;
5. but emptied himself, taking the form of a slave,
6. and became obedient to the point of death—
7. so that at the name of Jesus every knee should bend,
   [*omit* ————————————]

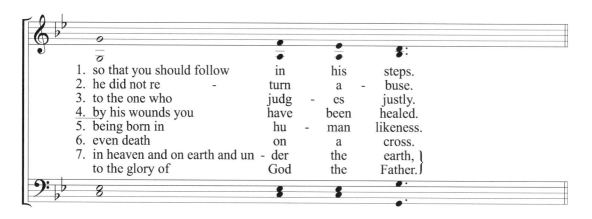

1. so that you should follow in his steps.
2. he did not re - turn a - buse.
3. to the one who judg - es justly.
4. by his wounds you have been healed.
5. being born in hu - man likeness.
6. even death on a cross.
7. in heaven and on earth and un - der the earth, ⎫
   to the glory of God the Father. ⎭

36   Christ, Our Pasch

♩ = 84   *Adaptations from Psalm 66*

Cantor: *All:*

1. Christ, our pasch, is sa - cri - ficed, al - le - lu - ia.
2. Make a joy - ful noise to God,
3. Won - drous are your deeds, O Lord,
4. Come and see what God has done,

Cantor: *All:*

1. Un - lea - vened bread will be our feast, al - le - lu - ia.
2. O sing the glo - ry of God's name,
3. and all the earth will wor - ship you,
4. How awe - some are God's deeds for us,

Cantor: *All:*

1. Bread of truth and sin - ce - ri - ty, al - le - lu - ia,
2. Praise the Lord for his ma - jes - ty,
3. They will sing prais - es to your name,
4. We re - joice in God's might - y pow'r,

al - le - lu - ia, al - le - lu - ia!

Christ the Lord Is Risen Again

♩ = 84   *Adaptations from Psalm 95*

1. Christ the Lord is ris'n a - gain,
2. Christ the Lord is ris'n in - deed,
3. Cry a - loud to God with joy,
4. Peo - ple of the Lord our God,
5. Faith - ful to the end of time,

al - le - lu - ia,

1. his hand on us to keep us safe,
2. All pow'r and glo - ry be to him,
3. let earth with glad - ness serve the Lord,
4. who made all things up - on the earth,
5. is God, whose mer - cy co - vers us,

al - le - lu - ia.

1. How his wis - dom is won - der - ful!
2. Praise his name to the end of time,
3. come to God with our songs of joy,
4. sing with praise and thanks - giv - ing,
5. and whose love is e - ter - nal,

al - le - lu - ia,

al - le - lu - ia, al - le - lu - ia!

38   Clothed in Christ, One in Christ

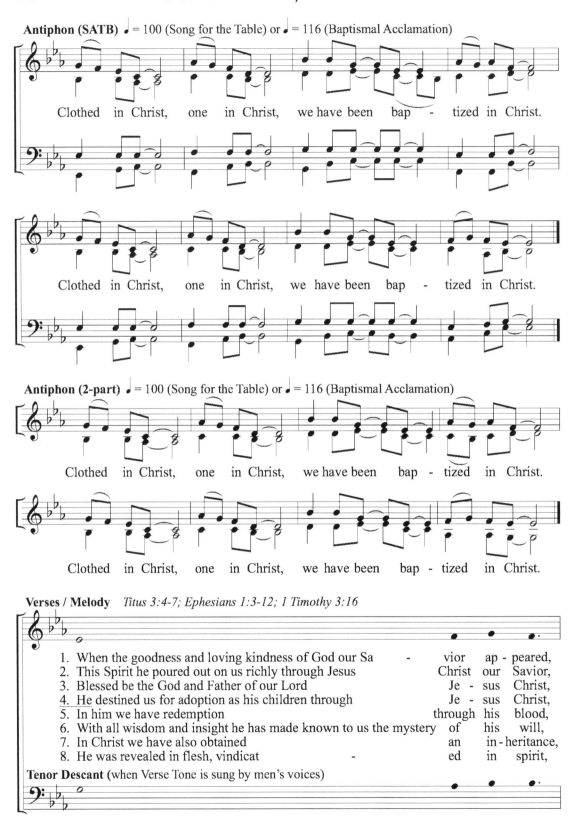

Antiphon (SATB) ♩ = 100 (Song for the Table) or ♩ = 116 (Baptismal Acclamation)

Clothed in Christ, one in Christ, we have been bap - tized in Christ.

Clothed in Christ, one in Christ, we have been bap - tized in Christ.

Antiphon (2-part) ♩ = 100 (Song for the Table) or ♩ = 116 (Baptismal Acclamation)

Clothed in Christ, one in Christ, we have been bap - tized in Christ.

Clothed in Christ, one in Christ, we have been bap - tized in Christ.

Verses / Melody   *Titus 3:4-7; Ephesians 1:3-12; 1 Timothy 3:16*

1. When the goodness and loving kindness of God our Sa - vior ap - peared,
2. This Spirit he poured out on us richly through Jesus Christ our Savior,
3. Blessed be the God and Father of our Lord Je - sus Christ,
4. He destined us for adoption as his children through Je - sus Christ,
5. In him we have redemption through his blood,
6. With all wisdom and insight he has made known to us the mystery of his will,
7. In Christ we have also obtained an in - heritance,
8. He was revealed in flesh, vindicat - ed in spirit,

Tenor Descant (when Verse Tone is sung by men's voices)

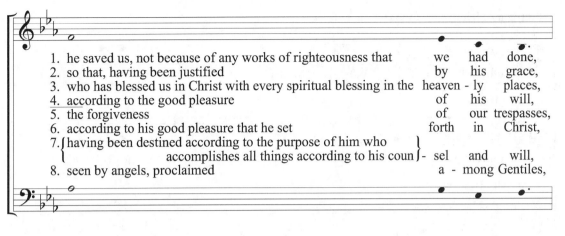

1. he saved us, not because of any works of righteousness that we had done,
2. so that, having been justified by his grace,
3. who has blessed us in Christ with every spiritual blessing in the heaven - ly places,
4. according to the good pleasure of his will,
5. the forgiveness of our trespasses,
6. according to his good pleasure that he set forth in Christ,
7. { having been destined according to the purpose of him who
   accomplishes all things according to his coun - sel and will,
8. seen by angels, proclaimed a - mong Gentiles,

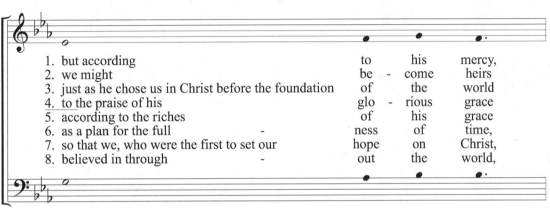

1. but according to his mercy,
2. we might be - come heirs
3. just as he chose us in Christ before the foundation of the world
4. to the praise of his glo - rious grace
5. according to the riches of his grace
6. as a plan for the full - ness of time,
7. so that we, who were the first to set our hope on Christ,
8. believed in through - out the world,

1. through the water of rebirth and renewal by the Ho - ly Spirit.
2. according to the hope of e - ter - nal life.
3. to be holy and blameless before him in love.
4. that he freely bestowed on us in the Be - loved.
5. that he la - vished on us.
6. to gather up all things in him, things in heaven and things on earth.
7. might live for the praise of his glory.
8. taken up in glory.

Performance Notes

During the Rite of Baptism, the antiphon may be used as an acclamation immediately after each baptism, or at the clothing with a white garment, or at both moments in the Rite.
Verses are used on the Baptism of the Lord, Years A and B.

Come, All You Good and Faithful Servants

Antiphon / Melody Not too fast ($\quad$ = 48)

Come, all you good and faith-ful ser-vants, share in the joy, the joy of the Lord.

Soprano Descant

Come, all you good and faith-ful ser-vants, Share in the joy, the joy of the Lord.

Tenor /Alto Descant

Come, all you good and faith-ful ser-vants, Share in the joy, the joy of the Lord.

Come, all you good and faith-ful ser-vants, share in the joy of the Lord.

Come, all you good and faith-ful ser-vants, Share in the joy of the Lord.

Come, all you good and faith-ful ser-vants, Share in the joy of the Lord.

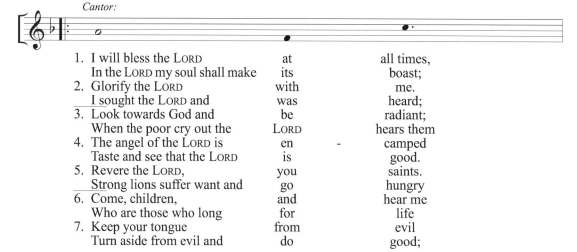

Verses   *Psalms 34:1-15, 16-23; 73:23-26, 28*

Cantor:

1. I will bless the LORD   at   all times,
   In the LORD my soul shall make   its   boast;
2. Glorify the LORD   with   me.
   I sought the LORD and   was   heard;
3. Look towards God and   be   radiant;
   When the poor cry out the   LORD   hears them
4. The angel of the LORD is   en   -   camped
   Taste and see that the LORD   is   good.
5. Revere the LORD,   you   saints.
   Strong lions suffer want and   go   hungry
6. Come, children,   and   hear me
   Who are those who long   for   life
7. Keep your tongue   from   evil
   Turn aside from evil and   do   good;

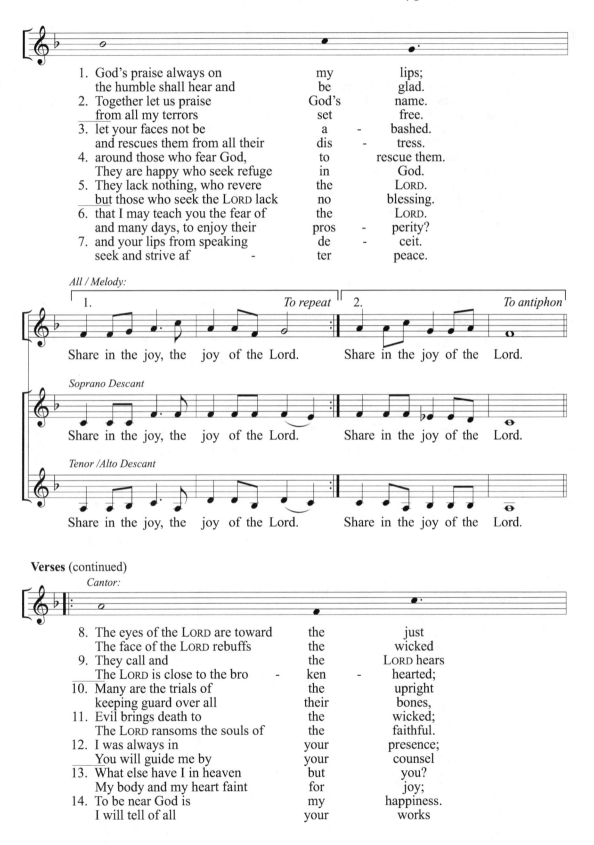

1. God's praise always on   my   lips;
   the humble shall hear and   be   glad.
2. Together let us praise   God's   name.
   from all my terrors   set   free.
3. let your faces not be   a -   bashed.
   and rescues them from all their   dis -   tress.
4. around those who fear God,   to   rescue them.
   They are happy who seek refuge   in   God.
5. They lack nothing, who revere   the   LORD.
   but those who seek the LORD lack   no   blessing.
6. that I may teach you the fear of   the   LORD.
   and many days, to enjoy their   pros -   perity?
7. and your lips from speaking   de -   ceit.
   seek and strive af -   ter   peace.

All / Melody:

1. | *To repeat* | 2. | *To antiphon*

Share in the joy, the joy of the Lord. Share in the joy of the Lord.

Soprano Descant

Share in the joy, the joy of the Lord. Share in the joy of the Lord.

Tenor /Alto Descant

Share in the joy, the joy of the Lord. Share in the joy of the Lord.

Verses (continued)

Cantor:

8. The eyes of the LORD are toward   the   just
   The face of the LORD rebuffs   the   wicked
9. They call and   the   LORD hears
   The LORD is close to the bro - ken - hearted;
10. Many are the trials of   the   upright
    keeping guard over all   their   bones,
11. Evil brings death to   the   wicked;
    The LORD ransoms the souls of   the   faithful.
12. I was always in   your   presence;
    You will guide me by   your   counsel
13. What else have I in heaven   but   you?
    My body and my heart faint   for   joy;
14. To be near God is   my   happiness.
    I will tell of all   your   works

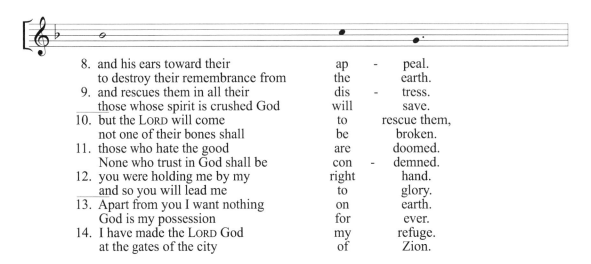

8.	and his ears toward their	ap -	peal.
	to destroy their remembrance from	the	earth.
9.	and rescues them in all their	dis -	tress.
	those whose spirit is crushed God	will	save.
10.	but the LORD will come	to	rescue them,
	not one of their bones shall	be	broken.
11.	those who hate the good	are	doomed.
	None who trust in God shall be	con -	demned.
12.	you were holding me by my	right	hand.
	and so you will lead me	to	glory.
13.	Apart from you I want nothing	on	earth.
	God is my possession	for	ever.
14.	I have made the LORD God	my	refuge.
	at the gates of the city	of	Zion.

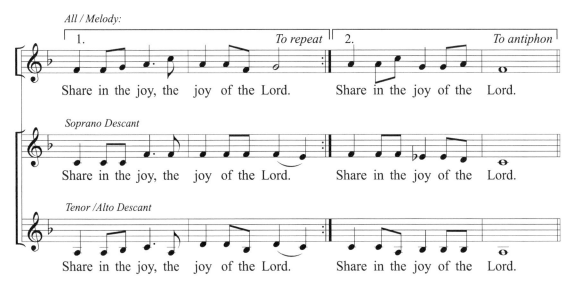

All / Melody:

1. Share in the joy, the joy of the Lord. *To repeat* **2.** Share in the joy of the Lord. *To antiphon*

Soprano Descant

Share in the joy, the joy of the Lord. Share in the joy of the Lord.

Tenor /Alto Descant

Share in the joy, the joy of the Lord. Share in the joy of the Lord.

Antiphon / Melody $\half = $ ca. 60

Come, come to the ban-quet: all that I have is yours.

Alto Descant

Come, come to the ban-quet: all is yours.

Come, come to the ban-quet: all that I have is yours.

Come, come to the ban-quet: all I have is yours.

Verses (*Option A) *Psalm 78:13-16, 23-29, 35, 52-53*

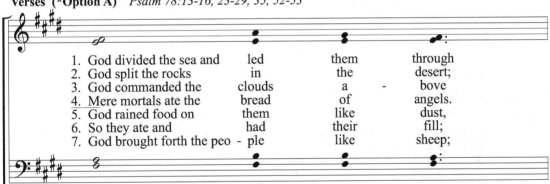

1. God divided the sea and led them through
2. God split the rocks in the desert;
3. God commanded the clouds a - bove
4. Mere mortals ate the bread of angels.
5. God rained food on them like dust,
6. So they ate and had their fill;
7. God brought forth the peo - ple like sheep;

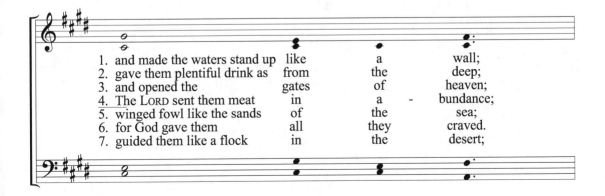

1. and made the waters stand up like a wall;
2. gave them plentiful drink as from the deep;
3. and opened the gates of heaven;
4. The LORD sent them meat in a - bundance;
5. winged fowl like the sands of the sea;
6. for God gave them all they craved.
7. guided them like a flock in the desert;

1. leading them by day with a cloud,
2. made streams flow out from the rock,
3. rained down manna for their food,
4. made the east wind blow from heaven
5. let it fall in the midst of their camp
6. They remembered that God was their rock,
7. led them safely with no - thing to fear,

1. by night, with a light of fire.
2. and made waters run down like rivers.
3. and gave them bread from heaven.
4. and roused the south wind with might.
5. and all around their tents.
6. God, the Most High, their re - deemer.
7. while the sea engulfed their foes.

Verses (*Option B) *Psalm 32*

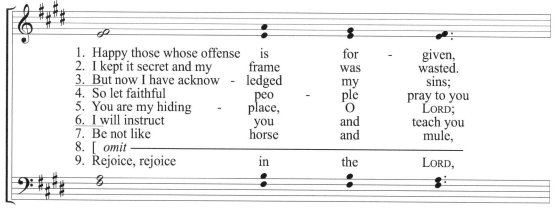

1. Happy those whose offense is for - given,
2. I kept it secret and my frame was wasted.
3. But now I have acknow - ledged my sins;
4. So let faithful peo - ple pray to you
5. You are my hiding - place, O LORD;
6. I will instruct you and teach you
7. Be not like horse and mule,
8. [omit ———————————————
9. Rejoice, rejoice in the LORD,

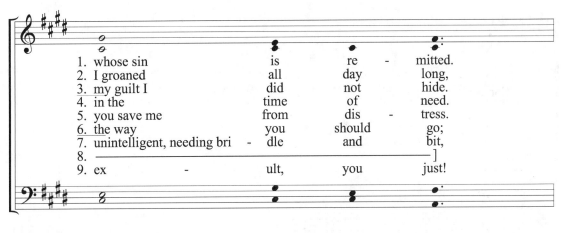

1. whose sin   is   re - mitted.
2. I groaned   all   day   long,
3. my guilt I   did   not   hide.
4. in the   time   of   need.
5. you save me   from   dis - tress.
6. the way   you   should   go;
7. unintelligent, needing bri - dle   and   bit,
8. —————————————————]
9. ex - ult,   you   just!

1. O happy those to whom the LORD im - putes   no   guilt,
2. for night and day your hand was hea - vy   up - on me.
3. I said: "I will confess my offense   to   the   LORD."
4. The floods of water   may   reach   high
5. [*omit* ———————————————]
6. I will   give   you   counsel
7. [*omit* ———————————————]
8. Many sorrows   have   the   wicked,
9. O come, ring   out   your   joy,

1. in whose spirit is   no   guile.
2. Indeed my strength was dried up as by the sum - mer's   heat.
3. And you, LORD, have forgiven the guilt of   my   sin.
4. but they shall stand   se - cure.
5. You surround me with cries of   de - liverance.
6. with my eye   up - on you.
7. else they will not   ap - proach you.
8. but those who trust in the LORD are surrounded with lov - ing   mercy.
9. all you upright   of   heart.

Performance Notes

Option A verses are used on the Fourth Sunday of Lent, Year C, and the Eighteenth Sunday in Ordinary Time, Year A. Option B verses are used on the Twenty-fourth Sunday in Ordinary Time, Year C.

Come, Lord, and Save Us

Antiphon ♩ = ca. 72

Come, Lord, and save us.

Verses *Psalm 146:6c-10b*

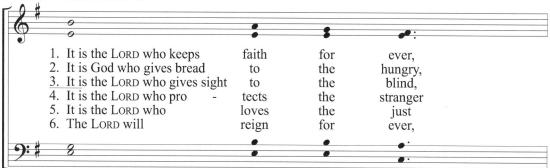

1. It is the LORD who keeps   faith   for   ever,
2. It is God who gives bread   to   the   hungry,
3. It is the LORD who gives sight   to   the   blind,
4. It is the LORD who pro - tects   the   stranger
5. It is the LORD who   loves   the   just
6. The LORD will   reign   for   ever,

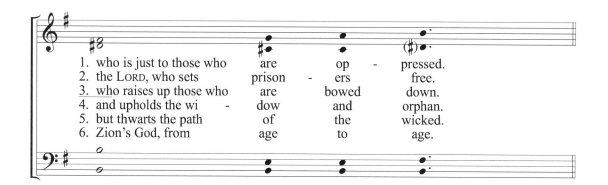

1. who is just to those who   are   op - pressed.
2. the LORD, who sets   prison - ers   free.
3. who raises up those who   are   bowed   down.
4. and upholds the wi - dow   and   orphan.
5. but thwarts the path   of   the   wicked.
6. Zion's God, from   age   to   age.

Performance Notes

The antiphon is in 5/8 time.

Come, My Children

Verses (Superimposed) *Jeremiah 31:10-14*

1. Hear the word of the LORD,   O
2. say, "He who scattered Israel   will
3. For the LORD has ran   -   somed
4. They shall come and sing aloud on the height   of
5. over the grain, the wine, and   the
6. their life shall become like a wa   -   tered
7. Then shall the young women rejoice in   the
8. I will turn their mourning in   -   to
9. I will give the priests their fill   of

Antiphon / Melody ♩ = ca. 92

Come, my child-ren, come to me!

1. nations,   and declare it to the coastlands
2. gather him,   and will keep him as a shep   -
3. Jacob,   and has redeemed him from hands too
4. Zion,   and they shall be radiant over the goodness
5. oil,   and over the young of the flock
6. garden,   and they shall never lan   -
7. dance,   and the young men and the old
8. joy,   I will comfort them, and give them glad   -
9. fatness,   and my people shall be satisfied with my bounty,

Come, my child-ren, come to me!

To repeat (verses) | *Final time*

1. far   a - way;
2. herd   a   flock."
3. strong for   him.
4. of   the   LORD,
5. and   the   herd;
6. guish   a - gain.
7. shall   be   merry.
8. ness   for   sorrow.
9. says   the   LORD.

Come, my child-ren, come to me.

Performance Notes

The cantor's verses overlap the repeated refrains of the assembly. It may be helpful to have a second cantor sing with and direct the assembly if a choir is not present. Establish the assembly refrain before adding the verses.

"Come," Says My Heart

Antiphon ♩ = 72

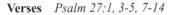

"Come," says my heart, "come, seek his face." Your face, O Lord, I seek.

Verses *Psalm 27:1, 3-5, 7-14*

1. The LORD is my light and my	help;	whom shall I	fear?
2. Though an army encamp a -	gainst me	my heart would not	fear.
3. ⌠There is one thing I ask of		⌠to live in the house of the	
⌡ the LORD, for this I⌡	long,	⌡ LORD all the days of my⌡	life,
4. For God makes me safe in his	tent	in the day of	evil.
5. O LORD, hear my voice when I	call;	have mercy and	answer.
6. It is your face, O LORD, that I	seek;	hide not your	face.
7. Do not abandon or for -	sake me,	O God my	help!
8. Instruct me, LORD, in your	way;	on an even path	lead me.
9. I am sure I shall see the LORD's	goodness	in the land of the	living.

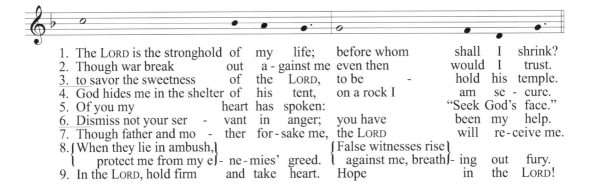

1. The LORD is the stronghold of	my life;	before whom shall I	shrink?
2. Though war break out	a - gainst me even then	would I	trust.
3. to savor the sweetness of	the LORD, to be -	hold his	temple.
4. God hides me in the shelter of	his tent,	on a rock I am	se - cure.
5. Of you my	heart has spoken:	"Seek God's	face."
6. Dismiss not your ser -	vant in anger;	you have been my	help.
7. Though father and mo -	ther for - sake me,	the LORD will	re - ceive me.
8. ⌠When they lie in ambush,⌡		⌠False witnesses rise⌡	
⌡ protect me from my e⌡ - ne - mies'	greed.	⌡ against me, breath⌡ - ing	out fury.
9. In the LORD, hold firm	and take heart.	Hope in the	LORD!

Come to Me and Drink

Antiphon ♩ = ca. 108

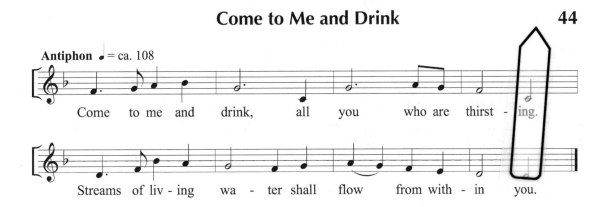

Come to me and drink, all you who are thirst - ing.

Streams of liv - ing wa - ter shall flow from with - in you.

Verses *Psalms 63:2-9; 42:2-3, 8-9*

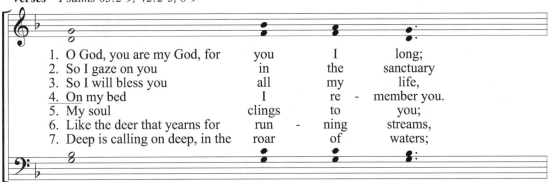

1. O God, you are my God, for you I long;
2. So I gaze on you in the sanctuary
3. So I will bless you all my life,
4. On my bed I re - member you.
5. My soul clings to you;
6. Like the deer that yearns for run - ning streams,
7. Deep is calling on deep, in the roar of waters;

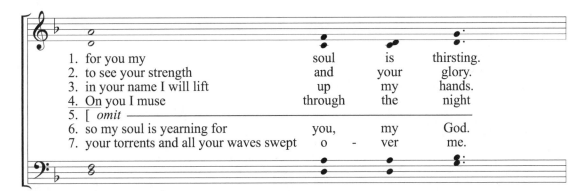

1. for you my soul is thirsting.
2. to see your strength and your glory.
3. in your name I will lift up my hands.
4. On you I muse through the night
5. [*omit* ———————————————————
6. so my soul is yearning for you, my God.
7. your torrents and all your waves swept o - ver me.

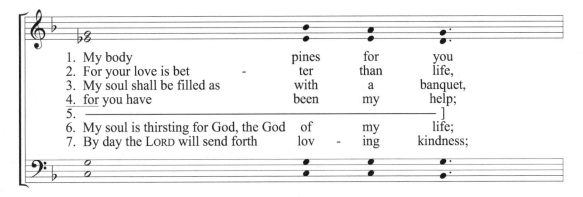

1. My body pines for you
2. For your love is bet - ter than life,
3. My soul shall be filled as with a banquet,
4. for you have been my help;
5. ————————————————————————]
6. My soul is thirsting for God, the God of my life;
7. By day the Lord will send forth lov - ing kindness;

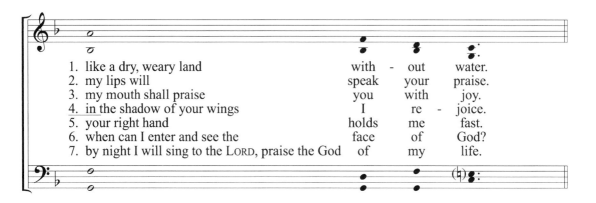

1. like a dry, weary land   with - out   water.
2. my lips will   speak   your   praise.
3. my mouth shall praise   you   with   joy.
4. <u>in</u> the shadow of your wings   I   re - joice.
5. your right hand   holds   me   fast.
6. when can I enter and see the   face   of   God?
7. by night I will sing to the LORD, praise the God   of   my   life.

Come to Me and You Shall Never Hunger

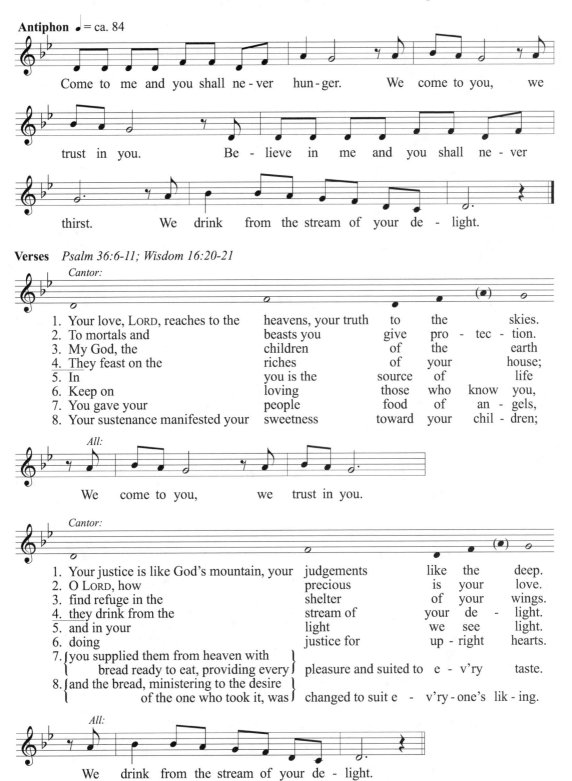

Antiphon ♩ = ca. 84

Come to me and you shall ne‑ver hun‑ger. We come to you, we trust in you. Be‑lieve in me and you shall ne‑ver thirst. We drink from the stream of your de‑light.

Verses *Psalm 36:6-11; Wisdom 16:20-21*

Cantor:

1. Your love, LORD, reaches to the heavens, your truth to the skies.
2. To mortals and beasts you give pro - tec - tion.
3. My God, the children of the earth
4. They feast on the riches of your house;
5. In you is the source of life
6. Keep on loving those who know you,
7. You gave your people food of an - gels,
8. Your sustenance manifested your sweetness toward your chil - dren;

All:

We come to you, we trust in you.

Cantor:

1. Your justice is like God's mountain, your judgements like the deep.
2. O LORD, how precious is your love.
3. find refuge in the shelter of your wings.
4. they drink from the stream of your de - light.
5. and in your light we see light.
6. doing justice for up - right hearts.
7. { you supplied them from heaven with bread ready to eat, providing every } pleasure and suited to e - v'ry taste.
8. { and the bread, ministering to the desire of the one who took it, was } changed to suit e - v'ry‑one's lik - ing.

All:

We drink from the stream of your de - light.

Courage! Get Up!

Antiphon / Melody ♩ = ca. 100

Cou - rage! Get up! Je - sus is call - ing you! Take

Alto Descant

Cou - rage! Get up! Je - sus is call - ing you! Take

Tenor Descant

Cou - rage! Get up! Je - sus is call - ing you! Take

cou - rage! Get up, and be on your way!

cou - rage! Get up, and be on your way!

cou - rage! Get up, and be on your way!

Verses *Psalm 20:2-3, 5-6ab, 7-10*

1. May the LORD answer in time of trial; may the name of Jacob's God pro - tect you.
2. May God send you help from the shrine and give you sup - port from Zion.
3. May God give you your heart's de - sire and fulfill every one of your plans.
4. May we ring out our joy at your victory and rejoice in the name of our God.
5. {I am sure now that the} {will reply from his holy}
   {LORD will give victory to} his a - nointed, {heaven with a mighty vic} - tor - ious hand.
6. Some trust in char - iots or horses, but we in the name of the LORD.
7. They will col - lapse and fall, but we shall hold and stand firm.
8. Give victory to the king, O LORD, give answer on the day we call.

Do Not Abandon Me, Lord!

Verses (Superimposed)   *Psalm 38*

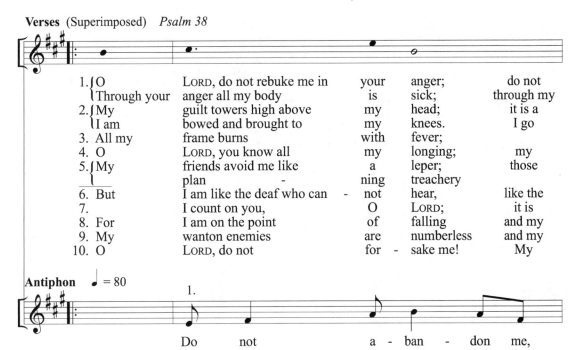

1. {O / Through your} LORD, do not rebuke me in your anger; do not / anger all my body is sick; through my
2. {My / I am} guilt towers high above my head; it is a / bowed and brought to my knees. I go
3. All my frame burns with fever;
4. O LORD, you know all my longing; my
5. {My friends avoid me like a leper; those / plan - ning treachery}
6. But I am like the deaf who can - not hear, like the
7. I count on you, O LORD; it is
8. For I am on the point of falling and my
9. My wanton enemies are numberless and my
10. O LORD, do not for - sake me! My

Antiphon   ♩ = 80

1. Do not a - ban - don me,

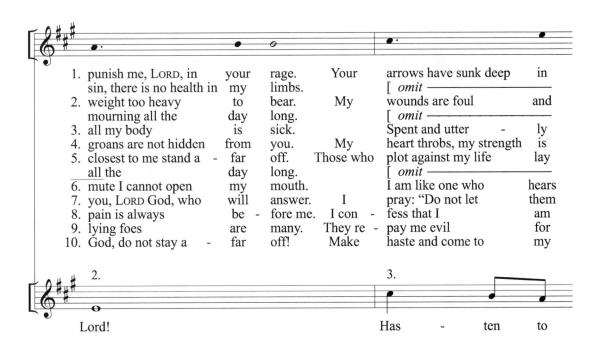

1. punish me, LORD, in your rage. Your arrows have sunk deep in
   sin, there is no health in my limbs. [*omit* ——————
2. weight too heavy to bear. My wounds are foul and
   mourning all the day long. [*omit* ——————
3. all my body is sick. Spent and utter - ly
4. groans are not hidden from you. My heart throbs, my strength is
5. closest to me stand a - far off. Those who plot against my life lay
   all the day long. [*omit* ——————
6. mute I cannot open my mouth. I am like one who hears
7. you, LORD God, who will answer. I pray: "Do not let them
8. pain is always be - fore me. I con - fess that I am
9. lying foes are many. They re - pay me evil for
10. God, do not stay a - far off! Make haste and come to my

2. Lord!

3. Has - ten to

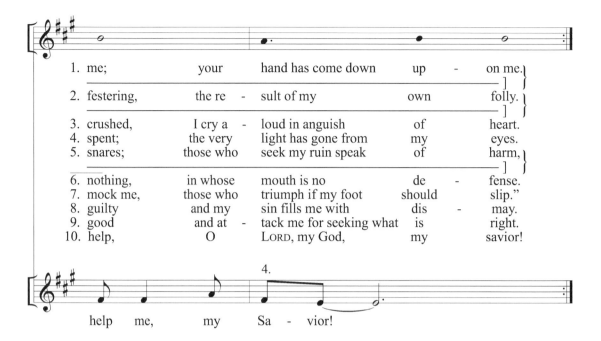

1. me; your hand has come down up - on me.
2. festering, the re - sult of my own folly.
3. crushed, I cry a - loud in anguish of heart.
4. spent; the very light has gone from my eyes.
5. snares; those who seek my ruin speak of harm,
6. nothing, in whose mouth is no de - fense.
7. mock me, those who triumph if my foot should slip."
8. guilty and my sin fills me with dis - may.
9. good and at - tack me for seeking what is right.
10. help, O LORD, my God, my savior!

4.

help me, my Sa - vior!

Performance Notes

The antiphon can be sung as a round as indicated.

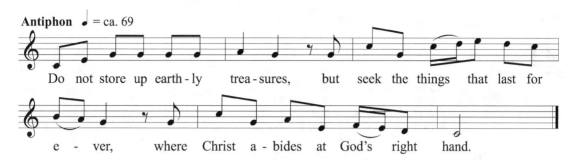

Antiphon ♩ = ca. 69

Do not store up earth-ly trea-sures, but seek the things that last for e - ver, where Christ a - bides at God's right hand.

Verses (*Option A) *Psalms 36:6-11; 63:2-6, 8-9*

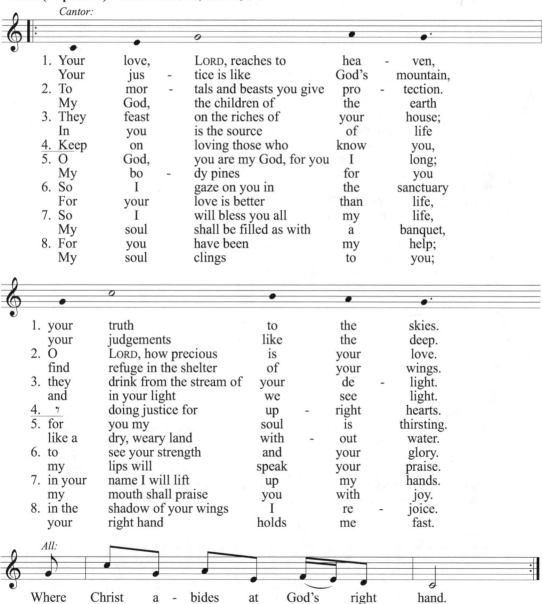

Cantor:

1. Your love, LORD, reaches to hea - ven,
   Your jus - tice is like God's mountain,
2. To mor - tals and beasts you give pro - tection.
   My God, the children of the earth
3. They feast on the riches of your house;
   In you is the source of life
4. Keep on loving those who know you,
5. O God, you are my God, for you I long;
   My bo - dy pines for you
6. So I gaze on you in the sanctuary
   For your love is better than life,
7. So I will bless you all my life,
   My soul shall be filled as with a banquet,
8. For you have been my help;
   My soul clings to you;

1. your truth to the skies.
   your judgements like the deep.
2. O LORD, how precious is your love.
   find refuge in the shelter of your wings.
3. they drink from the stream of your de - light.
   and in your light we see light.
4. ⁊ doing justice for up - right hearts.
5. for you my soul is thirsting.
   like a dry, weary land with - out water.
6. to see your strength and your glory.
   my lips will speak your praise.
7. in your name I will lift up my hands.
   my mouth shall praise you with joy.
8. in the shadow of your wings I re - joice.
   your right hand holds me fast.

All:

Where Christ a - bides at God's right hand.

Verses (*Option B) *Psalm 37:3-6, 18-19, 23-24, 27-29*

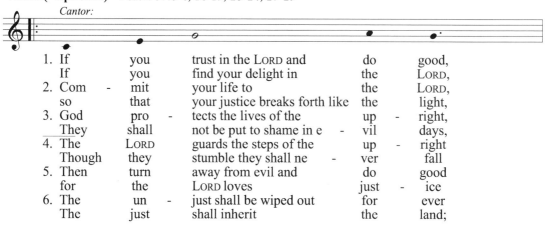

Cantor:

1. If you trust in the LORD and do good,
   If you find your delight in the LORD,
2. Com - mit your life to the LORD,
   so that your justice breaks forth like the light,
3. God pro - tects the lives of the up - right,
   They shall not be put to shame in e - vil days,
4. The LORD guards the steps of the up - right
   Though they stumble they shall ne - ver fall
5. Then turn away from evil and do good
   for the LORD loves just - ice
6. The un - just shall be wiped out for ever
   The just shall inherit the land;

If additional verses are required, sing the first four stanzas from Option A, Psalm 36:6-11.

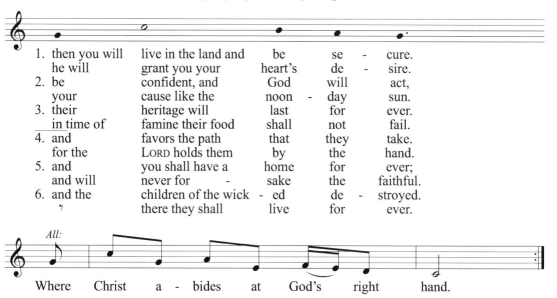

1. then you will live in the land and be se - cure.
   he will grant you your heart's de - sire.
2. be confident, and God will act,
   your cause like the noon - day sun.
3. their heritage will last for ever.
   in time of famine their food shall not fail.
4. and favors the path that they take.
   for the LORD holds them by the hand.
5. and you shall have a home for ever;
   and will never for - sake the faithful.
6. and the children of the wick - ed de - stroyed.
   there they shall live for ever.

All:

Where Christ a - bides at God's right hand.

Performance Notes

Option A verses are used on the Eighteenth Sunday in Ordinary Time, Year C. Option B verses are used on the Twenty-fifth Sunday in Ordinary Time, Year C.

This setting is designed for unaccompanied singing in neo-plainsong style, the recommended option, keeping the music flowing, as indicated by the metronome marking. It would of course be possible to sing the Wachet auf *chorale tune to the slower J.S. Bach harmonization found in many hymn books.*

The tone is sung twice through for each stanza except stanza 4 of Option A.

Don't Be Afraid

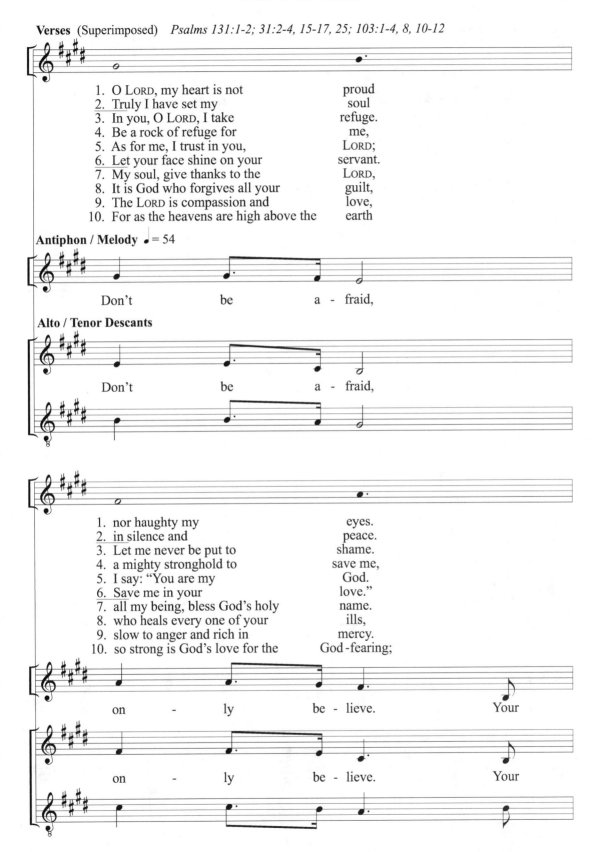

Verses (Superimposed) *Psalms 131:1-2; 31:2-4, 15-17, 25; 103:1-4, 8, 10-12*

1. O LORD, my heart is not proud
2. Truly I have set my soul
3. In you, O LORD, I take refuge.
4. Be a rock of refuge for me,
5. As for me, I trust in you, LORD;
6. Let your face shine on your servant.
7. My soul, give thanks to the LORD,
8. It is God who forgives all your guilt,
9. The LORD is compassion and love,
10. For as the heavens are high above the earth

Antiphon / Melody ♩ = 54

Don't be a - fraid,

Alto / Tenor Descants

Don't be a - fraid,

1. nor haughty my eyes.
2. in silence and peace.
3. Let me never be put to shame.
4. a mighty stronghold to save me,
5. I say: "You are my God.
6. Save me in your love."
7. all my being, bless God's holy name.
8. who heals every one of your ills,
9. slow to anger and rich in mercy.
10. so strong is God's love for the God-fearing;

on - ly be - lieve. Your

on - ly be - lieve. Your

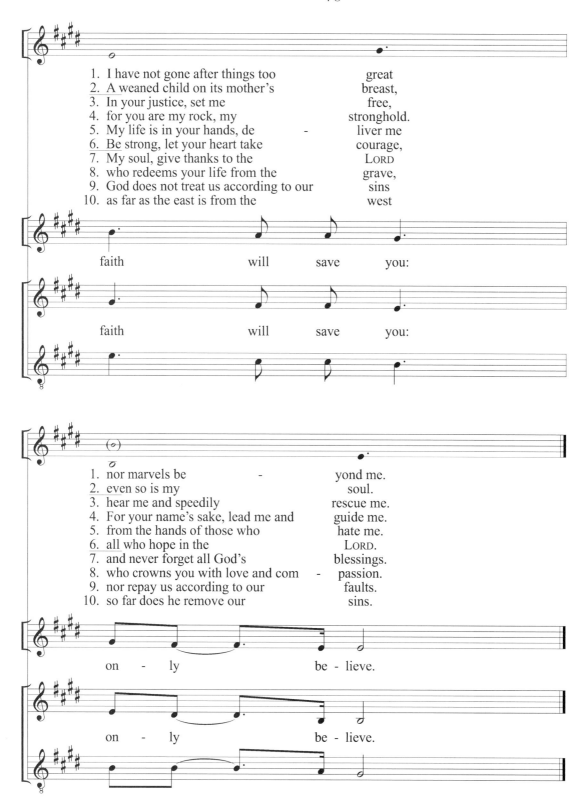

1. I have not gone after things too   great
2. A weaned child on its mother's   breast,
3. In your justice, set me   free,
4. for you are my rock, my   stronghold.
5. My life is in your hands, de - liver me
6. Be strong, let your heart take   courage,
7. My soul, give thanks to the   Lord
8. who redeems your life from the   grave,
9. God does not treat us according to our   sins
10. as far as the east is from the   west

faith   will   save   you:

faith   will   save   you:

1. nor marvels be - yond me.
2. even so is my   soul.
3. hear me and speedily   rescue me.
4. For your name's sake, lead me and   guide me.
5. from the hands of those who   hate me.
6. all who hope in the   Lord.
7. and never forget all God's   blessings.
8. who crowns you with love and com - passion.
9. nor repay us according to our   faults.
10. so far does he remove our   sins.

on - ly   be - lieve.

on - ly   be - lieve.

Verses (continued)   *Psalms 103:13-14, 17-18; 31:20-22b, 24ab, 25; 73:1-2, 23-26*

11. As parents have compassion on their   children,
12. The love of the LORD is ever   -   lasting
13. How great is the goodness,   LORD,
14. You hide them in the shelter of your   presence
15. Love the LORD, all you   saints.
16. How good is God to   Israel,
17. Yet I was always in your   presence;
18. What else have I in heaven but   you?

11. the LORD has pity on those who are   God-fearing
12. upon those who fear the   LORD.
13. that you keep for those who   fear you,
14. from human   plots;
15. The LORD guards the   faithful.
16. to those who are pure of   heart.
17. you were holding me by my right   hand.
18. Apart from you I want nothing on   earth.

11. for he knows of what we are   made,
12. God's justice reaches out to children's   children
13. that you show to those who   trust you
14. you keep them safe within your   tent
15. Be strong, let your heart take   courage,
16. Yet my feet came close to   stumbling,
17. You will guide me by your   counsel
18. My body and my heart faint for   joy;

11. and remembers that we are   dust.
12. when they keep his covenant in   truth.
13. in the sight of   all.
14. from disputing   tongues.
15. all who hope in the   LORD.
16. my steps had almost   slipped.
17. and so you will lead me to   glory.
18. God is my possession for   ever.

Performance Notes

Verses 3–12 are used on the Nineteenth Sunday in Ordinary Time, Years A and C.
Verses 1–12 are used on the Thirteenth Sunday in Ordinary Time, Year B.
Verses 3–6 and 13–18 are used on the Thirty-third Sunday in Ordinary Time, Year C.
As the cantor sings the verses, the other voices may vocalize to 'oo' under the superimposed tone instead of
singing the words.

Eat My Flesh and Drink My Blood

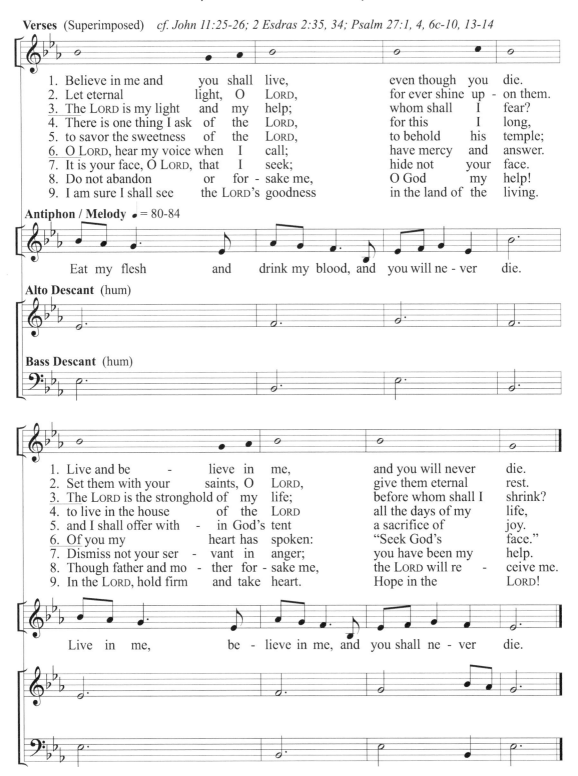

Verses (Superimposed)   *cf. John 11:25-26; 2 Esdras 2:35, 34; Psalm 27:1, 4, 6c-10, 13-14*

1. Believe in me and   you shall   live,   even though you   die.
2. Let eternal   light, O   LORD,   for ever shine up - on them.
3. The LORD is my light   and my   help;   whom shall   I   fear?
4. There is one thing I ask   of   the   LORD,   for this   I   long,
5. to savor the sweetness   of   the   LORD,   to behold   his   temple;
6. O LORD, hear my voice when   I   call;   have mercy   and   answer.
7. It is your face, O LORD, that   I   seek;   hide not   your   face.
8. Do not abandon   or   for - sake me,   O God   my   help!
9. I am sure I shall see   the LORD's goodness   in the land of the   living.

Antiphon / Melody ♩. = 80-84

Eat my flesh   and   drink my blood, and   you will ne - ver   die.

Alto Descant (hum)

Bass Descant (hum)

1. Live and be - lieve in   me,   and you will never   die.
2. Set them with your   saints, O   LORD,   give them eternal   rest.
3. The LORD is the stronghold of   my   life;   before whom shall I   shrink?
4. to live in the house   of   the   LORD   all the days of my   life,
5. and I shall offer with -   in God's tent   a sacrifice of   joy.
6. Of you my   heart has   spoken: "Seek God's   face."
7. Dismiss not your ser - vant in   anger;   you have been my   help.
8. Though father and mo - ther for - sake me,   the LORD will re - ceive me.
9. In the LORD, hold firm   and take heart.   Hope in the   LORD!

Live in   me,   be - lieve in me, and   you shall ne - ver   die.

Everlasting Is Your Love

Antiphon ♩ = ca. 80

E - ver - last - ing is your love; do not for - sake what your

hands have made, Lord. hands have made. E - ver - last - ing is your love;

do not for - sake what your hands have made.

Verses *Psalm 138:1-3, 6, 8bc*

1. I thank you, LORD, with all my heart, {you have heard the words of} my mouth.
2. I thank you for your faithful-ness and love {which excel all we e -} ver knew of you.
3. The LORD is high yet looks on the lowly {and the haughty God knows from} a - far.

1. {In the presence of the angels} I will bless you. I will adore before your ho - ly temple.
2. On the day I called, you answered; you increased the strength of my soul.
3. Your love, O LORD, is e - ternal, discard not the work of your hands.

Every Valley Shall Be Filled

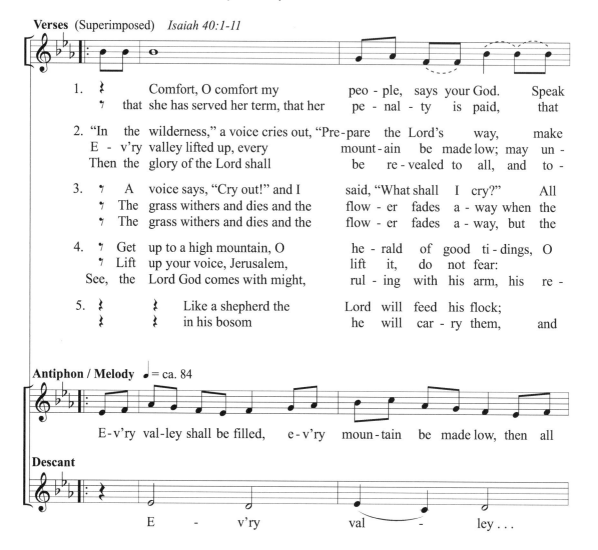

Verses (Superimposed)   *Isaiah 40:1-11*

1. Comfort, O comfort my peo - ple, says your God. Speak
   that she has served her term, that her pe - nal - ty is paid, that

2. "In the wilderness," a voice cries out, "Pre - pare the Lord's way, make
   E - v'ry valley lifted up, every mount - ain be made low; may un -
   Then the glory of the Lord shall be re - vealed to all, and to -

3. A voice says, "Cry out!" and I said, "What shall I cry?" All
   The grass withers and dies and the flow - er fades a - way when the
   The grass withers and dies and the flow - er fades a - way, but the

4. Get up to a high mountain, O he - rald of good ti - dings, O
   Lift up your voice, Jerusalem, lift it, do not fear:
   See, the Lord God comes with might, rul - ing with his arm, his re -

5. Like a shepherd the Lord will feed his flock;
   in his bosom he will car - ry them, and

Antiphon / Melody ♩ = ca. 84

E-v'ry val-ley shall be filled, e - v'ry moun-tain be made low, then all

Descant

E - v'ry val - ley . . .

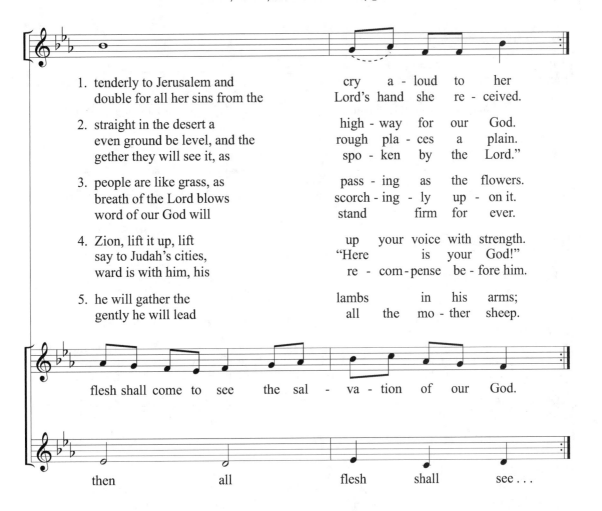

1. tenderly to Jerusalem and   cry   a - loud   to   her
   double for all her sins from the   Lord's hand   she   re - ceived.

2. straight in the desert a   high - way   for   our   God.
   even ground be level, and the   rough   pla - ces   a   plain.
   gether they will see it, as   spo - ken   by   the   Lord."

3. people are like grass, as   pass - ing   as   the   flowers.
   breath of the Lord blows   scorch - ing - ly   up - on it.
   word of our God will   stand   firm   for   ever.

4. Zion, lift it up, lift   up   your voice with strength.
   say to Judah's cities,   "Here   is   your   God!"
   ward is with him, his   re - com - pense   be - fore him.

5. he will gather the   lambs   in   his   arms;
   gently he will lead   all   the   mo - ther   sheep.

flesh shall come to see   the sal - va - tion   of   our   God.

then   all   flesh   shall   see . . .

Father, into Your Hands

Antiphon / Melody ♩ = 66

Fa-ther, in-to your hands, in-to your hands I com-mend my spi-rit.

Descant

Fa-ther, in-to your hands I com-mend my spi-rit.

Verses *Psalm 31:2, 6, 12-13, 15-17, 25*

1. In you, O LORD, I take refuge.
   Let me never be put to shame. In your justice, set me free.
2. In the face of all my foes I am a re-proach,
3. Those who see me in the street run far a - way from me.
4. But as for me, I trust in you, LORD; I say: "You are my God.
5. Let your face shine on your servant. Save me in your love."

1. Into your hands I com - mend my spirit. It is you who will re-deem me, LORD.
2. an object of scorn to my neighbors and of fear to my friends.
3. I am like the dead, forgot-ten by all, like a thing thrown a - way.
4. My life is in your hands, de - liver me from the hands of those who hate me.
5. Be strong, let your heart take courage, all who hope in the LORD.

Antiphon ♩ = ca. 50

Fin - est food! Choic-est wine! All we need, our God pro-vides.

Fin - est food! Choic-est wine! Come, the ban-quet is rea - dy!

Verses *Psalms 125:1-4, 5c; 96:1-10*

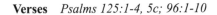

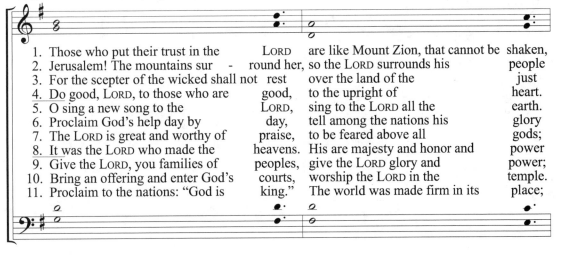

1. Those who put their trust in the LORD are like Mount Zion, that cannot be shaken,
2. Jerusalem! The mountains sur - round her, so the LORD surrounds his people
3. For the scepter of the wicked shall not rest over the land of the just
4. Do good, LORD, to those who are good, to the upright of heart.
5. O sing a new song to the LORD, sing to the LORD all the earth.
6. Proclaim God's help day by day, tell among the nations his glory
7. The LORD is great and worthy of praise, to be feared above all gods;
8. It was the LORD who made the heavens. His are majesty and honor and power
9. Give the LORD, you families of peoples, give the LORD glory and power;
10. Bring an offering and enter God's courts, worship the LORD in the temple.
11. Proclaim to the nations: "God is king." The world was made firm in its place;

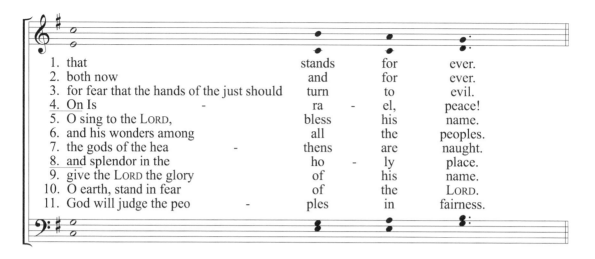

1. that stands for ever.
2. both now and for ever.
3. for fear that the hands of the just should turn to evil.
4. On Is - ra - el, peace!
5. O sing to the LORD, bless his name.
6. and his wonders among all the peoples.
7. the gods of the hea - thens are naught.
8. and splendor in the ho - ly place.
9. give the LORD the glory of his name.
10. O earth, stand in fear of the LORD.
11. God will judge the peo - ples in fairness.

55 For Ever, For Ever, We Praise You For Ever

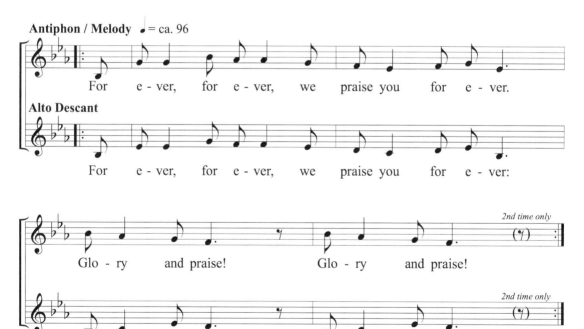

Antiphon / Melody ♩ = ca. 96

For e - ver, for e - ver, we praise you for e - ver.

Alto Descant

For e - ver, for e - ver, we praise you for e - ver:

Glo - ry and praise! Glo - ry and praise!

2nd time only

Glo - ry and praise! Glo - ry and praise!

2nd time only

Verses   *Daniel 3:52-56*

1. Blest are you, Lord, the God of our fore-bears.
2. Blest are you in the tem-ple of your glo-ry,
3. Blest are you from the throne of your king-dom.

Ah . . .

Glo-ry and praise! Glo-ry and praise!
Glo-ry and praise! Glo-ry and praise!

1. Blest your ho-ly and
2. who look to the depths from your
3. Blest are you in the

Ah . . .

1. glo-ri-ous name, Lord.
2. throne with the an-gels.
3. fir-ma-ment of hea-ven.

Glo-ry and praise! Glo-ry and praise!
Glo-ry and praise! Glo-ry and praise!

Performance Notes

A variety of styles possible here, from a detached Gospel style to a smoother and more relaxed rendition.
The tempo may be faster or slower than that indicated.

For You My Soul Is Thirsting

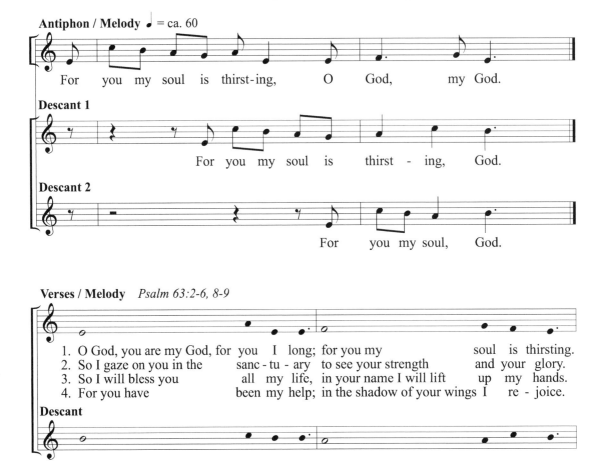

Antiphon / Melody ♩ = ca. 60

For you my soul is thirst-ing, O God, my God.

Descant 1

For you my soul is thirst - ing, God.

Descant 2

For you my soul, God.

Verses / Melody   *Psalm 63:2-6, 8-9*

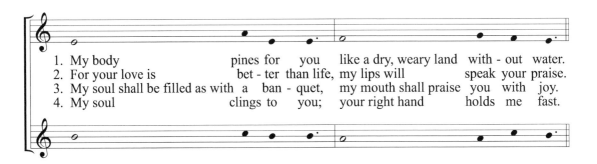

1. O God, you are my God, for you I long; for you my soul is thirsting.
2. So I gaze on you in the sanc - tu - ary to see your strength and your glory.
3. So I will bless you all my life, in your name I will lift up my hands.
4. For you have been my help; in the shadow of your wings I re - joice.

Descant

1. My body pines for you like a dry, weary land with - out water.
2. For your love is bet - ter than life, my lips will speak your praise.
3. My soul shall be filled as with a ban - quet, my mouth shall praise you with joy.
4. My soul clings to you; your right hand holds me fast.

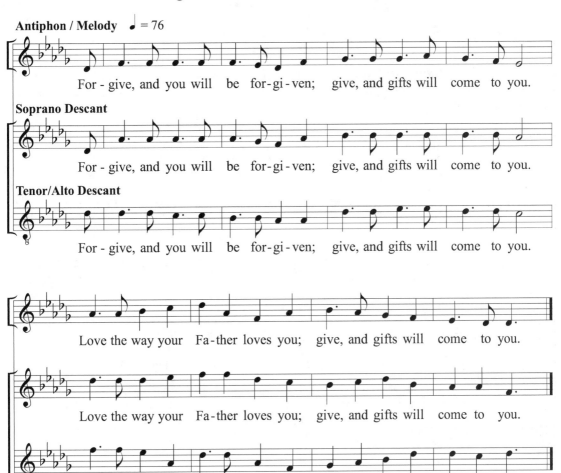

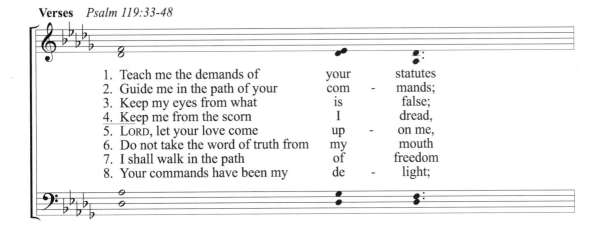

Verses *Psalm 119:33-48*

1. Teach me the demands of your statutes
2. Guide me in the path of your com - mands;
3. Keep my eyes from what is false;
4. Keep me from the scorn I dread,
5. LORD, let your love come up - on me,
6. Do not take the word of truth from my mouth
7. I shall walk in the path of freedom
8. Your commands have been my de - light;

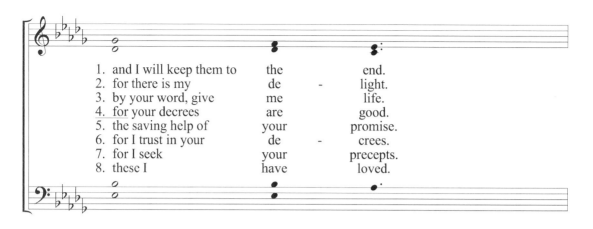

1. and I will keep them to the end.
2. for there is my de - light.
3. by your word, give me life.
4. for your decrees are good.
5. the saving help of your promise.
6. for I trust in your de - crees.
7. for I seek your precepts.
8. these I have loved.

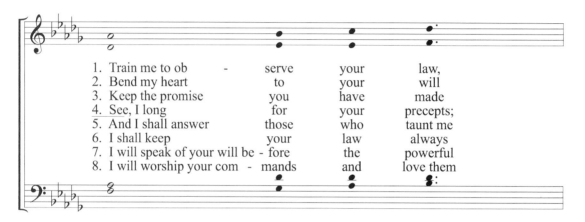

1. Train me to ob - serve your law,
2. Bend my heart to your will
3. Keep the promise you have made
4. See, I long for your precepts;
5. And I shall answer those who taunt me
6. I shall keep your law always
7. I will speak of your will be - fore the powerful
8. I will worship your com - mands and love them

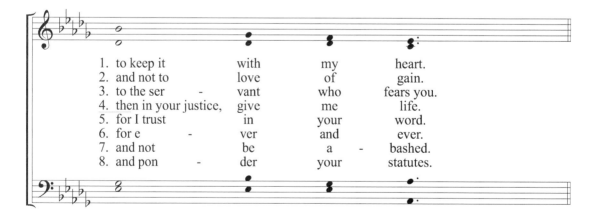

1. to keep it with my heart.
2. and not to love of gain.
3. to the ser - vant who fears you.
4. then in your justice, give me life.
5. for I trust in your word.
6. for e - ver and ever.
7. and not be a - bashed.
8. and pon - der your statutes.

Antiphon / Melody ♩ = 66

From the east and west, from the north and south, we will

Alto Descant

East, west, north, south,

come to the ta-ble and feast, where the first are last and the

come to the ta-ble and feast. First, last,

last are first, and the great-est be-come the least.

last, first, great-est be-come the least.

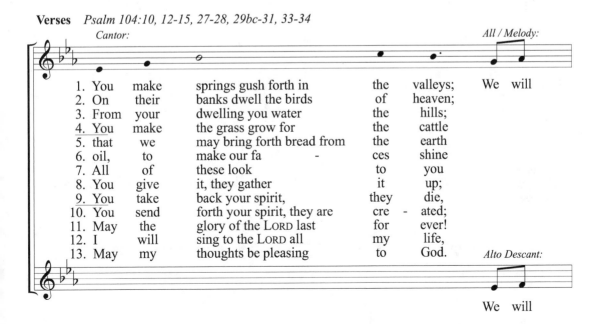

Verses *Psalm 104:10, 12-15, 27-28, 29bc-31, 33-34*

Cantor: *All / Melody:*

1. You	make	springs gush forth in	the	valleys;	We will
2. On	their	banks dwell the birds	of	heaven;	
3. From	your	dwelling you water	the	hills;	
4. You	make	the grass grow for	the	cattle	
5. that	we	may bring forth bread from	the	earth	
6. oil,	to	make our fa -	ces	shine	
7. All	of	these look	to	you	
8. You	give	it, they gather	it	up;	
9. You	take	back your spirit,	they	die,	
10. You	send	forth your spirit, they are	cre -	ated;	
11. May	the	glory of the LORD last	for	ever!	
12. I	will	sing to the LORD all	my	life,	
13. May	my	thoughts be pleasing	to	God.	

Alto Descant:

We will

come to the ta - ble and feast.

come to the ta - ble and feast.

Cantor: *All / Melody:*

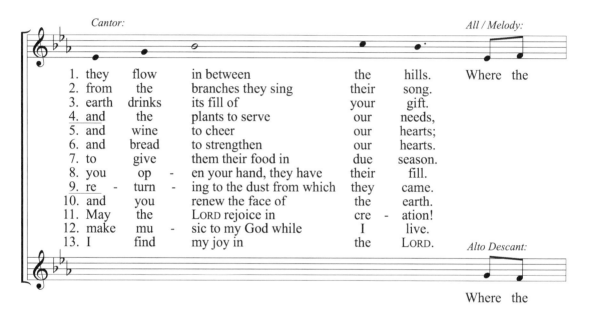

1. they flow in between the hills. Where the
2. from the branches they sing their song.
3. earth drinks its fill of your gift.
4. and the plants to serve our needs,
5. and wine to cheer our hearts;
6. and bread to strengthen our hearts.
7. to give them their food in due season.
8. you op - en your hand, they have their fill.
9. re - turn - ing to the dust from which they came.
10. and you renew the face of the earth.
11. May the LORD rejoice in cre - ation!
12. make mu - sic to my God while I live.
13. I find my joy in the LORD.

Alto Descant:

Where the

great - est be - come the least.

great - est be - come the least.

Performance Notes

The antiphon melody is adapted from the first half of the anonymous English carol tune NOEL, *traditionally sung in England to "It came upon the midnight clear."*

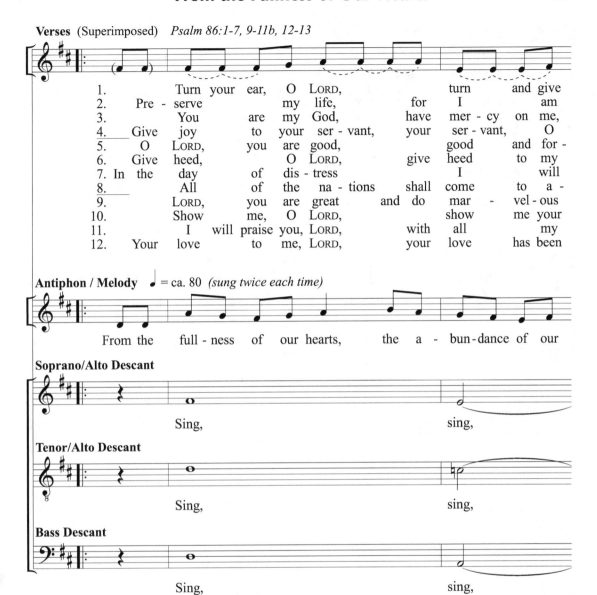

Verses (Superimposed)   *Psalm 86:1-7, 9-11b, 12-13*

1. Turn your ear, O LORD, turn and give
2. Pre - serve my life, for I am
3. You are my God, have mer - cy on me,
4. Give joy to your ser - vant, your ser - vant, O
5. O LORD, you are good, good and for -
6. Give heed, O LORD, give heed to my
7. In the day of dis - tress I will
8. All of the na - tions shall come to a -
9. LORD, you are great and do mar - vel - ous
10. Show me, O LORD, show me your
11. I will praise you, LORD, with all my
12. Your love to me, LORD, your love has been

Antiphon / Melody   ♩ = ca. 80 *(sung twice each time)*

From the full - ness of our hearts, the a - bun-dance of our

Soprano/Alto Descant

Sing,   sing,

Tenor/Alto Descant

Sing,   sing,

Bass Descant

Sing,   sing,

1. an - swer,   for   I   am   poor   and   need-y.
2. faith-ful, save the   ser - vant who trusts   in   you.
3. LORD,   for   I   cry   to   you   all   the   day   long.
4. LORD,   for   to   you   I   lift   up   my   soul.
5. giv - ing, full   of   love   to   all   who   call.
6. prayer   and   at - tend   to   the sound   of   my   voice.
7. call   and   sure - ly   you   will   re - ply.
8. dore you   and   glo - ri - fy your name,   O   LORD.
9. deeds,   you   who   a - lone   are   God.
10. way   so   that   I   may   walk   in   your   truth.
11. heart   and   glo - ri - fy your name,   for   e - ver.
12. great,   you have saved me from the depths   of   the   grave.

hearts,   let   us   sing   of   the   good-ness   of   the   Lord.

to   the   Lord.

O   sing,   to   the   Lord.

sing   to   the   Lord.

Performance Notes

The antiphon and descant parts are hummed when the verse is superimposed.
The psalm text has been slightly adapted for performance purposes.

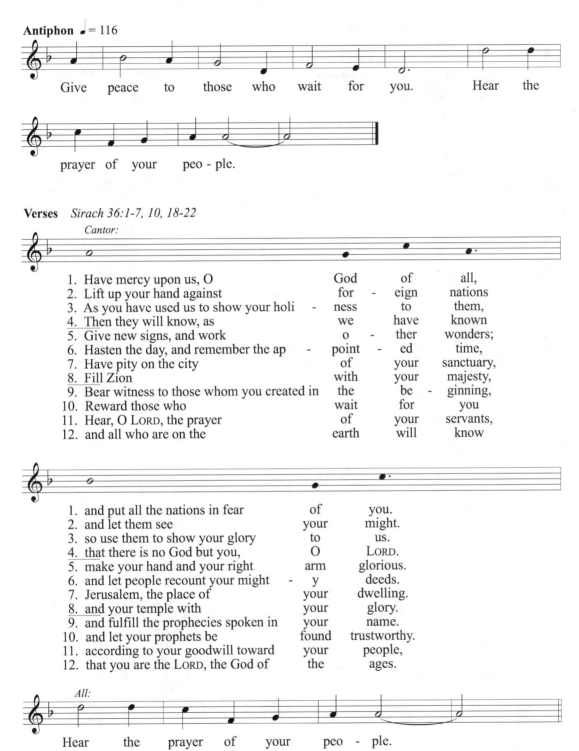

Antiphon ♩ = 116

Give peace to those who wait for you. Hear the prayer of your peo-ple.

Verses *Sirach 36:1-7, 10, 18-22*

Cantor:

1. Have mercy upon us, O God of all,
2. Lift up your hand against for - eign nations
3. As you have used us to show your holi - ness to them,
4. Then they will know, as we have known
5. Give new signs, and work o - ther wonders;
6. Hasten the day, and remember the ap - point - ed time,
7. Have pity on the city of your sanctuary,
8. Fill Zion with your majesty,
9. Bear witness to those whom you created in the be - ginning,
10. Reward those who wait for you
11. Hear, O Lord, the prayer of your servants,
12. and all who are on the earth will know

1. and put all the nations in fear of you.
2. and let them see your might.
3. so use them to show your glory to us.
4. that there is no God but you, O Lord.
5. make your hand and your right arm glorious.
6. and let people recount your might - y deeds.
7. Jerusalem, the place of your dwelling.
8. and your temple with your glory.
9. and fulfill the prophecies spoken in your name.
10. and let your prophets be found trustworthy.
11. according to your goodwill toward your people,
12. that you are the Lord, the God of the ages.

All:

Hear the prayer of your peo-ple.

61 Give Thanks to the Lord, Alleluia (I)

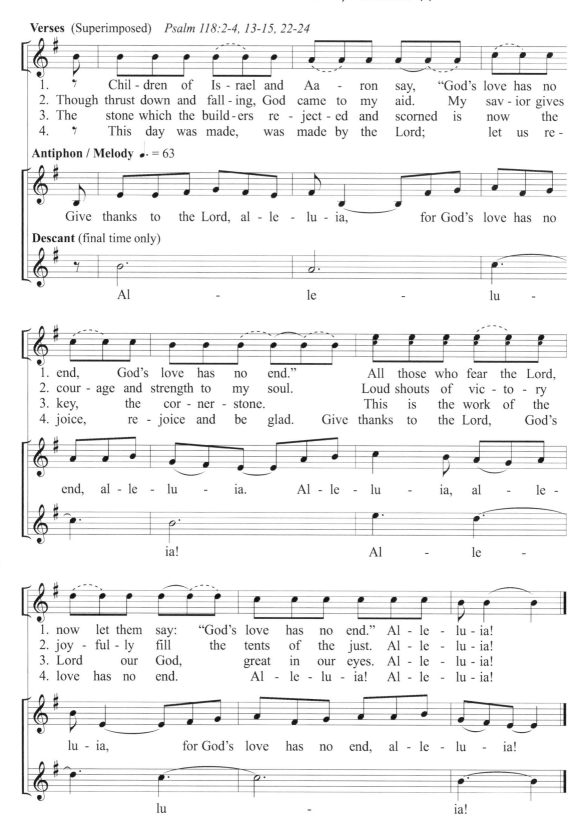

Give Thanks to the Lord, Alleluia (II)

Antiphon / Melody ♩ = 66

Give thanks to the Lord, al-le-lu - ia, who is love with-out end, al-le-lu - ia!

Descant

Thanks to the Lord! Love with-out end!

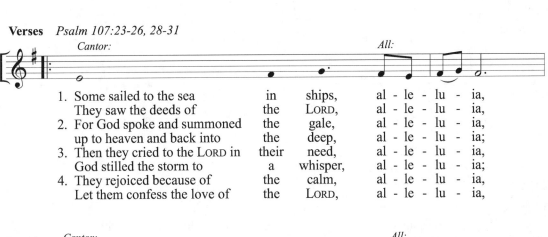

Verses *Psalm 107:23-26, 28-31*

Cantor: All:

1. Some sailed to the sea in ships, al - le - lu - ia,
   They saw the deeds of the LORD, al - le - lu - ia,
2. For God spoke and summoned the gale, al - le - lu - ia,
   up to heaven and back into the deep, al - le - lu - ia;
3. Then they cried to the LORD in their need, al - le - lu - ia,
   God stilled the storm to a whisper, al - le - lu - ia;
4. They rejoiced because of the calm, al - le - lu - ia,
   Let them confess the love of the LORD, al - le - lu - ia,

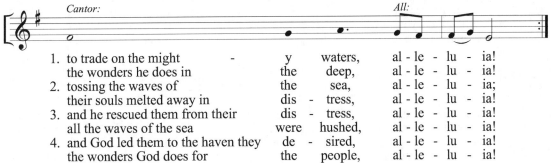

Cantor: All:

1. to trade on the might - y waters, al - le - lu - ia!
   the wonders he does in the deep, al - le - lu - ia!
2. tossing the waves of the sea, al - le - lu - ia;
   their souls melted away in dis - tress, al - le - lu - ia!
3. and he rescued them from their dis - tress, al - le - lu - ia!
   all the waves of the sea were hushed, al - le - lu - ia!
4. and God led them to the haven they de - sired, al - le - lu - ia!
   the wonders God does for the people, al - le - lu - ia!

Give the Lord Power

Antiphon / Melody ♩. = 65

Give the Lord pow - er, give the Lord glo - ry;

Tenor Descant   *sung only on the repeat of the antiphon*

Pow - er, glo - ry;

great is the Lord and worth - y of praise.

great is the Lord! Worth - y of praise!

Verses   *Psalm 96:1, 3-5, 7-10a, 10c*

1. O sing a new song to   the LORD,   sing to the LORD,   all   the   earth.
2. The LORD is great and worthy   of   praise,   to be feared a - bove   all   gods;
3. Give the LORD, you families   of   peoples,   give the LORD glo - ry   and   power;
4. Worship the LORD in   the   temple.   O earth, stand in fear   of   the   LORD.

1. Tell among the nations   God's   glory   and his wonders among all   the   peoples.
2. the gods of the heathens   are   naught.   It was the LORD who made   the   heavens.
3. give the LORD the glory of   his   name.   Bring an offering and enter God's   courts.
4. Proclaim to the nations: "God   is   king."   God will judge the peoples   in   fairness.

Performance Notes

The antiphon is sung twice each time, with the tenor descant added on the repeat.

Give Us Living Water

Verses (Superimposed) *John 4:13-14, 34; Psalm 34:2-15*

1. Everyone who drinks of this wa - ter
2. Those who drink of the water that I will give them
3. water that I will give will be - come in them a spring of
4. food is to do the will of him who sent me
5. bless the LORD at all times,
6. LORD my soul shall make its boast; the

7. Glori - fy the LORD with me. To -
8. sought the LORD and was heard; from
9. Look towards God and be ra - diant;
10. When the poor cry out the LORD hears them and
11. The angel of the LORD is en - camped a -
12. Taste and see that the LORD is good.

13. vere the LORD, you his saints.
14. Strong lions suffer want and go hungry but
15. Come, children, and hear me that
16. Who are those who long for life and
17. Keep your tongue from e - vil and your
18. Turn a - side from evil and do good;

Antiphon / Melody ♩ = 72

Give us liv - ing wa - ter, well - ing up with - in us:

Alto / Tenor Descant

Give us liv - ing wa - ter well - ing

Bass Descant

Give us wa - ter, well with - in us,

1. will be thirsty a - gain.
2. will never be thirst - y. 3. The
3. water gushing up to e - ternal life. 4. My
4. and to com - plete his work. 5. I will
5. God's praise always on my lips; 6. In the
6. humble shall hear and be glad.

7. gether let us praise God's name. 8. I
8. all my terrors set free.
9. let your faces not be a - bashed.
10. rescues them from all their dis - tress.
11. round those who fear God, to rescue them.
12. They are happy who seek refuge in God. 13. Re -

13. They lack nothing, who re - vere the LORD.
14. those who seek the LORD lack no blessing.
15. I may teach you the fear of the LORD.
16. many days to en - joy their pros - perity?
17. lips from speaking de - ceit.
18. seek and strive after peace.

fill us with your Spi - rit, fill us with your truth.

deep with - in us, with your Spi - rit and truth.

fill us with your Spi - rit and truth.

Antiphon / Melody ♩ = 72

Give: your Fa-ther sees. Pray: your Fa-ther hears.

Descant

Give: your Fa-ther sees. Pray: your Fa-ther—

Hun - ger and thirst, for your Fa - ther will fill you.

Hun - ger and thirst, for your Fa - ther will fill you.

Verses *Matthew 5:3-10*

1. Blessed are the poor in spirit, for theirs is the king - dom of heaven.
2. Blessed are the meek, for they will inher - it the earth.
3. Blessed are the merciful, for they will re - ceive mercy.
4. Blessed are the peacemakers, for they will be called child - ren of God.

1. Blessed are those who mourn, for they will be comforted.
2. { Blessed are those who hunger and } thirst for righteousness, for they will be filled.
3. Blessed are the pure in heart, for they will see God.
4. { Blessed are those who are persecuted for right - } eous-ness' sake, { for theirs is the king - } dom of heaven.

Go to the Ends of the Earth

Antiphon / Melody ♩. = 63-69

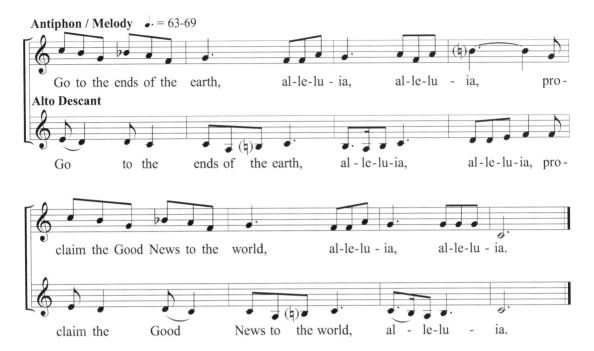

Alto Descant

Go to the ends of the earth, al-le-lu - ia, al-le-lu - ia, pro-

Go to the ends of the earth, al - le-lu-ia, al-le-lu-ia, pro-

claim the Good News to the world, al-le-lu - ia, al-le-lu - ia.

claim the Good News to the world, al - le-lu - ia.

Verses *Psalm 117*

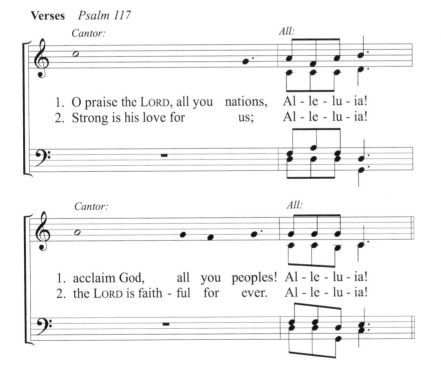

Cantor: / All:

1. O praise the LORD, all you nations, Al - le - lu - ia!
2. Strong is his love for us; Al - le - lu - ia!

Cantor: / All:

1. acclaim God, all you peoples! Al - le - lu - ia!
2. the LORD is faith - ful for ever. Al - le - lu - ia!

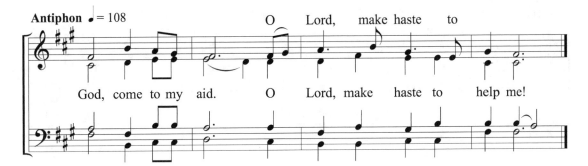

Verses *Psalm 40:2-4, 18*

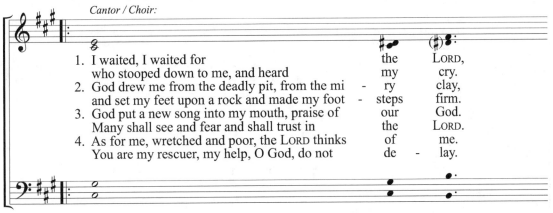

1. I waited, I waited for   the   Lᴏʀᴅ,
   who stooped down to me, and heard   my   cry.
2. God drew me from the deadly pit, from the mi - ry   clay,
   and set my feet upon a rock and made my foot - steps   firm.
3. God put a new song into my mouth, praise of   our   God.
   Many shall see and fear and shall trust in   the   Lᴏʀᴅ.
4. As for me, wretched and poor, the Lᴏʀᴅ thinks   of   me.
   You are my rescuer, my help, O God, do not   de - lay.

God, Come to My Aid (II)

Antiphon ♩ = 108

O Lord, make haste to God, come to my aid. O Lord, make haste to help me!

You are the one who sus-tains me: O Lord, do not de-lay!

Verses   *Psalm 70*

Cantor / Choir: *All:*   Lord, make haste to

1. O God, make haste to   my rescue, O   Lord, make   haste to   help me!
2. Let there be shame and   con-fusion,
3. O let them turn back in   con-fusion,
4. Let them retreat, covered with shame,
5. Let there be rejoicing   and gladness
6. Let them say for ever: "God is   great,"
7. As for me, wretched   and   poor,
8. You are my rescuer,   my   help,

Cantor / Choir: *All:*

1. LORD, come to   my   aid. O   Lord, do not de-lay!
2. on those who seek   my   life.
3. who delight in   my   harm.
4. who jeer at   my   lot.
5. for all   who   seek you.
6. who love your sav - ing   help.
7. come to me,   O   God.
8. O LORD, do not   de - lay.

Antiphon ♩ = 46

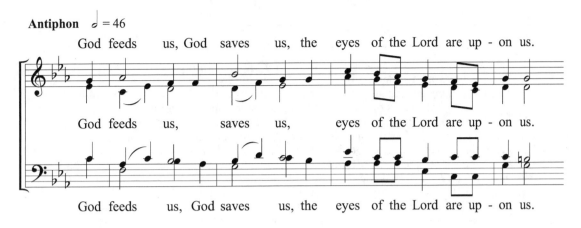

God feeds us, God saves us, the eyes of the Lord are up - on us.

God feeds us, saves us, eyes of the Lord are up - on us.

God feeds us, God saves us, the eyes of the Lord are up - on us.

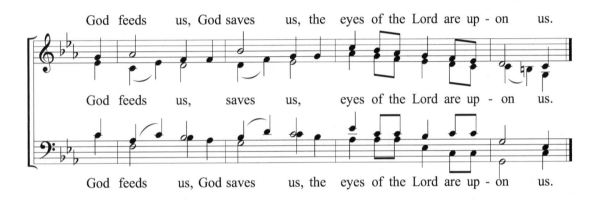

God feeds us, God saves us, the eyes of the Lord are up - on us.

God feeds us, saves us, eyes of the Lord are up - on us.

God feeds us, God saves us, the eyes of the Lord are up - on us.

Verses *Psalm 33*

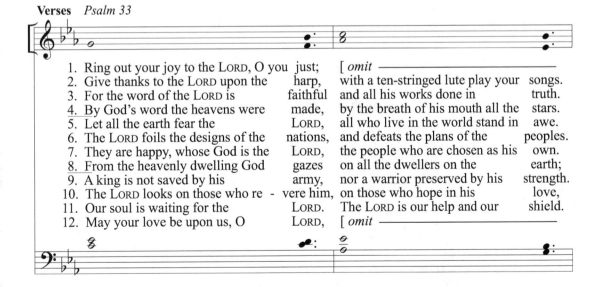

1. Ring out your joy to the LORD, O you just; [*omit* ——————————————
2. Give thanks to the LORD upon the harp, with a ten-stringed lute play your songs.
3. For the word of the LORD is faithful and all his works done in truth.
4. By God's word the heavens were made, by the breath of his mouth all the stars.
5. Let all the earth fear the LORD, all who live in the world stand in awe.
6. The LORD foils the designs of the nations, and defeats the plans of the peoples.
7. They are happy, whose God is the LORD, the people who are chosen as his own.
8. From the heavenly dwelling God gazes on all the dwellers on the earth;
9. A king is not saved by his army, nor a warrior preserved by his strength.
10. The LORD looks on those who re - vere him, on those who hope in his love,
11. Our soul is waiting for the LORD. The LORD is our help and our shield.
12. May your love be upon us, O LORD, [*omit* ——————————————

1. —————————————————] for praise is fitting for   loy - al hearts.
2. Sing to the LORD a song that is   new, play loudly, with   all your skill.
3. The LORD loves justice and   right and fills the earth   with his love.
4. God collects the waves of the   ocean, and stores up the depths   of the sea.
5. For God spoke; it came to   be. God commanded; it sprang   in - to being.
6. The counsel of the LORD stands for - ever, the plans of God's heart from age to age.
7. From the heavens the LORD looks   forth and sees all the peoples   of the earth.
8. God who shapes the hearts of them   all and considers   all their deeds.
9. A vain hope for safety is the   horse; despite its power it   can - not save.
10. to rescue their souls from   death, to keep them a - live in famine.
11. Our hearts find joy in the   LORD. We trust in God's   ho - ly name.
12. —————————————————] as we place all our   hope in you.

70   God Goes Up with Shouts of Joy

Antiphon / Melody 𝅗𝅥 = 84

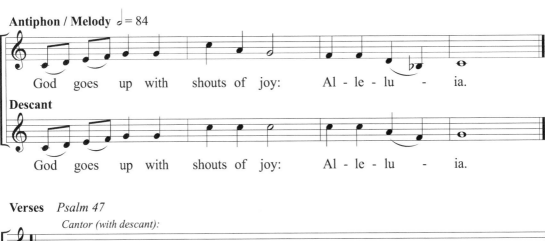

God goes up with shouts of joy: Al - le - lu - ia.

Descant

God goes up with shouts of joy: Al - le - lu - ia.

Verses   *Psalm 47*

Cantor (with descant):

1. All peoples,   clap   your   hands,
    For the LORD, the Most High,   we   must   fear,
2. God subdues   peo - ples   under us
    Our inheritance, our glory   is   from   God,
3. God goes up with   shouts   of   joy;
    Sing praise for   God,   sing   praise,
4. God is king of   all   the   earth,
    God is king o - ver   the   nations;
5. The leaders of the people   are   as - sembled
    The rulers of the earth be - long   to   God,

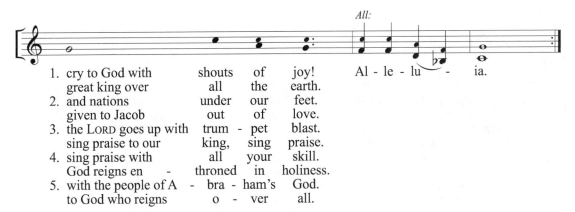

1. cry to God with   shouts   of   joy!   Al - le - lu - ia.
    great king over   all   the   earth.
2. and nations   under   our   feet.
    given to Jacob   out   of   love.
3. the LORD goes up with   trum - pet   blast.
    sing praise to our   king,   sing   praise.
4. sing praise with   all   your   skill.
    God reigns en - throned   in   holiness.
5. with the people of A - bra - ham's   God.
    to God who reigns   o - ver   all.

Performance Notes

Verses 1, 3, and 4 are the Lectionary selections for the Ascension of the Lord.
Cue-size notes in the last two measures of the verse are the descant part.

God Heals the Broken   71

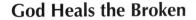

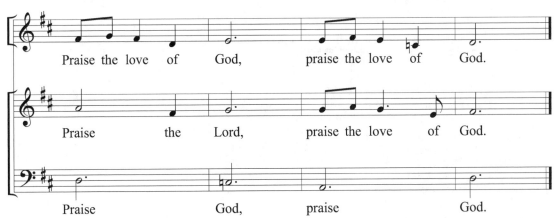

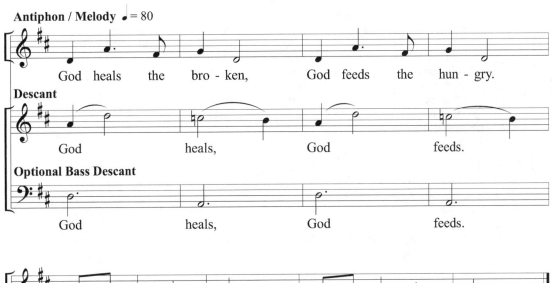

Verses   *Psalm 146:2–10b*

1. I will praise the LORD all my days,
2. Put no trust in the powerful,
3. Take their breath, they re - turn to clay
4. They are happy who are helped by Ja - cob's God,
5. the LORD who alone made heav'n and˜ earth,
6. It is the LORD who keeps faith for ever,
7. It is God who gives bread to the hungry,
8. the LORD who gives sight to the blind,
9. the LORD, who pro - tects the stranger
10. It is the LORD who loves the just
11. The LORD will reign for ever,

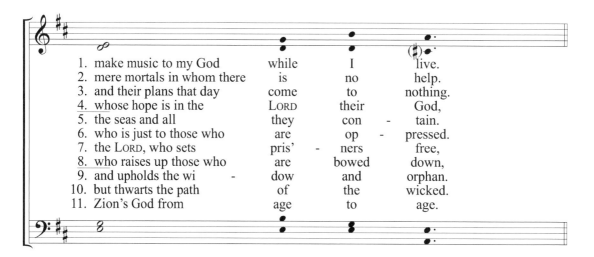

1. make music to my God while I live.
2. mere mortals in whom there is no help.
3. and their plans that day come to nothing.
4. whose hope is in the LORD their God,
5. the seas and all they con - tain.
6. who is just to those who are op - pressed.
7. the LORD, who sets pris' - ners free,
8. who raises up those who are bowed down,
9. and upholds the wi - dow and orphan.
10. but thwarts the path of the wicked.
11. Zion's God from age to age.

Performance Notes

Verses 6–11 are the Lectionary selections for the Twenty-sixth Sunday in Ordinary Time, Year C. On this day, verses should be sung in sets of two.

God, Let All the Peoples Praise You

Antiphon / Melody ♩ = 88

"Alleluia" may be sung during Eastertide.

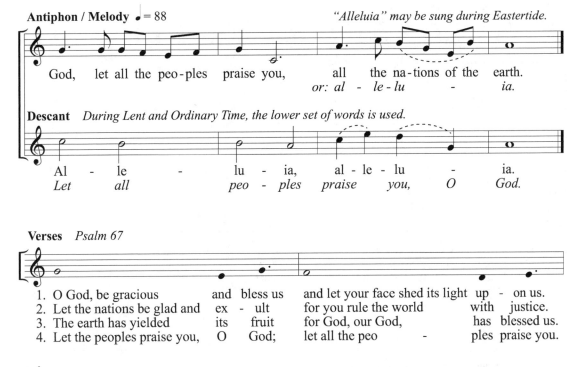

God,   let all the peo-ples   praise you,   all   the na-tions of the   earth.
or: al - le-lu - ia.

Descant   *During Lent and Ordinary Time, the lower set of words is used.*

Al - le - lu - ia,   al - le - lu - ia.
Let   all   peo - ples   praise   you,   O   God.

Verses   *Psalm 67*

1. O God, be gracious   and bless us   and let your face shed its light up - on us.
2. Let the nations be glad and   ex - ult   for you rule the world   with justice.
3. The earth has yielded   its   fruit   for God, our God,   has blessed us.
4. Let the peoples praise you,   O   God;   let all the peo -   ples praise you.

1. So will your ways be known up - on   earth   and all nations learn your sav - ing   help.
2. With fairness you   rule the peoples,   you guide the   nations on   earth.
3. May God still   give us blessing   till the ends of the earth stand in   awe.
4. Let the peoples praise   you, O   God,   let all the   peo - ples praise you.

Performance Notes

Verses 1, 2, and 4 are the Lectionary selections for the Twentieth Sunday in Ordinary Time, Year A, and the Sixth Sunday of Easter, Year C.

God of Hosts, Bring Us Back

Antiphon *Strong, not too fast* ♩ = 126

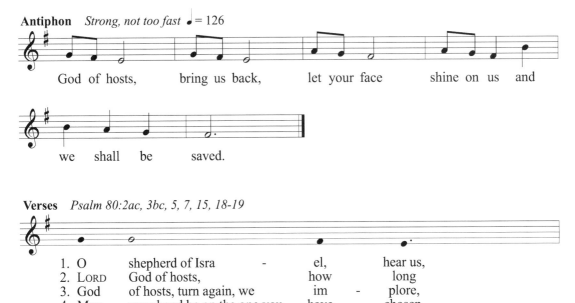

God of hosts, bring us back, let your face shine on us and
we shall be saved.

Verses *Psalm 80:2ac, 3bc, 5, 7, 15, 18-19*

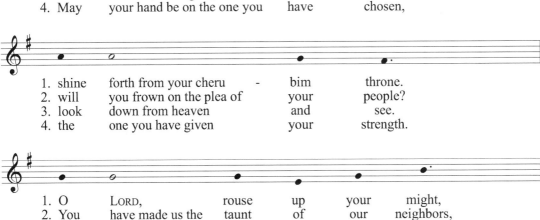

1. O shepherd of Isra - el, hear us,
2. LORD God of hosts, how long
3. God of hosts, turn again, we im - plore,
4. May your hand be on the one you have chosen,

1. shine forth from your cheru - bim throne.
2. will you frown on the plea of your people?
3. look down from heaven and see.
4. the one you have given your strength.

1. O LORD, rouse up your might,
2. You have made us the taunt of our neighbors,
3. Visit this vine and pro - tect it,
4. And we shall never for - sake you a - gain;

1. O LORD, come to our help.
2. our enemies laugh us to scorn.
3. the vine your right hand has planted.
4. give us life that we may call on your name.

Performance Notes

Verses 1, 3, and 4 are the Lectionary selections for the First Sunday of Advent, Year B, and the Fourth Sunday of Advent, Year C.

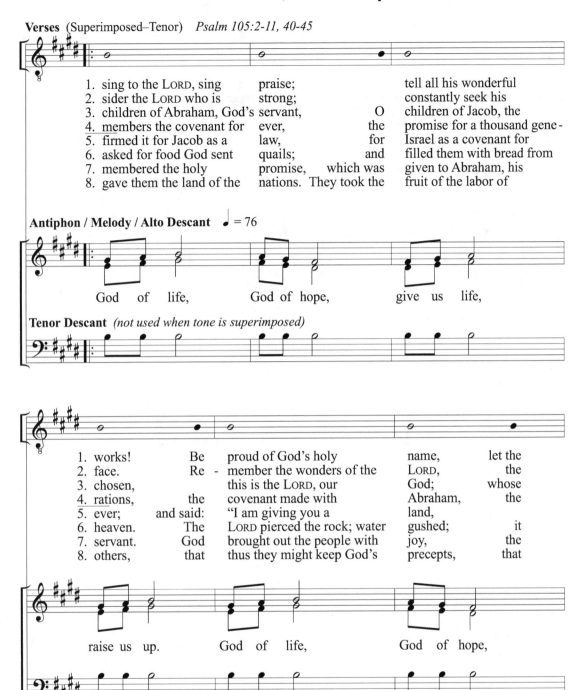

Verses (Superimposed–Tenor)   *Psalm 105:2-11, 40-45*

1. sing to the LORD, sing praise; tell all his wonderful
2. sider the LORD who is strong; constantly seek his
3. children of Abraham, God's servant, O children of Jacob, the
4. members the covenant for ever, the promise for a thousand gene -
5. firmed it for Jacob as a law, for Israel as a covenant for
6. asked for food God sent quails; and filled them with bread from
7. membered the holy promise, which was given to Abraham, his
8. gave them the land of the nations. They took the fruit of the labor of

Antiphon / Melody / Alto Descant   ♩ = 76

God of life,   God of hope,   give us life,

Tenor Descant *(not used when tone is superimposed)*

1. works! Be proud of God's holy name, let the
2. face. Re - member the wonders of the LORD, the
3. chosen, this is the LORD, our God; whose
4. rations, the covenant made with Abraham, the
5. ever; and said: "I am giving you a land,
6. heaven. The LORD pierced the rock; water gushed; it
7. servant. God brought out the people with joy, the
8. others, that thus they might keep God's precepts, that

raise us up.   God of life,   God of hope,

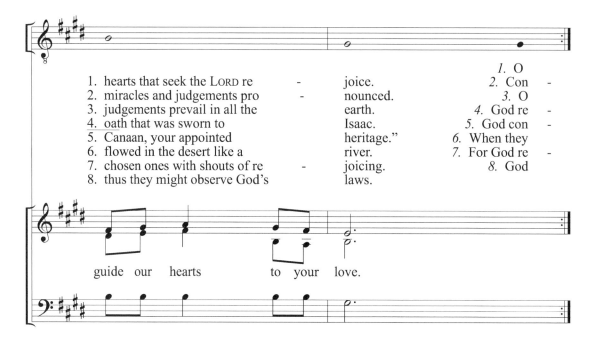

1. hearts that seek the LORD re - joice.
2. miracles and judgements pro - nounced.
3. judgements prevail in all the earth.
4. oath that was sworn to Isaac.
5. Canaan, your appointed heritage."
6. flowed in the desert like a river.
7. chosen ones with shouts of re - joicing.
8. thus they might observe God's laws.

1. O
2. Con -
3. O
4. God re -
5. God con -
6. When they
7. For God re -
8. God

guide our hearts to your love.

Performance Notes

Each verse begins on the pick-up note in the last measure.

Antiphon / Melody ♩ = 72-76

God re - mem - bers his co - ve - nant for e - ver.

Descant

God re - mem - bers his co - ve - nant for e - ver.

Verses   *Psalm 105:1–9*

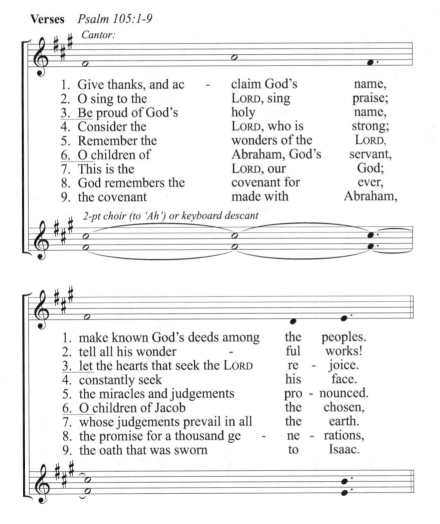

Cantor:

1. Give thanks, and ac - claim God's name,
2. O sing to the LORD, sing praise;
3. Be proud of God's holy name,
4. Consider the LORD, who is strong;
5. Remember the wonders of the LORD,
6. O children of Abraham, God's servant,
7. This is the LORD, our God;
8. God remembers the covenant for ever,
9. the covenant made with Abraham,

2-pt choir (to 'Ah') or keyboard descant

1. make known God's deeds among the peoples.
2. tell all his wonder - ful works!
3. let the hearts that seek the LORD re - joice.
4. constantly seek his face.
5. the miracles and judgements pro - nounced.
6. O children of Jacob the chosen,
7. whose judgements prevail in all the earth.
8. the promise for a thousand ge - ne - rations,
9. the oath that was sworn to Isaac.

Performance Notes

Verses 1–6 and 8–9 are the Lectionary selections for the feast of the Holy Family, Year B.

God, Who Raised Jesus from the Dead

Antiphon ♩ = ca. 92

God, who raised Je-sus from the dead will give our bo-dies life by the
Spi - rit with - in.

Verses *Psalm 16:1-2, 5-11*

1. {Preserve me, God, I take   refuge in   you.
I say to you,   LORD: "You are my   God.}
2. O LORD, it is you who are my   portion and   cup,
3. The lot marked out for   me is my de - light,
4. I will bless you,   LORD, you give me   counsel,
5. I keep you, LORD,   ever in my   sight;
6. And so my heart re - joices, my soul is   glad;
7. For you will not leave my   soul among the   dead,
8. You will show me the   path of   life,

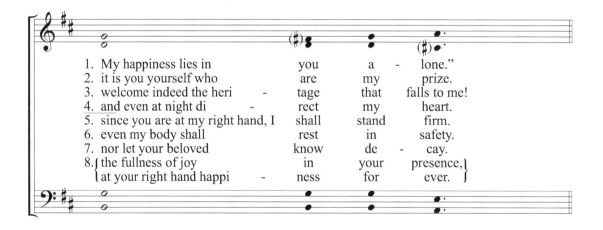

1. My happiness lies in   you   a - lone."
2. it is you yourself who   are   my   prize.
3. welcome indeed the heri - tage   that   falls to me!
4. and even at night di - rect   my   heart.
5. since you are at my right hand, I   shall   stand   firm.
6. even my body shall   rest   in   safety.
7. nor let your beloved   know   de - cay.
8. {the fullness of joy   in   your   presence,
at your right hand happi - ness   for   ever. }

Antiphon ♩ = 88

Cantor then all:

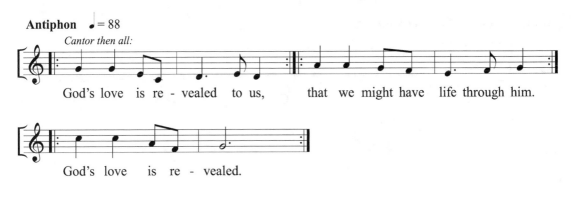

God's love is re - vealed to us, that we might have life through him.

God's love is re - vealed.

Verses *Psalm 98; Ephesians 1:3-4*

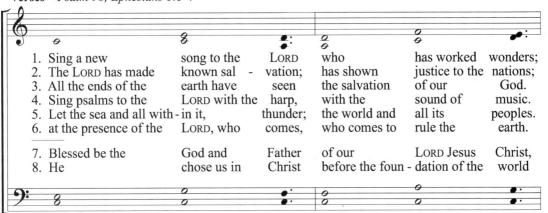

1. Sing a new song to the LORD who has worked wonders;
2. The LORD has made known sal - vation; has shown justice to the nations;
3. All the ends of the earth have seen the salvation of our God.
4. Sing psalms to the LORD with the harp, with the sound of music.
5. Let the sea and all with - in it, thunder; the world and all its peoples.
6. at the presence of the LORD, who comes, who comes to rule the earth.

7. Blessed be the God and Father of our LORD Jesus Christ,
8. He chose us in Christ before the foun - dation of the world

1. whose right hand and ho - ly arm have brought sal - vation.
2. has remembered truth and love for the house of Israel.
3. Shout to the LORD, all the earth, ring out your joy.
4. With trumpets and the sound of the horn acclaim the King, the LORD.
5. Let the rivers clap their hands and the hills ring out their joy
6. God will rule the world with justice and the peo - ples with fairness.

7. who has blessed us in Christ {with every spiritual blessing in the} hea - v'nly places.

8. to be holy and blameless before him in love.

Optional Coda to the Final Antiphon

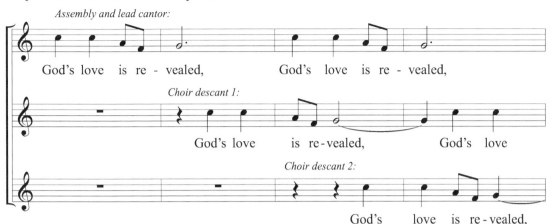

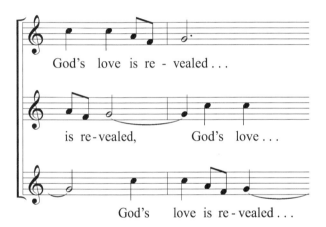

Performance Notes

Verses 1–4 are the Lectionary selections for Christmas.
Verses 7 and 8 are sung on the Baptism of the Lord, Year C, only; omit these verses on Christmas.
Each two-measure phrase of the antiphon is sung first by a cantor and then repeated by all.
Instead of repeating the last two measures of the final antiphon, use the optional three-part coda above at a
distance of two quarter-notes to create the effect of gently pealing bells, as shown. The top line is the assembly,
led by a cantor, the lower two lines being taken by other members of the choir.
The canon may be repeated at any time as desired, gradually fading out.

God's Tender Mercy

Antiphon ♩ = 76

1. 2.
God's ten - der mer - cy, a - ris - ing like the sun,

3. 4.
vi - sit us with light, set your peo - ple free.

Verses *Psalms 92:2-6, 13-16; 103:1-4, 8, 10-14*

1. It is good to give thanks to the LORD, to make music to your name, O Most High,
2. Your deeds, O LORD, have made me glad; for the work of your hands I shout with joy.
3. The just will flourish like the palm tree and grow like a Lebanon cedar.
4. still bearing fruit when they are old, still full of sap, still green,
5. My soul, give thanks to the LORD; all my being, bless his holy name.
6. It is God who forgives all your guilt, who heals every one of your ills,
7. The LORD is compassion and love, slow to anger and rich in mercy.
8. As the heavens are high above the earth so strong is God's love for the God-fearing.
9. As parents have compassion on their children, the LORD has pity on those who are God-fearing

1. to proclaim your love in the morning and your truth in the watches of the night,
   on the ten-stringed lyre and the lute, with the murmuring sound of the harp.
2. O LORD, how great are your works! How deep are your de - signs!
3. Planted in the house of the LORD they will flourish in the courts of our God,
4. to proclaim that the LORD is just, my rock, in whom there is no wrong.
5. My soul, give thanks to the LORD and never forget all God's blessings.
6. who redeems your life from the grave, who crowns you with love and com - passion.
7. God does not treat us according to our sins nor repay us according to our faults.
8. As far as the east is from the west so far does he remove our sins.
9. for he knows of what we are made, and remembers that we are dust.

Performance Notes
The antiphon could be sung as a four-part round, if desired.

Great in Our Midst Is the Holy One

Verses (Superimposed)   *cf. Isaiah 12:2-6*

1. Tru - ly God is our sal - va - tion, we
   LORD is our strength and our song:
2. Joy - ful - ly you will draw wa - ter,
3. And we will say on that day: Give pro -
   Make known God's name a - mong na - tions;
4. praise to the LORD for his glo - rious deeds;
   loud and sing joy - ful - ly, Zi - on, for

Antiphon / Melody ♩. = 63

Great in our midst is the Ho - ly One:

Descant

Great in our midst is the Ho - ly One:

Bass *(vocalize to 'Ah')*

1. trust, we shall not fear; for the
   he has be - come our sal - va - tion.
2. deep from sal - va - tion's springs.
3. thanks to the LORD, bless his name.
   claim that God's name is ex - alt - ed.   4. Sing
4. tell them to all of the earth. Shout a -
   great in our midst is the Ho - ly One!

cry out with glad - ness and joy.

cry out with glad - ness and joy.

Performance Notes

The verses can be superimposed on the antiphon as shown, or they may be sung separately (but still in rhythm) using a simple chordal accompaniment.

Antiphon ♩ = ca. 92

Guard me as the ap-ple of your eye! Hide me in the sha-dow of your wings!

Antiphon (alternate setting)

Cantor/Group I:

Guard me as the ap - ple of your eye!

wings!

Cantor/Group II:

Hide me in the sha-dow of your

Verses   *Psalm 17:1-3b, 5-7, 15*

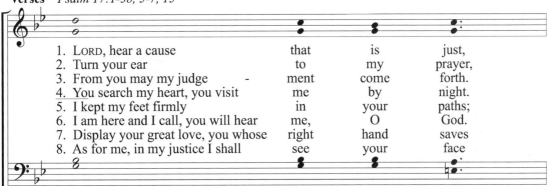

1. Lord, hear a cause	that	is	just,
2. Turn your ear	to	my	prayer,
3. From you may my judge - ment	come	forth.	
4. You search my heart, you visit	me	by	night.
5. I kept my feet firmly	in	your	paths;
6. I am here and I call, you will hear	me,	O	God.
7. Display your great love, you whose	right	hand	saves
8. As for me, in my justice I shall	see	your	face

1. pay heed	to	my	cry.
2. no deceit is	on	my	lips.
3. Your eyes dis -	cern	the	truth.
4. You test me and you find in	me	no	wrong.
5. there was no faltering	in	my	steps.
6. Turn your ear to me;	hear	my	words.
7. your friends from those who re -	bel	a - gainst them.	
8. and be filled, when I awake, with the sight	of	your	glory.

Performance Notes

Once the antiphon is well known by the assembly, it could be sung in two overlapping parts as shown in the alternate setting. If two cantors are available, the assembly could be divided into two groups, with one cantor leading each section. Or a cantor could sing the upper line, with choir/assembly singing the lower line. Or male voices on one line, female voices on the other.

Happy Are They Who Dwell in Your House

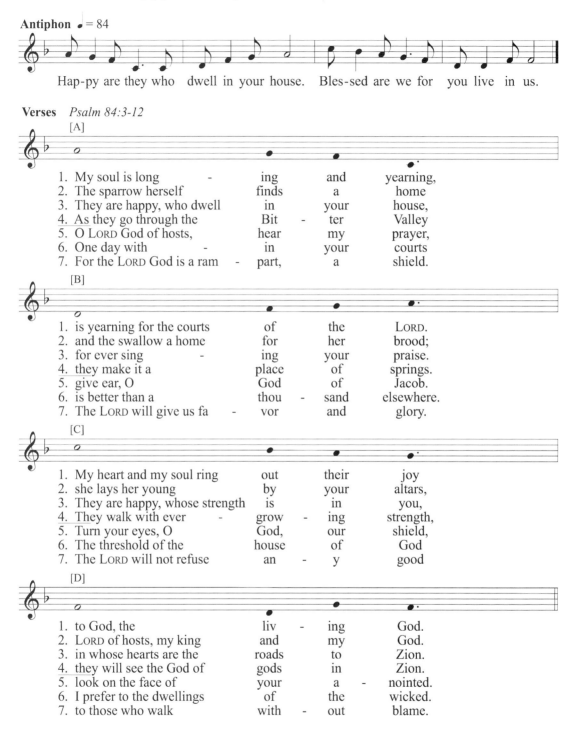

Antiphon ♩ = 84

Hap-py are they who dwell in your house. Bles-sed are we for you live in us.

Verses   *Psalm 84:3-12*

[A]

1. My soul is long - ing and yearning,
2. The sparrow herself finds a home
3. They are happy, who dwell in your house,
4. As they go through the Bit - ter Valley
5. O Lord God of hosts, hear my prayer,
6. One day with - in your courts
7. For the Lord God is a ram - part, a shield.

[B]

1. is yearning for the courts of the Lord.
2. and the swallow a home for her brood;
3. for ever sing - ing your praise.
4. they make it a place of springs.
5. give ear, O God of Jacob.
6. is better than a thou - sand elsewhere.
7. The Lord will give us fa - vor and glory.

[C]

1. My heart and my soul ring out their joy
2. she lays her young by your altars,
3. They are happy, whose strength is in you,
4. They walk with ever - grow - ing strength,
5. Turn your eyes, O God, our shield,
6. The threshold of the house of God
7. The Lord will not refuse an - y good

[D]

1. to God, the liv - ing God.
2. Lord of hosts, my king and my God.
3. in whose hearts are the roads to Zion.
4. they will see the God of gods in Zion.
5. look on the face of your a - nointed.
6. I prefer to the dwellings of the wicked.
7. to those who walk with - out blame.

Performance Notes

Verses 1, 3, and 5 are the Lectionary selections for the feast of the Holy Family, Year C.
Verses 1, 2, 3ab, 5cd, and 6 are the Lectionary selections for the Anniversary of the Dedication of a Church.

Happy Are They Who Follow

Antiphon / Melody ♩ = ca. 88-92

Hap-py are they who fol-low, who fol-low the law of the Lord.

Descant

Hap - py they who fol - low God's law.

Bass Descant (optional)

Hap - py they who fol - low God's law.

Verses *Psalm 119:1-2, 4-5, 17-18, 33-34*

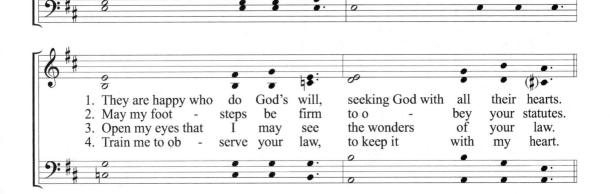

1. They are happy whose life is blameless, who fol - low God's law!
2. You have laid down your precepts to be o - beyed with care.
3. Bless your servant and I shall live and o - bey your word.
4. Teach me the demands of your statutes and I will keep them to the end.

1. They are happy who do God's will, seeking God with all their hearts.
2. May my foot - steps be firm to o - bey your statutes.
3. Open my eyes that I may see the wonders of your law.
4. Train me to ob - serve your law, to keep it with my heart.

Happy Are They Whose God Is the Lord

Antiphon ♩ = 84

Hap-py are they whose God is the Lord. Bles-sed are we, the cho-sen of God.

Verses (*Option A) *Psalm 33:1, 12, 18-20, 22*

1. Ring out your joy to the Lord, O you just; for praise is fitting for loy - al hearts.
2. The Lord looks on those who fear him, on those who hope in his love,
3. Our soul is waiting for the Lord. The Lord is our help and our shield.

1. They are happy, whose God is the Lord, the people who are chosen as his own.
2. to rescue their souls from death, to keep them a - live in famine.
3. May your love be upon us, O Lord, as we place all our hope in you.

Verses (*Option B) *Psalm 33:4-6, 9, 18-20, 22*

1. The word of the Lord is faithful and all his works done in truth.
2. By God's word the heav'ns were made, by the breath of his mouth all the stars.
3. The Lord looks on those who fear him, on those who hope in his love,
4. Our soul is waiting for the Lord. The Lord is our help and our shield.

1. The Lord loves jus - tice and right and fills the earth with his love.
2. For God spoke; it came to be. God commanded; it sprang in - to being.
3. to rescue their souls from death, to keep them a - live in famine.
4. May your love be upon us, O Lord, as we place all our hope in you.

Performance Notes

Option A verses are used on the Nineteenth Sunday in Ordinary Time, Year C, and Option B verses are used on Trinity Sunday, Year B.

Heal Me in Your Mercy

Antiphon ♩ = 76-80

Heal me in your mer - cy, save me in your love.

Verses *Psalm 103*

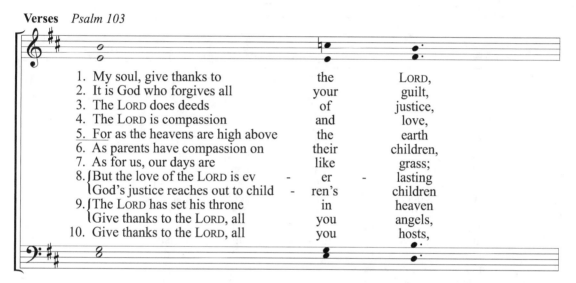

1. My soul, give thanks to the LORD,
2. It is God who forgives all your guilt,
3. The LORD does deeds of justice,
4. The LORD is compassion and love,
5. For as the heavens are high above the earth
6. As parents have compassion on their children,
7. As for us, our days are like grass;
8. But the love of the LORD is ev - er - lasting
   God's justice reaches out to child - ren's children
9. The LORD has set his throne in heaven
   Give thanks to the LORD, all you angels,
10. Give thanks to the LORD, all you hosts,

1. all my being, bless God's ho - ly name.
2. who heals every one of your ills,
3. gives judgement for all who are op - pressed.
4. slow to anger and rich in mercy.
5. so strong is God's love for the God-fearing;
6. the LORD has pity on those who are God-fearing
7. we flower like the flower of the field;
8. upon those who fear the LORD.
   when they keep his cove - nant in truth,
9. and his kingdom rules o - ver all.
   mighty in power, fulfill - ing God's word,
10. you servants who do God's will.

1. My soul, give thanks to the LORD
2. { who redeems your life from the grave,
   { who fills your life with good things,
3. The LORD's ways were made known to Moses;
4. { The LORD will not al - ways chide,
   { God does not treat us according to our sins
5. as far as the east is from the west
6. for he knows of what we are made,
7. the wind blows and we are gone
8. [*omit* ————————————]
9. [*omit* ————————————]
10. Give thanks to the LORD, all his works,

1. and never forget all God's blessings.
2. who crowns you with love and com - passion, }
   renewing your youth like an eagle's. }
3. the LORD's deeds to Is - rael's children.
4. will not be an - gry for - ever. }
   nor repay us according to our faults. }
5. so far does he re - move our sins.
6. and remembers that we are dust.
7. and our place never sees us a - gain.
8. when they keep his will in their mind.
9. who heed the voice of that word.
10. { in every place where God rules. }
    { My soul, give thanks to the LORD! }

Performance Notes

The antiphon may be sung twice each time if desired.

Heal My Soul

Antiphon ♩ = 58

Heal my soul, for I have sinned a - gainst you.

you.

you.

Verses *Psalm 41:2-5, 13-14*

1. Happy are those who consider the poor and the weak.
2. The LORD will give them strength in their pain,
3. If you uphold me, I shall be un - harm'd

1. The LORD will save them in the e - vil day,
2. will bring them back from sick - ness to health.
3. and set in your presence for e - ver - more.

1. will guard them, give them life, make them happy in the land
2. As for me, I said: "LORD, have mer - cy on me,
3. Blessed be the LORD, the God of Israel

1. and will not give them up to the will of their foes.
2. heal my soul for I have sinn'd a - gainst you."
3. from age to age. A - men. A - men.

Heaven and Earth Will Fade Away

Antiphon ♩. = ca. 58

Hea - ven and earth will fade a - way: my words will

ne - ver fade a - way, ne - ver fade a - way.

Verses *Psalm 119:7-16, 27-28, 35-38, 49-50, 57, 72, 89-91, 103, 105-112, 129-131, 133-135, 142, 144*

1. I will thank you with an up - right heart as I learn your de - crees.
2. How shall the young re - main sinless? By obey - ing your word.
3. I treasure your promise in my heart lest I sin a - gainst you.
4. With my tongue I have re - counted the decrees of your lips.
5. I will ponder all your precepts and consi - der your paths.
6. Make me grasp the way of your precepts and I will muse on your wonders.
7. Guide me in the path of your com - mands; for there is my de - light.
8. Keep my eyes from what is false; by your word, give me life.

1. I will o - bey your statutes; do not for - sake me.
2. I have sought you with all my heart; let me not stray from your com - mands.
3. Blessed are you, O LORD; teach me your statutes.
4. I rejoiced to do your will as though all rich - es were mine.
5. I take delight in your statutes; I will not for - get your word.
6. My soul pines a - way with grief; by your word raise me up.
7. Bend my heart to your will and not to love of gain.
8. Keep the promise you have made to the ser - vant who fears you.

Verses (continued)

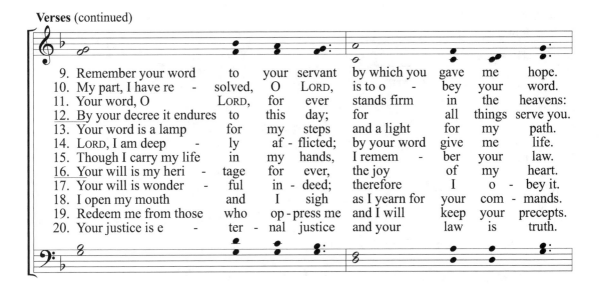

9. Remember your word	to	your servant	by which you	gave me hope.
10. My part, I have re - solved,	O	LORD,	is to o -	bey your word.
11. Your word, O	LORD,	for ever	stands firm	in the heavens:
12. By your decree it endures to	this	day;	for	all things serve you.
13. Your word is a lamp	for	my steps	and a light	for my path.
14. LORD, I am deep - ly	af - flicted;	by your word	give me life.
15. Though I carry my life	in	my hands,	I remem - ber	your law.
16. Your will is my heri - tage	for	ever,	the joy	of my heart.
17. Your will is wonder - ful	in - deed;	therefore	I o - bey it.
18. I open my mouth	and	I sigh	as I yearn for	your com - mands.
19. Redeem me from those	who	op - press me	and I will	keep your precepts.
20. Your justice is e - ter -	nal	justice	and your	law is truth.

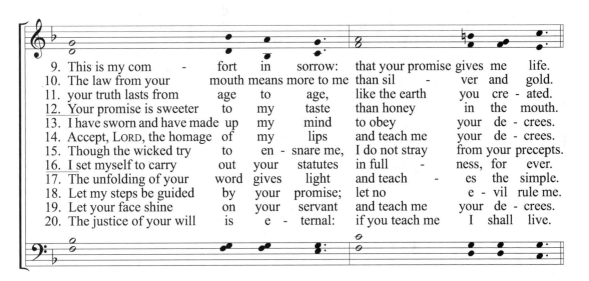

9. This is my com - fort	in	sorrow:	that your promise gives me	life.
10. The law from your	mouth means more to me	than sil - ver	and gold.
11. your truth lasts from	age	to age,	like the earth	you cre - ated.
12. Your promise is sweeter	to	my taste	than honey	in the mouth.
13. I have sworn and have made up	my	mind	to obey	your de - crees.
14. Accept, LORD, the homage of	my	lips	and teach me	your de - crees.
15. Though the wicked try	to	en - snare me,	I do not stray	from your precepts.
16. I set myself to carry	out	your statutes	in full - ness,	for ever.
17. The unfolding of your	word	gives light	and teach - es	the simple.
18. Let my steps be guided	by	your promise;	let no	e - vil rule me.
19. Let your face shine	on	your servant	and teach me	your de - crees.
20. The justice of your will	is	e - ternal:	if you teach me	I shall live.

Performance Notes

Verses 1–16 are used on the Sixth Sunday in Ordinary Time, Year A.
Verses 13–20 are used on the Thirty-third Sunday in Ordinary Time, Year B.

87 Here I Am

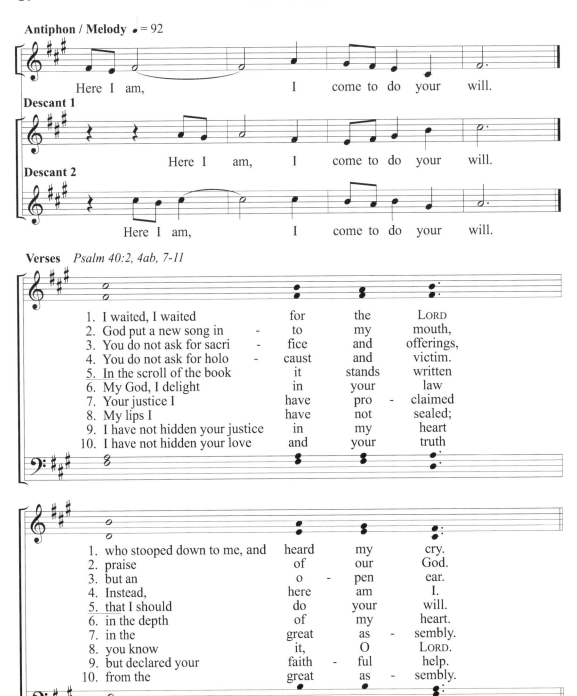

Antiphon / Melody ♩ = 92

Here I am, I come to do your will.

Descant 1

Here I am, I come to do your will.

Descant 2

Here I am, I come to do your will.

Verses *Psalm 40:2, 4ab, 7-11*

1. I waited, I waited for the LORD
2. God put a new song in - to my mouth,
3. You do not ask for sacri - fice and offerings,
4. You do not ask for holo - caust and victim.
5. In the scroll of the book it stands written
6. My God, I delight in your law
7. Your justice I have pro - claimed
8. My lips I have not sealed;
9. I have not hidden your justice in my heart
10. I have not hidden your love and your truth

1. who stooped down to me, and heard my cry.
2. praise of our God.
3. but an o - pen ear.
4. Instead, here am I.
5. that I should do your will.
6. in the depth of my heart.
7. in the great as - sembly.
8. you know it, O LORD.
9. but declared your faith - ful help.
10. from the great as - sembly.

Performance Notes

Verses 1–8 are the Lectionary selections for the Second Sunday in Ordinary Time, Years A and B.
The antiphon may be sung twice each time if desired.
The descants are intended for equal voices.

Antiphon / Melody ♩ = ca. 63

Here in your pre-sence we eat of this bread:

Descant 1

Here in your pre-sence, may

Antiphon / Melody

may we en - ter in - to your rest.

Descant 1

we en - ter in - to your rest.

Descant 2

May we en - ter in - to your rest.

Descant 3

Here in your pre - sence we rest.

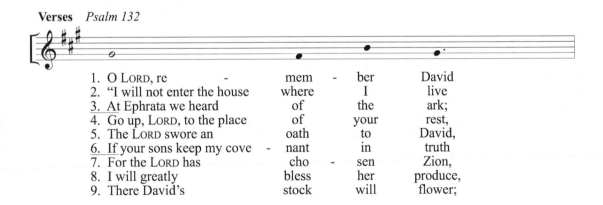

Verses *Psalm 132*

1. O LORD, re - mem - ber David
2. "I will not enter the house where I live
3. At Ephrata we heard of the ark;
4. Go up, LORD, to the place of your rest,
5. The LORD swore an oath to David,
6. If your sons keep my cove - nant in truth
7. For the LORD has cho - sen Zion,
8. I will greatly bless her produce,
9. There David's stock will flower;

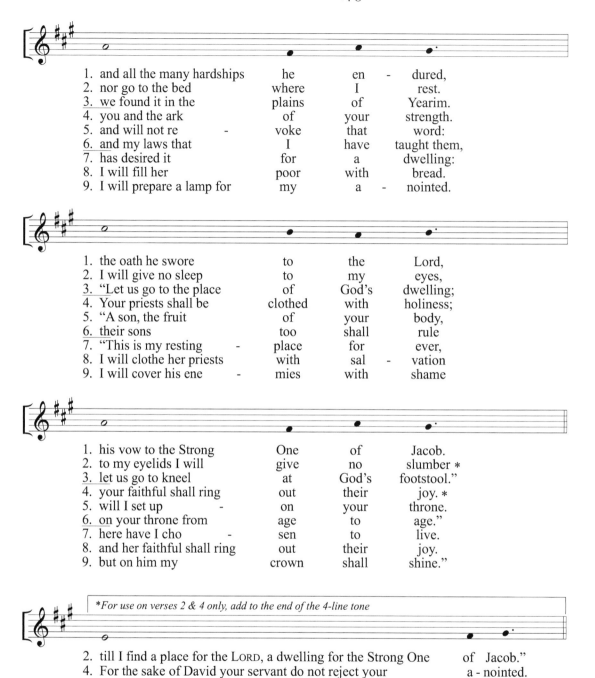

1. and all the many hardships   he   en - dured,
2. nor go to the bed   where   I   rest.
3. we found it in the   plains   of   Yearim.
4. you and the ark   of   your   strength.
5. and will not re -   voke   that   word:
6. and my laws that   I   have   taught them,
7. has desired it   for   a   dwelling:
8. I will fill her   poor   with   bread.
9. I will prepare a lamp for   my   a - nointed.

1. the oath he swore   to   the   Lord,
2. I will give no sleep   to   my   eyes,
3. "Let us go to the place   of   God's   dwelling;
4. Your priests shall be   clothed   with   holiness;
5. "A son, the fruit   of   your   body,
6. their sons   too   shall   rule
7. "This is my resting -   place   for   ever,
8. I will clothe her priests   with   sal - vation
9. I will cover his ene -   mies   with   shame

1. his vow to the Strong   One   of   Jacob.
2. to my eyelids I will   give   no   slumber ✱
3. let us go to kneel   at   God's   footstool."
4. your faithful shall ring   out   their   joy. ✱
5. will I set up -   on   your   throne.
6. on your throne from   age   to   age."
7. here have I cho -   sen   to   live.
8. and her faithful shall ring   out   their   joy.
9. but on him my   crown   shall   shine."

*For use on verses 2 & 4 only, add to the end of the 4-line tone

2. till I find a place for the LORD, a dwelling for the Strong One   of   Jacob."
4. For the sake of David your servant do not reject your   a - nointed.

Here Is My Servant, Here Is My Son

Antiphon ♩ = 63-66

Here is my ser - vant, here is my Son, here is my cho-sen Be - lov - ed One.

Verses *Isaiah 40:1-11*

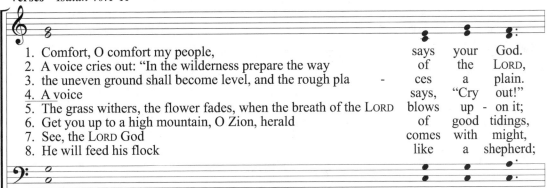

1. Comfort, O comfort my people,   says your God.
2. A voice cries out: "In the wilderness prepare the way   of the LORD,
3. the uneven ground shall become level, and the rough pla - ces a plain.
4. A voice   says, "Cry out!"
5. The grass withers, the flower fades, when the breath of the LORD   blows up - on it;
6. Get you up to a high mountain, O Zion, herald   of good tidings,
7. See, the LORD God   comes with might,
8. He will feed his flock   like a shepherd;

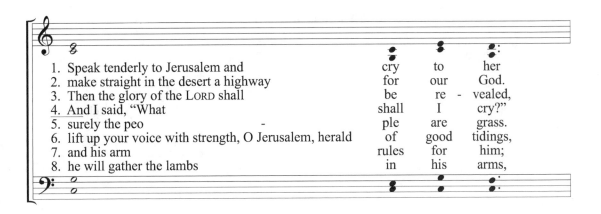

1. Speak tenderly to Jerusalem and   cry to her
2. make straight in the desert a highway   for our God.
3. Then the glory of the LORD shall   be re - vealed,
4. And I said, "What   shall I cry?"
5. surely the peo - ple   are grass.
6. lift up your voice with strength, O Jerusalem, herald   of good tidings,
7. and his arm   rules for him;
8. he will gather the lambs   in his arms,

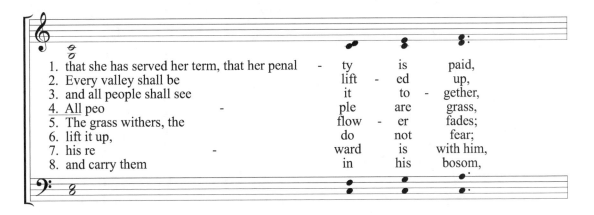

1. that she has served her term, that her penal - ty is paid,
2. Every valley shall be   lift - ed up,
3. and all people shall see   it to - gether,
4. All peo - ple   are grass,
5. The grass withers, the   flow - er fades;
6. lift it up,   do not fear;
7. his re - ward   is with him,
8. and carry them   in his bosom,

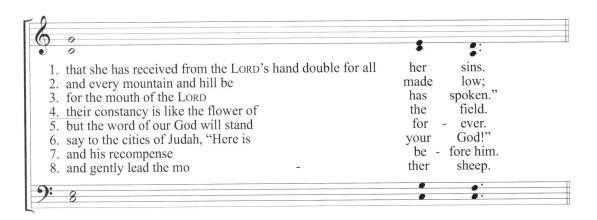

1. that she has received from the LORD's hand double for all   her   sins.
2. and every mountain and hill be   made   low;
3. for the mouth of the LORD   has   spoken."
4. their constancy is like the flower of   the   field.
5. but the word of our God will stand   for - ever.
6. say to the cities of Judah, "Here is   your   God!"
7. and his recompense   be - fore him.
8. and gently lead the mo -   ther   sheep.

Performance Notes

As indicated, the antiphon may be sung as a round.

90   Home for the Lonely

Antiphon / Melody ♩ = 80

Home for the lone - ly, strength for the peo - ple:

Descant

God is home, God is strength.

Optional Bass

God is home, God is strength.

bles-sed be our God, bles-sed be our God.

Bless our God, bles-sed be our God.

Bless our God, bless our God.

Verses *Psalm 68:4-5a, 5c-7b, 10-11, 20, 36bc*

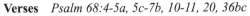

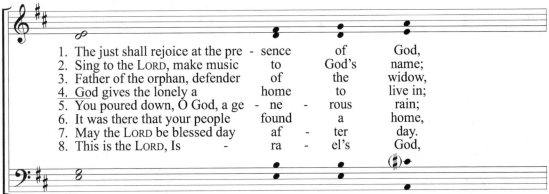

1. The just shall rejoice at the pre - sence of God,
2. Sing to the LORD, make music to God's name;
3. Father of the orphan, defender of the widow,
4. God gives the lonely a home to live in;
5. You poured down, O God, a ge - ne - rous rain;
6. It was there that your people found a home,
7. May the LORD be blessed day af - ter day.
8. This is the LORD, Is - ra - el's God,

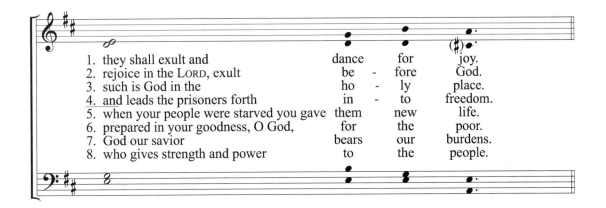

1. they shall exult and dance for joy.
2. rejoice in the LORD, exult be - fore God.
3. such is God in the ho - ly place.
4. and leads the prisoners forth in - to freedom.
5. when your people were starved you gave them new life.
6. prepared in your goodness, O God, for the poor.
7. God our savior bears our burdens.
8. who gives strength and power to the people.

Performance Notes
Verses 1–6 are the Lectionary selections for the Twenty-second Sunday in Ordinary Time, Year C.

Hosanna, Hosanna, Hosanna in the Highest

Antiphon ♩. = 72-76

Ho - san - na, ho - san - na, ho - san - na in the high - est. Ho -
san - na, hos - san - na, ho - san - na in the high - est.

Verses

1. The children of Je - ru - salem   welcomed Christ   the   King.
2. The children of Je - ru - salem   welcomed Christ   the   King.
3. Hosanna to the Son of   Da - vid!   Blessed is he   who   comes
4. The children of Je - ru - salem   welcomed Christ   the   King.
5. Waving olive   bran - ches,   they loudly praised   the   Lord:
6. When the people heard   that   Jesus   was entering Je - ru - salem,
7. Waving olive   bran - ches,   they loudly praised   the   Lord:

*

1. They carried olive branches and loudly   praised   the   Lord.
2. They spread their cloaks before him and loudly   praised   the   Lord.
3. in the name   of   the   Lord!
4. They proclaimed the resurrec - tion   of   life.
5. Hosanna   in   the   highest.
6. they   went   to   meet him.
7. Hosanna   in   the   highest.

Performance Notes

* *Final note of verse: sing either G or high C or low C.*

Antiphon ♩ = ca. 76

How hap - py   are you who fear the Lord!

Verses   *Psalm 128*

1. O blessed are you who fear   the   LORD
2. By the labor of your hands you   shall   eat.
3. Your wife like a fruit   -   ful   vine
4. your children like shoots of   the   olive,
5. Indeed thus shall   be   blessed
6. May the LORD bless you   from   Zion
7. May you see your children's children in a happy   Je - rusalem!

1. and walk in   God's   ways!
2. You will be happy   and   prosper.
3. in the heart of   your   house;
4. around   your   table.
5. those who fear   the   LORD.
6. all the days of   your   life!
7. On Isra - el,   peace!

How I Thirst for You

Antiphon ♩ = ca. 72

How I thirst for you, the liv-ing God! When shall I see you face to face?

Verses *Psalms 42:2-3, 5cdef; 43:3-5*

Cantor:

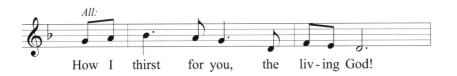

1. Like the deer that yearns for   run - ning   streams,
2. My soul is thirsting for God, the God   of   my   life;
3. I would lead the rejoicing crowd into the   house   of   God,
4. O send forth your light and your truth; let these   be   my   guide.
5. And I will come to your altar, O God, the God   of   my   joy.
6. Why are you cast down, my soul, why   groan   with - in me?

All:

How I thirst for you, the liv - ing God!

Cantor:

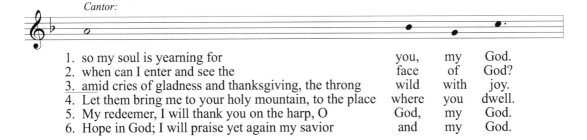

1. so my soul is yearning for   you,   my   God.
2. when can I enter and see the   face   of   God?
3. amid cries of gladness and thanksgiving, the throng   wild   with   joy.
4. Let them bring me to your holy mountain, to the place   where   you   dwell.
5. My redeemer, I will thank you on the harp, O   God,   my   God.
6. Hope in God; I will praise yet again my savior   and   my   God.

All:

When shall I see you face to face?

How Wonderful Your Name, O Lord

I Am the Resurrection

Antiphon ♩ = ca. 120

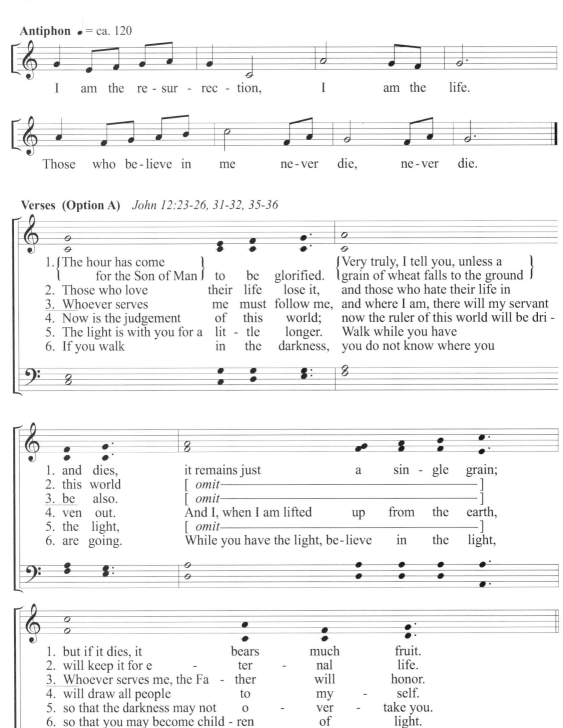

I am the re - sur - rec - tion, I am the life.

Those who be-lieve in me ne-ver die, ne-ver die.

Verses (Option A) *John 12:23-26, 31-32, 35-36*

1. {The hour has come for the Son of Man} to be glorified. {Very truly, I tell you, unless a grain of wheat falls to the ground}
2. Those who love their life lose it, and those who hate their life in
3. Whoever serves me must follow me, and where I am, there will my servant
4. Now is the judgement of this world; now the ruler of this world will be dri -
5. The light is with you for a lit - tle longer. Walk while you have
6. If you walk in the darkness, you do not know where you

1. and dies, it remains just a sin - gle grain;
2. this world [omit————————————————————]
3. be also. [omit————————————————————]
4. ven out. And I, when I am lifted up from the earth,
5. the light, [omit————————————————————]
6. are going. While you have the light, be-lieve in the light,

1. but if it dies, it bears much fruit.
2. will keep it for e - ter - nal life.
3. Whoever serves me, the Fa - ther will honor.
4. will draw all people to my - self.
5. so that the darkness may not o - ver - take you.
6. so that you may become child - ren of light.

Verses (Option B) *Psalm 34*

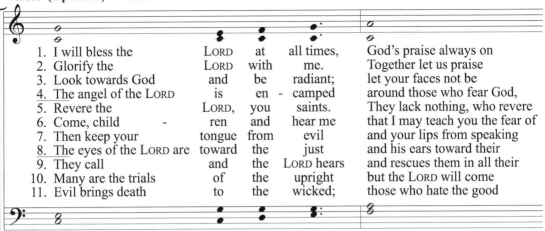

1. I will bless the LORD at all times, God's praise always on
2. Glorify the LORD with me. Together let us praise
3. Look towards God and be radiant; let your faces not be
4. The angel of the LORD is en - camped around those who fear God,
5. Revere the LORD, you saints. They lack nothing, who revere
6. Come, child - ren and hear me that I may teach you the fear of
7. Then keep your tongue from evil and your lips from speaking
8. The eyes of the LORD are toward the just and his ears toward their
9. They call and the LORD hears and rescues them in all their
10. Many are the trials of the upright but the LORD will come
11. Evil brings death to the wicked; those who hate the good

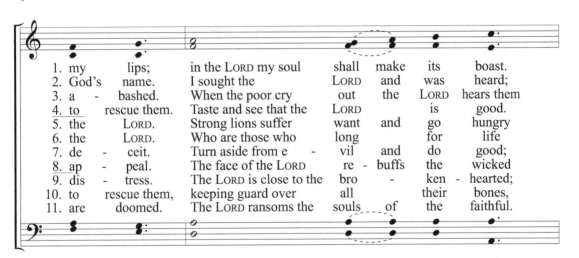

1. my lips; in the LORD my soul shall make its boast.
2. God's name. I sought the LORD and was heard;
3. a - bashed. When the poor cry out the LORD hears them
4. to rescue them. Taste and see that the LORD is good.
5. the LORD. Strong lions suffer want and go hungry
6. the LORD. Who are those who long for life
7. de - ceit. Turn aside from e - vil and do good;
8. ap - peal. The face of the LORD re - buffs the wicked
9. dis - tress. The LORD is close to the bro - ken - hearted;
10. to rescue them, keeping guard over all their bones,
11. are doomed. The LORD ransoms the souls of the faithful.

1. The humble shall hear and be glad.
2. from all my ter - rors set free.
3. and rescues them from all their dis - tress.
4. They are happy who seek re - fuge in God.
5. but those who seek the LORD lack no blessing.
6. and many days, to enjoy their pros - perity?
7. seek and strive af - ter peace.
8. to destroy their remembrance from the earth.
9. those whose spirit is crushed God will save.
10. not one of their bones shall be broken.
11. None who trust in God shall be con - demned.

96 I Am the Way: Follow Me

Antiphon / Melody ♩. = 52

I am the Way: fol - low me. I am the Truth: be -

Tenor/Alto Descant

I am the Way, I am the

Bass Descant

I am the Way, I am the

lieve in me. I am the Life: dwell in me, al - le - lu - ia.

Truth, I am the Life, al - le - lu - ia.

Truth, I am the Life, al - le - lu - ia.

Verses *Cf. John 15:5; 10:11; 14:27; Revelation 19:5; 12:10; Romans 6:8; Psalm 71:8, 23a;*
2 Corinthians 5:15; Revelation 5:12; Colossians 2:12; John 17:20-21

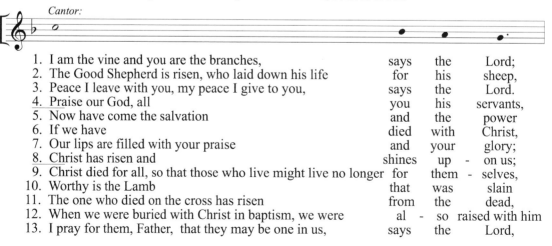

Cantor:

1. I am the vine and you are the branches,	says	the	Lord;
2. The Good Shepherd is risen, who laid down his life	for	his	sheep,
3. Peace I leave with you, my peace I give to you,	says	the	Lord.
4. Praise our God, all	you	his	servants,
5. Now have come the salvation	and	the	power
6. If we have	died	with	Christ,
7. Our lips are filled with your praise	and	your	glory;
8. Christ has risen and	shines	up -	on us;
9. Christ died for all, so that those who live might live no longer for	them -	selves,
10. Worthy is the Lamb	that	was	slain
11. The one who died on the cross has risen	from	the	dead,
12. When we were buried with Christ in baptism, we were	al -	so raised with him
13. I pray for them, Father, that they may be one in us,	says	the	Lord,

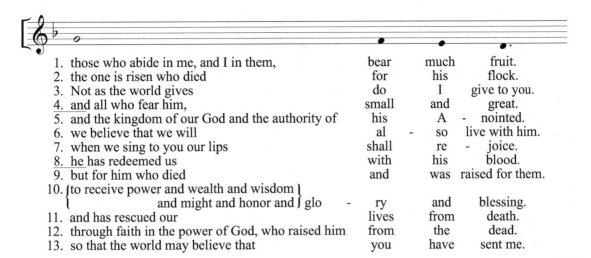

1. those who abide in me, and I in them,	bear	much	fruit.
2. the one is risen who died	for	his	flock.
3. Not as the world gives	do	I	give to you.
4. and all who fear him,	small	and	great.
5. and the kingdom of our God and the authority of	his	A -	nointed.
6. we believe that we will	al -	so	live with him.
7. when we sing to you our lips	shall	re -	joice.
8. he has redeemed us	with	his	blood.
9. but for him who died	and	was	raised for them.
10. {to receive power and wealth and wisdom			
and might and honor and} glo -	ry	and	blessing.
11. and has rescued our	lives	from	death.
12. through faith in the power of God, who raised him	from	the	dead.
13. so that the world may believe that	you	have	sent me.

All / Melody:

Al - le - lu - ia.

Tenor / Alto Descant:

Al - le - lu - ia.

Bass Descant:

Al - le - lu - ia.

I Am with You

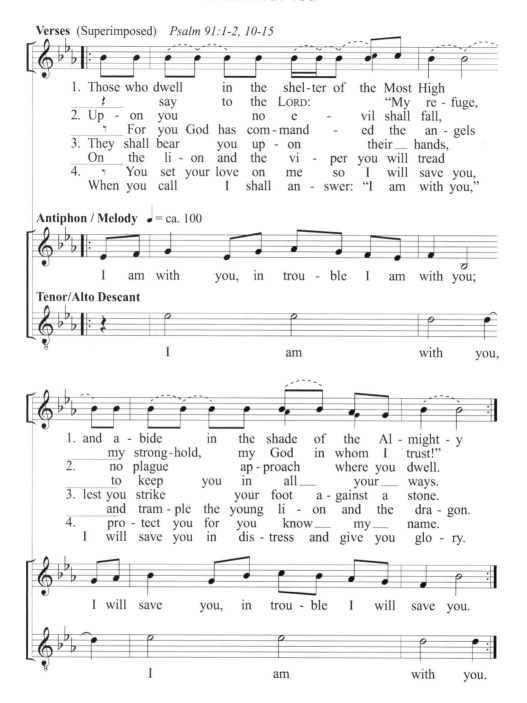

Verses (Superimposed)   *Psalm 91:1-2, 10-15*

1. Those who dwell in the shel-ter of the Most High
   say to the LORD: "My re-fuge,
2. Up - on you no e - vil shall fall,
   For you God has com-mand - ed the an - gels
3. They shall bear you up - on their hands,
   On the li - on and the vi - per you will tread
4. You set your love on me so I will save you,
   When you call I shall an - swer: "I am with you,"

Antiphon / Melody   ♩ = ca. 100

I am with you, in trou - ble I am with you;

Tenor/Alto Descant

I am with you,

1. and a - bide in the shade of the Al - might - y
   my strong-hold, my God in whom I trust!"
2. no plague ap - proach where you dwell.
   to keep you in all your ways.
3. lest you strike your foot a - gainst a stone.
   and tram - ple the young li - on and the dra - gon.
4. pro - tect you for you know my name.
   I will save you in dis - tress and give you glo - ry.

I will save you, in trou - ble I will save you.

I am with you.

Performance Notes

The verses are chanted rhythmically and may be sung superimposed on the antiphon, or separately without the antiphon being sung beneath (though still with accompaniment if accompaniment is being used).

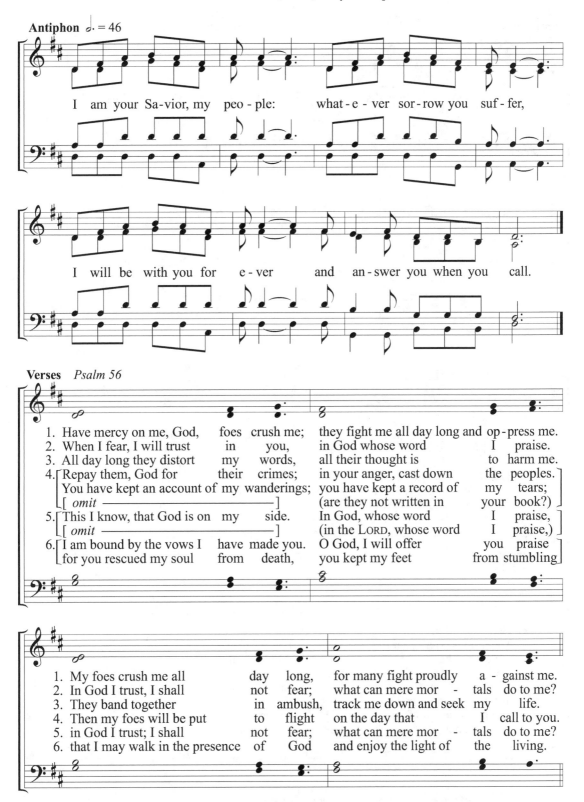

Antiphon ♩. = 46

I am your Sa-vior, my peo-ple: what-e-ver sor-row you suf-fer,

I will be with you for e-ver and an-swer you when you call.

Verses *Psalm 56*

1. Have mercy on me, God, foes crush me; they fight me all day long and op-press me.
2. When I fear, I will trust in you, in God whose word I praise.
3. All day long they distort my words, all their thought is to harm me.
4. [Repay them, God for their crimes; in your anger, cast down the peoples.
   You have kept an account of my wanderings; you have kept a record of my tears;
   [omit ——————————————————] (are they not written in your book?)]
5. [This I know, that God is on my side. In God, whose word I praise,
   [omit ——————————————————] (in the LORD, whose word I praise,)]
6. [I am bound by the vows I have made you. O God, I will offer you praise
   for you rescued my soul from death, you kept my feet from stumbling]

1. My foes crush me all day long, for many fight proudly a - gainst me.
2. In God I trust, I shall not fear; what can mere mor - tals do to me?
3. They band together in ambush, track me down and seek my life.
4. Then my foes will be put to flight on the day that I call to you.
5. in God I trust; I shall not fear; what can mere mor - tals do to me?
6. that I may walk in the presence of God and enjoy the light of the living.

I Called in My Distress

Antiphon ♩ = 92

God set me free.

I called in my dis - tress; God set me free. From

God set me free.

e - v'ry kind of fear God set me free.

Verses *Psalm 34:2-9*

Cantor / Choir:

1. I will bless the LORD at all times,
   In the LORD my soul shall make its boast.
2. Glorify the LORD with me.
   I sought the LORD and was heard;
3. Look towards God and be radiant;
   When the poor cry out the LORD hears them
4. The angel of the LORD is en - camped
   Taste and see that the LORD is good.

All: me free.

1. God's praise always on my lips; God set me free.
   The humble shall hear and be glad.
2. Together let us praise God's name.
   from all my ter - rors set free.
3. let your faces not be a - bashed.
   and rescues them from all their dis - tress.
4. around those who fear God, to rescue them.
   They are happy who seek re - fuge in God.

I Know I Shall See the Goodness of the Lord

Antiphon ♩ = 72

I know I shall see the good-ness of the Lord in the land, in the land of the liv - ing.

Verses *Psalm 27:1, 3-5, 7-14*

1. The LORD is my light and my help; whom shall I fear?
2. Though an army encamp a - gainst me my heart would not fear.
3. {There is one thing I ask of the LORD, for this I} long, {to live in the house of the LORD, all the days of my} life,
4. For God makes me safe in his tent in the day of evil.
5. O LORD, hear my voice when I call; have mercy and answer.
6. It is your face, O LORD, that I seek; hide not your face.
7. Do not abandon or for - sake me, O God my help!
8. Instruct me, LORD, in your way; on an even path lead me.
9. I am sure I shall see the LORD's goodness in the land of the living.

1. The LORD is the stronghold of my life; before whom shall I shrink?
2. Though war break out a - gainst me even then would I trust.
3. to savor the sweetness of the LORD, to be - hold his temple.
4. God hides me in the shelter of his tent, on a rock I am se - cure.
5. Of you my heart has spoken: "Seek God's face."
6. Dismiss not your ser - vant in anger; you have been my help.
7. Though father and mo - ther for - sake me, the LORD will re - ceive me.
8. {When they lie in ambush, protect me from my e} - ne-mies' greed. {False witnesses rise against me, breath -}ing out fury.
9. In the LORD, hold firm and take heart. Hope in the LORD!

Performance Notes

Verses 1, 3, and 5 are the Lectionary selections for the Seventh Sunday of Easter, Year A.

I Love You, Lord / The Strong Lord Sets Me Free

Antiphon I ♩ = ca. 76

I love you, Lord, love you, Lord, how I love you, Lord, my strength!

Antiphon II (alternate setting) ♩ = ca. 76

The strong Lord sets me free, in his love de-lights in me.

Verses *Psalm 18:2-4, 47, 51ab*

1. I love you, LORD, my strength,
2. God, you are the rock where I take refuge;
3. LORD, you are worthy of all praise,
4. Long life to you, LORD, my rock!
5. You have given great victories to your king

1. my rock, my fort - ress, my savior.
2. my shield, my mighty help, my stronghold.
3. when I call I am saved from my foes.
4. Praise to you, God, who saves me.
5. and shown your love for your a - nointed.

Antiphon ♩ = ca. 72   (optional 4-part round)

[1] I loved wis-dom more than health or beau-ty,

[2] and I chose her e-ven o-ver light;

[3] for her ra-diance ne-ver cea-ses,

[4] and I chose her e-ven o-ver light.

Verses *Wisdom 9:9-11, 13-14, 17*

1. With you is wisdom, she who knows your works
2. Send her forth from the holy heavens,
3. For she knows and under - stands all things,
4. For who can learn the counsel of God?
5. Who has learned your counsel,

1. and was present when you made the world;
2. from the throne of your glory send her,
3. she will guide me wisely in my actions
4. Who can discern what the LORD wills?
5. unless you have given wisdom

1. she understands what is pleasing in your sight
2. that she may labor at my side,
3. [omit ——————————————————]
4. For the reasoning of mortals is worthless,
5. [omit ——————————————————]

1. and what is right according to your com - mandments.
2. that I may learn what is pleas - ing to you.
3. and guard me with her glory.
4. and our designs are like - ly to fail.
5. and sent your holy spirit from on high?

I Shall Dwell in the House of the Lord

Antiphon / Melody ♩ = ca. 80

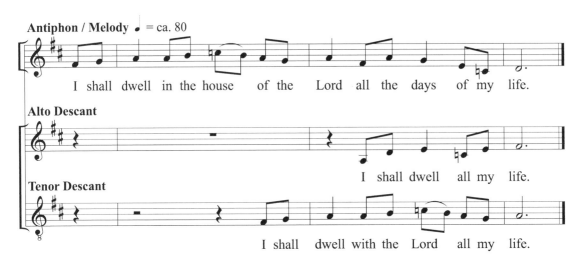

I shall dwell in the house of the Lord all the days of my life.

Alto Descant

I shall dwell all my life.

Tenor Descant

I shall dwell with the Lord all my life.

Verses *Psalm 23*

1. LORD, you are my shepherd; there is noth-ing I shall want.
2. Near restful waters you lead me, to re-vive my droop-ing spirit.
3. If I should walk in the valley of darkness no ___ e - vil would I fear.
4. You have prepared a banquet for me in the sight ___ of my foes.
5. Surely goodness and kindness shall follow me all the days ___ of my life.

1. Fresh and green are the pastures where you give me re - pose.
2. You guide me along the right path; you are true to your name.
3. You are there with your crook and your staff; with these you give me comfort.
4. My head you have anointed with oil; my cup is o - ver-flowing.
5. In the LORD's own house shall I dwell for e - ver and ever.

I Thank You, Lord, with All My Heart

Verses (Superimposed–Soprano) *Psalm 138*

1. ′ I thank you, LORD, with all my
2. ′ I thank you for your faith - ful
3. All the ru - lers on the earth shall
4. The LORD is high yet looks on the
5. ′ You stretch out your hand and

Antiphon / Melody ♩ = ca. 80

I thank you, Lord, with

Soprano/Alto Descants *(Soprano descant omitted when tone is superimposed)*

Tenor Descant

1. heart, you have heard the words of my
2. love which ex - cels all we e - ver
3. thank you when they hear the words of your
4. low - ly, and the haugh - ty God knows from a -
5. save me, your hand will do all things for

all my heart: you have heard my

Performance Notes

The vocal descants hum to 'n' or vocalize to 'oo'.
Whenever the tone is superimposed on the antiphon, this tone replaces the soprano descant.
The cue-notes in measures 2 and 3 are used with verses 3, 4, and 5.

I Will Dwell with You

Verses (Superimposed) *Revelation 21:1a, 2-5ab, 6; 22:17*

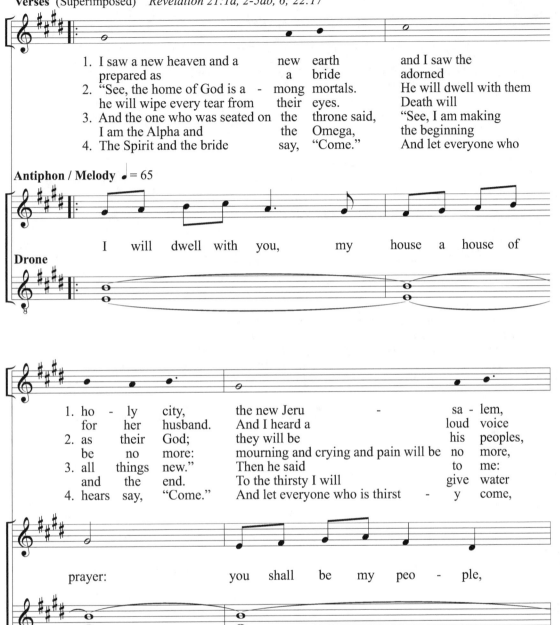

1. I saw a new heaven and a new earth and I saw the
prepared as a bride adorned
2. "See, the home of God is a - mong mortals. He will dwell with them
he will wipe every tear from their eyes. Death will
3. And the one who was seated on the throne said, "See, I am making
I am the Alpha and the Omega, the beginning
4. The Spirit and the bride say, "Come." And let everyone who

Antiphon / Melody ♩ = 65

I will dwell with you, my house a house of

Drone

1. ho - ly city, the new Jeru - sa - lem,
for her husband. And I heard a loud voice
2. as their God; they will be his peoples,
be no more: mourning and crying and pain will be no more,
3. all things new." Then he said to me:
and the end. To the thirsty I will give water
4. hears say, "Come." And let everyone who is thirst - y come,

prayer: you shall be my peo - ple,

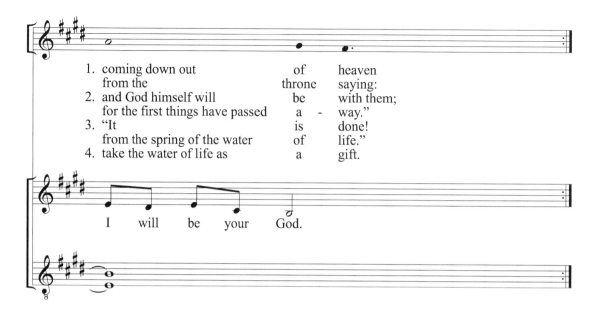

1. coming down out — of heaven
   from the — throne saying:
2. and God himself will — be with them;
   for the first things have passed — a - way."
3. "It — is done!
   from the spring of the water — of life."
4. take the water of life as — a gift.

I will be your God.

Performance Notes

The drone is preferably hummed (to an 'n' sound rather than an 'm' sound), but may also be sustained on the organ or played by guitars strumming an E chord without the 3rd on the first beat of every measure only.
If desired, the verses could be chanted independently on the tone given and not superimposed over the antiphon.
Note the correct accentuation of "Omega" in verse 3, with the stress on the first and not the second syllable.

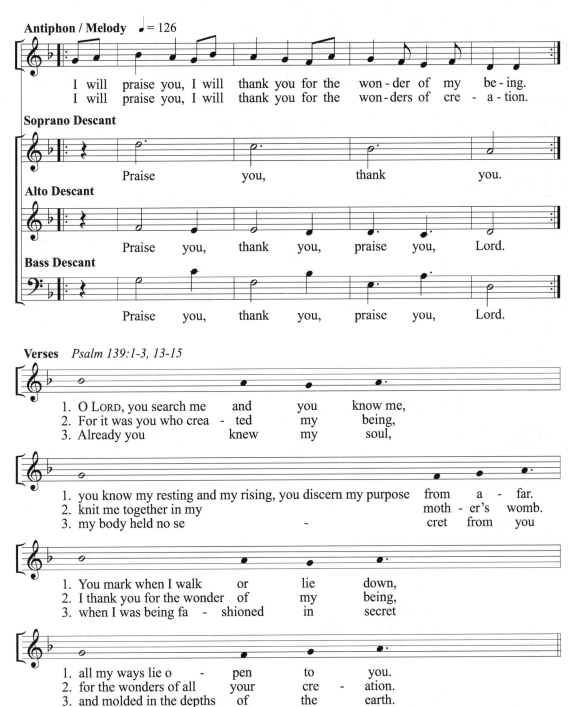

Performance Notes

In the first two full measures of the antiphon, the alto/bass descant rhythms could be sung as two dotted quarter notes (as in the third full measure) instead of half note followed by quarter note.

107   I Will Praise You, Lord

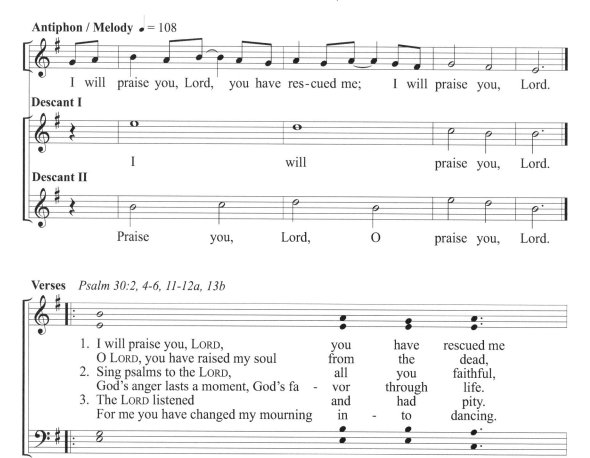

Antiphon / Melody ♩ = 108

I will praise you, Lord, you have res-cued me; I will praise you, Lord.

Descant I

I will praise you, Lord.

Descant II

Praise you, Lord, O praise you, Lord.

Verses *Psalm 30:2, 4-6, 11-12a, 13b*

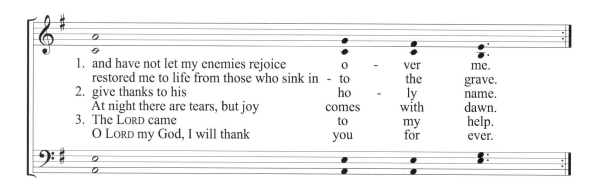

1. I will praise you, LORD, you have rescued me
   O LORD, you have raised my soul from the dead,
2. Sing psalms to the LORD, all you faithful,
   God's anger lasts a moment, God's fa - vor through life.
3. The LORD listened and had pity.
   For me you have changed my mourning in - to dancing.

1. and have not let my enemies rejoice o - ver me.
   restored me to life from those who sink in - to the grave.
2. give thanks to his ho - ly name.
   At night there are tears, but joy comes with dawn.
3. The LORD came to my help.
   O LORD my God, I will thank you for ever.

Antiphon / Melody ♩ = ca. 60

I will praise your name for e - ver, my God and king for e - ver.

Melody

Al - le - lu - ia, al - le - lu - ia, al - le - lu - ia.

Descants

Al - le - lu - ia, al - le - lu - ia, al - le - lu - ia.

Verses *Psalm 145:8-13*

Cantor:

1. You are kind and full of com - passion,
2. How good you are, LORD, to all,
3. All your creatures shall thank you, O LORD,
4. They shall speak of the glory of your reign
5. Let them make known to all your might - y deeds
6. Yours is an ever - last - ing kingdom;

1. slow to anger, abound - ing in love.
2. compassionate to all your creatures.
3. and your friends shall re - peat their blessing.
4. and declare your might, O God.
5. and the glorious splendor of your reign.
6. your rule lasts from age to age.

All / Melody:

Al - le - lu - ia, al - le - lu - ia, al - le - lu - ia.

Descants:

Al - le - lu - ia, al - le - lu - ia, al - le - lu - ia.

109

I Will Praise Your Name For Ever (II)

Antiphon / Melody ♩ = ca. 60

I will praise your name for e - ver, my God and king for e - ver.

Melody

Al - le - lu - ia, al-le-lu - ia, I will praise your name.

Descants

Al - le - lu - ia, al-le-lu - ia, I will praise your name.

Verses *Psalm 145:1-2, 8-11, 13c-14*

Cantor:

1. I will give you glory, O God my king,
2. I will bless you day af - ter day
3. You are kind and full of com - passion,
4. How good you are, Lord, to all,
5. All your creatures shall thank you, O Lord,
6. They shall speak of the glory of your reign
7. You are faithful in all your words
8. You support all those who are falling

1. I will bless your name for ever.
2. and praise your name for ever.
3. slow to anger, abound - ing in love.
4. compassionate to all your creatures.
5. and your friends shall re - peat their blessing.
6. and declare your might, O God.
7. and loving in all your deeds.
8. and raise up all who are bowed down.

All / Melody:

Al - le - lu - ia, al-le-lu - ia, I will praise your name.

Descants:

Al - le - lu - ia, al-le-lu - ia, I will praise your name.

Verses *cf. John 14:18; 16:22; Revelation 1:17-18; John 14:26; 16:7; 16:13; 15:26-27; Acts 1:8*

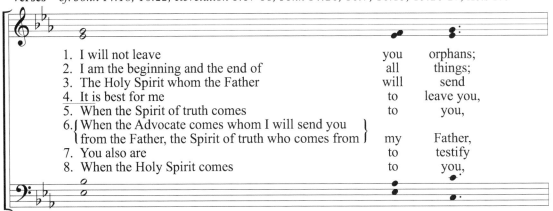

1. I will not leave   you   orphans;
2. I am the beginning and the end of   all   things;
3. The Holy Spirit whom the Father   will   send
4. It is best for me   to   leave you,
5. When the Spirit of truth comes   to   you,
6. { When the Advocate comes whom I will send you
   { from the Father, the Spirit of truth who comes from }   my   Father,
7. You also are   to   testify
8. When the Holy Spirit comes   to   you,

1. I will come back to you and your hearts   will   re - joice.
2. I have met death, but I   am   a - live.
3. will teach you, and remind you of all   I   have   said.
4. because if I do not go the Spirit   will   not   come to you.
5. you will be led to the full - ness   of   truth.
6. he will testify on   my   be - half.
7. because you have been with me from   the   be - ginning.
8. you will be my witnesses to   all   the   world.

I Will Show God's Salvation

Antiphon / Melody ♩ = 76

I will show God's sal-va-tion, I will show God's sal-va-tion, I will

Tenor / Baritone Descant

I will show, I will show,

show God's sal-va-tion to the up-right of heart.

show God's sal-va-tion to the up-right of heart.

Verses *Psalm 50:1, 8, 12-15*

1. The God of gods, the LORD, has spoken and summoned the earth,
2. Were I hungry, I would not tell you,
3. Offer to God your sacrifice;

1. from the rising of the sun to its setting. "I find no fault
2. for I own the world and all it holds. Do you think I eat the
3. to the Most High pay your vows. Call on me in the day

1. with your sacrifices, your offerings are al-ways be-fore me.
2. flesh of bulls, or drink the blood of goats?
3. of dis-tress. I will free you and you shall honor me."

112　I Will Sing For Ever of Your Love

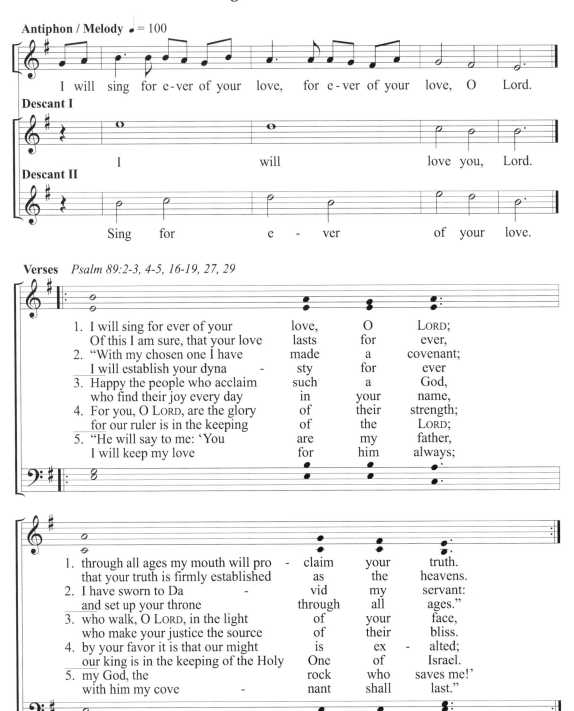

Performance Notes

Verses 1, 3, and 4 are the Lectionary selections for the Thirteenth Sunday in Ordinary Time, Year A.
Verses 1, 2, and 5 are the Lectionary selections for the Fourth Sunday of Advent, Year B.

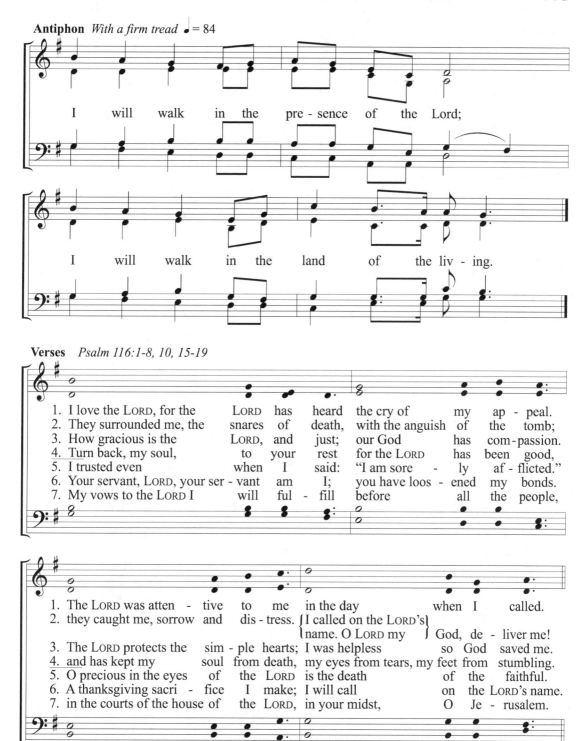

Performance Notes

Verses 5–7 are the Lectionary selections for the Second Sunday of Lent, Year B.
Verses 1–4 are the Lectionary selections for the Twenty-fourth Sunday in Ordinary Time, Year B.

If I Must Drink This Cup

Antiphon ♩ = ca. 72

If I must drink this cup, if it may not pass me by,

Fa-ther, let your will be done.

Verses *Psalm 116*

1. I love the LORD, for the LORD has heard the cry of my ap - peal.
2. The LORD was atten - tive to me in the day when I called.
3. They surrounded me, the snares of death, with the anguish of the tomb;
4. they caught me, sorrow and dis - tress. I called on the LORD's name.
5. O LORD, my God, de - liver me! O LORD, my God, de - liver me!
6. How gracious is the LORD and just; our God has com - passion.
7. The LORD protects the sim - ple hearts; I was helpless so God saved me.
8. Turn back, my soul, to your rest for the LORD has been good.
9. The LORD has kept my soul from death, {my eyes from tears, my} feet from stumbling.
10. I will walk in the presence of the LORD in the land of the living.

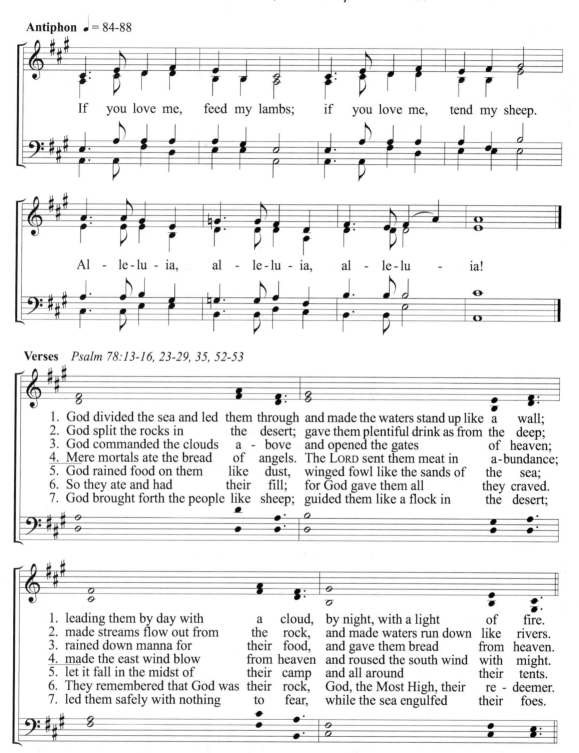

Antiphon ♩ = 84-88

If you love me, feed my lambs; if you love me, tend my sheep.

Al - le-lu - ia, al - le-lu - ia, al - le-lu - ia!

Verses *Psalm 78:13-16, 23-29, 35, 52-53*

1. God divided the sea and led them through and made the waters stand up like a wall;
2. God split the rocks in the desert; gave them plentiful drink as from the deep;
3. God commanded the clouds a - bove and opened the gates of heaven;
4. Mere mortals ate the bread of angels. The LORD sent them meat in a-bundance;
5. God rained food on them like dust, winged fowl like the sands of the sea;
6. So they ate and had their fill; for God gave them all they craved.
7. God brought forth the people like sheep; guided them like a flock in the desert;

1. leading them by day with a cloud, by night, with a light of fire.
2. made streams flow out from the rock, and made waters run down like rivers.
3. rained down manna for their food, and gave them bread from heaven.
4. made the east wind blow from heaven and roused the south wind with might.
5. let it fall in the midst of their camp and all around their tents.
6. They remembered that God was their rock, God, the Most High, their re - deemer.
7. led them safely with nothing to fear, while the sea engulfed their foes.

116   If You Love Me, Feed My Lambs (II)

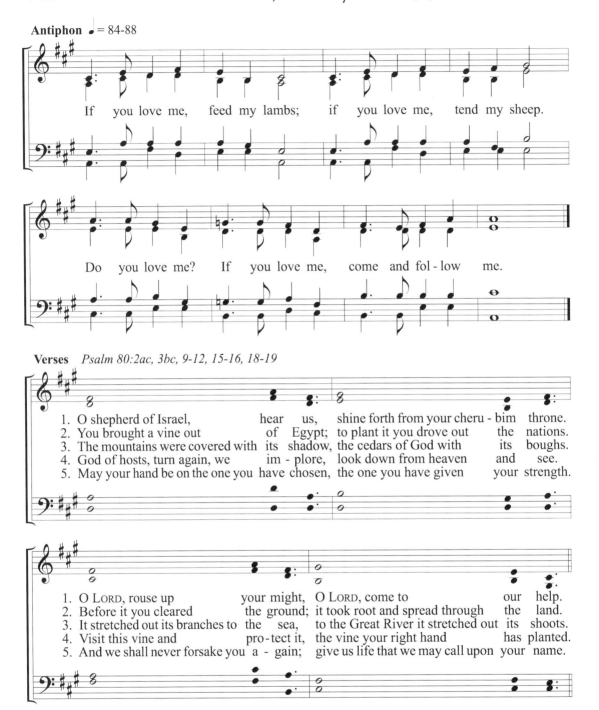

Antiphon ♩ = 84-88

If you love me, feed my lambs; if you love me, tend my sheep.

Do you love me? If you love me, come and fol - low me.

Verses *Psalm 80:2ac, 3bc, 9-12, 15-16, 18-19*

1. O shepherd of Israel,   hear us, shine forth from your cheru - bim throne.
2. You brought a vine out   of Egypt; to plant it you drove out   the nations.
3. The mountains were covered with its shadow, the cedars of God with   its boughs.
4. God of hosts, turn again, we   im - plore, look down from heaven   and see.
5. May your hand be on the one you have chosen, the one you have given   your strength.

1. O LORD, rouse up   your might, O LORD, come to   our help.
2. Before it you cleared   the ground; it took root and spread through   the land.
3. It stretched out its branches to the sea, to the Great River it stretched out its shoots.
4. Visit this vine and   pro - tect it, the vine your right hand   has planted.
5. And we shall never forsake you a - gain; give us life that we may call upon your name.

If You Will Love Each Other

Verses   *Romans 12:1-2, 4-5, 9-17, 20ab, 21; 13:8, 9a, 9g-10; 14:8-9; 15:5-7*

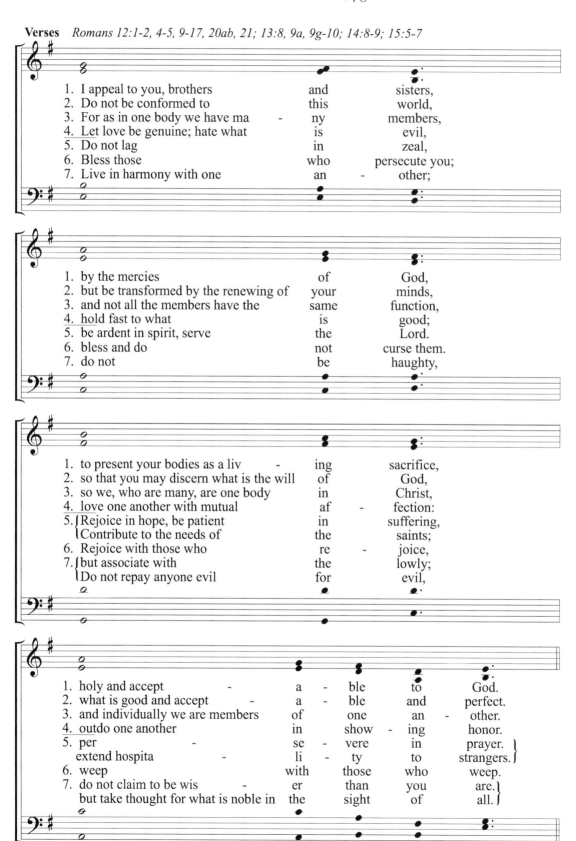

1. I appeal to you, brothers and sisters,
2. Do not be conformed to this world,
3. For as in one body we have ma - ny members,
4. Let love be genuine; hate what is evil,
5. Do not lag in zeal,
6. Bless those who persecute you;
7. Live in harmony with one an - other;

1. by the mercies of God,
2. but be transformed by the renewing of your minds,
3. and not all the members have the same function,
4. hold fast to what is good;
5. be ardent in spirit, serve the Lord.
6. bless and do not curse them.
7. do not be haughty,

1. to present your bodies as a liv - ing sacrifice,
2. so that you may discern what is the will of God,
3. so we, who are many, are one body in Christ,
4. love one another with mutual af - fection:
5. ∫ Rejoice in hope, be patient in suffering,
   ∖ Contribute to the needs of the saints;
6. Rejoice with those who re - joice,
7. ∫ but associate with the lowly;
   ∖ Do not repay anyone evil for evil,

1. holy and accept - a - ble to God.
2. what is good and accept - a - ble and perfect.
3. and individually we are members of one an - other.
4. outdo one another in show - ing honor.
5. per - se - vere in prayer. ∖
   extend hospita - li - ty to strangers. ∫
6. weep with those who weep.
7. do not claim to be wis - er than you are. ∖
   but take thought for what is noble in the sight of all. ∫

Verses (continued)

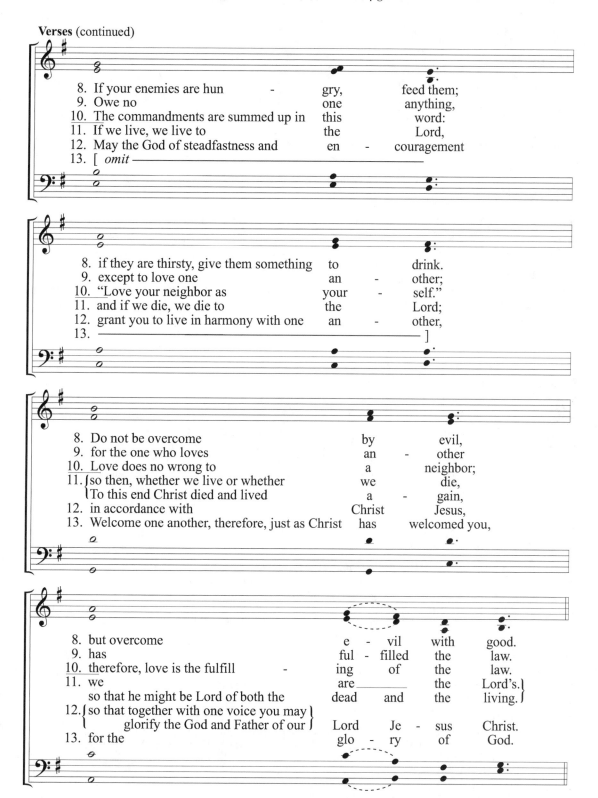

8. If your enemies are hun - gry, feed them;
9. Owe no one anything,
10. The commandments are summed up in this word:
11. If we live, we live to the Lord,
12. May the God of steadfastness and en - couragement
13. [*omit* ⸻

8. if they are thirsty, give them something to drink.
9. except to love one an - other;
10. "Love your neighbor as your - self."
11. and if we die, we die to the Lord;
12. grant you to live in harmony with one an - other,
13. ⸻]

8. Do not be overcome by evil,
9. for the one who loves an - other
10. Love does no wrong to a neighbor;
11. { so then, whether we live or whether we die,
    { To this end Christ died and lived a - gain,
12. in accordance with Christ Jesus,
13. Welcome one another, therefore, just as Christ has welcomed you,

8. but overcome e - vil with good.
9. has ful - filled the law.
10. therefore, love is the fulfill - ing of the law.
11. we are____ the Lord's. }
    so that he might be Lord of both the dead and the living. }
12. { so that together with one voice you may }
    { glorify the God and Father of our } Lord Je - sus Christ.
13. for the glo - ry of God.

In Every Age, O Lord, You Have Been Our Refuge

Antiphon / Melody ♩ = ca. 69

In ev'ry age, O Lord, you have been our re - fuge.

Soprano Descant

In ev'ry age, you have been our re - fuge.

Alto Descant

You have been our re - fuge.

Bass Descant

You have been our re - fuge.

Verses *Psalm 90:3-4, 5-6, 12-13, 14, 17*

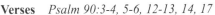

1. You turn us back into dust and say: "Go back, children of the earth."
2. You sweep us away like a dream, like grass which springs up in the morning.
3. Make us know the shortness of our life that we may gain wisdom of heart.
4. In the morning, fill us with your love; we shall exult and rejoice all our days.

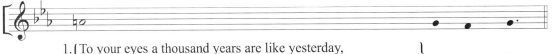

1. {To your eyes a thousand years are like yesterday, come and gone, no more than a watch} in the night.
2. In the morning it springs up and flowers; by evening it wi - thers and fades.
3. LORD, relent! Is your anger for ever? Show pity to your servants.
4. Let the favor of the LORD be upon us: give success to the work of our hands.

Performance Notes
The cantor may hold on the last note of the verse to overlap the beginning of the antiphon.

In God Alone Is My Soul at Rest

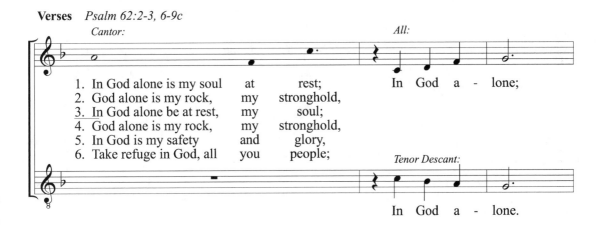

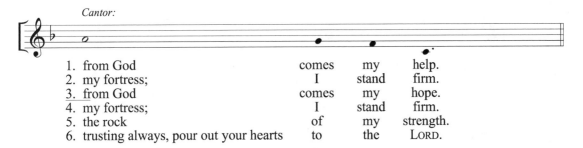

In the Presence of the Angels

Performance Notes

At the end of the piece, the antiphon may be repeated using the Alleluias in italics instead of the usual text.
Verses 1–3 and 5 are the Lectionary selections for the Fifth Sunday in Ordinary Time, Year C.
Verses 1–2 and 4–5 are the Lectionary selections for the Seventeenth Sunday in Ordinary Time, Year C.

121

In Your Abundant Love

Antiphon ♩ = ca. 80

In your a - bun - dant love, an - swer me, O God.

an - swer me, O God.

Verses *Psalm 69:8-10, 14, 17, 33-35*

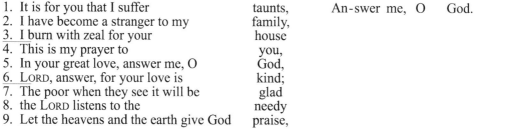

Cantor: *All:*

1. It is for you that I suffer   taunts,   An-swer me, O God.
2. I have become a stranger to my   family,
3. I burn with zeal for your   house
4. This is my prayer to   you,
5. In your great love, answer me, O   God,
6. LORD, answer, for your love is   kind;
7. The poor when they see it will be   glad
8. the LORD listens to the   needy
9. Let the heavens and the earth give God   praise,

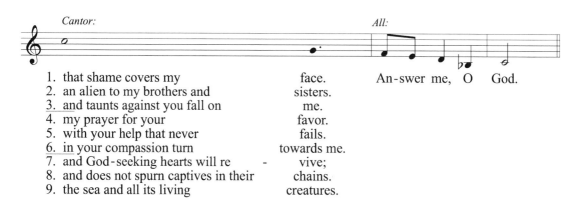

Cantor: *All:*

1. that shame covers my   face.   An-swer me, O God.
2. an alien to my brothers and   sisters.
3. and taunts against you fall on   me.
4. my prayer for your   favor.
5. with your help that never   fails.
6. in your compassion turn   towards me.
7. and God-seeking hearts will re - vive;
8. and does not spurn captives in their   chains.
9. the sea and all its living   creatures.

It Is Good to Give You Thanks, O Lord

123   Jesus Christ, the Same Today, Yesterday and Evermore

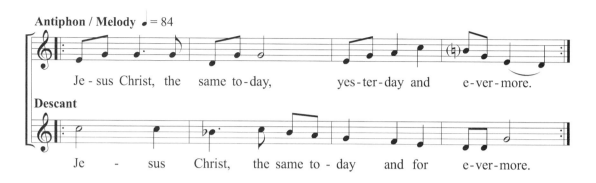

Antiphon / Melody ♩ = 84

Je - sus Christ, the same to-day,   yes-ter-day and   e-ver-more.

Descant

Je - sus Christ, the same to - day and for e-ver-more.

Verses   *Colossians 1:11-20*

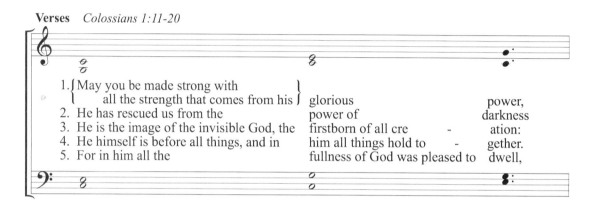

1. May you be made strong with all the strength that comes from his | glorious power,
2. He has rescued us from the | power of darkness
3. He is the image of the invisible God, the | firstborn of all cre - ation:
4. He himself is before all things, and in | him all things hold to - gether.
5. For in him all the | fullness of God was pleased to dwell,

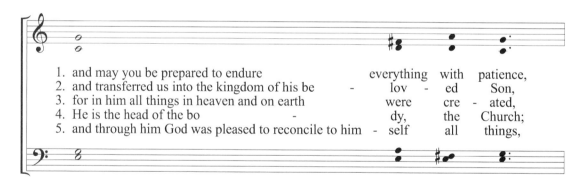

1. and may you be prepared to endure everything with patience,
2. and transferred us into the kingdom of his be - lov - ed Son,
3. for in him all things in heaven and on earth were cre - ated,
4. He is the head of the bo - dy, the Church;
5. and through him God was pleased to reconcile to him - self all things,

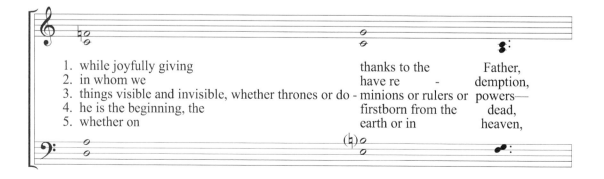

1. while joyfully giving thanks to the Father,
2. in whom we have re - demption,
3. things visible and invisible, whether thrones or do - minions or rulers or powers—
4. he is the beginning, the firstborn from the dead,
5. whether on earth or in heaven,

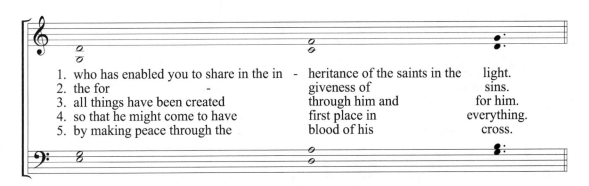

1. who has enabled you to share in the in - heritance of the saints in the light.
2. the for - giveness of sins.
3. all things have been created through him and for him.
4. so that he might come to have first place in everything.
5. by making peace through the blood of his cross.

Jesus, Mighty Lord, Come Save Us 124

Antiphon ♩ = 69

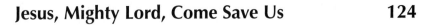

Je - sus, might - y Lord, come save us;

God - a - mong - us, set us free.

Verses *Psalm 19*

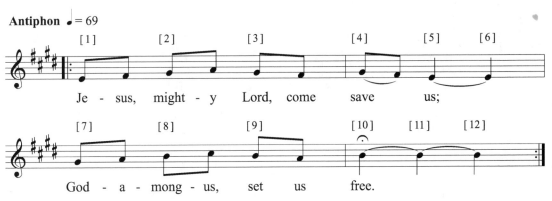

1. The heavens proclaim the glo - ry of God,
2. No speech, no word, no voice is heard
3. There God has placed a tent for the sun;
4. At the end of the sky is the rising of the sun;
5. The law of the LORD is perfect,
6. The precepts of the LORD are right,

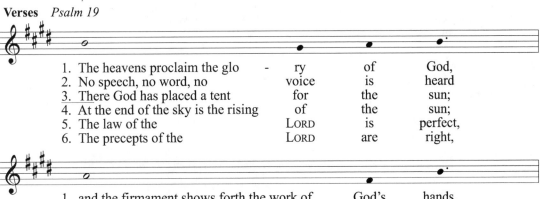

1. and the firmament shows forth the work of God's hands.
2. yet their span extends through all the earth,
3. it comes forth like a bridegroom coming from his tent,
4. to the furthest end of the sky is its course.
5. it revives the soul.
6. they gladden the heart.

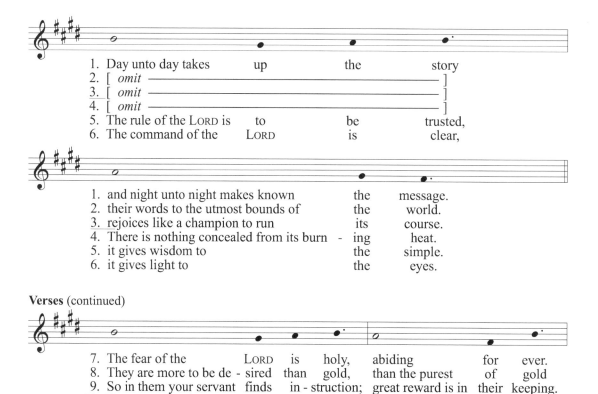

1. Day unto day takes up the story
2. [omit ————————————————————]
3. [omit ————————————————————]
4. [omit ————————————————————]
5. The rule of the LORD is to be trusted,
6. The command of the LORD is clear,

1. and night unto night makes known the message.
2. their words to the utmost bounds of the world.
3. rejoices like a champion to run its course.
4. There is nothing concealed from its burn - ing heat.
5. it gives wisdom to the simple.
6. it gives light to the eyes.

Verses (continued)

7. The fear of the LORD is holy, abiding for ever.
8. They are more to be de - sired than gold, than the purest of gold
9. So in them your servant finds in - struction; great reward is in their keeping.
10. From presumption re - strain your servant and let it not rule me.
11. May the spoken words of my mouth, the thoughts of my heart,

7. The decrees of the LORD are truth and all of them just.
8. and sweeter are they than honey, than honey from the comb.
9. But can we discern all our errors? From hidden faults ac - quit us.
10. Then shall I be blameless, clean from grave sin.
11. win favor in your sight, O LORD, my rescuer, my rock!

Performance Notes

The antiphon may be sung in unison or as a round:

    2-part round: begin at 1 and 7
    3 or 4-part round: begin at 1, 4, 7, and 10
    5 or 6-part round: begin at 1, 3, 5, 7, 9, and 11
    7–12 multi-part round: begin as indicated

The melody of the antiphon is derived from the hymn tune Divinum Mysterium *("Of the Father's love begotten").*

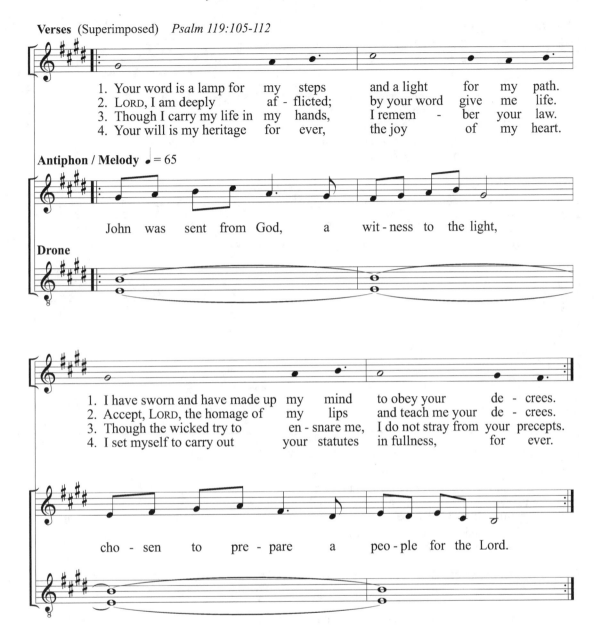

Verses (Superimposed) *Psalm 119:105-112*

1. Your word is a lamp for my steps and a light for my path.
2. LORD, I am deeply af - flicted; by your word give me life.
3. Though I carry my life in my hands, I remem - ber your law.
4. Your will is my heritage for ever, the joy of my heart.

Antiphon / Melody ♩ = 65

John was sent from God, a wit - ness to the light,

Drone

1. I have sworn and have made up my mind to obey your de - crees.
2. Accept, LORD, the homage of my lips and teach me your de - crees.
3. Though the wicked try to en - snare me, I do not stray from your precepts.
4. I set myself to carry out your statutes in fullness, for ever.

cho - sen to pre - pare a peo - ple for the Lord.

Performance Notes

The drone is preferably hummed (to an 'n' sound rather than an 'm' sound), but may also be sustained by the organ or guitar.
If desired, the verses could be chanted independently on the tone given and not superimposed over the antiphon.

126   Joyfully You Will Draw Water

Performance Notes

The psalm-tone can be superimposed on the antiphon as shown, or it may be sung separately (but still in rhythm).

Justice Shall Flourish

Antiphon ♩ = ca. 82

flou - rish,   full - ness,

Just - ice shall flou - rish,   peace in its full - ness,

just - ice shall flou - rish in his time, in his time.

time.

time.

Verses *Psalm 72:1-4b, 5-14, 15c-19*

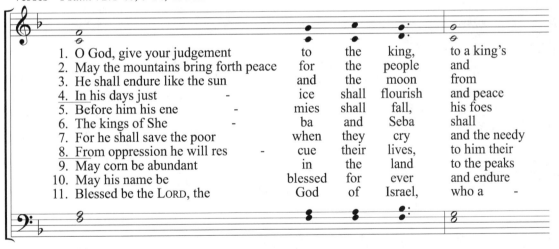

1. O God, give your judgement	to	the king,	to a king's
2. May the mountains bring forth peace	for	the people	and
3. He shall endure like the sun	and	the moon	from
4. In his days just -	ice	shall flourish	and peace
5. Before him his ene -	mies	shall fall,	his foes
6. The kings of She -	ba	and Seba	shall
7. For he shall save the poor	when	they cry	and the needy
8. From oppression he will res -	cue	their lives,	to him their
9. May corn be abundant	in	the land	to the peaks
10. May his name be	blessed	for ever	and endure
11. Blessed be the LORD, the	God	of Israel,	who a -

1. son your justice, that he may judge your peo - ple in justice
2. the hills, justice. May he defend the poor of the people
3. age to age. He shall descend like rain on the meadow,
4. till the moon fails. He shall rule from sea to sea,
5. lick the dust. The kings of Tarshish and the seacoasts
6. bring him gifts. Before him all rulers shall fall prostrate,
7. who are helpless. He will have pity on the weak
8. blood is dear. They shall pray for him with - out ceasing
9. of the mountains. May its fruit rus - tle like Lebanon;
10. like the sun. Every tribe shall be blessed in him,
11. lone works wonders, ever blessed God's glo - rious name.

1. and your poor in right judgement.
2. and save the children of the needy.
3. like raindrops on the earth.
4. from the Great River to earth's bounds.
5. shall pay him tribute.
6. all na - tions shall serve him.
7. and save the lives of the poor.
8. and bless him all the day.
9. may people flourish in the cities like grass on the earth.
10. all nations bless his name.
11. Let his glory fill the earth. A - men! A - men!

Performance Notes

Verses 1, 4, 7, and 10 are the Lectionary selections for the Second Sunday of Advent, Year A.

Keep My Soul in Peace

Antiphon / Melody ♩ = ca. 80-84

Keep my soul in peace, Lord, al-ways in your pre-sence.

Soprano Descant

Keep my soul in peace, al-ways in your pre-sence.

Alto Descant

Keep my soul in your pre-sence.

Bass Descant

Keep my soul in peace, Lord.

Verses *Psalm 131*

1. O LORD, my heart is not proud nor haughty my eyes.
2. Truly I have set my soul in silence and peace.
3. [*omit*]

1. I have not gone after things too great nor marvels be - yond me.
3. A weaned child on its mother's breast, even so is my soul.
3. O Israel, hope in the LORD both now and for ever.

129   Keep These Words in Your Heart and Soul

Antiphon ♩ = 82

Keep these words in your heart and soul, bind these words to your head and hand, lis-ten and do my Fa-ther's will.

Verses   *Psalm 17:1-9, 15*

1. LORD, hear a cause that is just, pay heed to
2. From you may my judgement come forth. Your eyes discern
3. My words are not sinful like human words. I kept from violence because of
4. I am here and I call, you will hear me, O God. Turn your ear to me; hear
5. Guard me as the apple of your eye. Hide me in the shadow of
6. As for me, in my justice, I shall see

1. my cry. Turn your ear to my prayer,
2. the truth. You search my heart, you visit me by night.
3. your word, I kept my feet firmly in your paths;
4. my words. Display your great love, you whose right hand saves
5. your wings from the violent at - tack of the wicked.
6. your face and be filled, when I a - wake,

1. no deceit is on my lips.
2. You test me and you find in me no wrong.
3. there was no falter - ing in my steps.
4. your friends from those who re - bel a - gainst them.
5. My foes encircle me with deadly in - tent.
6. with the sight of your glory.

Keep Us in Your Name

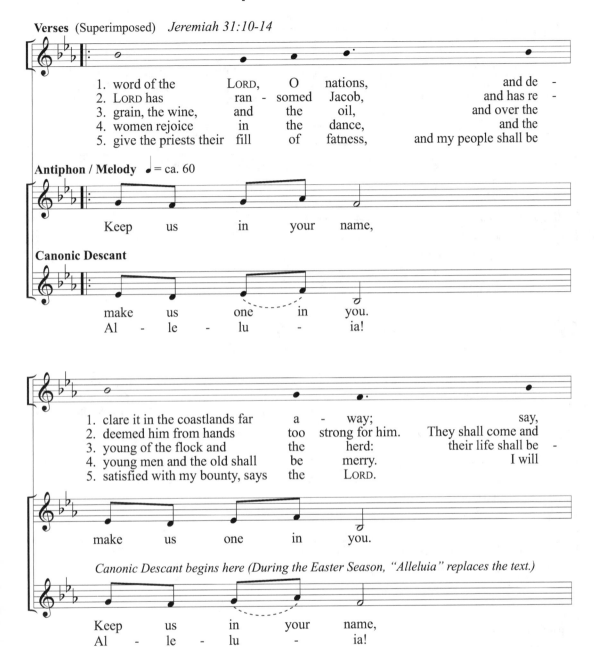

Verses (Superimposed)   *Jeremiah 31:10-14*

1. word of the LORD, O nations, and de -
2. LORD has ran - somed Jacob, and has re -
3. grain, the wine, and the oil, and over the
4. women rejoice in the dance, and the
5. give the priests their fill of fatness, and my people shall be

Antiphon / Melody ♩ = ca. 60

Keep us in your name,

Canonic Descant

make us one in you.
Al - le - lu - ia!

1. clare it in the coastlands far a - way; say,
2. deemed him from hands too strong for him. They shall come and
3. young of the flock and the herd: their life shall be -
4. young men and the old shall be merry. I will
5. satisfied with my bounty, says the LORD.

make us one in you.

Canonic Descant begins here (During the Easter Season, "Alleluia" replaces the text.)

Keep us in your name,
Al - le - lu - ia!

1. "He who scattered Israel will gather him, and will
2. sing aloud on the height of Zion, and they shall be
3. come like a wa - tered garden, and they shall
4. turn their mourning in - to joy, I will comfort
5. [omit —————

Keep us in your name,

make us one in you.
Al - le - lu - ia!

1. keep him as a shepherd a flock." *1. Hear the*
2. radiant over the goodness of the LORD, *2. For the*
3. never languish a - gain. *3. over the*
4. them and give them gladness for sorrow. *4. Then shall the young*
5. —————————————— *5. I will*
 ]

make us one in you.

Keep us in your name,
Al - le - lu - ia!

Performance Notes
Verses begin on the final beat of the last measure (a pickup beat to the first measure).

Laughter Fills Our Mouths

Performance Notes

Both antiphon and verses are repeated each time they are sung.

Lead Me, Guide Me

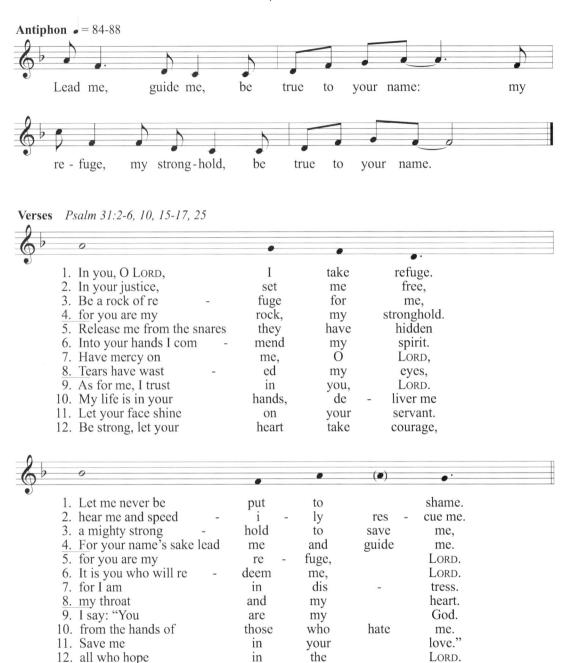

Antiphon ♩ = 84-88

Lead me, guide me, be true to your name: my re-fuge, my strong-hold, be true to your name.

Verses *Psalm 31:2-6, 10, 15-17, 25*

1. In you, O LORD, I take refuge.
2. In your justice, set me free,
3. Be a rock of re - fuge for me,
4. for you are my rock, my stronghold.
5. Release me from the snares they have hidden
6. Into your hands I com - mend my spirit.
7. Have mercy on me, O LORD,
8. Tears have wast - ed my eyes,
9. As for me, I trust in you, LORD.
10. My life is in your hands, de - liver me
11. Let your face shine on your servant.
12. Be strong, let your heart take courage,

1. Let me never be put to shame.
2. hear me and speed - i - ly res - cue me.
3. a mighty strong - hold to save me,
4. For your name's sake lead me and guide me.
5. for you are my re - fuge, LORD.
6. It is you who will re - deem me, LORD.
7. for I am in dis - tress.
8. my throat and my heart.
9. I say: "You are my God.
10. from the hands of those who hate me.
11. Save me in your love."
12. all who hope in the LORD.

Let All the Earth Cry Out Your Praises/
Let All the Earth Adore and Praise You

Antiphon ♩ = 138

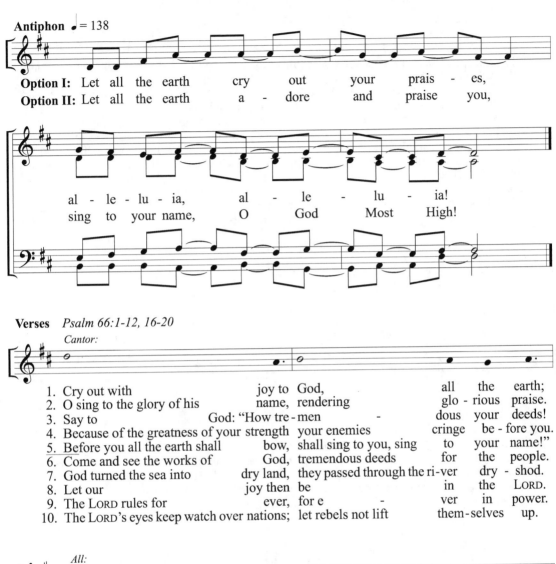

Option I: Let all the earth cry out your prais - es,
Option II: Let all the earth a - dore and praise you,

al - le - lu - ia, al - le - lu - ia!
sing to your name, O God Most High!

Verses *Psalm 66:1-12, 16-20*

Cantor:

1. Cry out with joy to God, all the earth;
2. O sing to the glory of his name, rendering glo - rious praise.
3. Say to God: "How tre - men - dous your deeds!
4. Because of the greatness of your strength your enemies cringe be - fore you.
5. Before you all the earth shall bow, shall sing to you, sing to your name!"
6. Come and see the works of God, tremendous deeds for the people.
7. God turned the sea into dry land, they passed through the ri - ver dry - shod.
8. Let our joy then be in the LORD.
9. The LORD rules for ever, for e - ver in power.
10. The LORD's eyes keep watch over nations; let rebels not lift them - selves up.

All:

Al - le - lu - ia, al - le - lu - ia!
Sing to your name, O God Most High!

Verses (continued)

11. O peoples, bless our   God, let the   voice of God's   praise   re - sound.
12. Praise God who gave life to our   souls   and kept our   feet   from stumbling.
13. For you, our God, have   tested us,   you have tried us as sil - ver   is   tried;
14. you led us, God, into the   snare;   you laid a heavy burden on   our   backs.
15. You let foes ride over our   heads;   we went through fire   and   through water
16. but then you   brought us,   you brought   us   re - lief.
17. Come and hear, all who fear   God,   I will tell what God did   for   my   soul;
18. to God I cried a   -   loud,   with high praise ready   on   my   tongue.
19. If there had been evil in my   heart,   the Lord would   not   have   listened.
20. But truly God has   listened;   has heeded the voice   of   my   prayer.
21. Blessed be   God who has   not re   -   ject - ed   me.
22. Blessed be   God who has not with - held his   love   from   me.

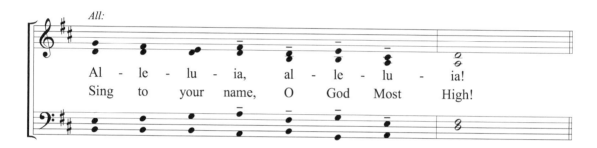

Al - le - lu - ia, al - le - lu - ia!
Sing to your name, O God Most High!

Performance Notes

Option I antiphon is used on the Third Sunday of Easter, Years A, B, and C, and on the Sixth Sunday of Easter, Year A (verses 1–10, 17, 21, and 22 are the Lectionary selections).
Option II antiphon is used on the Second Sunday in Ordinary Time, Years A, B, and C, and on the Fourteenth Sunday in Ordinary Time, Year C (verses 1–3, 5–9, 17, and 21–22 are the Lectionary selections).
Since the psalm verses are fairly short and brisk, it is recommended that the antiphon only be sung after every two or three verses.

Let My Prayer Come Before You, Lord

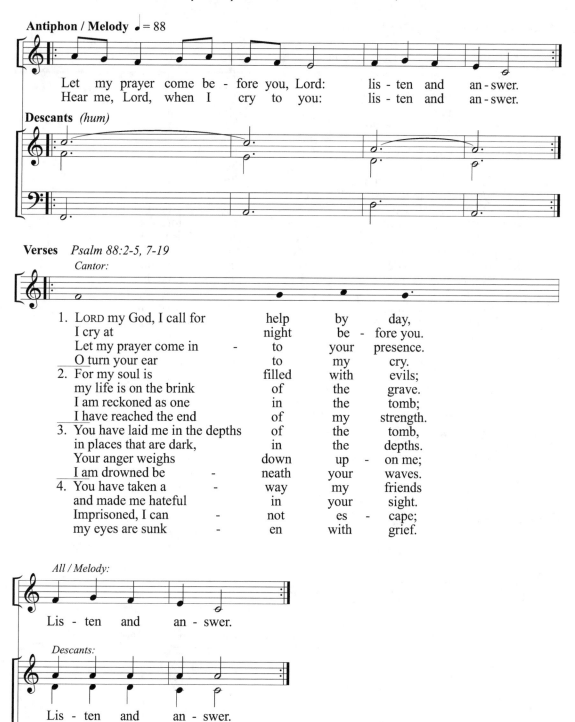

Antiphon / Melody ♩ = 88

Let my prayer come be - fore you, Lord: lis - ten and an - swer.
Hear me, Lord, when I cry to you: lis - ten and an - swer.

Descants *(hum)*

Verses *Psalm 88:2-5, 7-19*

Cantor:

1. LORD my God, I call for		help	by	day,
I cry at		night	be -	fore you.
Let my prayer come in	-	to	your	presence.
O turn your ear		to	my	cry.
2. For my soul is		filled	with	evils;
my life is on the brink		of	the	grave.
I am reckoned as one		in	the	tomb;
I have reached the end		of	my	strength.
3. You have laid me in the depths		of	the	tomb,
in places that are dark,		in	the	depths.
Your anger weighs		down	up -	on me;
I am drowned be -	-	neath	your	waves.
4. You have taken a	-	way	my	friends
and made me hateful		in	your	sight.
Imprisoned, I can	-	not	es -	cape;
my eyes are sunk	-	en	with	grief.

All / Melody:

Lis - ten and an - swer.

Descants:

Lis - ten and an - swer.

Verses (continued)

Cantor:

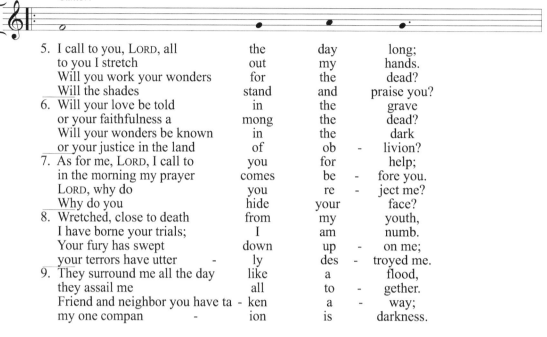

5. I call to you, LORD, all	the	day	long;
to you I stretch	out	my	hands.
Will you work your wonders	for	the	dead?
Will the shades	stand	and	praise you?
6. Will your love be told	in	the	grave
or your faithfulness a	mong	the	dead?
Will your wonders be known	in	the	dark
or your justice in the land	of	ob -	livion?
7. As for me, LORD, I call to	you	for	help;
in the morning my prayer	comes	be -	fore you.
LORD, why do	you	re -	ject me?
Why do you	hide	your	face?
8. Wretched, close to death	from	my	youth,
I have borne your trials;	I	am	numb.
Your fury has swept	down	up -	on me;
your terrors have utter -	ly	des -	troyed me.
9. They surround me all the day	like	a	flood,
they assail me	all	to -	gether.
Friend and neighbor you have ta - ken	a -	way;
my one compan -	ion	is	darkness.

All / Melody:

Lis - ten and an - swer.

Descants:

Lis - ten and an - swer.

Let the King of Glory Come In

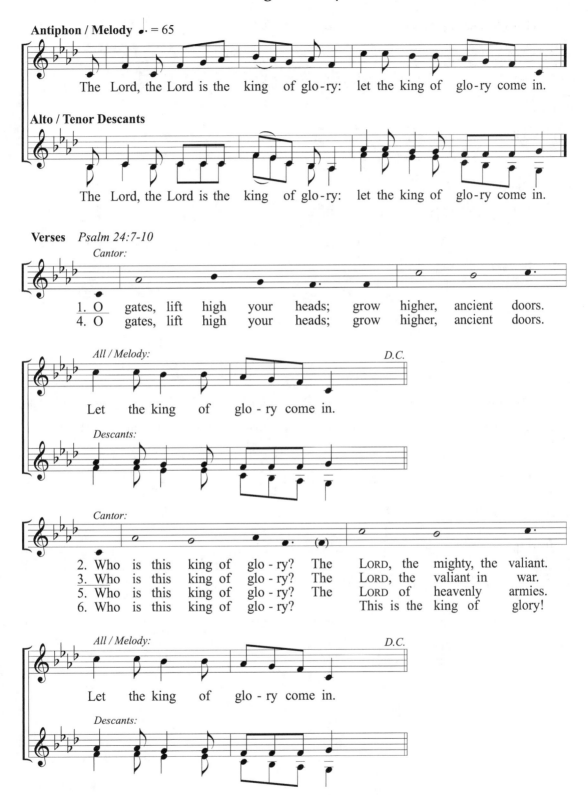

Let the Word Make a Home in Your Heart

Verses *Psalms 146; 127; 45:17-18*

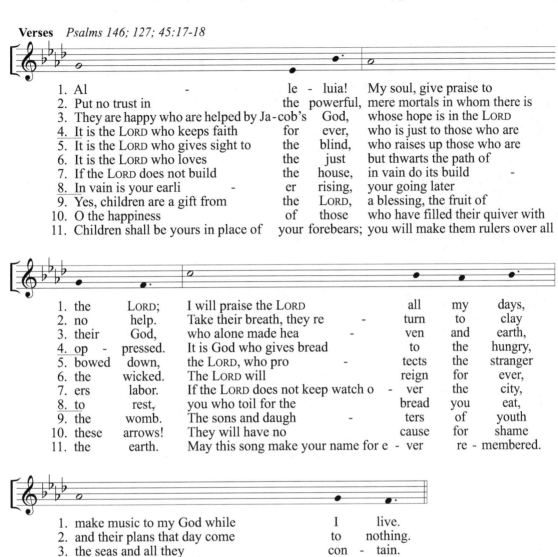

1. Al - le - luia! My soul, give praise to
2. Put no trust in the powerful, mere mortals in whom there is
3. They are happy who are helped by Ja-cob's God, whose hope is in the LORD
4. It is the LORD who keeps faith for ever, who is just to those who are
5. It is the LORD who gives sight to the blind, who raises up those who are
6. It is the LORD who loves the just but thwarts the path of
7. If the LORD does not build the house, in vain do its build -
8. In vain is your earli - er rising, your going later
9. Yes, children are a gift from the LORD, a blessing, the fruit of
10. O the happiness of those who have filled their quiver with
11. Children shall be yours in place of your forebears; you will make them rulers over all

1. the LORD; I will praise the LORD all my days,
2. no help. Take their breath, they re - turn to clay
3. their God, who alone made hea - ven and earth,
4. op - pressed. It is God who gives bread to the hungry,
5. bowed down, the LORD, who pro - tects the stranger
6. the wicked. The LORD will reign for ever,
7. ers labor. If the LORD does not keep watch o - ver the city,
8. to rest, you who toil for the bread you eat,
9. the womb. The sons and daugh - ters of youth
10. these arrows! They will have no cause for shame
11. the earth. May this song make your name for e - ver re - membered.

1. make music to my God while I live.
2. and their plans that day come to nothing.
3. the seas and all they con - tain.
4. the LORD, who sets pris - 'ners free.
5. and upholds the widow and orphan.
6. Zion's God, from age to age.
7. in vain do the watchers keep vigil.
8. when God pours gifts on the beloved while they slumber.
9. are like arrows in the hand of a warrior.
10. when they dispute with their foes in the gateways.
11. May the peoples praise you from age to age.

Performance Notes
The descant may be sung an octave lower as a tenor part, the tenor part being sung (at tenor pitch) by altos.

Let Us Go Rejoicing

Antiphon / Melody ♩ = ca. 100

Let us go re - joic - ing to the house of the Lord;

Descant 1 (Alto)

Let us go up to God's house,

Descant 2 (Tenor or Soprano)

Let us go re - joic - ing to the house of the Lord;

let us go re - joic - ing to the house of the Lord.

let us go up to God's house.

let us go re - joic - ing to the house of the Lord.

Verses *Psalm 122*

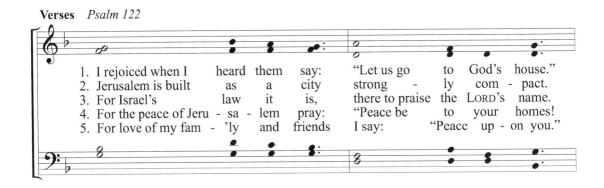

1. I rejoiced when I heard them say: "Let us go to God's house."
2. Jerusalem is built as a city strong - ly com - pact.
3. For Israel's law it is, there to praise the LORD's name.
4. For the peace of Jeru - sa - lem pray: "Peace be to your homes!
5. For love of my fam - 'ly and friends I say: "Peace up - on you."

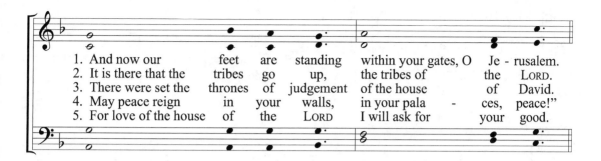

1. And now our feet are standing within your gates, O Je - rusalem.
2. It is there that the tribes go up, the tribes of the LORD.
3. There were set the thrones of judgement of the house of David.
4. May peace reign in your walls, in your pala - ces, peace!"
5. For love of the house of the LORD I will ask for your good.

Performance Notes

Verses 1, 2, and 5 are the Lectionary selections for the Anniversary of the Dedication of a Church.

138   Let Your Love Be Upon Us, O Lord

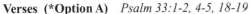

Antiphon ♩ = 88

Let your love be up-on us, O Lord. We hope in you! We hope in you!

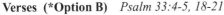

Verses (*Option A)   *Psalm 33:1-2, 4-5, 18-19*

1. Ring out your joy to the LORD, O you just; for praise is fitting for loy-al hearts.
   Give thanks to the LORD upon the harp, with a ten-stringed lute play your songs.
2. The word of the LORD is faithful and all his works done in truth.
   The LORD loves justice and right and fills the earth with love.
3. The LORD looks on those who fear him, on those who hope in his love,
   to rescue their souls from death, to keep them a - live in famine.

Verses (*Option B)   *Psalm 33:4-5, 18-21*

1. The word of the LORD is faithful and all his works done in truth.
2. The LORD loves justice and right and fills the earth with love.
3. The LORD looks on those who fear him, on those who hope in his love,
4. to rescue their souls from death, to keep them a - live in famine.
5. Our soul is waiting for the LORD. The LORD is our help and our shield.
6. Our hearts find joy in the LORD. We trust in God's ho - ly name.

Performance Notes

*Option A verses are used as the Song for the Word on the Fifth Sunday of Easter, Year A.

Option B verses are used as the Song for the Word on the Second Sunday of Lent, Year A, and the Twenty-ninth Sunday in Ordinary Time, Year B.

Lift Up Your Heads, Stand and Believe

Verses (Superimposed) *Luke 21:9a, 10a, 18, 17, 19-20a, 22b, 23b, 24c-25a, 27a, 28a, 31b, 33, 36ac*

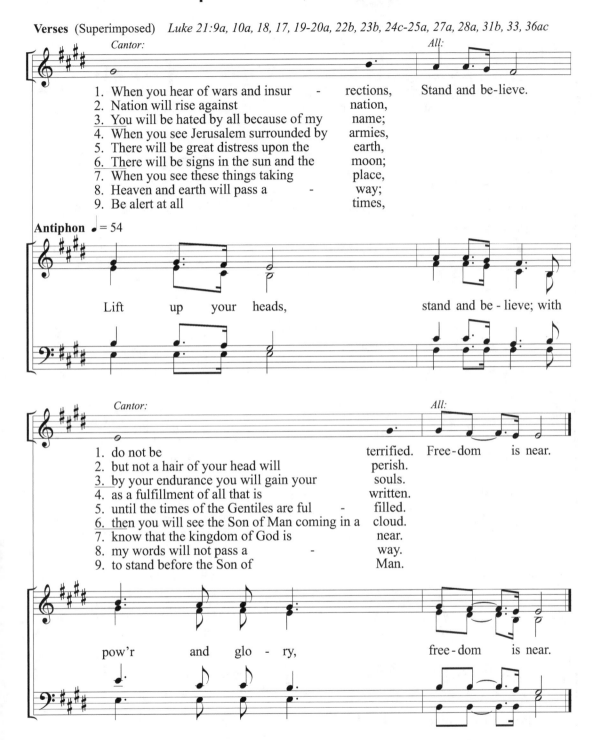

Cantor: *All:*

1. When you hear of wars and insur - rections,   Stand and be-lieve.
2. Nation will rise against nation,
3. You will be hated by all because of my name;
4. When you see Jerusalem surrounded by armies,
5. There will be great distress upon the earth,
6. There will be signs in the sun and the moon;
7. When you see these things taking place,
8. Heaven and earth will pass a - way;
9. Be alert at all times,

Antiphon ♩ = 54

Lift   up   your   heads,   stand and be - lieve; with

Cantor: *All:*

1. do not be terrified. Free-dom is near.
2. but not a hair of your head will perish.
3. by your endurance you will gain your souls.
4. as a fulfillment of all that is written.
5. until the times of the Gentiles are ful - filled.
6. then you will see the Son of Man coming in a cloud.
7. know that the kingdom of God is near.
8. my words will not pass a - way.
9. to stand before the Son of Man.

pow'r   and   glo - ry,   free - dom   is near.

Performance Notes

As the cantor sings the verses, the other voices may vocalize to 'oo' under measures 1 and 3 of the superimposed tone instead of singing the words.

Light of the World

Verses (*Option A)   *Isaiah 9:2-6; Psalm 27:1, 3, 13-14*

Cantor:

1. ⁊ The peo-ple in dark - ness have seen a great
2. You have filled them with glad - ness and joy in a -
3. For the yoke of their bur - den, the rod of op -
4. For the boots of the bat - tle, the cloaks rolled in
5. For a child has been born for us, a son has been
6. He is Won - der - ful Coun - sel - lor, Might - y
7. ⁊ The Lord is my light, the Lord is my
8. Though an ar - my be - siege me, my heart shall not
9. ⁊ I know I shall see the good - ness of

Descants:

Ah . . .   Ah . . .

All / Melody:

1. light.   You are the light of the world.
2. bun - dance.
3. pres - sion,
4. blood,
5. giv'n.
6. God,
7. help.
8. fear.
9. God.

You are the light of the world.

Cantor:

1. On the dwell - ers in sha - dow a light has
2. ⁊ They sing now be - fore you the joy of the
3. ⁊ the bar on their shoul - ders you shat - ter to
4. ⁊ are burnt and con - sumed as fuel for the
5. ⁊ The rule of the na - tions is laid on his
6. ⁊ Fa - ther E - ter - nal, Prince of
7. ⁊ The Lord is my strong - hold: whom shall I
8. Though a war rage a - gainst me, I shall stand
9. ⁊ Wait for the Lord, be strong and take

Ah . . .   Ah . . .

All / Melody: D.C.

1. shone.   We are the light of the world.
2. har - vest.
3. pie - ces.
4. fire.
5. shoul - ders.
6. Peace.
7. fear?
8. firm.
9. heart.

D.C.

We are the light of the world.

Verses (*Option B) *Isaiah 58:7-11; Matthew 5:13a, 14; Psalm 27:1, 3, 13-14*

Performance Notes

Option A verses are used on the Third Sunday in Ordinary Time, Year A. Option B verses are used on the Fifth Sunday in Ordinary Time, Year A.

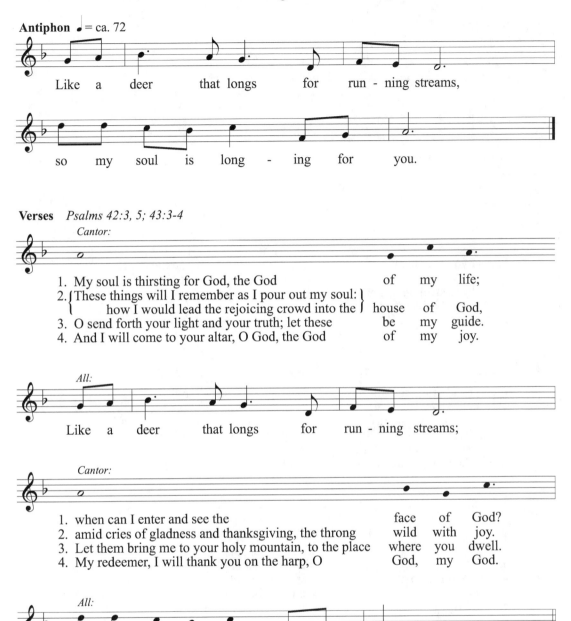

Antiphon ♩ = ca. 72

Like a deer that longs for run - ning streams,

so my soul is long - ing for you.

Verses *Psalms 42:3, 5; 43:3-4*

Cantor:

1. My soul is thirsting for God, the God of my life;
2. {These things will I remember as I pour out my soul: how I would lead the rejoicing crowd into the} house of God,
3. O send forth your light and your truth; let these be my guide.
4. And I will come to your altar, O God, the God of my joy.

All:

Like a deer that longs for run - ning streams;

Cantor:

1. when can I enter and see the face of God?
2. amid cries of gladness and thanksgiving, the throng wild with joy.
3. Let them bring me to your holy mountain, to the place where you dwell.
4. My redeemer, I will thank you on the harp, O God, my God.

All:

So my soul is long - ing for you.

Like Newborn Children

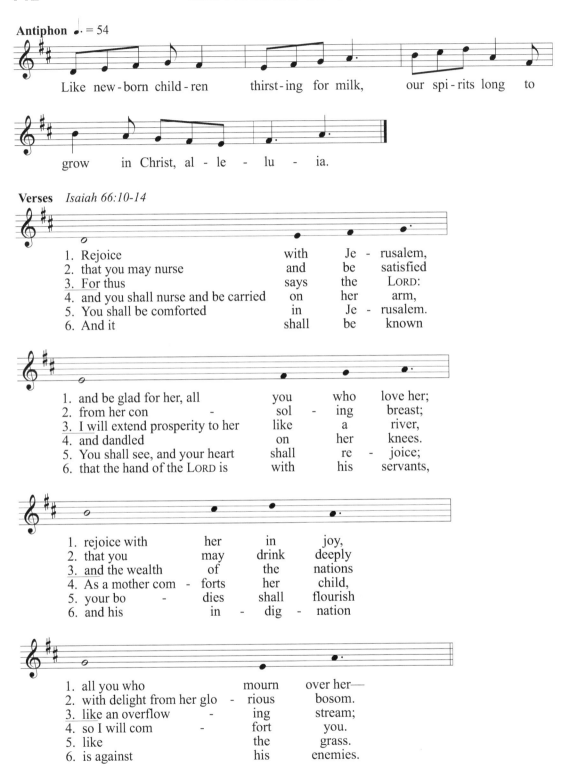

Antiphon ♩. = 54

Like new-born child-ren thirst-ing for milk, our spi-rits long to grow in Christ, al - le - lu - ia.

Verses *Isaiah 66:10-14*

1. Rejoice with Je - rusalem,
2. that you may nurse and be satisfied
3. For thus says the LORD:
4. and you shall nurse and be carried on her arm,
5. You shall be comforted in Je - rusalem.
6. And it shall be known

1. and be glad for her, all you who love her;
2. from her con - sol - ing breast;
3. I will extend prosperity to her like a river,
4. and dandled on her knees.
5. You shall see, and your heart shall re - joice;
6. that the hand of the LORD is with his servants,

1. rejoice with her in joy,
2. that you may drink deeply
3. and the wealth of the nations
4. As a mother com - forts her child,
5. your bo - dies shall flourish
6. and his in - dig - nation

1. all you who mourn over her—
2. with delight from her glo - rious bosom.
3. like an overflow - ing stream;
4. so I will com - fort you.
5. like the grass.
6. is against his enemies.

Verses (Superimposed)   *Sirach 14:20-26; 15:1-6*

1. Happy are you who meditate on wisdom,
2. Happy are you who reflect in your heart on wisdom's ways,
3. Happy are you who pursue wisdom like a hunter,
4. Happy are you who peer through wisdom's windows,
5. Happy are you who camp near wisdom's house,
6. Happy are you who pitch your tent near wisdom,
7. Happy you who place your children under wisdom's shelter,
8. Whoever fears the Lord will act in this way;
9. She will come to meet him like a loving mother,
10. She will feed him with the bread of learning,
11. He will lean on her and he will not fall,
12. She will exalt him above all his neighbors,
13. He will find gladness and a crown of rejoicing,

Antiphon / Melody ♩ = ca. 78

Lis - ten: I stand at the door and knock.

Soprano / Alto Descants

Lis - ten: I stand at the door and knock.

Bass Descant

O - pen, and we shall feast.

O - pen, and we shall feast.

1. happy are you who   reason with   in - tel - li - gence.
2. happy are you who   ponder   her   se - crets.
3. happy are you who lie in   wait on   her   paths.
4. happy are you who   listen at   her   doors.
5. you who fasten your   tent peg to   her   walls.
6. who so occupy an   excel - lent   lodg - ing place.
7. happy are you who lodge   under wis - dom's   boughs.
8. whoever holds to the law   will ob - tain   wis - dom.
9. like a young bride   wisdom   will   wel - come him.
10. she will give him the water of   wisdom   to   drink.
11. he will rely on her and   not be put   to   shame.
12. she will open his mouth in the   midst of the   as - sem - bly.
13. he will inherit an   everlast - ing   name.

Lis - ten: I stand at the door and knock.

Lis - ten: I stand at the door and knock.

O - pen and we shall feast.

O - pen, and we shall feast.

Performance Notes

When the antiphon is sung alone, sing all the text; when the verse is superimposed, vocalize to "oo" in measures 1–2 and 5–6 while the cantor sings the verse text.

Listen! Listen! Open Your Hearts!

Antiphon ♩ = ca. 100

Lis-ten! Lis-ten! O-pen your hearts! Lis-ten! Lis-ten! O-pen your hearts!

Verses *Psalm 95:1-9*

1. Come, ring out our joy to the   LORD;
2. Let us come before God, giving   thanks;
3. A mighty God is the   LORD,
4. In God's hands are the depths of the   earth;
5. The sea belongs to God, who   made it
6. Come in; let us bow and bend   low;
7. This is our God, and we the people who belong to his   pasture,
8. ⎧O that today you would listen to God's   voice!
   ⎨as on that day at Massah in the   desert

1. hail the rock   who   saves us.
2. with songs let us hail   the   LORD.
3. a great king above   all   gods.
4. the heights of the mountains   as   well.
5. and the dry land shaped by   his   hands.
6. let us kneel before the God   who   made us.
7. the flock that is led by   his   hand.
8. "Harden not your hearts as at   Me - ribah,⎫
   ⎧when your ancestors put me to the test; ⎬
   ⎨ when they tried me, though they saw ⎭ my   work."

Performance Notes

Verses 1, 2, 6, 7, and 8 are the Lectionary selections for the Third Sunday of Lent, Year A. They are also used in Ordinary Time on the the Twenty-third Sunday, Year A, the Fourth Sunday, Year B, and the Twenty-seventh Sunday, Year C.

Listen, Listen to the Voice of Jesus

Antiphon ♩ = ca. 40

Lis - ten, lis - ten to the voice of Je - sus, who

is, who was, and who is to come.

Verses (*Option A) *Isaiah 58:6-8b, 9ab, 10-11ab,11def*

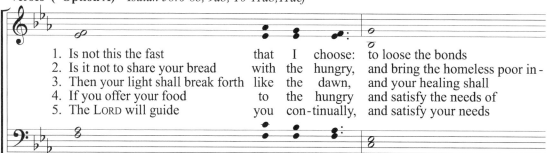

1. Is not this the fast that I choose: to loose the bonds
2. Is it not to share your bread with the hungry, and bring the homeless poor in -
3. Then your light shall break forth like the dawn, and your healing shall
4. If you offer your food to the hungry and satisfy the needs of
5. The LORD will guide you con - tinually, and satisfy your needs

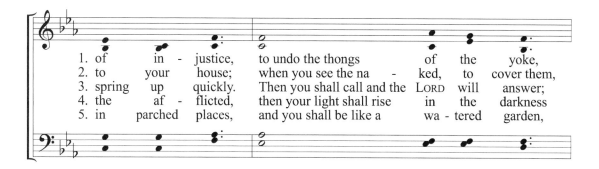

1. of in - justice, to undo the thongs of the yoke,
2. to your house; when you see the na - ked, to cover them,
3. spring up quickly. Then you shall call and the LORD will answer;
4. the af - flicted, then your light shall rise in the darkness
5. in parched places, and you shall be like a wa - tered garden,

1. to let the oppressed go free, and to break e - v'ry yoke?
2. and not to hide yourself from your own kin?
3. you shall cry for help, and he will say, Here I am.
4. and your gloom be like the noonday.
5. like a spring of water, whose waters ne - ver fail.

Verses (*Option B)   *Psalm 29*

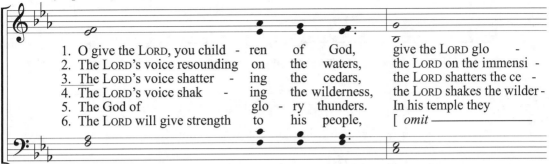

1. O give the LORD, you child - ren   of   God,   give the LORD glo -
2. The LORD's voice resounding   on   the   waters,   the LORD on the immensi -
3. The LORD's voice shatter - ing   the   cedars,   the LORD shatters the ce -
4. The LORD's voice shak - ing   the   wilderness,   the LORD shakes the wilder -
5. The God of   glo - ry   thunders.   In his temple they
6. The LORD will give strength   to   his   people,   [*omit* —————————

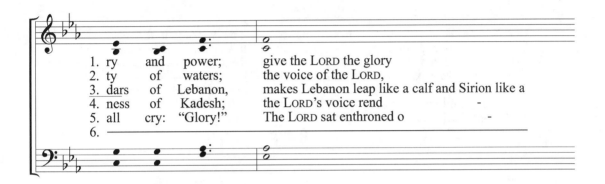

1. ry   and   power;   give the LORD the glory
2. ty   of   waters;   the voice of the LORD,
3. dars   of   Lebanon,   makes Lebanon leap like a calf and Sirion like a
4. ness   of   Kadesh;   the LORD's voice rend   -
5. all   cry: "Glory!"   The LORD sat enthroned o   -
6. ————————————

1. of   his   name.   Adore the LORD, resplen - dent   and   holy.
2. full   of   power;   the voice of the LORD,   full   of   splendor.
3. young   wild   ox.   The LORD's voice flashes   flames   of   fire.
4. ing   the   oak tree   and stripping the   for - est   bare.
5. ver   the   flood;   the LORD sits as   king   for   ever.
6. ———————]   the LORD will bless his peo - ple   with   peace.

Performance Notes

Option A verses are used as the Song for the Table on Christ the King, Year A, and Option B verses for that same solemnity in Year B.

As indicated, the antiphon may be sung as a 4-part round if desired.

146 Listen, Listen to the Words of Jesus

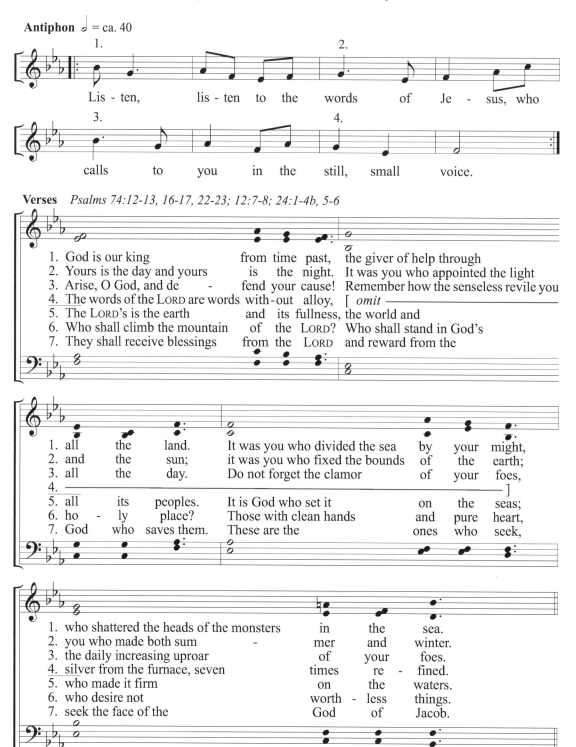

Antiphon ♩ = ca. 40

Lis - ten, lis - ten to the words of Je - sus, who
calls to you in the still, small voice.

Verses *Psalms 74:12-13, 16-17, 22-23; 12:7-8; 24:1-4b, 5-6*

1. God is our king from time past, the giver of help through
2. Yours is the day and yours is the night. It was you who appointed the light
3. Arise, O God, and de - fend your cause! Remember how the senseless revile you
4. The words of the LORD are words with-out alloy, [*omit* ———————
5. The LORD's is the earth and its fullness, the world and
6. Who shall climb the mountain of the LORD? Who shall stand in God's
7. They shall receive blessings from the LORD and reward from the

1. all the land. It was you who divided the sea by your might,
2. and the sun; it was you who fixed the bounds of the earth;
3. all the day. Do not forget the clamor of your foes,
4. ———————————————————]
5. all its peoples. It is God who set it on the seas;
6. ho - ly place? Those with clean hands and pure heart,
7. God who saves them. These are the ones who seek,

1. who shattered the heads of the monsters in the sea.
2. you who made both sum - mer and winter.
3. the daily increasing uproar of your foes.
4. silver from the furnace, seven times re - fined.
5. who made it firm on the waters.
6. who desire not worth - less things.
7. seek the face of the God of Jacob.

Performance Notes

As indicated, the antiphon may be sung as a 4-part round if desired.

Live on in My Love

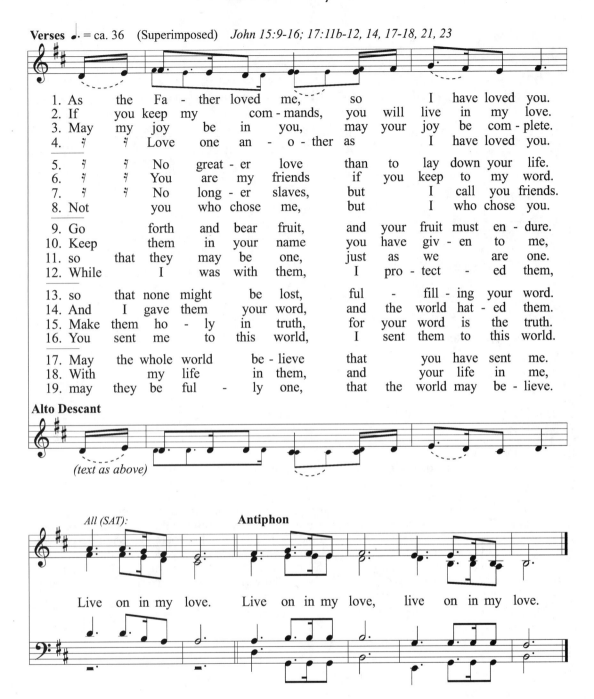

Verses ♩. = ca. 36 (Superimposed) *John 15:9-16; 17:11b-12, 14, 17-18, 21, 23*

1. As the Fa - ther loved me, so I have loved you.
2. If you keep my com - mands, you will live in my love.
3. May my joy be in you, may your joy be com - plete.
4. Love one an - o - ther as I have loved you.

5. No great - er love than to lay down your life.
6. You are my friends if you keep to my word.
7. No long - er slaves, but I call you friends.
8. Not you who chose me, but I who chose you.

9. Go forth and bear fruit, and your fruit must en - dure.
10. Keep them in your name you have giv - en to me,
11. so that they may be one, just as we are one.
12. While I was with them, I pro - tect - ed them,

13. so that none might be lost, ful - fill - ing your word.
14. And I gave them your word, and the world hat - ed them.
15. Make them ho - ly in truth, for your word is the truth.
16. You sent me to this world, I sent them to this world.

17. May the whole world be - lieve that you have sent me.
18. With my life in them, and your life in me,
19. may they be ful - ly one, that the world may be - lieve.

Alto Descant

(text as above)

All (SAT): **Antiphon**

Live on in my love. Live on in my love, live on in my love.

Performance Notes

Verses 1–9 are used on the Sixth Sunday of Easter, Years A, B, and C.

148   Look on My Toil

Antiphon / Melody ♩ = ca. 92

Look on my toil, lift me from my shame,

Descant

Look on my toil, lift me from my

teach me how to walk your way.

shame, let me walk your way.

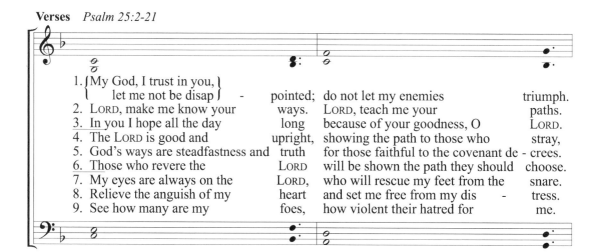

Verses   *Psalm 25:2-21*

1. {My God, I trust in you, / let me not be disap} - pointed; do not let my enemies triumph.
2. LORD, make me know your ways. LORD, teach me your paths.
3. In you I hope all the day long because of your goodness, O LORD.
4. The LORD is good and upright, showing the path to those who stray,
5. God's ways are steadfastness and truth for those faithful to the covenant de - crees.
6. Those who revere the LORD will be shown the path they should choose.
7. My eyes are always on the LORD, who will rescue my feet from the snare.
8. Relieve the anguish of my heart and set me free from my dis - tress.
9. See how many are my foes, how violent their hatred for me.

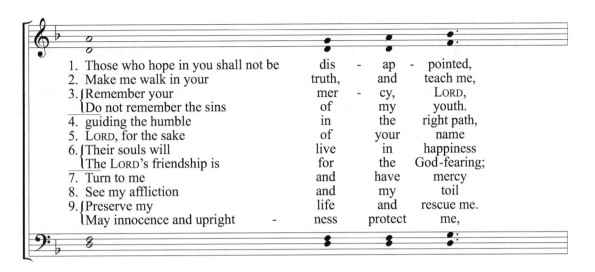

1. Those who hope in you shall not be dis - ap - pointed,
2. Make me walk in your truth, and teach me,
3. {Remember your mer - cy, LORD,
   {Do not remember the sins of my youth.
4. guiding the humble in the right path,
5. LORD, for the sake of your name
6. {Their souls will live in happiness
   {The LORD's friendship is for the God-fearing;
7. Turn to me and have mercy
8. See my affliction and my toil
9. {Preserve my life and rescue me.
   {May innocence and upright - ness protect me,

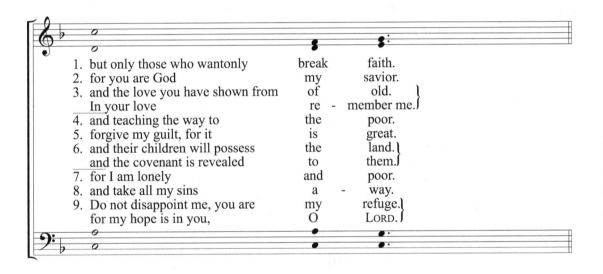

1. but only those who wantonly break faith.
2. for you are God my savior.
3. and the love you have shown from of old. }
   In your love re - member me.}
4. and teaching the way to the poor.
5. forgive my guilt, for it is great.
6. and their children will possess the land.}
   and the covenant is revealed to them.}
7. for I am lonely and poor.
8. and take all my sins a - way.
9. Do not disappoint me, you are my refuge.}
   for my hope is in you, O LORD.}

149

Lord, Cleanse My Heart

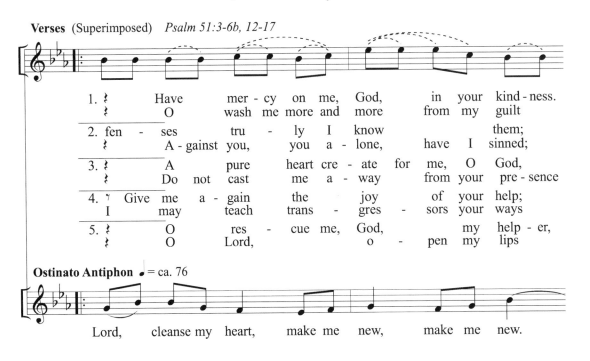

Verses (Superimposed) *Psalm 51:3-6b, 12-17*

1. Have mer - cy on me, God, in your kind - ness.
   O wash me more and more from my guilt

2. fen - ses tru - ly I know them;
   A - gainst you, you a - lone, have I sinned;

3. A pure heart cre - ate for me, O God,
   Do not cast me a - way from your pre - sence

4. Give me a - gain the joy of your help;
   I may teach trans - gres - sors your ways

5. O res - cue me, God, my help - er,
   O Lord, o - pen my lips

Ostinato Antiphon ♩ = ca. 76

Lord, cleanse my heart, make me new, make me new.

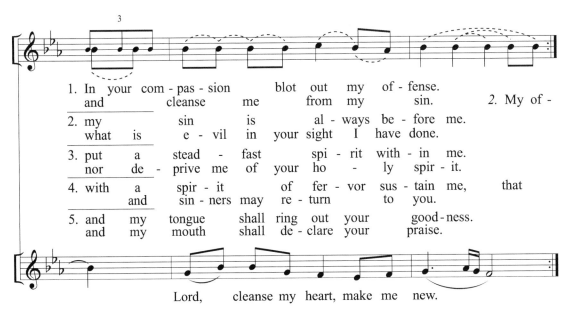

3

1. In your com - pas - sion blot out my of - fense.
   and cleanse me from my sin.   *2.* My of -

2. my sin is al - ways be - fore me.
   what is e - vil in your sight I have done.

3. put a stead - fast spi - rit with - in me.
   nor de - prive me of your ho - ly spir - it.

4. with a spir - it of fer - vor sus - tain me, that
   and sin - ners may re - turn to you.

5. and my tongue shall ring out your good - ness.
   and my mouth shall de - clare your praise.

Lord, cleanse my heart, make me new.

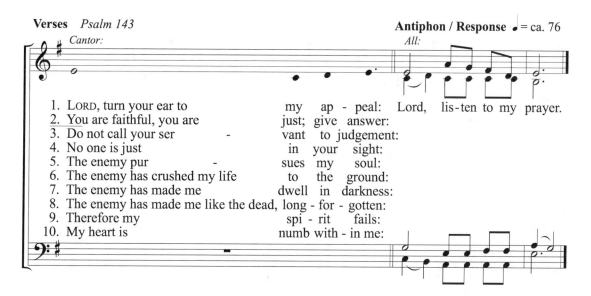

Verses *Psalm 143*   Antiphon / Response ♩ = ca. 76

1. LORD, turn your ear to my ap-peal: Lord, lis-ten to my prayer.
2. You are faithful, you are just; give answer:
3. Do not call your ser - vant to judgement:
4. No one is just in your sight:
5. The enemy pur - sues my soul:
6. The enemy has crushed my life to the ground:
7. The enemy has made me dwell in darkness:
8. The enemy has made me like the dead, long - for - gotten:
9. Therefore my spi - rit fails:
10. My heart is numb with - in me:

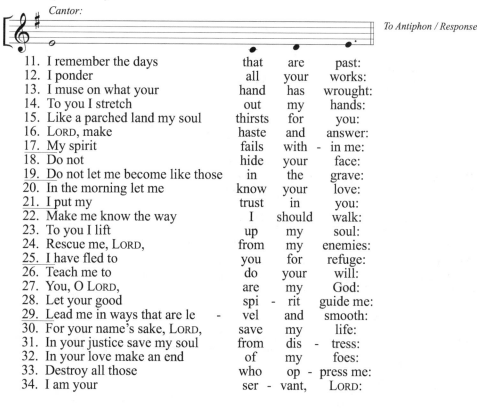

Verses (continued)

Cantor: *To Antiphon / Response*

11. I remember the days that are past:
12. I ponder all your works:
13. I muse on what your hand has wrought:
14. To you I stretch out my hands:
15. Like a parched land my soul thirsts for you:
16. LORD, make haste and answer:
17. My spirit fails with - in me:
18. Do not hide your face:
19. Do not let me become like those in the grave:
20. In the morning let me know your love:
21. I put my trust in you:
22. Make me know the way I should walk:
23. To you I lift up my soul:
24. Rescue me, LORD, from my enemies:
25. I have fled to you for refuge:
26. Teach me to do your will:
27. You, O LORD, are my God:
28. Let your good spi - rit guide me:
29. Lead me in ways that are le - vel and smooth:
30. For your name's sake, LORD, save my life:
31. In your justice save my soul from dis - tress:
32. In your love make an end of my foes:
33. Destroy all those who op - press me:
34. I am your ser - vant, LORD:

Performance Notes
Verses 1, 2, 11–17, 20, 21, and 26–29 are the Lectionary selections for All Souls Day.

151   Lord, This Is the People

Antiphon ♩ = 63

Lord, this is the peo-ple that longs to see your face, that

longs to see your face.

Verses *Psalm 24:1-6*

1. The LORD's is the   earth and its   fullness,
2. Who shall climb the   mountain of the   LORD?
3. They shall receive   blessings from the   LORD

1. the world and all   its   peoples.
2. Who shall stand in God's ho - ly   place?
3. and reward from the God   who   saves them.

1. It is God who set it on   the   seas,
2. Those with clean hands and   pure   hearts,
3. These are the ones   who   seek,

1. who made it firm   on   the   waters.
2. who desire not   worth - less   things.
3. seek the face of the   God   of   Jacob.

Lord, You Are Close

Lord, You Are Close, pg. 2

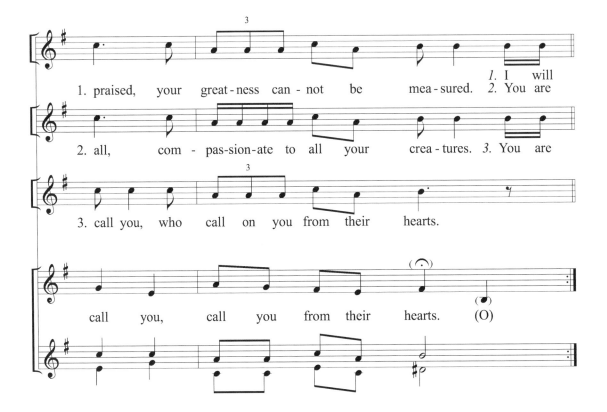

1. praised, your great-ness can-not be mea-sured. *1. I will*

2. all, com-pas-sion-ate to all your crea-tures. *3. You are*

3. call you, who call on you from their hearts.

call you, call you from their hearts. (O)

Performance Notes

Verses begin on the final beat of the last measure (a pickup beat to the first measure).

In measure 2, the cue-size notes in parentheses may be substituted if necessary.

The superimposed tone for a tenor cantor is intended as an alternative to the tenor descant—the two should not be sung concurrently.

The antiphon melody is derived from the Gavotte in Bach's Suite #2 in B minor for flute and strings.

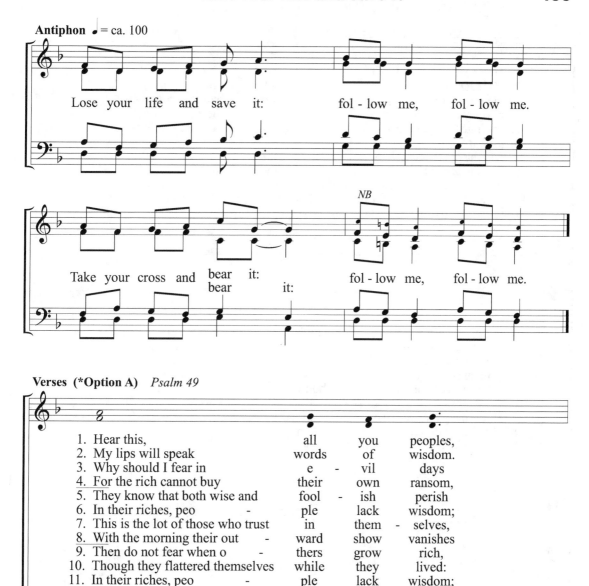

Antiphon ♩ = ca. 100

Lose your life and save it: fol - low me, fol - low me.

NB

Take your cross and bear it: / bear it: fol - low me, fol - low me.

Verses (*Option A) *Psalm 49*

1. Hear this,	all	you	peoples,
2. My lips will speak	words	of	wisdom.
3. Why should I fear in	e - vil	days	
4. For the rich cannot buy	their	own	ransom,
5. They know that both wise and	fool - ish	perish	
6. In their riches, peo -	ple	lack	wisdom;
7. This is the lot of those who trust	in	them - selves,	
8. With the morning their out -	ward	show	vanishes
9. Then do not fear when o -	thers	grow	rich,
10. Though they flattered themselves	while	they	lived:
11. In their riches, peo -	ple	lack	wisdom;

NB: *The cue-size notes are an optional descant and are used when the antiphon is sung in unison, not when SATB voices are sung.*

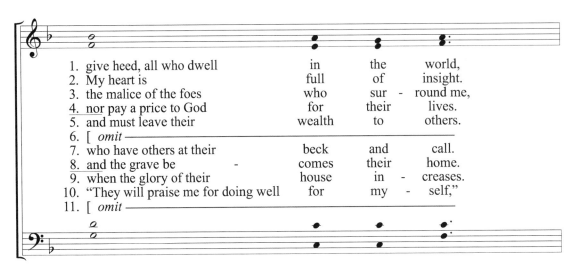

1. give heed, all who dwell   in   the   world,
2. My heart is   full   of   insight.
3. the malice of the foes   who   sur - round me,
4. <u>nor</u> pay a price to God   for   their   lives.
5. and must leave their   wealth   to   others.
6. [*omit* ——————
7. who have others at their   beck   and   call.
8. and the grave be   -   comes   their   home.
9. when the glory of their   house   in - creases.
10. "They will praise me for doing well   for   my - self,"
11. [*omit* ——————————————————————

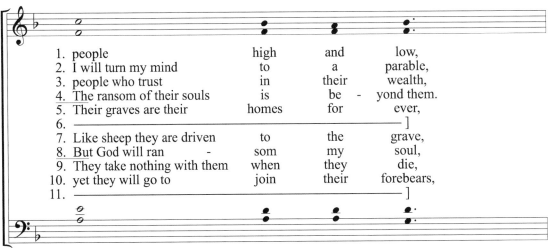

1. people   high   and   low,
2. I will turn my mind   to   a   parable,
3. people who trust   in   their   wealth,
4. <u>The</u> ransom of their souls   is   be - yond them.
5. Their graves are their   homes   for   ever,
6. ————————————————————————]
7. Like sheep they are driven   to   the   grave,
8. But God will ran   -   som   my   soul,
9. They take nothing with them   when   they   die,
10. yet they will go to   join   their   forebears,
11. ————————————————————————]

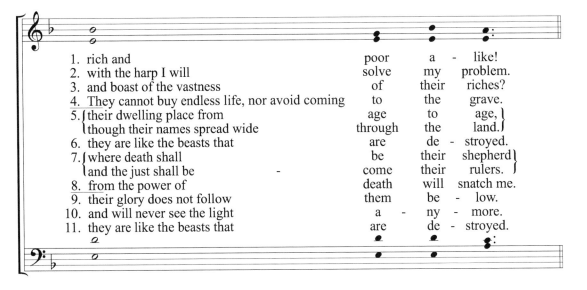

1. rich and   poor   a - like!
2. with the harp I will   solve   my   problem.
3. and boast of the vastness   of   their   riches?
4. <u>They</u> cannot buy endless life, nor avoid coming   to   the   grave.
5. { their dwelling place from   age   to   age, }
   { though their names spread wide   through   the   land. }
6. they are like the beasts that   are   de - stroyed.
7. { where death shall   be   their   shepherd }
  { and the just shall be   -   come   their   rulers. }
8. <u>from</u> the power of   death   will   snatch me.
9. their glory does not follow   them   be - low.
10. and will never see the light   a - ny - more.
11. they are like the beasts that   are   de - stroyed.

Verses (*Option B)   *Psalm 116:1-9, 10-19*

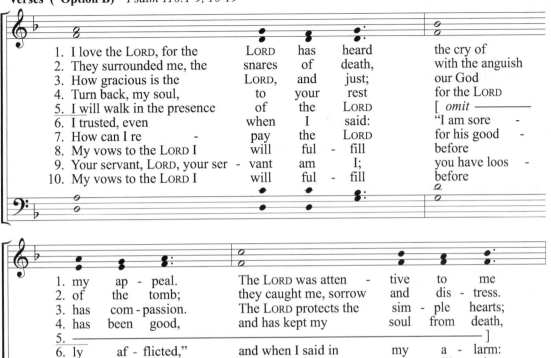

1. I love the LORD, for the LORD has heard the cry of my ap - peal. The LORD was atten - tive to me in the day when I called.
2. They surrounded me, the snares of death, with the anguish of the tomb; they caught me, sorrow and dis - tress. I called on the LORD's name. O LORD my God, de - liver me!
3. How gracious is the LORD, and just; our God has com - passion. The LORD protects the sim - ple hearts; I was helpless so God saved me.
4. Turn back, my soul, to your rest for the LORD has been good, and has kept my soul from death, my eyes from tears, my feet from stumbling.
5. I will walk in the presence of the LORD [omit ———————] in the land of the living.
6. I trusted, even when I said: "I am sore - ly af - flicted," and when I said in my a - larm: "There is no one I can trust."
7. How can I re - pay the LORD for his good - ness to me? The cup of salvation I will raise; I will call on the LORD's name.
8. My vows to the LORD I will ful - fill before all the people. O precious in the eyes of the LORD is the death of the faithful.
9. Your servant, LORD, your ser - vant am I; you have loos - ened my bonds. A thanksgiving sacri - fice I make; I will call on the LORD's name.
10. My vows to the LORD I will ful - fill before all the people, in the courts of the house of the LORD, in your midst, O Je - rusalem.

Performance Notes

*Option A verses are used as the Song for the Table on the Twenty-third Sunday in Ordinary Time, Year C.
Option B verses are used as the Song for the Table on the Exaltation of the Holy Cross; the Thirteenth and Twenty-second Sundays in Ordinary Time, Year A; the Twenty-fourth Sunday in Ordinary Time, Year B (verses 6–10 only); and the Twelfth Sunday in Ordinary Time, Year C.*

Love Bears All Things

Antiphon / Melody ♩ = 65

Love bears all things, be - lieves all things, hopes all

Soprano / Alto Descants

Love bears all things, be - lieves all things, hopes all

Bass Descant

things, en - dures all things. Love bears all things, be -

things, en - dures all things. Bears all things, be -

lieves all things, hopes all things, en - dures all things.

lieves all things, hopes all things, en - dures all things.

Verses *John 15:16-17; 1 Corinthians 13:4-5a, 13, 8a; 14:1a*

1. You did not choose me
2. And I appointed you to go and bear fruit,
3. so that the Father will give you
4. I am giving you these com - mands
5. Love is patient; love is kind;
6. Love does not rejoice in wrongdoing,
7. Faith, hope and love abide, these three;
8. Love ne - ver ends.

1. but I chose you.
2. fruit that will last,
3. whatever you ask him in my name.
4. so that you may love one an - other.
5. love is not envious or boastful or arro - gant or rude.
6. but rejoices in the truth.
7. and the greatest of these is love.
8. Pursue love and strive for the spi - ri - tual gifts.

Love Is My Desire

Antiphon / Melody ♩ = 78-80

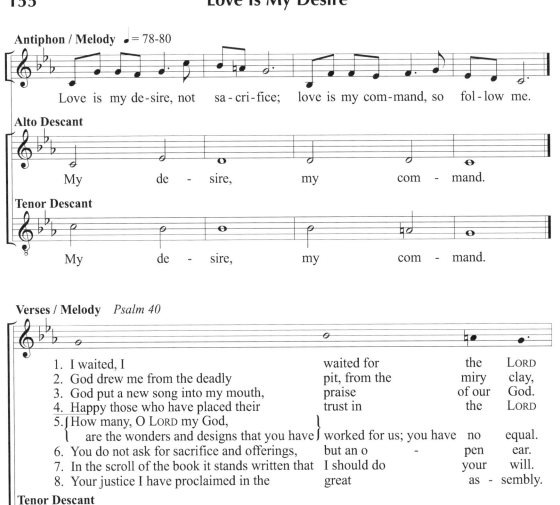

Love is my de-sire, not sa-cri-fice; love is my com-mand, so fol-low me.

Alto Descant

My de - sire, my com - mand.

Tenor Descant

My de - sire, my com - mand.

Verses / Melody *Psalm 40*

1. I waited, I waited for the LORD
2. God drew me from the deadly pit, from the miry clay,
3. God put a new song into my mouth, praise of our God.
4. Happy those who have placed their trust in the LORD
5. How many, O LORD my God,
   are the wonders and designs that you have worked for us; you have no equal.
6. You do not ask for sacrifice and offerings, but an o - pen ear.
7. In the scroll of the book it stands written that I should do your will.
8. Your justice I have proclaimed in the great as - sembly.

Tenor Descant

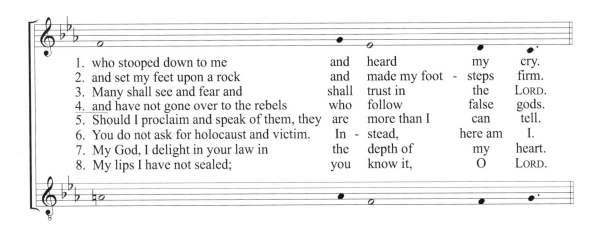

1. who stooped down to me and heard my cry.
2. and set my feet upon a rock and made my foot - steps firm.
3. Many shall see and fear and shall trust in the LORD.
4. and have not gone over to the rebels who follow false gods.
5. Should I proclaim and speak of them, they are more than I can tell.
6. You do not ask for holocaust and victim. In - stead, here am I.
7. My God, I delight in your law in the depth of my heart.
8. My lips I have not sealed; you know it, O LORD.

Verses (continued)

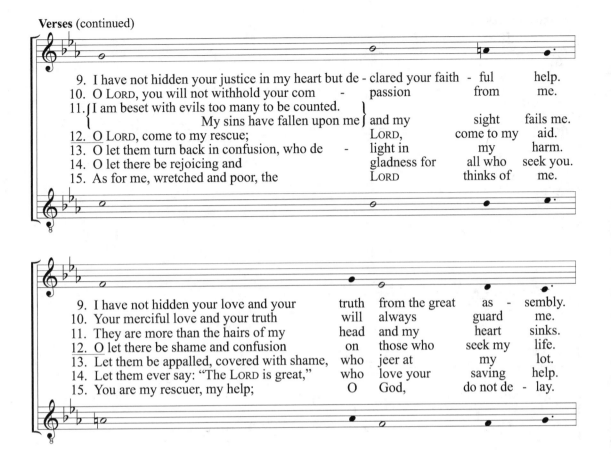

9. I have not hidden your justice in my heart but de - clared your faith - ful help.
10. O Lᴏʀᴅ, you will not withhold your com - passion from me.
11. {I am beset with evils too many to be counted.
    My sins have fallen upon me} and my sight fails me.
12. O Lᴏʀᴅ, come to my rescue; Lᴏʀᴅ, come to my aid.
13. O let them turn back in confusion, who de - light in my harm.
14. O let there be rejoicing and gladness for all who seek you.
15. As for me, wretched and poor, the Lᴏʀᴅ thinks of me.

9. I have not hidden your love and your truth from the great as - sembly.
10. Your merciful love and your truth will always guard me.
11. They are more than the hairs of my head and my heart sinks.
12. O let there be shame and confusion on those who seek my life.
13. Let them be appalled, covered with shame, who jeer at my lot.
14. Let them ever say: "The Lᴏʀᴅ is great," who love your saving help.
15. You are my rescuer, my help; O God, do not de - lay.

Love the Lord Your God

Verses *Psalm 119:1-8*

Cantor:

1. They are happy whose life is blameless, who fol - low God's law!
2. They are happy who do God's will, seeking God with all their hearts.
3. They never do a - ny - thing evil but walk in God's ways.
4. You have laid down your precepts to be o - beyed with care.
5. May my foot - steps be firm to o - bey your statutes.
6. Then I shall not be put to shame as I heed your com - mands.
7. I will thank you with an up - right heart as I learn your de - crees.
8. I will o - bey your statutes; do not for - sake me.

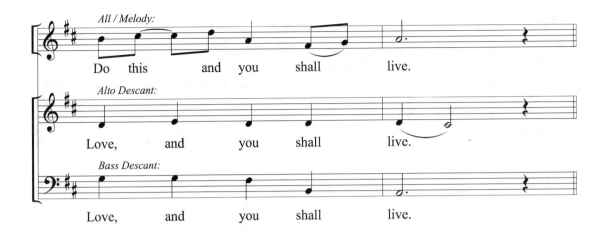

All / Melody:

Do this and you shall live.

Alto Descant:

Love, and you shall live.

Bass Descant:

Love, and you shall live.

May God Bless Us in Mercy

Antiphon / Melody ♩ = 88

May God bless us in mer-cy; may God bless us in love.

Descant

May God bless us, bless us in love.

Verses *Psalm 67*

1. O God, be gracious and bless us and let your face shed its light
2. Let the nations be glad and ex - ult for you rule the world
3. The earth has yielded its fruit for God, our God,
4. Let the peoples praise you, O God; let all the peo -

1. up - on us. So will your ways be known up - on earth
2. with justice. With fairness you rule the peoples,
3. has blessed us. May God still give us blessing
4. ples praise you. Let the peoples praise you, O God,

1. and all nations learn your sav - ing help.
2. you guide the nations on earth.
3. till the ends of the earth stand in awe.
4. let all the peo - ples praise you.

Performance Notes

Verses 1, 2, and 4 are the Lectionary selections for the solemnity of Mary, Mother of God.

May God Grant Us Joy of Heart

1. pre - sence of the an - gels I a -
2. day I called, you an - swered, you in -
3. sing of the Lord's ways: "How
4. walk in af - flic - tion, you give me
5. love, O Lord, is e - ter - nal, e -
6. *lu - ia, al - le - lu - ia!*

good - ness last for e - ver:
lu - ia, al - le - lu - ia!

lu - *ia!*

good - ness last for e - ver:
lu - ia, al - le - lu - ia!

1. dore be - fore your tem - ple.
2. creased my strength of soul.
3. great the glo - ry of the Lord!"
4. life and con - found my foes.
5. ter - nal is your mer - cy.
6. *Bless the Lord of all!*

bless the Lord of all!
Bless the Lord of all!

Bless the Lord of all!

bless the Lord of all!
Bless the Lord of all!

Performance Notes
At the end of the piece, the antiphon may be repeated using the Alleluias in italics instead of the usual text or humming.

Merciful and Tender

Antiphon ♩ = 76-80

Mer - ci - ful and ten - der, faith - ful is the Lord.

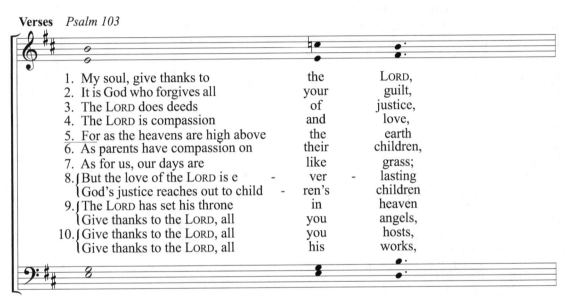

Verses *Psalm 103*

1. My soul, give thanks to the Lord,
2. It is God who forgives all your guilt,
3. The Lord does deeds of justice,
4. The Lord is compassion and love,
5. For as the heavens are high above the earth
6. As parents have compassion on their children,
7. As for us, our days are like grass;
8. { But the love of the Lord is e - ver - lasting
   { God's justice reaches out to child - ren's children
9. { The Lord has set his throne in heaven
   { Give thanks to the Lord, all you angels,
10. { Give thanks to the Lord, all you hosts,
    { Give thanks to the Lord, all his works,

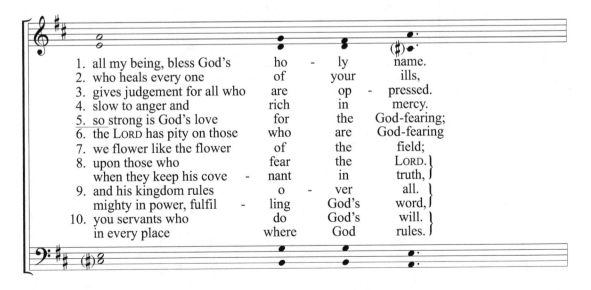

1. all my being, bless God's ho - ly name.
2. who heals every one of your ills,
3. gives judgement for all who are op - pressed.
4. slow to anger and rich in mercy.
5. so strong is God's love for the God-fearing;
6. the Lord has pity on those who are God-fearing
7. we flower like the flower of the field;
8. upon those who fear the Lord. }
   when they keep his cove - nant in truth, }
9. and his kingdom rules o - ver all. }
   mighty in power, fulfil - ling God's word, }
10. you servants who do God's will. }
    in every place where God rules. }

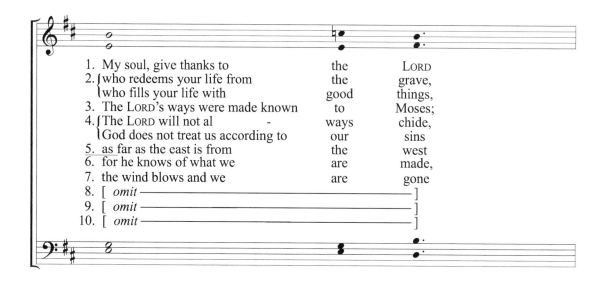

1. My soul, give thanks to the LORD
2. { who redeems your life from the grave,
   { who fills your life with good things,
3. The LORD's ways were made known to Moses;
4. { The LORD will not al - ways chide,
   { God does not treat us according to our sins
5. as far as the east is from the west
6. for he knows of what we are made,
7. the wind blows and we are gone
8. [omit ————————————————]
9. [omit ————————————————]
10. [omit ————————————————]

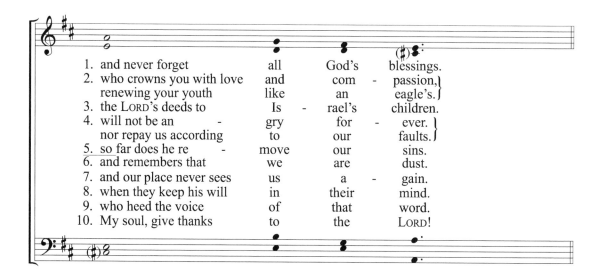

1. and never forget all God's blessings.
2. who crowns you with love and com - passion, }
   renewing your youth like an eagle's. }
3. the LORD's deeds to Is - rael's children.
4. will not be an - gry for - ever. }
   nor repay us according to our faults. }
5. so far does he re - move our sins.
6. and remembers that we are dust.
7. and our place never sees us a - gain.
8. when they keep his will in their mind.
9. who heed the voice of that word.
10. My soul, give thanks to the LORD!

See the Performance Notes on the next page for Lectionary verse options.

Verses (Lectionary Selections)   *Psalm 103:1-2, 3-4, 9-10, 11-12, 6, 8, 10*

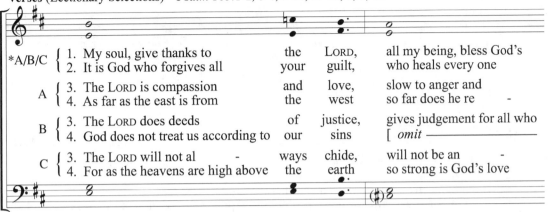

*A/B/C
1. My soul, give thanks to the LORD, all my being, bless God's
2. It is God who forgives all your guilt, who heals every one

A
3. The LORD is compassion and love, slow to anger and
4. As far as the east is from the west so far does he re -

B
3. The LORD does deeds of justice, gives judgement for all who
4. God does not treat us according to our sins [omit ——————

C
3. The LORD will not al - ways chide, will not be an -
4. For as the heavens are high above the earth so strong is God's love

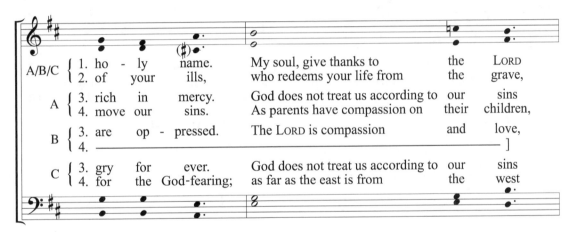

A/B/C
1. ho - ly name. My soul, give thanks to the LORD
2. of your ills, who redeems your life from the grave,

A
3. rich in mercy. God does not treat us according to our sins
4. move our sins. As parents have compassion on their children,

B
3. are op - pressed. The LORD is compassion and love,
4. ————————————————————————————————]

C
3. gry for ever. God does not treat us according to our sins
4. for the God-fearing; as far as the east is from the west

A/B/C
1. and never forget all God's blessings.
2. who crowns you with love and com - passion.

A
3. nor repay us according to our faults.
4. the LORD has pity on those who are God-fearing.

B
3. slow to anger and rich in mercy.
4. nor repay us according to our faults.

C
3. nor repay us according to our faults.
4. so far does he re - move our sins.

Performance Notes
**Option A verses are the Lectionary selections during Ordinary Time on the Seventh Sunday, Years A and C;
the Eighth Sunday, Year B; and the Third Sunday of Lent, Year C.
Option B verses are the Lectionary selections for the solemnity of the Sacred Heart, Year A.
Option C verses are the Lectionary selections for the Twenty-fourth Sunday in Ordinary Time, Year A.*

160

My God, My God

Psalm text: The Grail (England), © 1963, 1986, 1993, 2000, The Grail, GIA Publications, Inc., agent. All rights reserved. Used with permission.

Music and antiphon text: © 2005, The Collegeville Composers Group. Published and administered by Liturgical Press, Collegeville, MN 56321. All rights reserved.

Antiphon ♩ = 54

My God, my God, why have you a - ban-doned me, my God?

Verses *Psalm 22:8-9, 17-18a, 19-20, 23-24*

1. All who see me de - ride me. They curl their lips, they toss their heads.
2. Many dogs have sur - round-ed me, a band of the wicked be - set me.
3. They divide my clothing a - mong them. They cast lots for my robe.
4. I will tell of your name to my people and praise you where they are as - sembled.

1. "He trusted in the LORD, let him save him, and release him if this is his friend."
2. They tear holes in my hands and my feet. I can count every one of my bones.
3. O LORD, do not leave me a - lone, my strength, make haste to help me.
4. "You who fear the LORD, give praise; {all children of Jacob, give glory. Revere God, children} of Israel."

Antiphon ♩ = 76

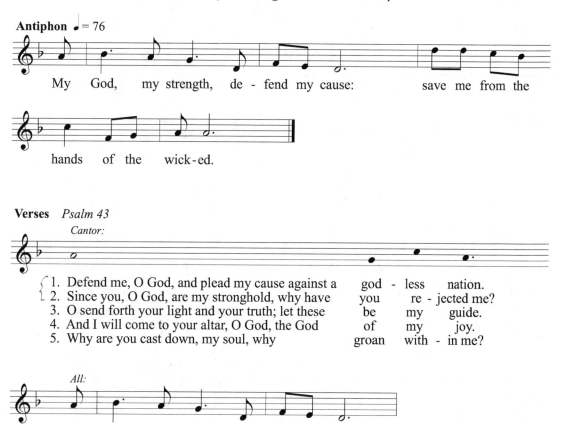

My God, my strength, de-fend my cause: save me from the hands of the wick-ed.

Verses *Psalm 43*

Cantor:

1. Defend me, O God, and plead my cause against a god - less nation.
2. Since you, O God, are my stronghold, why have you re - jected me?
3. O send forth your light and your truth; let these be my guide.
4. And I will come to your altar, O God, the God of my joy.
5. Why are you cast down, my soul, why groan with - in me?

All:

My God, my strength, de - fend my cause.

Cantor:

1. From a deceitful and cunning people rescue me, O God.
2. Why do I go mourning, oppressed by the foe?
3. Let them bring me to your holy mountain, to the place where you dwell.
4. My redeemer, I will thank you on the harp, O God, my God.
5. Hope in God; I will praise yet again my savior and my God.

All:

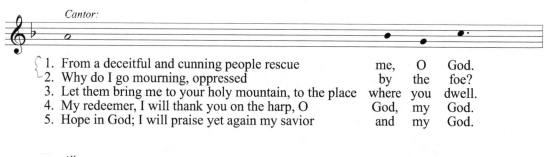

Save me from the hands of the wick-ed.

My Grace Is Enough

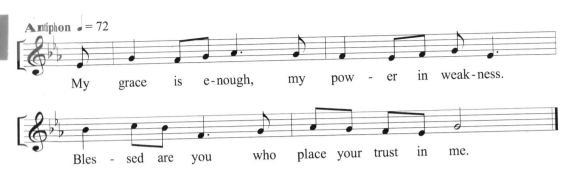

Antiphon ♩ = 72

My grace is e-nough, my pow - er in weak-ness.

Bles - sed are you who place your trust in me.

Verses *Psalm 25:2-21*

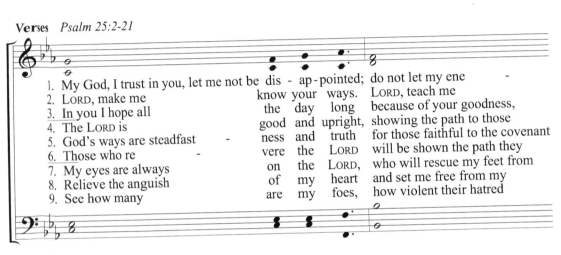

1. My God, I trust in you, let me not be dis - ap-pointed; do not let my ene -
2. Lord, make me   know your ways. Lord, teach me
3. In you I hope all   the day long because of your goodness,
4. The Lord is   good and upright, showing the path to those
5. God's ways are steadfast - ness and truth for those faithful to the covenant
6. Those who re - vere the Lord will be shown the path they
7. My eyes are always on the Lord, who will rescue my feet from
8. Relieve the anguish of my heart and set me free from my
9. See how many are my foes, how violent their hatred

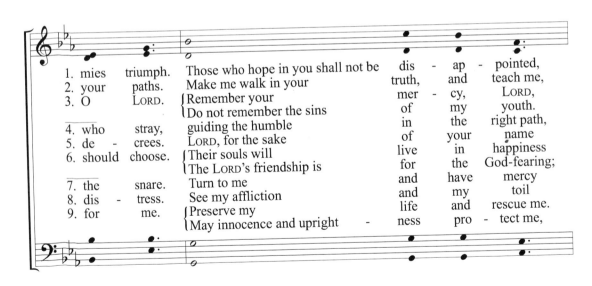

1. mies   triumph.   Those who hope in you shall not be   dis - ap - pointed,
2. your   paths.   Make me walk in your   truth, and teach me,
3. O   Lord.   ⎰Remember your   mer - cy, Lord,
   ⎱Do not remember the sins   of my youth.
4. who   stray,   guiding the humble   in the right path,
5. de - crees.   Lord, for the sake   of your name
6. should   choose.   ⎰Their souls will   live in happiness
   ⎱The Lord's friendship is   for the God-fearing;
7. the   snare.   Turn to me   and have mercy
8. dis - tress.   See my affliction   and my toil
9. for   me.   ⎰Preserve my   life and rescue me.
   ⎱May innocence and upright - ness pro - tect me,

1. but only those who wantonly   break   faith.
2. for you are God   my   savior.
3. and the love you have shown from   of   old. ⎫
   In your love   re - member me. ⎭
4. and teaching the way to   the   poor.
5. forgive my guilt, for it   is   great.
6. and their children will possess   the   land. ⎫
   and the covenant is revealed   to   them. ⎭
7. for I am lonely   and   poor.
8. and take all my sins   a - way.
9. Do not disappoint me, you are   my   refuge. ⎫
   for my hope is in you,   O   LORD. ⎭

My Lips Will Tell of Your Justice

Antiphon ♩. = ca. 60

My lips will tell, will tell of your just - ice.

my mouth will sing of your sav - ing help.

Verses *Psalm 71:1-4a, 5-6b, 15ab, 17*

Cantor:

1. In you, O LORD, I take refuge; let me never be put to shame.
2. Be a rock where I can take refuge, a mighty strong - hold to save me.
3. It is you, O LORD, who are my hope, my trust, O LORD, since my youth.
4. My lips will tell of your justice and day by day of your help.

All:

My lips will tell, will tell of your just - ice.

Cantor:

1. In your justice rescue me, free me; pay heed to me and save me.
2. For you are my rock, my stronghold. Free me from the hand of the wicked.
3. On you I have leaned from my birth; from my mother's womb you have been my help.
4. O God, you have taught me from my youth and I pro - claim your won-ders still.

All:

My mouth will sing of your sav - ing help.

165

My Portion and My Cup

Antiphon ♩ = ca. 76

My por - tion and my cup, my pro - mise and my song: my
heart re - joi - ces and my soul is glad.

Verses (*Option A) *Psalm 16:5, 8-11*

Flex measure for verses 3 and 5 only

1. [*omit* ————————————] O Lord, it is you who are my portion and cup,
2. [*omit* ————————————] I keep you, Lord, ever in my sight;
3. And so my heart re - joices, my soul is glad;
4. [*omit* ————————————] For you will not leave my soul among the dead,
5. You will show me the path of life, the fullness of joy in your presence,

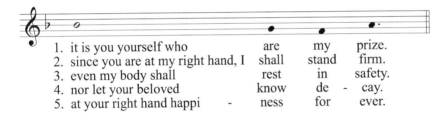

1. it is you yourself who are my prize.
2. since you are at my right hand, I shall stand firm.
3. even my body shall rest in safety.
4. nor let your beloved know de - cay.
5. at your right hand happi - ness for ever.

Verses (*Option B) *Psalm 16:1-2a, 5, 7-11*

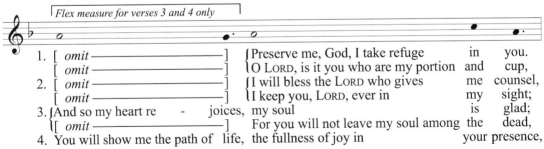

Flex measure for verses 3 and 4 only

1. [*omit* ————————————] {Preserve me, God, I take refuge in you.
   [*omit* ————————————] {O Lord, is it you who are my portion and cup,
2. [*omit* ————————————] {I will bless the Lord who gives me counsel,
   [*omit* ————————————] {I keep you, Lord, ever in my sight;
3. {And so my heart re - joices, my soul is glad;
   {[*omit* ————————————] For you will not leave my soul among the dead,
4. You will show me the path of life, the fullness of joy in your presence,

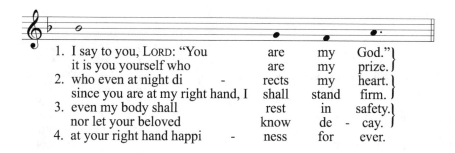

1. I say to you, LORD: "You are my God."
   it is you yourself who are my prize.
2. who even at night di - rects my heart.
   since you are at my right hand, I shall stand firm.
3. even my body shall rest in safety.
   nor let your beloved know de - cay.
4. at your right hand happi - ness for ever.

Performance Notes

Option A verses are used as the Song for the Word at the Easter Vigil, Response II, and on the Thirty-third Sunday in Ordinary Time, Year B.
Option B verses are used as the Song for the Word on the Thirteenth Sunday in Ordinary Time, Year C.

My Sheep I Will Pasture

166

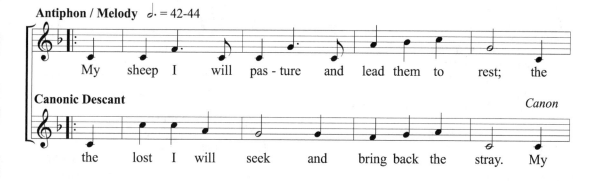

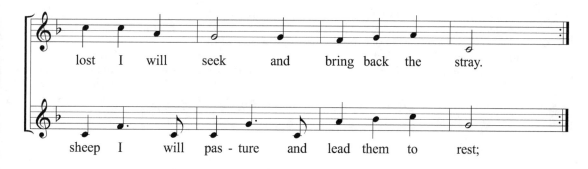

Verses *Ezekiel 36:24-28; 34:11-16*

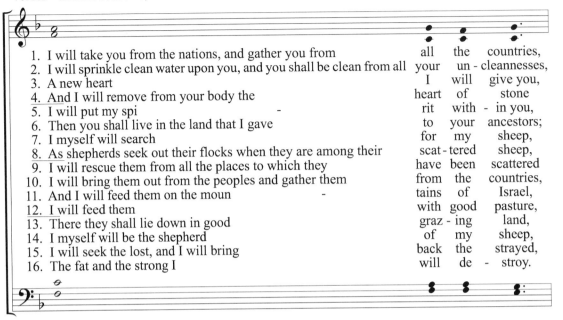

1. I will take you from the nations, and gather you from | all | the | countries,
2. I will sprinkle clean water upon you, and you shall be clean from all | your | un - cleannesses,
3. A new heart | I | will | give you,
4. And I will remove from your body the | heart | of | stone
5. I will put my spi | rit | with - in you,
6. Then you shall live in the land that I gave | to | your | ancestors;
7. I myself will search | for | my | sheep,
8. As shepherds seek out their flocks when they are among their | scat - tered | sheep,
9. I will rescue them from all the places to which they | have | been | scattered
10. I will bring them out from the peoples and gather them | from | the | countries,
11. And I will feed them on the moun | tains | of | Israel,
12. I will feed them | with | good | pasture,
13. There they shall lie down in good | graz - ing | land,
14. I myself will be the shepherd | of | my | sheep,
15. I will seek the lost, and I will bring | back | the | strayed,
16. The fat and the strong I | will | de - stroy.

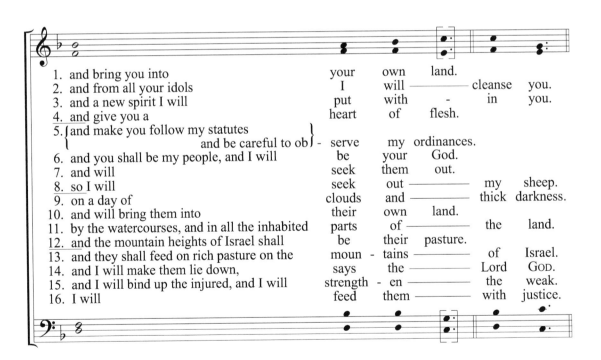

1. and bring you into | your | own | land.
2. and from all your idols | I | will — cleanse you.
3. and a new spirit I will | put | with - in | you.
4. and give you a | heart | of | flesh.
5. {and make you follow my statutes / and be careful to ob} - serve | my ordinances.
6. and you shall be my people, and I will | be | your | God.
7. and will | seek | them | out.
8. so I will | seek | out — my | sheep.
9. on a day of | clouds | and — thick | darkness.
10. and will bring them into | their | own | land.
11. by the watercourses, and in all the inhabited | parts | of — the | land.
12. and the mountain heights of Israel shall | be | their | pasture.
13. and they shall feed on rich pasture on the | moun - tains — of | Israel.
14. and I will make them lie down, | says | the — Lord | GOD.
15. and I will bind up the injured, and I will | strength - en — the | weak.
16. I will | feed | them — with | justice.

My Shepherd Is the Lord

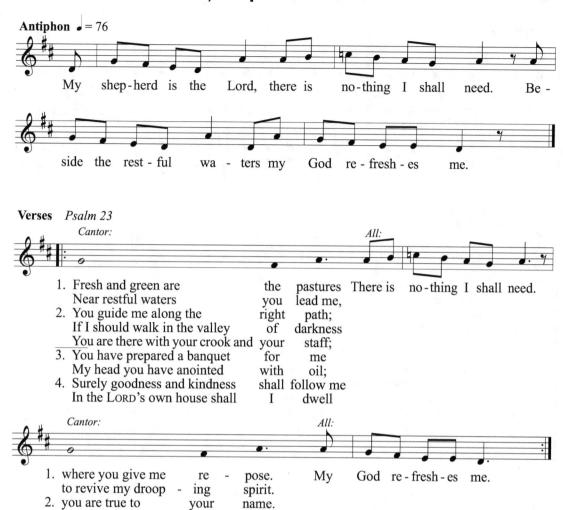

Antiphon ♩ = 76

My shep-herd is the Lord, there is no-thing I shall need. Be-
side the rest-ful wa-ters my God re-fresh-es me.

Verses *Psalm 23*

Cantor: ... *All:*

1. Fresh and green are   the   pastures There is no-thing I shall need.
   Near restful waters   you   lead me,
2. You guide me along the   right   path;
   If I should walk in the valley   of   darkness
   You are there with your crook and your   staff;
3. You have prepared a banquet   for   me
   My head you have anointed   with   oil;
4. Surely goodness and kindness   shall follow me
   In the LORD's own house shall   I   dwell

Cantor: ... *All:*

1. where you give me   re   -   pose.   My   God re-fresh-es me.
   to revive my droop   -   ing   spirit.
2. you are true to   your   name.
   no evil would   I   fear.
   with these you give   me   comfort.
3. in the sight of   my   foes.
   my cup is o   -   ver   -   flowing.
4. all the days of   my   life.
   for ever   and   ever.

My Soul Rejoices in God

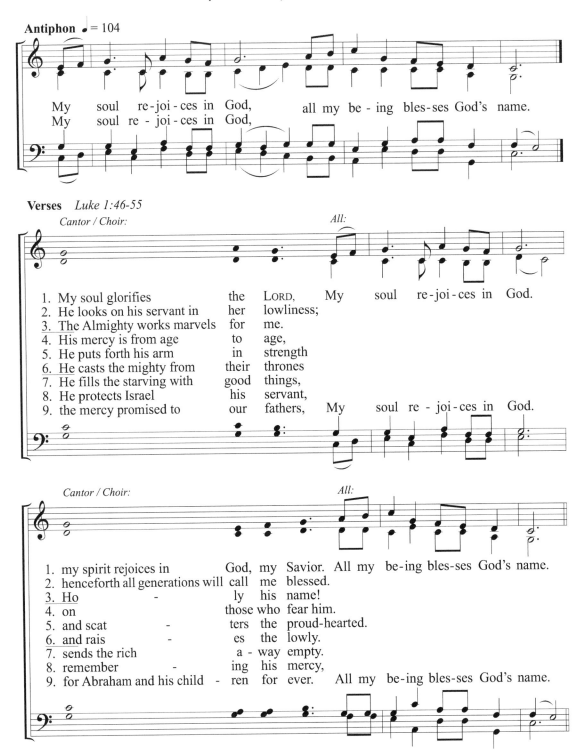

Antiphon ♩ = 104

My soul re-joi-ces in God, all my be-ing bles-ses God's name.
My soul re - joi-ces in God,

Verses *Luke 1:46-55*

Cantor / Choir: *All:*

1. My soul glorifies   the LORD,   My   soul re-joi-ces in God.
2. He looks on his servant in   her lowliness;
3. The Almighty works marvels   for me.
4. His mercy is from age   to age,
5. He puts forth his arm   in strength
6. He casts the mighty from   their thrones
7. He fills the starving with   good things,
8. He protects Israel   his servant,
9. the mercy promised to   our fathers, My soul re - joi-ces in God.

Cantor / Choir: *All:*

1. my spirit rejoices in   God, my Savior. All my be-ing bles-ses God's name.
2. henceforth all generations will call me blessed.
3. Ho -   ly   his name!
4. on   those who fear him.
5. and scat -   ters the proud-hearted.
6. and rais -   es   the lowly.
7. sends the rich   a - way empty.
8. remember -   ing his mercy,
9. for Abraham and his child - ren for ever. All my be-ing bles-ses God's name.

Performance Notes
Verses 1–4 and 7–8 are the Lectionary selections for the Third Sunday of Advent, Year B.

Not on Bread Alone Are We Nourished

* *The word* God *lasts for four beats only, unless Descant 1 is being sung,
  when it is prolonged for an additional measure.*

Verses / Melody   *Psalm 19*

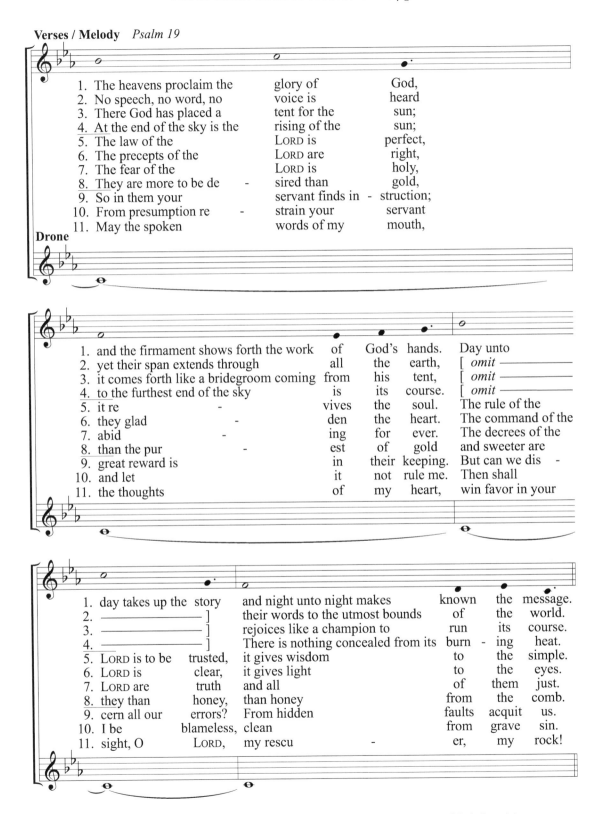

1. The heavens proclaim the glory of God,
2. No speech, no word, no voice is heard
3. There God has placed a tent for the sun;
4. At the end of the sky is the rising of the sun;
5. The law of the LORD is perfect,
6. The precepts of the LORD are right,
7. The fear of the LORD is holy,
8. They are more to be de - sired than gold,
9. So in them your servant finds in - struction;
10. From presumption re - strain your servant
11. May the spoken words of my mouth,

Drone

1. and the firmament shows forth the work of God's hands. Day unto
2. yet their span extends through all the earth, [omit ——
3. it comes forth like a bridegroom coming from his tent, [omit ——
4. to the furthest end of the sky is its course. [omit ——
5. it re - vives the soul. The rule of the
6. they glad - den the heart. The command of the
7. abid - ing for ever. The decrees of the
8. than the pur - est of gold and sweeter are
9. great reward is in their keeping. But can we dis -
10. and let it not rule me. Then shall
11. the thoughts of my heart, win favor in your

1. day takes up the story and night unto night makes known the message.
2. ——————] their words to the utmost bounds of the world.
3. ——————] rejoices like a champion to run its course.
4. ——————] There is nothing concealed from its burn - ing heat.
5. LORD is to be trusted, it gives wisdom to the simple.
6. LORD is clear, it gives light to the eyes.
7. LORD are truth and all of them just.
8. they than honey, than honey from the comb.
9. cern all our errors? From hidden faults acquit us.
10. I be blameless, clean from grave sin.
11. sight, O LORD, my rescu - er, my rock!

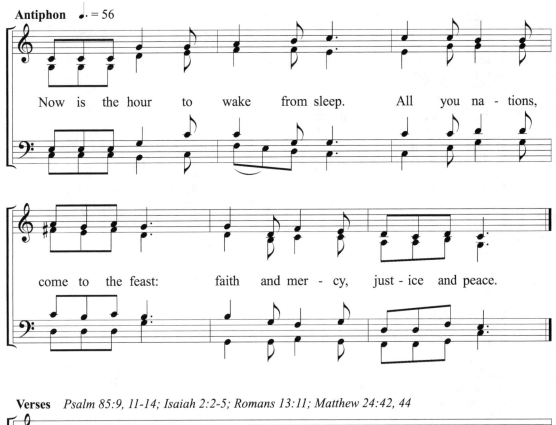

Antiphon ♩. = 56

Now is the hour to wake from sleep. All you na - tions,

come to the feast: faith and mer - cy, just - ice and peace.

Verses *Psalm 85:9, 11-14; Isaiah 2:2-5; Romans 13:11; Matthew 24:42, 44*

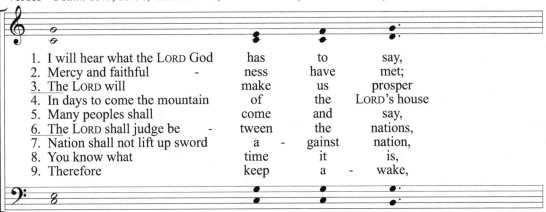

1. I will hear what the LORD God has to say,
2. Mercy and faithful - ness have met;
3. The LORD will make us prosper
4. In days to come the mountain of the LORD's house
5. Many peoples shall come and say,
6. The LORD shall judge be - tween the nations,
7. Nation shall not lift up sword a - gainst nation,
8. You know what time it is,
9. Therefore keep a - wake,

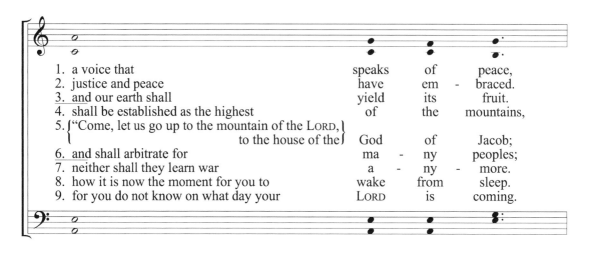

1. a voice that speaks of peace,
2. justice and peace have em - braced.
3. and our earth shall yield its fruit.
4. shall be established as the highest of the mountains,
5. {"Come, let us go up to the mountain of the LORD, to the house of the} God of Jacob;
6. and shall arbitrate for ma - ny peoples;
7. neither shall they learn war a - ny - more.
8. how it is now the moment for you to wake from sleep.
9. for you do not know on what day your LORD is coming.

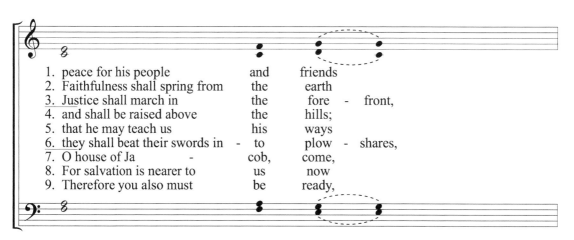

1. peace for his people and friends
2. Faithfulness shall spring from the earth
3. Justice shall march in the fore - front,
4. and shall be raised above the hills;
5. that he may teach us his ways
6. they shall beat their swords in - to plow - shares,
7. O house of Ja - cob, come,
8. For salvation is nearer to us now
9. Therefore you also must be ready,

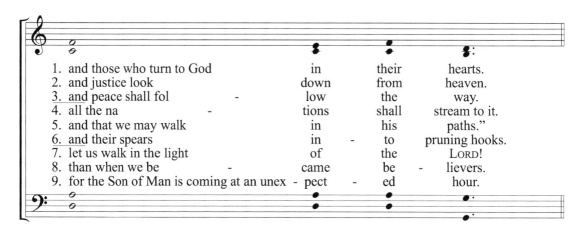

1. and those who turn to God in their hearts.
2. and justice look down from heaven.
3. and peace shall fol - low the way.
4. all the na - tions shall stream to it.
5. and that we may walk in his paths."
6. and their spears in - to pruning hooks.
7. let us walk in the light of the LORD!
8. than when we be - came be - lievers.
9. for the Son of Man is coming at an unex - pect - ed hour.

Antiphon ♩ = 72

O let my tongue   cleave to my mouth   if I re-mem-ber   you not!

Verses *Psalm 137:1-6*

1. By the rivers of Ba - by - lon
2. For it was there that they asked us,
3. O how could we sing the song of the LORD
4. O let my tongue cleave to my mouth

1. there we sat and wept, remembering Zi - on;
2. our captors for songs, our oppressors for joy.
3. on alien soil?
4. if I remember you not,

1. on the poplars that grew there
2. "Sing to us," they said,
3. If I forget you, Je - rusalem,
4. if I prize not Je - rusalem

1. we hung up our harps.
2. "one of Zi - on's songs."
3. let my right hand wither!
4. above all my joys.

172   O Praise the Lord, Jerusalem

Verses (Superimposed)   *Psalms 147B:13-20; 146:6c-10*

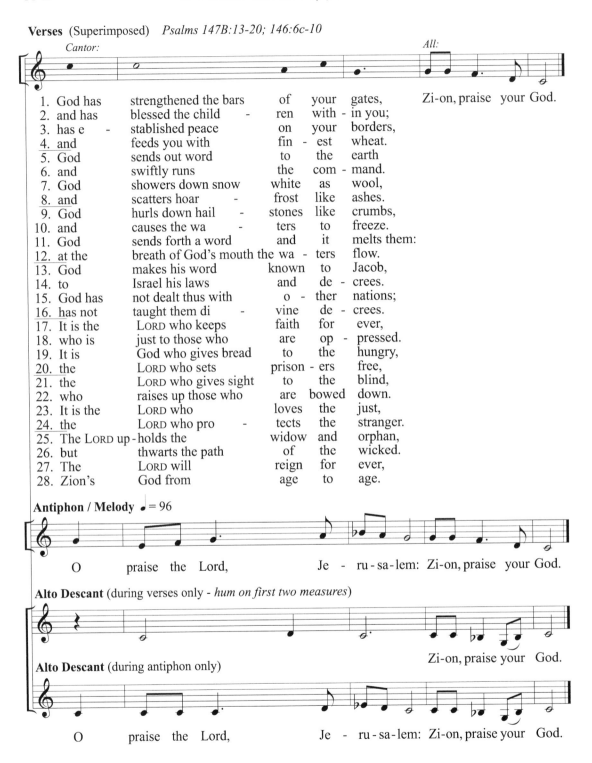

1. God has   strengthened the bars   of   your   gates,
2. and has   blessed the child - ren   with - in you;
3. has e - stablished peace   on   your   borders,
4. and   feeds you with   fin - est   wheat.
5. God   sends out word   to   the   earth
6. and   swiftly runs   the   com - mand.
7. God   showers down snow   white   as   wool,
8. and   scatters hoar - frost   like   ashes.
9. God   hurls down hail - stones   like   crumbs,
10. and   causes the wa - ters   to   freeze.
11. God   sends forth a word   and   it   melts them:
12. at the   breath of God's mouth the wa - ters   flow.
13. God   makes his word   known   to   Jacob,
14. to   Israel his laws   and   de - crees.
15. God has   not dealt thus with   o - ther   nations;
16. has not   taught them di - vine   de - crees.
17. It is the   LORD who keeps   faith   for   ever,
18. who is   just to those who   are   op - pressed.
19. It is   God who gives bread   to   the   hungry,
20. the   LORD who sets   prison - ers   free,
21. the   LORD who gives sight   to   the   blind,
22. who   raises up those who   are   bowed   down.
23. It is the   LORD who   loves   the   just,
24. the   LORD who pro - tects   the   stranger.
25. The LORD up - holds the   widow   and   orphan,
26. but   thwarts the path   of   the   wicked.
27. The   LORD will   reign   for   ever,
28. Zion's   God from   age   to   age.

Antiphon / Melody   ♩ = 96

O praise the Lord, Je - ru - sa - lem: Zi-on, praise your God.

Alto Descant (during verses only - *hum on first two measures*)

Zi-on, praise your God.

Alto Descant (during antiphon only)

O praise the Lord, Je - ru - sa - lem: Zi-on, praise your God.

Performance Notes
Verses 1–6 and 13–16 are the Lectionary selections for the Body and Blood of Christ, Year A.
Verses 17–28 are the Lectionary selections for the Twenty-third and Thirty-second Sundays in Ordinary Time, Year B.

Antiphon ♩ = 72

One thing I seek: to dwell in your house all the days of my life.

Verses *Psalm 27:1, 3-5, 7-14*

1. The LORD is my light and my help; whom shall I fear?
2. Though an army encamp a - gainst me my heart would not fear.
3. {There is one thing I ask of the LORD, {to live in the house of
   for this I long the LORD all the days of my life,
4. For God makes me safe in his tent in the day of evil.
5. O LORD, hear my voice when I call; have mercy and answer.
6. It is your face, O LORD, that I seek; hide not your face.
7. Do not abandon or for - sake me, O God my help!
8. Instruct me, LORD, in your way; on an even path lead me.
9. I am sure I shall see the LORD's goodness in the land of the living.

1. The LORD is the stronghold of my life; before whom shall I shrink?
2. Though war break out a - gainst me even then would I trust.
3. to savor the sweetness of the LORD, to be - hold his temple.
4. God hides me in the shelter of his tent, on a rock I am se - cure.
5. Of you my heart has spoken: "Seek God's face."
6. Dismiss not your ser - vant in anger; you have been my help.
7. Though father and mo - ther for-sake me, the LORD will re - ceive me.
8. {When they lie in ambush, {False witnesses rise
   protect me from my e - ne - mies' greed. against me, breath - ing out fury.
9. In the LORD, hold firm and take heart. Hope in the LORD!

Open, You Skies: Rain Down the Just One

Antiphon ♩. = 63

O-pen, you skies: rain down the Just One. O-pen, O earth, let sal-va-tion spring forth.

Verses *Psalm 72*

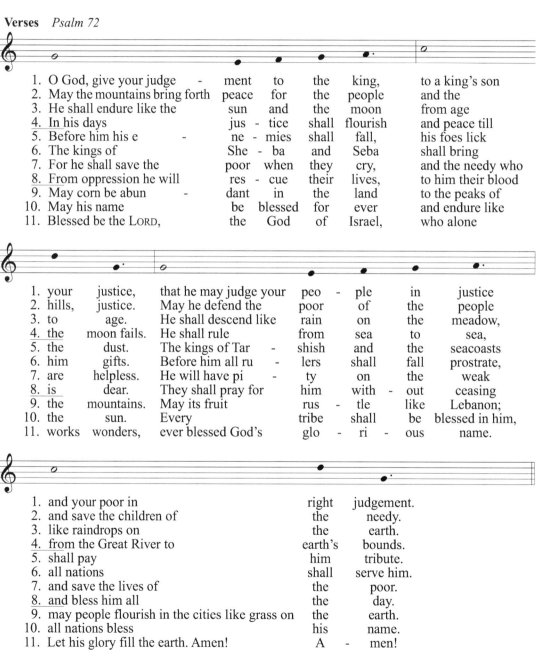

1. O God, give your judge - ment to the king, to a king's son
2. May the mountains bring forth peace for the people and the
3. He shall endure like the sun and the moon from age
4. In his days jus - tice shall flourish and peace till
5. Before him his e - ne - mies shall fall, his foes lick
6. The kings of She - ba and Seba shall bring
7. For he shall save the poor when they cry, and the needy who
8. From oppression he will res - cue their lives, to him their blood
9. May corn be abun - dant in the land to the peaks of
10. May his name be blessed for ever and endure like
11. Blessed be the LORD, the God of Israel, who alone

1. your justice, that he may judge your peo - ple in justice
2. hills, justice. May he defend the poor of the people
3. to age. He shall descend like rain on the meadow,
4. the moon fails. He shall rule from sea to sea,
5. the dust. The kings of Tar - shish and the seacoasts
6. him gifts. Before him all ru - lers shall fall prostrate,
7. are helpless. He will have pi - ty on the weak
8. is dear. They shall pray for him with - out ceasing
9. the mountains. May its fruit rus - tle like Lebanon;
10. the sun. Every tribe shall be blessed in him,
11. works wonders, ever blessed God's glo - ri - ous name.

1. and your poor in right judgement.
2. and save the children of the needy.
3. like raindrops on the earth.
4. from the Great River to earth's bounds.
5. shall pay him tribute.
6. all nations shall serve him.
7. and save the lives of the poor.
8. and bless him all the day.
9. may people flourish in the cities like grass on the earth.
10. all nations bless his name.
11. Let his glory fill the earth. Amen! A - men!

Open Your Hand, Lord

Verses (Superimposed) *Psalm 103:1-4, 8, 10-14, 17-18a*

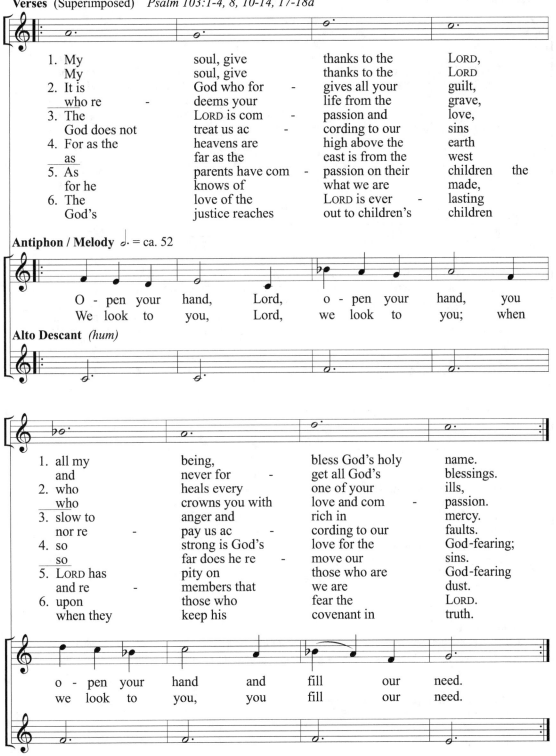

1. My soul, give thanks to the LORD,
   My soul, give thanks to the LORD
2. It is God who for - gives all your guilt,
   who re - deems your life from the grave,
3. The LORD is com - passion and love,
   God does not treat us ac - cording to our sins
4. For as the heavens are high above the earth
   as far as the east is from the west
5. As parents have com - passion on their children the
   for he knows of what we are made,
6. The love of the LORD is ever - lasting
   God's justice reaches out to children's children

Antiphon / Melody ♩. = ca. 52

O - pen your hand, Lord, o - pen your hand, you
We look to you, Lord, we look to you; when

Alto Descant *(hum)*

1. all my being, bless God's holy name.
   and never for - get all God's blessings.
2. who heals every one of your ills,
   who crowns you with love and com - passion.
3. slow to anger and rich in mercy.
   nor re - pay us ac - cording to our faults.
4. so strong is God's love for the God-fearing;
   so far does he re - move our sins.
5. LORD has pity on those who are God-fearing
   and re - members that we are dust.
6. upon those who fear the LORD.
   when they keep his covenant in truth.

o - pen your hand and fill our need.
we look to you, you fill our need.

Verses (alternate tone, if required)   *Psalm 103:1-4, 8, 10-14, 17-18a*

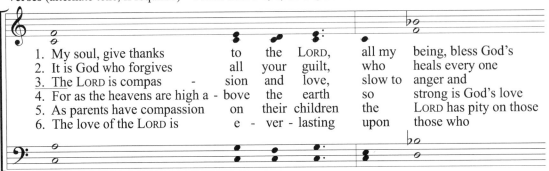

1. My soul, give thanks   to   the   LORD,   all my   being, bless God's
2. It is God who forgives   all   your guilt,   who   heals every one
3. The LORD is compas - sion   and   love,   slow to   anger and
4. For as the heavens are high a - bove the   earth   so   strong is God's love
5. As parents have compassion   on   their children the   LORD has pity on those
6. The love of the LORD is   e - ver - lasting upon   those who

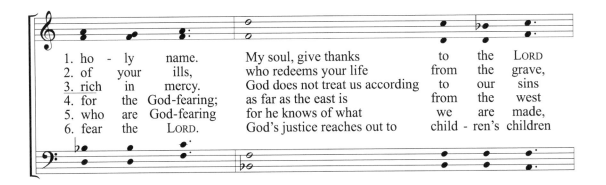

1. ho - ly   name.   My soul, give thanks   to   the   LORD
2. of   your   ills,   who redeems your life   from the   grave,
3. rich in   mercy.   God does not treat us according   to   our   sins
4. for   the God-fearing; as far as the east is   from the   west
5. who   are God-fearing   for he knows of what   we   are   made,
6. fear the LORD.   God's justice reaches out to   child - ren's children

1. and never forget   all   God's   blessings.
2. who crowns you with love   and   com - passion.
3. nor repay us according   to   our   faults.
4. so far does he re   -   move our   sins.
5. and remembers that   we   are   dust.
6. when they keep his cove -   nant in   truth.

Performance Notes

The psalm verses are pointed separately for use with either the superimposed tone or the alternate verse tone. When using the superimposed setting, the verse tone may be hummed as a tenor descant during the antiphon.

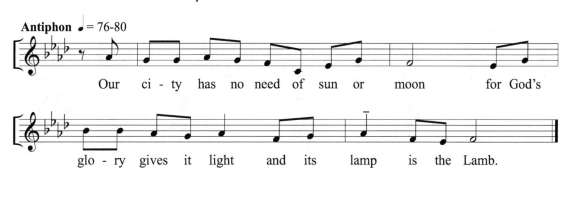

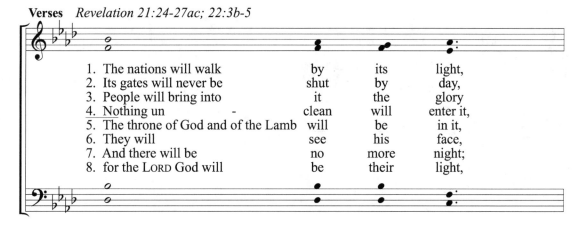

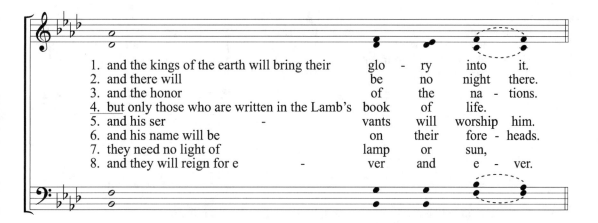

Our Cup of Blessing

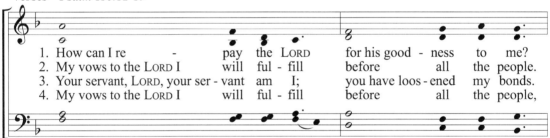

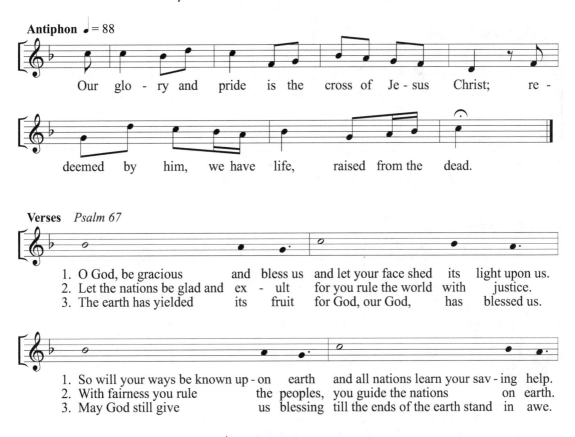

Antiphon ♩= 88

Our glo - ry and pride is the cross of Je - sus Christ; re -
deemed by him, we have life, raised from the dead.

Verses *Psalm 67*

1. O God, be gracious and bless us and let your face shed its light upon us.
2. Let the nations be glad and ex - ult for you rule the world with justice.
3. The earth has yielded its fruit for God, our God, has blessed us.

1. So will your ways be known up - on earth and all nations learn your sav - ing help.
2. With fairness you rule the peoples, you guide the nations on earth.
3. May God still give us blessing till the ends of the earth stand in awe.

1.–3. Let the peoples praise you, O God; let all the peo - ples praise you.

Our God Has Blessed Us

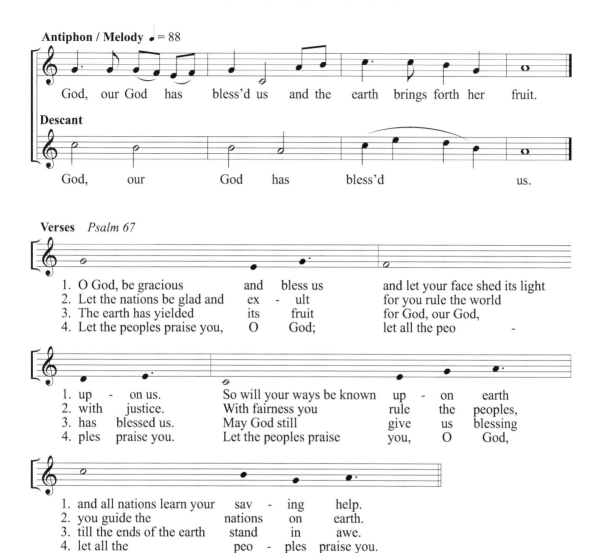

Antiphon / Melody ♩ = 88

God, our God has bless'd us and the earth brings forth her fruit.

Descant

God, our God has bless'd us.

Verses *Psalm 67*

1. O God, be gracious   and   bless us   and let your face shed its light
2. Let the nations be glad and   ex - ult   for you rule the world
3. The earth has yielded   its   fruit   for God, our God,
4. Let the peoples praise you,   O   God;   let all the peo -

1. up - on us.   So will your ways be known   up - on   earth
2. with   justice.   With fairness you   rule   the   peoples,
3. has   blessed us.   May God still   give   us   blessing
4. ples   praise you.   Let the peoples praise   you,   O   God,

1. and all nations learn your   sav - ing   help.
2. you guide the   nations   on   earth.
3. till the ends of the earth   stand   in   awe.
4. let all the   peo - ples   praise you.

Our Help Shall Come from the Lord

Antiphon ♩. = 66

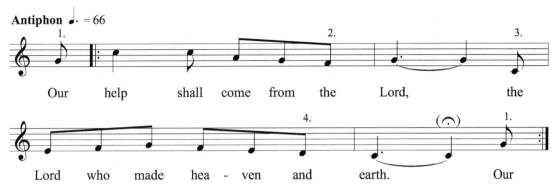

Our help shall come from the Lord, the Lord who made hea - ven and earth. Our

Verses *Psalm 121*

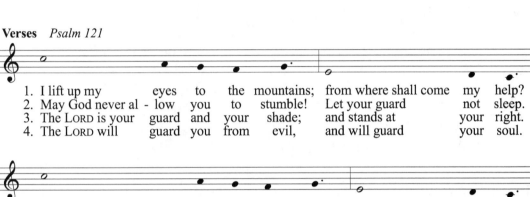

1. I lift up my eyes to the mountains; from where shall come my help?
2. May God never al - low you to stumble! Let your guard not sleep.
3. The LORD is your guard and your shade; and stands at your right.
4. The LORD will guard you from evil, and will guard your soul.

1. My help shall come from the LORD who made heaven and earth.
2. Behold, neither sleep - ing nor slumbering, Is - rael's guard.
3. By day the sun shall not smite you nor the moon in the night.
4. The LORD will guard your go - ing and coming both now and for ever.

Performance Notes

The antiphon may be sung as a round, if desired. When sung as a 4-part round, this piece works best divided into men - women - women - men.

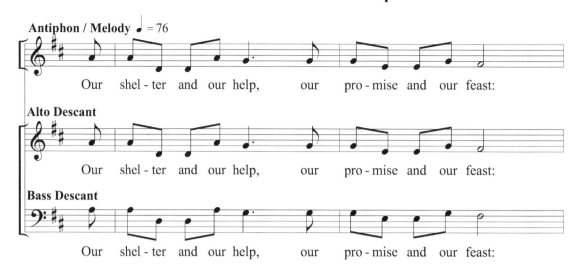

Antiphon / Melody ♩ = 76

Our shel-ter and our help, our pro-mise and our feast:

Alto Descant

Our shel-ter and our help, our pro-mise and our feast:

Bass Descant

Our shel-ter and our help, our pro-mise and our feast:

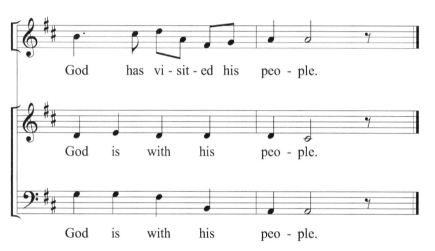

God has vi-sit-ed his peo-ple.

God is with his peo-ple.

God is with his peo-ple.

Verses   *Luke 1:68-79*

Cantor:

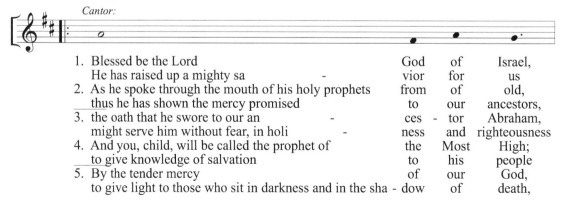

1. Blessed be the Lord God of Israel,
   He has raised up a mighty sa - vior for us
2. As he spoke through the mouth of his holy prophets from of old,
   thus he has shown the mercy promised to our ancestors,
3. the oath that he swore to our an - ces - tor Abraham,
   might serve him without fear, in holi - ness and righteousness
4. And you, child, will be called the prophet of the Most High;
   to give knowledge of salvation to his people
5. By the tender mercy of our God,
   to give light to those who sit in darkness and in the sha - dow of death,

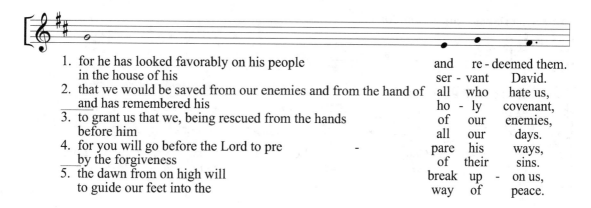

1. for he has looked favorably on his people and re-deemed them.
   in the house of his ser - vant David.
2. that we would be saved from our enemies and from the hand of all who hate us,
   and has remembered his ho - ly covenant,
3. to grant us that we, being rescued from the hands of our enemies,
   before him all our days.
4. for you will go before the Lord to pre - pare his ways,
   by the forgiveness of their sins.
5. the dawn from on high will break up - on us,
   to guide our feet into the way of peace.

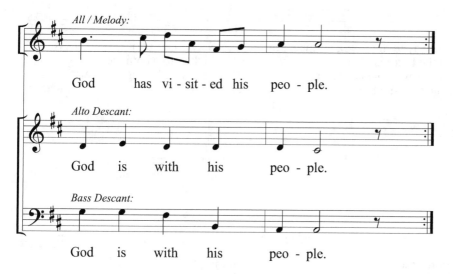

All / Melody:

God has vi - sit - ed his peo - ple.

Alto Descant:

God is with his peo - ple.

Bass Descant:

God is with his peo - ple.

People of God, Flock of the Lord

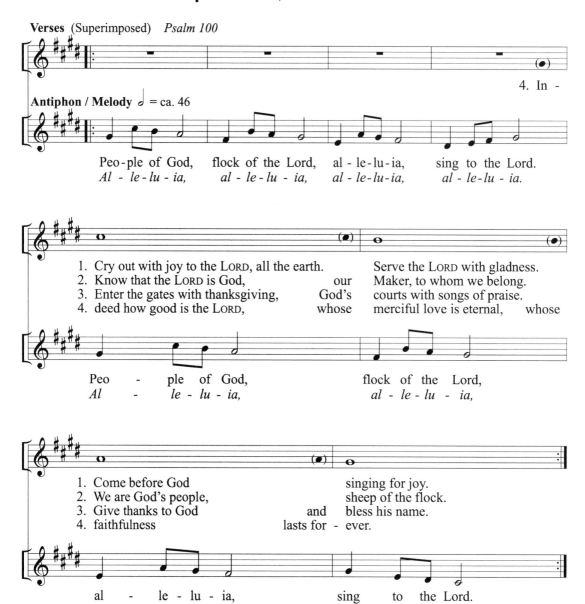

Verses (Superimposed) *Psalm 100*

4. In -

Antiphon / Melody ♩ = ca. 46

Peo-ple of God,   flock of the Lord,   al - le-lu - ia,   sing to the Lord.
Al - le-lu - ia,   al - le-lu - ia,   al - le-lu - ia,   al - le-lu - ia.

1. Cry out with joy to the LORD, all the earth.   Serve the LORD with gladness.
2. Know that the LORD is God,   our   Maker, to whom we belong.
3. Enter the gates with thanksgiving,   God's   courts with songs of praise.
4. deed how good is the LORD,   whose   merciful love is eternal,   whose

Peo - ple of God,   flock of the Lord,
Al - le - lu - ia,   al - le - lu - ia,

1. Come before God   singing for joy.
2. We are God's people,   sheep of the flock.
3. Give thanks to God   and   bless his name.
4. faithfulness   lasts for - ever.

al - le - lu - ia,   sing   to   the Lord.
al - le - lu - ia,   al - le - lu - ia.

Performance Notes

Verses 1, 2, and 4 are the Lectionary selections for the Eleventh Sunday in Ordinary Time, Year A, and the Fourth Sunday of Easter, Year C.
Descants for the antiphon are available on the next page.
The text in italics could be used for an additional final refrain instead of the main text, especially during the Easter Season.

183   **Planted Like a Tree**

Verses (Superimposed)   *Psalm 1:1-4, 6*

1. Happy indeed   are   those   who follow not the counsel
2. but whose delight is the law of   the   LORD   and who ponder God's law
3. that yields its fruit in   due   season   and whose leaves shall
4. For they like winnow   -   èd   chaff   shall be driven away

Antiphon / Melody ♩ = 65

Drone   Plant - ed   like   a   tree   be - side   a   flow - ing

1. of   the wicked,   nor linger in the way   of   sinners,
2. day   and night.   They are like a tree that   is   planted
3. ne - ver fade;   and all that they do   shall   prosper.
4. by   the wind.   For the LORD guards the way of   the   just

stream,   blest in - deed   are   they   whose

1. nor sit in the company   of   scorners,
2. beside the flow   -   ing   waters,
3. Not so are the wicked,   not   so!
4. but the way of the wicked leads   to   doom.

hope   is   in   the   Lord.

Performance Notes

The Drone is preferably hummed (to an 'n' sound rather than an 'm' sound). Verses are sung without pausing between stanzas. During the verses, the melody line of the antiphon may be vocalized to 'oo.'
If desired, the verses could be chanted independently on the tone given and not superimposed over the antiphon.
When the assembly sings the antiphon without a superimposed verse, choir voices may add the drones.

Praise the Lord, Alleluia!

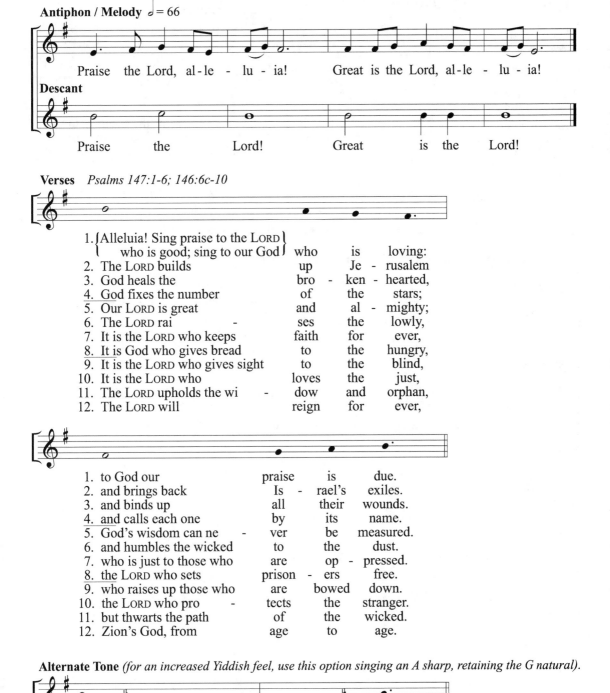

Antiphon / Melody ♩= 66

Praise the Lord, al-le - lu - ia! Great is the Lord, al-le - lu - ia!

Descant

Praise the Lord! Great is the Lord!

Verses *Psalms 147:1-6; 146:6c-10*

1. {Alleluia! Sing praise to the LORD
   who is good; sing to our God} who is loving:
2. The LORD builds up Je - rusalem
3. God heals the bro - ken - hearted,
4. God fixes the number of the stars;
5. Our LORD is great and al - mighty;
6. The LORD rai - ses the lowly,
7. It is the LORD who keeps faith for ever,
8. It is God who gives bread to the hungry,
9. It is the LORD who gives sight to the blind,
10. It is the LORD who loves the just,
11. The LORD upholds the wi - dow and orphan,
12. The LORD will reign for ever,

1. to God our praise is due.
2. and brings back Is - rael's exiles.
3. and binds up all their wounds.
4. and calls each one by its name.
5. God's wisdom can ne - ver be measured.
6. and humbles the wicked to the dust.
7. who is just to those who are op - pressed.
8. the LORD who sets prison - ers free.
9. who raises up those who are bowed down.
10. the LORD who pro - tects the stranger.
11. but thwarts the path of the wicked.
12. Zion's God, from age to age.

Alternate Tone *(for an increased Yiddish feel, use this option singing an A sharp, retaining the G natural).*

Performance Notes
Verses 1–6 are the Lectionary selections for the Fifth Sunday in Ordinary Time, Year B.
Verses 7–12 are the Lectionary selections for the Thirty-second Sunday in Ordinary Time, Year B.

185   Praise to God Who Lifts Up the Poor

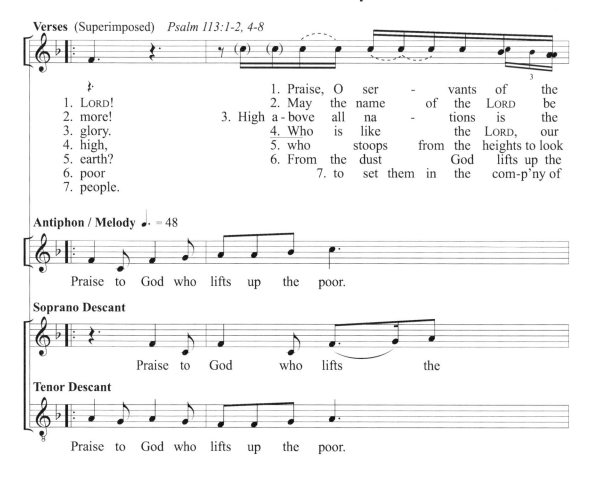

Verses (Superimposed)   *Psalm 113:1-2, 4-8*

1. LORD!
2. more!
3. glory.
4. high,
5. earth?
6. poor
7. people.

1. Praise, O ser - vants of the
2. May the name of the LORD be
3. High a - bove all na - tions is the
4. Who is like the LORD, our
5. who stoops from the heights to look
6. From the dust God lifts up the
7. to set them in the com-p'ny of

Antiphon / Melody ♩. = 48

Praise to God who lifts up the poor.

Soprano Descant

Praise to God who lifts the

Tenor Descant

Praise to God who lifts up the poor.

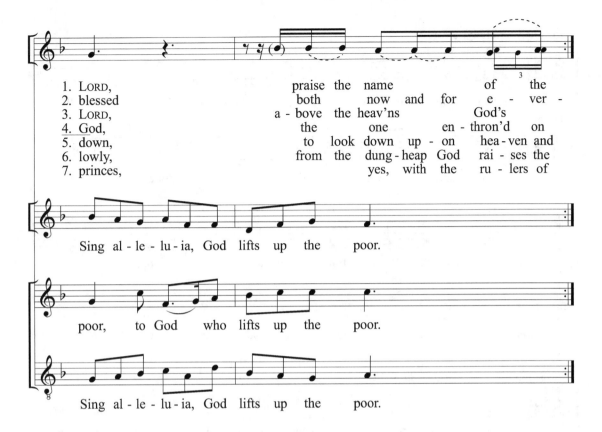

1. LORD,   praise the name   of   the
2. blessed   both   now and   for   e -   ver -
3. LORD,   a - bove the heav'ns   God's
4. <u>God,</u>   the   one   en - thron'd   on
5. down,   to   look down up - on   hea - ven and
6. lowly,   from   the   dung - heap God   rai - ses the
7. princes,   yes,   with   the   ru - lers of

Sing al - le - lu - ia, God lifts up the poor.

poor,   to God   who   lifts   up   the   poor.

Sing al - le - lu - ia, God lifts up the poor.

Performance Notes

In the superimposed tone, the note values shown are approximations, modifiable by natural speech rhythm.

Proclaim the Wonders God Has Done

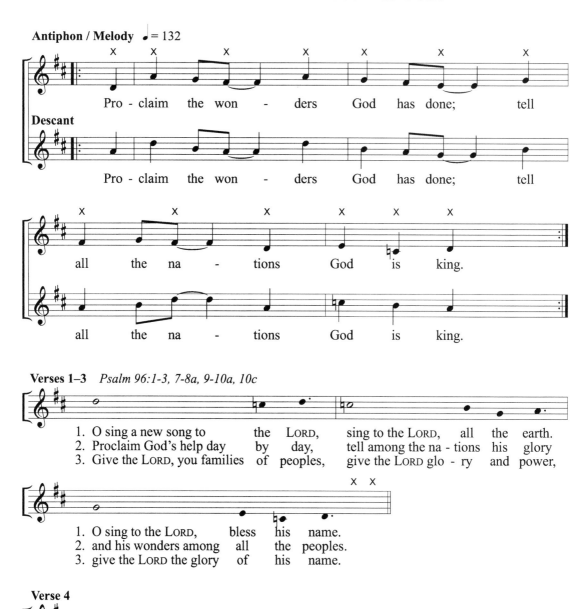

Antiphon / Melody ♩ = 132

Pro - claim the won - ders God has done; tell

Descant

Pro - claim the won - ders God has done; tell

all the na - tions God is king.

all the na - tions God is king.

Verses 1–3 *Psalm 96:1-3, 7-8a, 9-10a, 10c*

1. O sing a new song to the LORD, sing to the LORD, all the earth.
2. Proclaim God's help day by day, tell among the na - tions his glory
3. Give the LORD, you families of peoples, give the LORD glo - ry and power,

1. O sing to the LORD, bless his name.
2. and his wonders among all the peoples.
3. give the LORD the glory of his name.

Verse 4

4. Worship the LORD in the temple. O earth, stand in fear of the LORD.

4. Proclaim to the nations: "God is king." God will judge the peoples in fairness.

Performance Notes

Percussion or handclaps may be added, as indicated by the X's, both during the antiphon and at the end of the psalm verses to lead back into the antiphon.

Antiphon ♩ = 88

Put your hand here, Tho-mas, reach out and feel:

doubt no

doubt no long-er, but be - lieve, al - le - lu - ia.

Verses *Psalm 30*

1. I will praise you, LORD, you have rescued me [*omit*
2. O LORD, I cried to you for help   and you, my   God, have healed me.
3. Sing psalms to the   LORD, you faithful ones, give thanks to his ho - ly   name.
4. I said to myself in   my   good   fortune: "Nothing will e - ver dis - turb me."
5. To you,   LORD, I   cried,   to my God I   made ap - peal:
6. The LORD listened   and had   pity.   The LORD came   to my   help.

1. _____]
2. O LORD, you have raised my soul   from   the   dead,
3. God's anger lasts a moment, God's fa - vor   through   life.
4. Your favor had set me on a   moun - tain   fastness,
5. "What profit would my death be, my going   to   the   grave?
6. ⎧ For me you have changed my mourning   in - to   dancing,
   ⎩ So my soul sings psalms to   you   un - ceasingly.

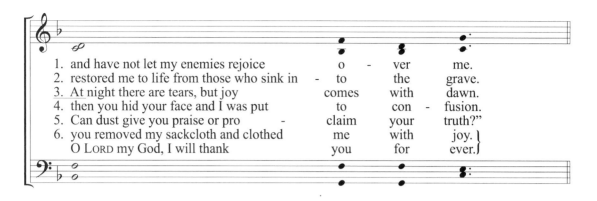

1. and have not let my enemies rejoice   o - ver   me.
2. restored me to life from those who sink in - to   the   grave.
3. At night there are tears, but joy   comes   with   dawn.
4. then you hid your face and I was put   to   con - fusion.
5. Can dust give you praise or pro -   claim   your   truth?"
6. you removed my sackcloth and clothed   me   with   joy.
    O LORD my God, I will thank   you   for   ever.

Raise the Cup of Salvation

Antiphon ♩ = 116

Raise the cup of sal - va - tion and call up-on the name of the Lord.

Verses *Psalm 116:12-19*

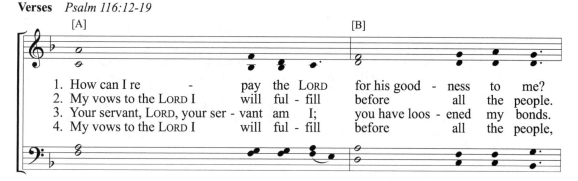

[A]   [B]

1. How can I re - pay the LORD for his good - ness to me?
2. My vows to the LORD I will ful - fill before all the people.
3. Your servant, LORD, your ser - vant am I; you have loos - ened my bonds.
4. My vows to the LORD I will ful - fill before all the people,

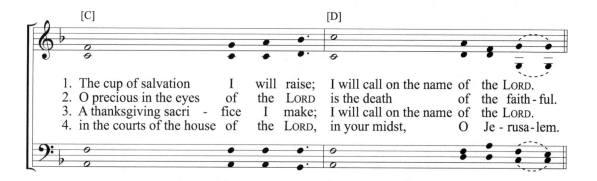

[C]   [D]

1. The cup of salvation I will raise; I will call on the name of the LORD.
2. O precious in the eyes of the LORD is the death of the faith - ful.
3. A thanksgiving sacri - fice I make; I will call on the name of the LORD.
4. in the courts of the house of the LORD, in your midst, O Je - rusa - lem.

Performance Notes

Verses 1, 2cd, 3, and 4ab are the Lectionary selections for the solemnity of the Body and Blood of Christ, Year B.

189   Rejoice in the Lord, Again Rejoice!

Antiphon ♩ = 138

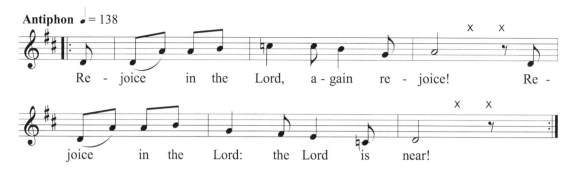

Re - joice in the Lord, a - gain re - joice! Re -

joice in the Lord: the Lord is near!

Verses 1–7   *Psalm 96*

1. O sing a new song to   the   LORD,   sing to the LORD,   all   the   earth.
2. Proclaim God's help day   by   day,   tell among the na   -   tions his   glory
3. The LORD is great and worthy   of   praise,   to be feared a   -   bove all   gods;
4. It was the LORD who made   the   heavens,   his are majesty and ho - nor and power
5. Give the LORD, you families   of   peoples,   give the LORD glo   -   ry   and power,
6. Bring an offering and enter   God's   courts,   worship the LORD   in   the temple.
7. Proclaim to the nations: "God   is   king."   The world was made firm in   its   place;

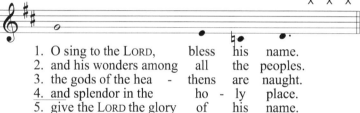

1. O sing to the LORD,   bless   his   name.
2. and his wonders among   all   the   peoples.
3. the gods of the hea   -   thens   are   naught.
4. and splendor in the   ho - ly   place.
5. give the LORD the glory   of   his   name.
6. O earth, stand in fear   of   the   LORD.
7. God will judge the peo - ple   in   fairness.

Verses 8–9

8. Let the heavens rejoice and earth be   glad,   let the sea and all within it thun - der praise,
9. at the presence of the LORD   who comes, who comes to   rule the earth,

8. let the land and all it bears re - joice,   all the trees of the wood shout for   joy,
9. comes with justice to rule the world,   and to judge the peoples   with truth.

Performance Notes

Both antiphon and verses are preferably sung unaccompanied. The antiphon is sung twice every time.

x = *fingersnaps/handclaps/other percussion on the 2nd and 3rd beats of the measure within the antiphon,*
and three strong beats at the end of each verse to lead back into the antiphon.

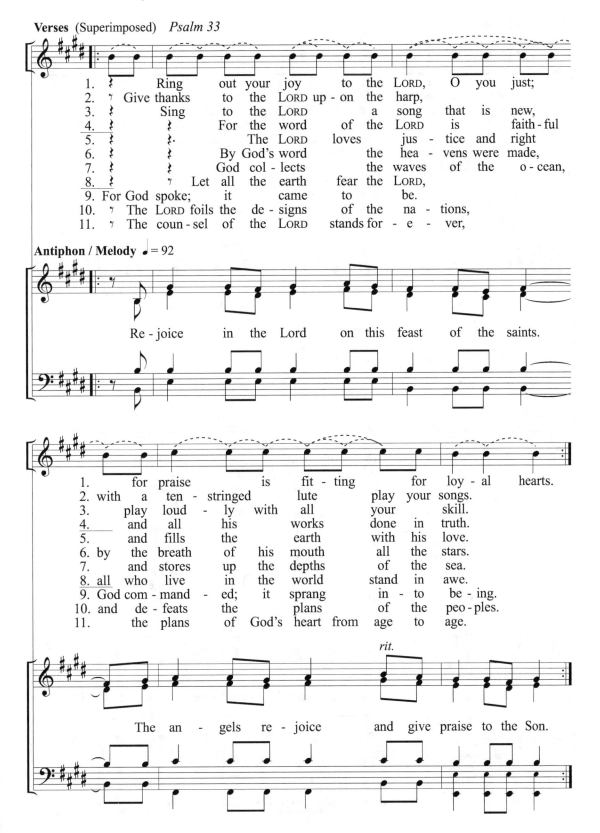

Verses (continued)

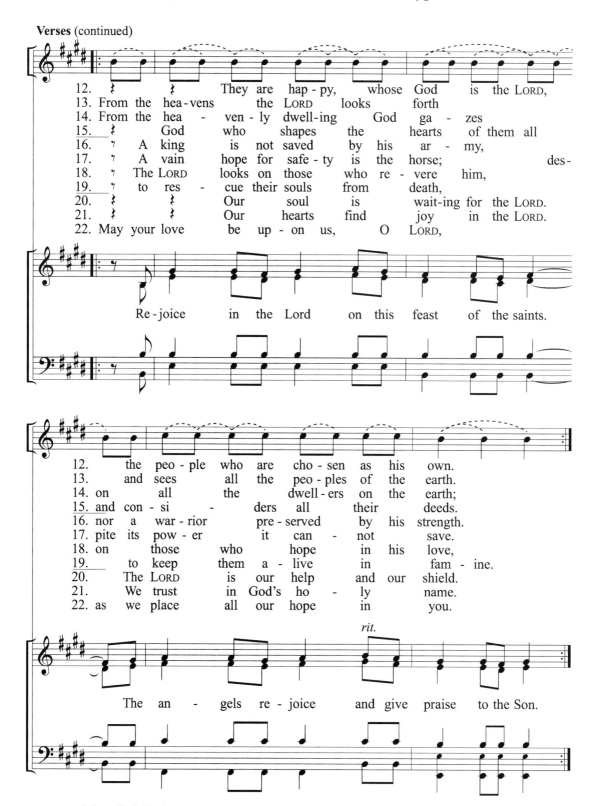

12.   They are hap-py, whose God is the LORD,
13. From the hea-vens the LORD looks forth
14. From the hea - ven-ly dwell-ing God ga - zes
15. God who shapes the hearts of them all
16. A king is not saved by his ar - my,
17. A vain hope for safe-ty is the horse; des-
18. The LORD looks on those who re - vere him,
19. to res - cue their souls from death,
20. Our soul is wait-ing for the LORD.
21. Our hearts find joy in the LORD.
22. May your love be up - on us, O LORD,

Re - joice in the Lord on this feast of the saints.

12. the peo - ple who are cho - sen as his own.
13. and sees all the peo - ples of the earth.
14. on all the dwell-ers on the earth;
15. and con - si - ders all their deeds.
16. nor a war-rior pre - served by his strength.
17. pite its pow - er it can - not save.
18. on those who hope in his love,
19. to keep them a - live in fam - ine.
20. The LORD is our help and our shield.
21. We trust in God's ho - ly name.
22. as we place all our hope in you.

rit.

The an - gels re - joice and give praise to the Son.

Rejoice, Rejoice, All You Who Love Jerusalem!

Re - joice, re - joice, all you who love Je - ru - sa - lem! Re -
joice, be glad, for you will be con - soled.

Verses *Psalm 122*

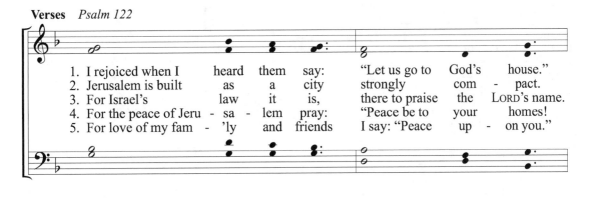

1. I rejoiced when I heard them say: "Let us go to God's house."
2. Jerusalem is built as a city strongly com - pact.
3. For Israel's law it is, there to praise the LORD's name.
4. For the peace of Jeru - sa - lem pray: "Peace be to your homes!
5. For love of my fam - 'ly and friends I say: "Peace up - on you."

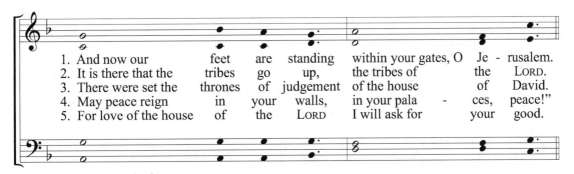

1. And now our feet are standing within your gates, O Je - rusalem.
2. It is there that the tribes go up, the tribes of the LORD.
3. There were set the thrones of judgement of the house of David.
4. May peace reign in your walls, in your pala - ces, peace!"
5. For love of the house of the LORD I will ask for your good.

192   Rejoice, Your Names Are Written in Heaven

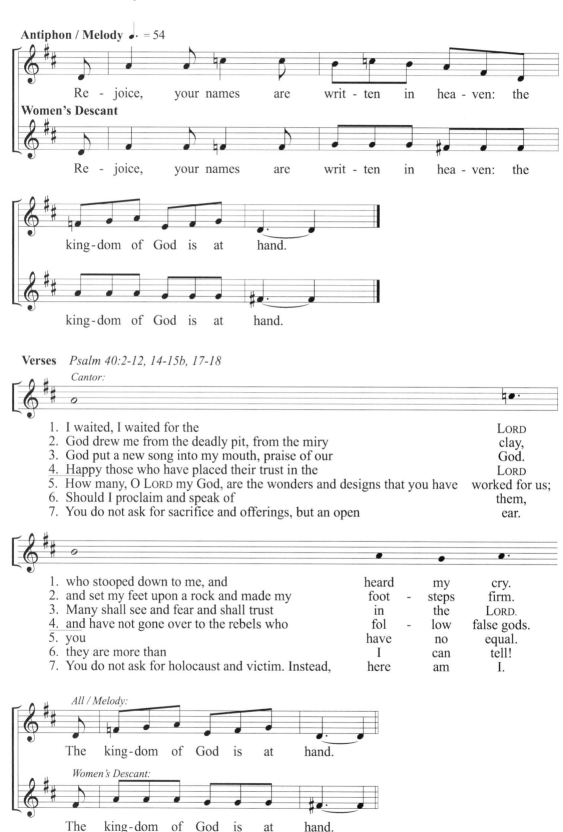

Antiphon / Melody ♩. = 54

Re - joice, your names are writ - ten in hea - ven: the king-dom of God is at hand.

Women's Descant

Re - joice, your names are writ - ten in hea - ven: the king-dom of God is at hand.

Verses *Psalm 40:2-12, 14-15b, 17-18*

Cantor:

1. I waited, I waited for the   Lord
2. God drew me from the deadly pit, from the miry   clay,
3. God put a new song into my mouth, praise of our   God.
4. Happy those who have placed their trust in the   Lord
5. How many, O Lord my God, are the wonders and designs that you have   worked for us;
6. Should I proclaim and speak of   them,
7. You do not ask for sacrifice and offerings, but an open   ear.

1. who stooped down to me, and   heard   my   cry.
2. and set my feet upon a rock and made my   foot - steps   firm.
3. Many shall see and fear and shall trust   in   the   Lord.
4. and have not gone over to the rebels who   fol - low   false gods.
5. you   have   no   equal.
6. they are more than   I   can   tell!
7. You do not ask for holocaust and victim. Instead,   here   am   I.

All / Melody:

The king-dom of God is at hand.

Women's Descant:

The king-dom of God is at hand.

Verses (continued)

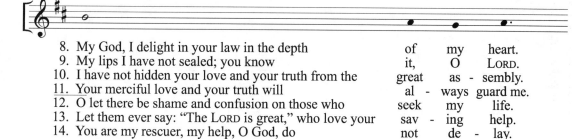

Cantor:

8. In the scroll of the book it stands written that I should do your   will.
9. Your justice I have proclaimed in the great as   -   sembly.
10. I have not hidden your justice in my heart but declared your faithful   help.
11. O Lord, you will not withhold your com   -   passion from me.
12. O Lord, come to my rescue; Lord, come to my   aid.
13. O let there be rejoicing and gladness for all who   seek you.
14. As for me, wretched and poor, the Lord thinks of   me.

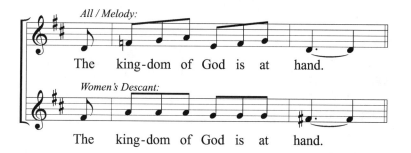

8. My God, I delight in your law in the depth   of   my   heart.
9. My lips I have not sealed; you know   it,   O   Lord.
10. I have not hidden your love and your truth from the   great   as - sembly.
11. Your merciful love and your truth will   al - ways guard me.
12. O let there be shame and confusion on those who   seek   my   life.
13. Let them ever say: "The Lord is great," who love your   sav - ing   help.
14. You are my rescuer, my help, O God, do   not   de - lay.

All / Melody:

The king-dom of God is at hand.

Women's Descant:

The king-dom of God is at hand.

193   Remember, Lord

Verses (Superimposed)   *Psalm 25:4-5b, 6, 7bc, 8-9*

1. LORD, make me know your ways. LORD,
2. member your mercy, LORD, and the
3. LORD is good and upright, showing the

Antiphon / Melody ♩ = ca. 65

Re - mem - ber, Lord, re -

Alto Descant   *Vocalize to 'oo'*

Tenor Descant   *Vocalize to 'oo'*

1. teach me your paths. Make me
2. love you have shown from of old. In your
3. path to those who stray,

mem - ber your mer - cy; re -

1. walk in your   truth and   teach me, for
2. love re -   member   me be -
3. guiding the   humble in the   right path, and

mem - ber,   Lord,   re -

1. you are God my   savior.   2. Re -
2. cause of your goodness, O   LORD.   3. The
3. teaching the way to the   poor.

mem - ber   not   our   sin.   Re -

194

Ring Out Your Joy

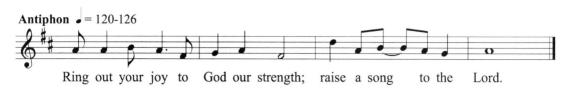

Antiphon ♩ = 120-126

Ring out your joy to God our strength; raise a song to the Lord.

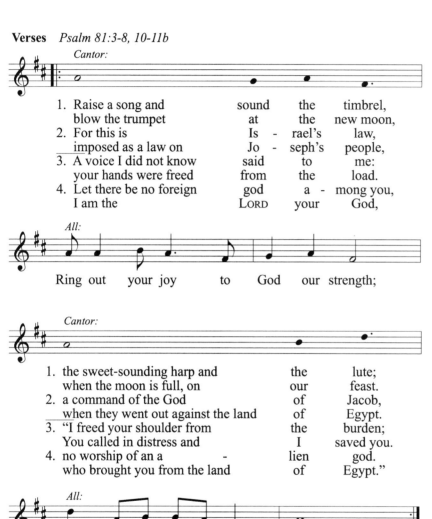

Verses *Psalm 81:3-8, 10-11b*

Cantor:

1. Raise a song and   sound   the   timbrel,
   blow the trumpet   at   the   new moon,
2. For this is   Is - rael's   law,
   imposed as a law on   Jo - seph's   people,
3. A voice I did not know   said   to   me:
   your hands were freed   from   the   load.
4. Let there be no foreign   god   a - mong you,
   I am the   LORD   your   God,

All:

Ring out   your joy   to   God   our strength;

Cantor:

1. the sweet-sounding harp and   the   lute;
   when the moon is full, on   our   feast.
2. a command of the God   of   Jacob,
   when they went out against the land   of   Egypt.
3. "I freed your shoulder from   the   burden;
   You called in distress and   I   saved you.
4. no worship of an a - lien   god.
   who brought you from the land   of   Egypt."

All:

Raise   a   song   to the   Lord.

Rise Up and Tell All Your Children

Antiphon / Melody ♩. = 58

Rise up and tell all your child - ren:

Descants

Rise up and tell all your child - ren:

Do not for - get the works of the Lord.

Do not for - get the Lord.

Do not, do not for - get!

Do not for - get! Do not for - get!

Do not for - get the Lord.

Verses *Psalm 78:1-2, 34-38*

Cantor:

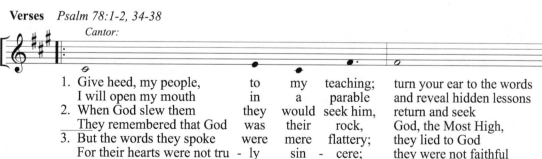

1. Give heed, my people, to my teaching; turn your ear to the words
   I will open my mouth in a parable and reveal hidden lessons
2. When God slew them they would seek him, return and seek
   They remembered that God was their rock, God, the Most High,
3. But the words they spoke were mere flattery; they lied to God
   For their hearts were not tru - ly sin - cere; they were not faithful
4. Yet the one who is full of com - passion forgave them their
   So often God held back the anger that might have been stirred

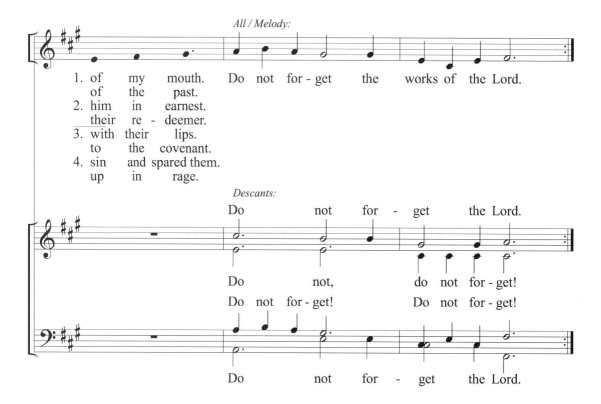

Performance Notes

Alto descant can be sung by tenor, and tenor and bass descants sung by divided basses.

Antiphon ♩. = 50

Rise up, O Lord, to the place of your rest,

you and the ark of your ho - li - ness.

Verses *Psalm 132:6-7, 9-10, 13-14*

1. At Ephrata we heard of the ark; we found it in the plains of Yearim.
2. Your priests shall be clothed with holiness; your faithful shall ring out their joy.
3. For the LORD has cho - sen Zion; has desired it for a dwelling:

1. "Let us go to the place of God's dwelling; let us go to kneel at God's footstool."
2. For the sake of Da - vid your servant do not reject your a - nointed.
3. "This is my resting - place for ever, here have I cho - sen to live."

Salvation Has Come to This House

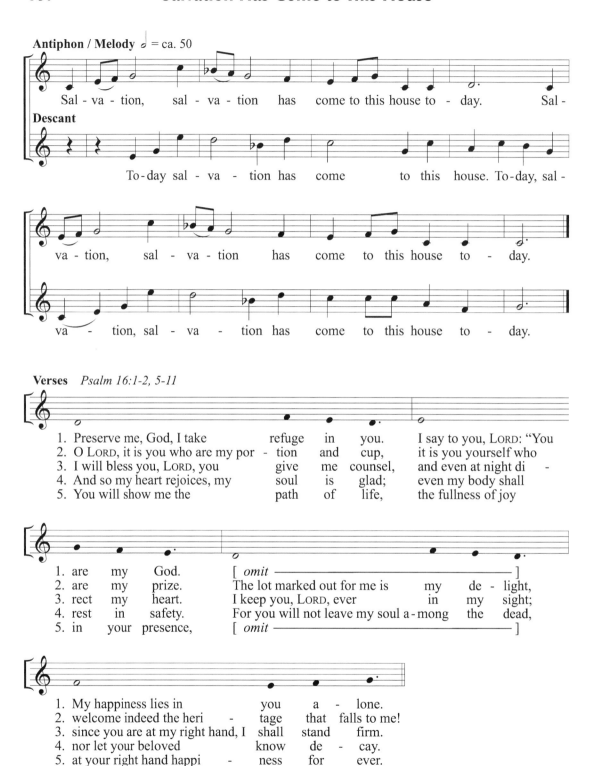

Antiphon / Melody ♩ = ca. 50

Sal - va - tion, sal - va - tion has come to this house to - day. Sal -

Descant

To-day sal - va - tion has come to this house. To-day, sal -

va - tion, sal - va - tion has come to this house to - day.

va - tion, sal - va - tion has come to this house to - day.

Verses *Psalm 16:1-2, 5-11*

1. Preserve me, God, I take refuge in you. I say to you, LORD: "You
2. O LORD, it is you who are my por - tion and cup, it is you yourself who
3. I will bless you, LORD, you give me counsel, and even at night di -
4. And so my heart rejoices, my soul is glad; even my body shall
5. You will show me the path of life, the fullness of joy

1. are my God. [*omit* —————————————————————]
2. are my prize. The lot marked out for me is my de - light,
3. rect my heart. I keep you, LORD, ever in my sight;
4. rest in safety. For you will not leave my soul a - mong the dead,
5. in your presence, [*omit* —————————————————————]

1. My happiness lies in you a - lone.
2. welcome indeed the heri - tage that falls to me!
3. since you are at my right hand, I shall stand firm.
4. nor let your beloved know de - cay.
5. at your right hand happi - ness for ever.

Save Me, O Lord

Antiphon / Melody ♩ = 72-76

Save me, O Lord; you are my rock. Lead me, O Lord; let me see you.

Descant Save me,

Verses *Psalm 31:2-4, 17, 25*

Descant:

You are my rock.

Cantor / Choir:

All:

1. In you, O Lord, I take refuge. Let me never be put to shame.
2. Be a rock of refuge for me, a mighty strong-hold to save me, You are my rock.
3. Let your face shine on your servant. Save me in your love.

Cantor / Choir:

1. In your justice set me free, hear me and speed - i - ly rescue me.
2. for you are my rock, my stronghold. For your name's sake, lead me and guide me.
3. Be strong, let your heart take courage, all who hope in the Lord.

Descant:

Lead me, O Lord; let me see you.

All:

Lead me, O Lord; let me see you.

Save Us, Lord (I)

199

Verses (Superimposed)   *Psalm 28*

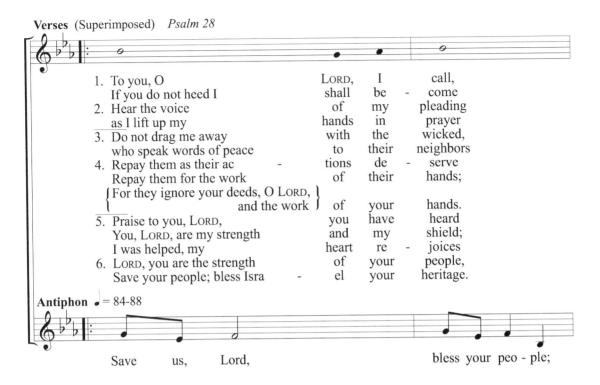

1. To you, O LORD, I call,
   If you do not heed I shall be - come
2. Hear the voice of my pleading
   as I lift up my hands in prayer
3. Do not drag me away with the wicked,
   who speak words of peace to their neighbors
4. Repay them as their ac - tions de - serve
   Repay them for the work of their hands;
   { For they ignore your deeds, O LORD,
   { and the work } of your hands.
5. Praise to you, LORD, you have heard
   You, LORD, are my strength and my shield;
   I was helped, my heart re - joices
6. LORD, you are the strength of your people,
   Save your people; bless Isra - el your heritage.

Antiphon ♩ = 84-88

Save   us,   Lord,   bless your peo - ple;

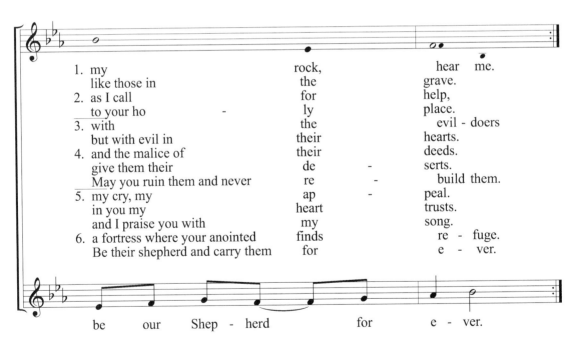

1. my rock, hear me.
   like those in the grave.
2. as I call for help,
   to your ho - ly place.
3. with the evil - doers
   but with evil in their hearts.
4. and the malice of their deeds.
   give them their de - serts.
   May you ruin them and never re - build them.
5. my cry, my ap - peal.
   in you my heart trusts.
   and I praise you with my song.
6. a fortress where your anointed finds re - fuge.
   Be their shepherd and carry them for e - ver.

be   our   Shep - herd   for   e - ver.

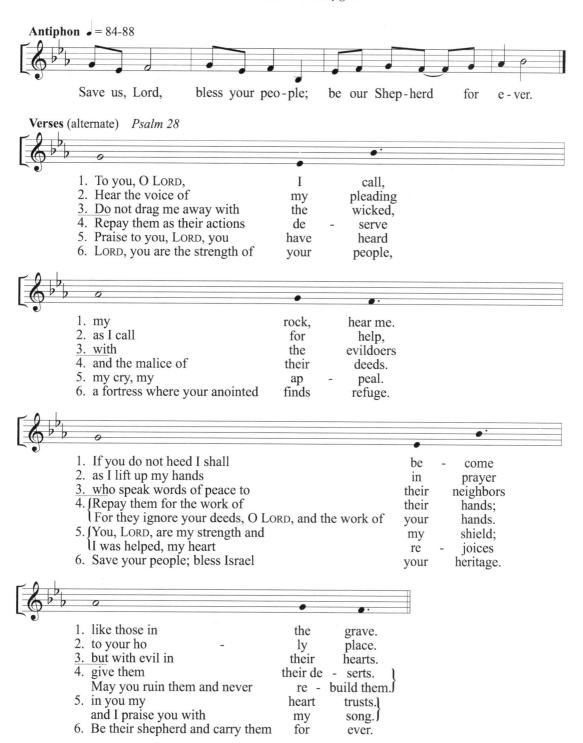

Antiphon ♩ = 84-88

Save us, Lord, bless your peo-ple; be our Shep-herd for e - ver.

Verses (alternate) *Psalm 28*

1. To you, O Lord, I call,
2. Hear the voice of my pleading
3. Do not drag me away with the wicked,
4. Repay them as their actions de - serve
5. Praise to you, Lord, you have heard
6. Lord, you are the strength of your people,

1. my rock, hear me.
2. as I call for help,
3. with the evildoers
4. and the malice of their deeds.
5. my cry, my ap - peal.
6. a fortress where your anointed finds refuge.

1. If you do not heed I shall be - come
2. as I lift up my hands in prayer
3. who speak words of peace to their neighbors
4. ⎰Repay them for the work of their hands;
   ⎱For they ignore your deeds, O Lord, and the work of your hands.
5. ⎰You, Lord, are my strength and my shield;
   ⎱I was helped, my heart re - joices
6. Save your people; bless Israel your heritage.

1. like those in the grave.
2. to your ho - ly place.
3. but with evil in their hearts.
4. give them their de - serts. ⎱
   May you ruin them and never re - build them.⎰
5. in you my heart trusts.⎱
   and I praise you with my song.⎰
6. Be their shepherd and carry them for ever.

Performance Notes

Either the superimposed verses or the separate verses on page 2 may be used.

200 Save Us, Lord (II)

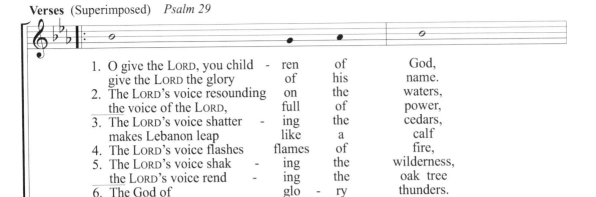

Verses (Superimposed) *Psalm 29*

1. O give the LORD, you child - ren of God,
   give the LORD the glory of his name.
2. The LORD's voice resounding on the waters,
   the voice of the LORD, full of power,
3. The LORD's voice shatter - ing the cedars,
   makes Lebanon leap like a calf
4. The LORD's voice flashes flames of fire,
5. The LORD's voice shak - ing the wilderness,
   the LORD's voice rend - ing the oak tree
6. The God of glo - ry thunders.
   The LORD sat enthroned o - ver the flood;
7. The LORD will give strength to his people,

Antiphon ♩ = 84-88

Save us, Lord, bless your peo - ple;

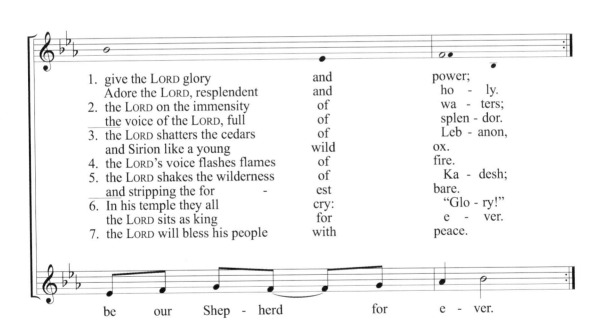

1. give the LORD glory and power;
   Adore the LORD, resplendent and ho - ly.
2. the LORD on the immensity of wa - ters;
   the voice of the LORD, full of splen - dor.
3. the LORD shatters the cedars of Leb - anon,
   and Sirion like a young wild ox.
4. the LORD's voice flashes flames of fire.
5. the LORD shakes the wilderness of Ka - desh;
   and stripping the for - est bare.
6. In his temple they all cry: "Glo - ry!"
   the LORD sits as king for e - ver.
7. the LORD will bless his people with peace.

be our Shep - herd for e - ver.

Antiphon ♩ = 84-88

Save us, Lord, bless your peo-ple; be our Shep-herd for e - ver.

Verses (alternate)   *Psalm 29*

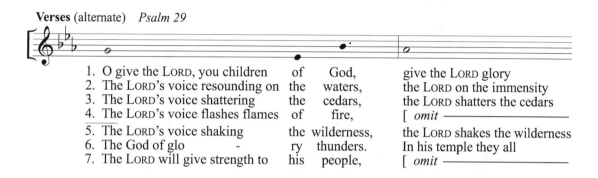

1. O give the LORD, you children of God, give the LORD glory
2. The LORD's voice resounding on the waters, the LORD on the immensity
3. The LORD's voice shattering the cedars, the LORD shatters the cedars
4. The LORD's voice flashes flames of fire, [*omit* ————————
5. The LORD's voice shaking the wilderness, the LORD shakes the wilderness
6. The God of glo - ry thunders. In his temple they all
7. The LORD will give strength to his people, [*omit* ————————

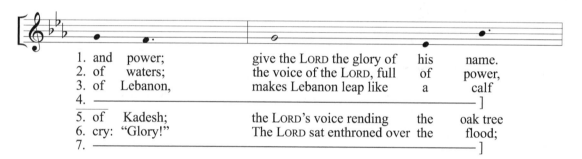

1. and power; give the LORD the glory of his name.
2. of waters; the voice of the LORD, full of power,
3. of Lebanon, makes Lebanon leap like a calf
4. ————————————————————————]
5. of Kadesh; the LORD's voice rending the oak tree
6. cry: "Glory!" The LORD sat enthroned over the flood;
7. ————————————————————————]

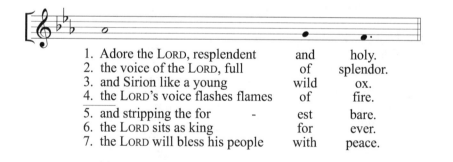

1. Adore the LORD, resplendent and holy.
2. the voice of the LORD, full of splendor.
3. and Sirion like a young wild ox.
4. the LORD's voice flashes flames of fire.
5. and stripping the for - est bare.
6. the LORD sits as king for ever.
7. the LORD will bless his people with peace.

Performance Notes
Either the superimposed verses or the separate verses on page 2 may be used.

201　Save Us, Lord (III)

Verses (Superimposed)　*Psalm 107:2-9, 19-22, 35-38, 41-42*

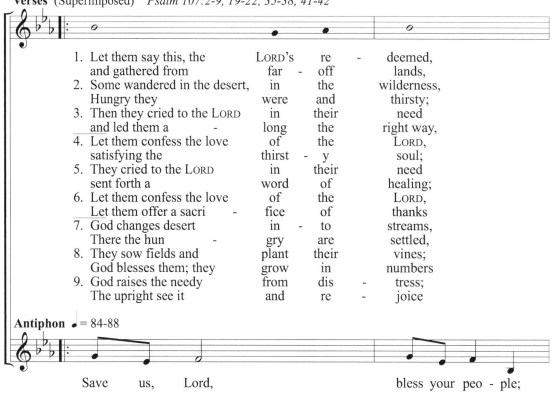

1. Let them say this, the LORD's re - deemed,
   and gathered from far - off lands,
2. Some wandered in the desert, in the wilderness,
   Hungry they were and thirsty;
3. Then they cried to the LORD in their need
   and led them a - long the right way,
4. Let them confess the love of the LORD,
   satisfying the thirst - y soul;
5. They cried to the LORD in their need
   sent forth a word of healing;
6. Let them confess the love of the LORD,
   Let them offer a sacri - fice of thanks
7. God changes desert in - to streams,
   There the hun - gry are settled,
8. They sow fields and plant their vines;
   God blesses them; they grow in numbers
9. God raises the needy from dis - tress;
   The upright see it and re - joice

Antiphon　♩ = 84-88

Save　us,　Lord,　　　　bless your peo - ple;

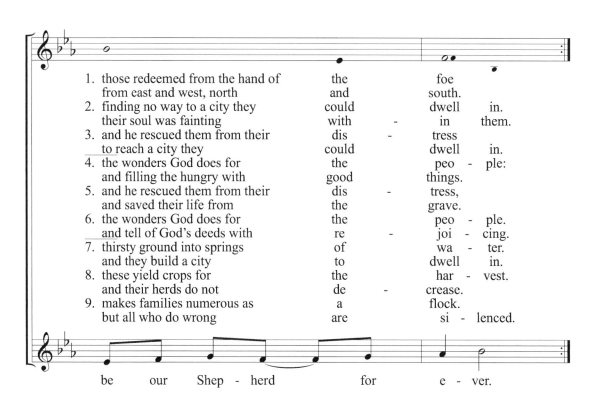

1. those redeemed from the hand of the foe
   from east and west, north and south.
2. finding no way to a city they could dwell in.
   their soul was fainting with - in them.
3. and he rescued them from their dis - tress
   to reach a city they could dwell in.
4. the wonders God does for the peo - ple:
   and filling the hungry with good things.
5. and he rescued them from their dis - tress,
   and saved their life from the grave.
6. the wonders God does for the peo - ple.
   and tell of God's deeds with re - joi - cing.
7. thirsty ground into springs of wa - ter.
   and they build a city to dwell in.
8. these yield crops for the har - vest
   and their herds do not de - crease.
9. makes families numerous as a flock.
   but all who do wrong are si - lenced.

be　our　Shep - herd　　for　e - ver.

Antiphon ♩ = 84-88

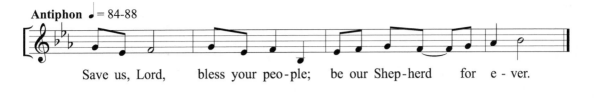

Save us, Lord, bless your peo-ple; be our Shep-herd for e - ver.

Verses (alternate) *Psalm 107:2-9, 19-22, 35-38, 41-42*

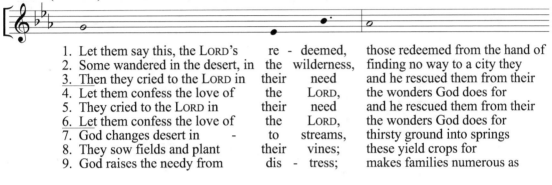

1. Let them say this, the LORD's re - deemed, those redeemed from the hand of
2. Some wandered in the desert, in the wilderness, finding no way to a city they
3. Then they cried to the LORD in their need and he rescued them from their
4. Let them confess the love of the LORD, the wonders God does for
5. They cried to the LORD in their need and he rescued them from their
6. Let them confess the love of the LORD, the wonders God does for
7. God changes desert in - to streams, thirsty ground into springs
8. They sow fields and plant their vines; these yield crops for
9. God raises the needy from dis - tress; makes families numerous as

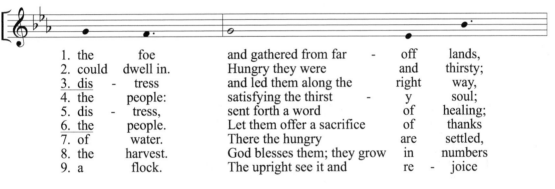

1. the foe and gathered from far - off lands,
2. could dwell in. Hungry they were and thirsty;
3. dis - tress and led them along the right way,
4. the people: satisfying the thirst - y soul;
5. dis - tress, sent forth a word of healing;
6. the people. Let them offer a sacrifice of thanks
7. of water. There the hungry are settled,
8. the harvest. God blesses them; they grow in numbers
9. a flock. The upright see it and re - joice

1. from east and west, north and south.
2. their soul was fainting with - in them.
3. to reach a city they could dwell in.
4. and filling the hungry with good things.
5. and saved their life from the grave.
6. and tell of God's deeds with re - joicing.
7. and they build a city to dwell in.
8. and their herds do not de - crease.
9. but all who do wrong are silenced.

Performance Notes

Either the superimposed verses or the separate verses on page 2 may be used.

Seek the Lord! Long for the Lord!

Antiphon ♩ = 69

Seek the Lord! Long for the Lord!

Search for the face of God!

Verses *Psalm 105:1-5, 8-10, 42, 45*

Cantor: All:

1. Give thanks and acclaim God's name al - ways,
2. O sing to the LORD, sing praise al - ways;
3. Be proud of God's holy name al - ways,
4. Consider the LORD, who is strong al - ways;
5. Remember the wonders of the LORD al - ways,
6. God remembers the covenant for e - ver al - ways,
7. God remembers the covenant made with Abra - ham al - ways,
8. God confirmed it for Jacob as a law al - ways,
9. God remembered the holy pro - mise al - ways,
10. Thus the people might keep God's pre - cepts al - ways,

Cantor: All:

1. make known God's deeds among the peo - ples al - ways.
2. tell all his wonderful works al - ways.
3. let the hearts that seek the LORD re - joice al - ways.
4. constantly seek his face al - ways.
5. the miracles and judgements pro - nounced al - ways.
6. the promise for a thousand genera - tions al - ways.
7. the oath that was sworn to Is - aac al - ways.
8. for Israel as a covenant for e - ver al - ways.
9. which was given to Abraham, his ser - vant, al - ways.
10. thus they might observe God's laws al - ways.

Send Out Your Spirit

Antiphon ♩ = 132

Send out your Spi-rit o-ver the wa-ters: you will re-new the face of the earth.

Verses *Psalm 104:1-2a, 5-6, 10, 12, 13-14, 24, 35c*

1. Bless the LORD,   my   soul!   LORD God, how   great   you   are,
2. You founded the earth on   its   base,   to stand firm from   age   to   age.
3. You make springs gush forth in the   valleys;   they flow in be -   tween   the   hills.
4. From your dwelling you water   the   hills;   earth drinks its fill   of   your   gift.
5. How many are your works,   O   LORD!   In wisdom you have   made   them   all.

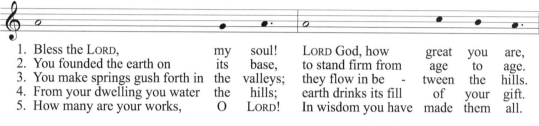

1. clothed in majesty   and   glory,   wrapped in light as in   a   robe!
2. You wrapped it with the ocean like a   cloak: the waters stood higher than the mountains.
3. On their banks dwell the birds   of   heaven; from the branches they sing their   song.
4. You make the grass grow for   the   cattle   and the plants to serve   our   needs.
5. The earth is full of   your riches. Bless the LORD,   my   soul.

Performance Notes

Percussion or handclaps may be added, as indicated by X's, both during the antiphon and at the end of the psalm verses to lead back into the antiphon.
The antiphon should be repeated every time it is sung.
The entire piece may be transposed down a whole step.

Set the Earth on Fire

Antiphon ♩ = 66-69

Set the earth on fire, burn with-in our hearts, with our eyes on you,

set the earth on fire.

Verses *Psalm 130:1-6b, 7b-8*

1. Out of the depths I cry to you, O LORD, LORD, hear my voice!
2. If you, O LORD, should mark our guilt, LORD, who would sur - vive?
3. My soul is waiting for the LORD, I count on God's word.
4. Because with the LORD there is mercy and fullness of re - demption,

1. O let your ears be at - tentive to the voice of my pleading.
2. But with you is found for - giveness: for this we re - vere you.
3. My soul is longing for the LORD more than those who watch for daybreak.
4. Israel in - deed God will re - deem from all its in - iquity.

Performance Notes

The antiphon may be sung as a round, as indicated.

Shine Out, O Lord; You Are My God

Antiphon / Melody ♩ = 72-76

Shine out, O Lord; you are my God. Save me, O Lord; let me see you.

Descant

Shine out, you are my God. Save me, O Lord; let me see you.

Verses *Psalm 31:2-19*

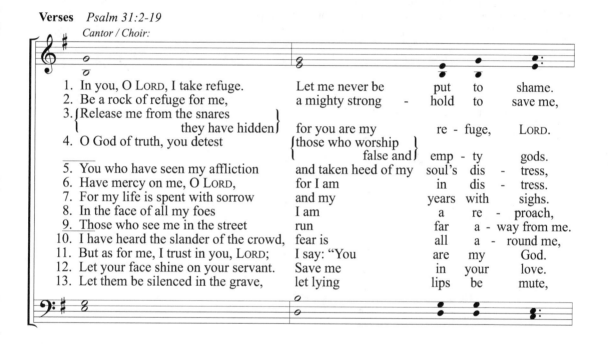

Cantor / Choir:

1. In you, O LORD, I take refuge.   Let me never be   put   to   shame.
2. Be a rock of refuge for me,   a mighty strong - hold   to   save me,
3. {Release me from the snares   they have hidden}   for you are my   re - fuge,   LORD.
4. O God of truth, you detest   {those who worship   false and}   emp - ty   gods.
5. You who have seen my affliction   and taken heed of my   soul's   dis - tress,
6. Have mercy on me, O LORD,   for I am   in   dis - tress.
7. For my life is spent with sorrow   and my   years   with   sighs.
8. In the face of all my foes   I am   a   re - proach,
9. Those who see me in the street   run   far   a - way from me.
10. I have heard the slander of the crowd,   fear is   all   a - round me,
11. But as for me, I trust in you, LORD;   I say: "You   are   my   God.
12. Let your face shine on your servant.   Save me   in   your   love.
13. Let them be silenced in the grave,   let lying   lips   be   mute,

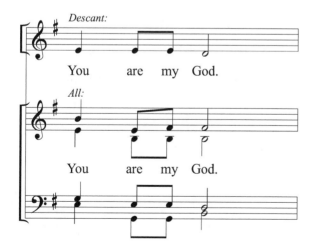

Descant:

You are my God.

All:

You are my God.

Cantor / Choir:

1. In your justice set me free, hear me and speed - i - ly rescue me.
2. for you are my rock, my stronghold. For your name's sake, lead me and guide me.
3. Into your hands I commend my spirit. It is you who will re - deem me, LORD.
4. As for me, I trust in the LORD; let me be glad and rejoice in your love.
5. have not handed me over to the enemy, but set my feet at large.
6. Tears have wasted my eyes, my throat and my heart.
7. Affliction has broken down my strength and my bones waste a - way.
8. an object of scorn to my neighbors and of fear to my friends.
9. I am like the dead, forgotten by all, like a thing thrown a - way.
10. as they plot together against me, as they plan to take my life.
11. My life is in your hands, deliver me from the hands of those who hate me.
12. Let me not be put to shame for I call you, let the wick - ed be shamed!
13. that speak haughtily against the just with pride and con - tempt."

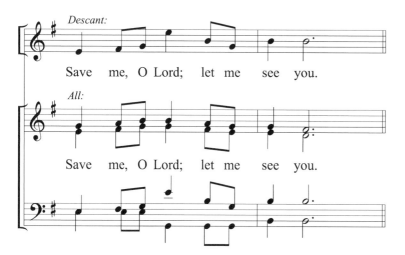

Descant:

Save me, O Lord; let me see you.

All:

Save me, O Lord; let me see you.

Performance Notes

The descant is for use only when SATB choir is not available.

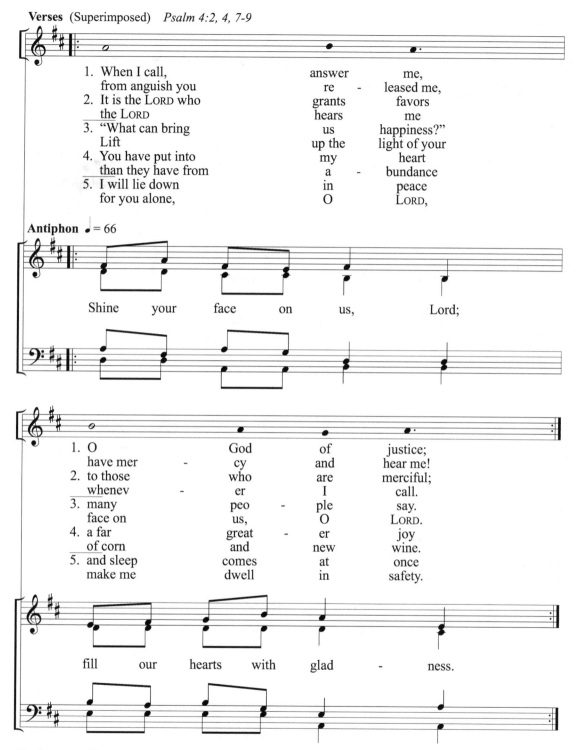

Verses (Superimposed) *Psalm 4:2, 4, 7-9*

1. When I call, answer me,
   from anguish you re - leased me,
2. It is the LORD who grants favors
   the LORD hears me
3. "What can bring us happiness?"
   Lift up the light of your
4. You have put into my heart
   than they have from a - bundance
5. I will lie down in peace
   for you alone, O LORD,

Antiphon ♩ = 66

Shine your face on us, Lord;

1. O God of justice;
   have mer - cy and hear me!
2. to those who are merciful;
   whenev - er I call.
3. many peo - ple say.
   face on us, O LORD.
4. a far great - er joy
   of corn and new wine.
5. and sleep comes at once
   make me dwell in safety.

fill our hearts with glad - ness.

Performance Notes

The psalm tone may be superimposed on an ostinato antiphon as shown; or tone and antiphon may be used separately, in which case the antiphon should be sung twice after each verse.

Shout to the Ends of the Earth

Antiphon ♩. = 69

Shout to the ends of the earth, al-le-lu - ia, al-le-lu - ia, the

Alto Descant

Shout to the ends of the earth, al - le-lu-ia, al-le-lu-ia, the

peo-ple re-deemed by the Lord, al-le-lu - ia, al-le-lu - ia.

peo-ple re - deemed by the Lord, al - le-lu - ia.

Verses 1–9 (*Option A) *Psalm 66:1-12, 16-20*

Cantor:

All:

1. Cry out with joy to God, all the earth.
2. Say to God: "How tremendous your deeds!
3. Before you all the earth shall bow,
4. Come and see the works of God,
5. God turned the sea into dry land,
6. Let our joy then be in the LORD,
7. The LORD's eyes keep watch over nations;
8. O peoples, bless our God,
9. Praise God who gave life to our souls

Al - le - lu - ia!

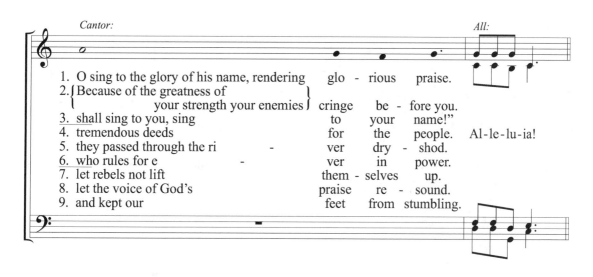

1. O sing to the glory of his name, rendering glo - rious praise.
2. ⎰ Because of the greatness of
   ⎱   your strength your enemies ⎰ cringe be - fore you.
3. shall sing to you, sing to your name!"
4. tremendous deeds for the people. Al-le-lu-ia!
5. they passed through the ri - ver dry - shod.
6. who rules for e - ver in power.
7. let rebels not lift them - selves up.
8. let the voice of God's praise re - sound.
9. and kept our feet from stumbling.

Verses 10–19 (*Option A)

10. For you, our God, have tested us, you have tried us as sil -
11. you led us, God, into the snare; you laid a heavy burden
12. You let foes ride over our heads; we went through fire
13. but then you brought us, you brought
14. Come and hear, all who fear God, Al-le-lu-ia! I will tell what God did
15. to God I cried a - loud, with high praise ready
16. If there had been evil in my heart, the LORD would
17. But truly God has listened; has heeded the voice
18. Blessed be God who has not re -
19. Blessed be God who has not withheld his

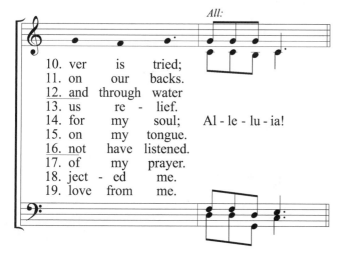

10. ver is tried;
11. on our backs.
12. and through water
13. us re - lief.
14. for my soul; Al - le - lu - ia!
15. on my tongue.
16. not have listened.
17. of my prayer.
18. ject - ed me.
19. love from me.

Verses (*Option B) *Psalm 98*

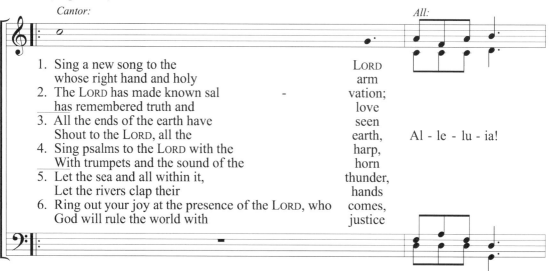

Cantor:

All:

1. Sing a new song to the LORD
   whose right hand and holy arm
2. The LORD has made known sal - vation;
   has remembered truth and love
3. All the ends of the earth have seen
   Shout to the LORD, all the earth,   Al - le - lu - ia!
4. Sing psalms to the LORD with the harp,
   With trumpets and the sound of the horn
5. Let the sea and all within it, thunder,
   Let the rivers clap their hands
6. Ring out your joy at the presence of the LORD, who comes,
   God will rule the world with justice

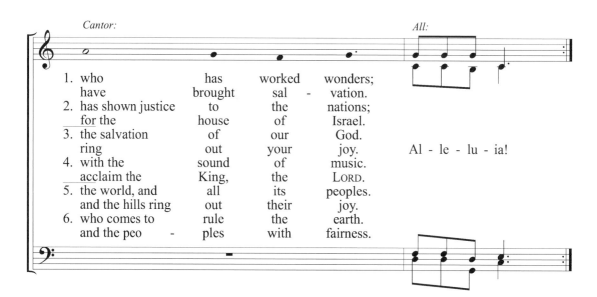

Cantor:

All:

1. who   has   worked   wonders;
   have   brought   sal -   vation.
2. has shown justice to   the   nations;
   for the   house   of   Israel.
3. the salvation of   our   God.
   ring   out   your   joy.   Al - le - lu - ia!
4. with the   sound   of   music.
   acclaim the King,   the   LORD.
5. the world, and all   its   peoples.
   and the hills ring out   their joy.
6. who comes to rule   the   earth.
   and the peo - ples   with   fairness.

Performance Notes

Option A verses are used on the Sixth Sunday of Easter, Years B and C, and the Seventh Sunday of Easter, Years A, B, and C. Option B verses are used on the Sixth Sunday of Easter, Year A.

Show Us, Lord, Your Kindness

Verses (Superimposed)   *Psalm 85:9-14*

1. I will hear what the LORD has   to   say,
   peace for his people and   his   friends
2. Salvation is near for   the   God-fearing,
3. Mercy and faithfulness   have   met;
   Faithfulness shall spring from   the   earth
4. The LORD will make   us   prosper
   Justice shall march in   the   forefront,

Antiphon ♩ = 66

Show   us,   Lord,   your   kind - ness,

1. a voice that   speaks   of   peace,
   and those who turn to God   in   their   hearts.
2. and his glory will dwell   in   our   land.
3. justice and peace   have   em - braced.
   and justice look   down   from   heaven.
4. and our earth shall   yield   its   fruit.
   and peace shall fol - low   the   way.

grant   us   your   sal - va - tion.

Performance Notes

The psalm tone may be superimposed on an ostinato antiphon as shown; or tone and antiphon may be used separately, in which case the antiphon should be sung twice after each verse.

Sing and Make Music

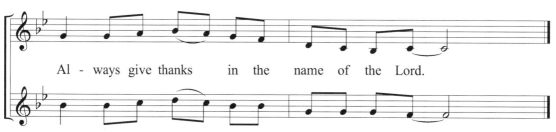

Antiphon / Melody ♩ = 120

Sing and make mu - sic to God in your hearts.

Descant

Al - ways give thanks in the name of the Lord.

Verses *Psalm 147*

1. Alleluia, allelu - ia!
2. Sing to our God who is loving:
3. The LORD builds up Je - rusalem
4. God heals the broken - hearted,
5. God fixes the number of the stars;
6. Our LORD is great and al - mighty;
7. The LORD raises the lowly;
8. O sing to the LORD, giving thanks;
9. God covers the heavens with clouds,

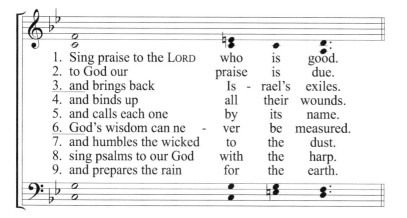

1. Sing praise to the LORD who is good.
2. to God our praise is due.
3. and brings back Is - rael's exiles.
4. and binds up all their wounds.
5. and calls each one by its name.
6. God's wisdom can ne - ver be measured.
7. and humbles the wicked to the dust.
8. sing psalms to our God with the harp.
9. and prepares the rain for the earth.

Verses (continued)

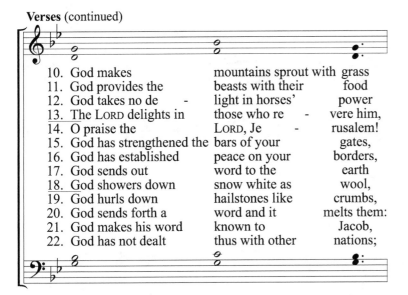

10. God makes	mountains sprout with	grass
11. God provides the	beasts with their	food
12. God takes no de -	light in horses'	power
13. The Lord delights in	those who re -	vere him,
14. O praise the	Lord, Je -	rusalem!
15. God has strengthened the	bars of your	gates,
16. God has established	peace on your	borders,
17. God sends out	word to the	earth
18. God showers down	snow white as	wool,
19. God hurls down	hailstones like	crumbs,
20. God sends forth a	word and it	melts them:
21. God makes his word	known to	Jacob,
22. God has not dealt	thus with other	nations;

10. and with plants to	serve	our needs.
11. and the young ravens	when	they cry.
12. nor pleasure in	war -	riors' strength.
13. in those who wait	for	his love.
14. Zion,	praise	your God!
15. and has blessed the child -	ren	with - in you.
16. and feeds you with	fin -	est wheat.
17. and swiftly runs	the	com - mand.
18. and scatters hoar -	frost	like ashes.
19. and causes the wa -	ters	to freeze.
20. at the breath of God's mouth the	wa -	ters flow.
21. to Israel his laws	and	de - crees.
22. has not taught them divine decrees. Al -	le -	luia!

Sing to God a New Song

Antiphon ♩ = 100

A new song, a new song, sing to God a new song! What

won - der, what pow - er! Sing al - le - lu - ia!

Verses *Psalm 98*

Cantor:

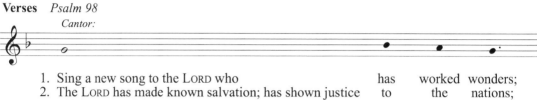

1. Sing a new song to the Lord who   has   worked wonders;
2. The Lord has made known salvation; has shown justice   to   the   nations;
3. All the ends of the earth have seen the salvation   of   our   God.
4. Sing psalms to the Lord with the harp, with the   sound   of   music.
5. Let the sea and all within it thunder; the world, and   all   its   peoples.
6. at the presence of the Lord who comes, who comes to   rule   the   earth.

All: *Cantor:*

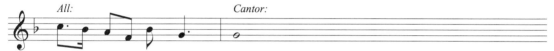

Sing to God a new song!
1. whose right hand and holy arm have
2. has remembered truth and love for the
3. Shout to the Lord, all the earth, ring
4. With trumpets and the sound of the horn acclaim the
5. Let the rivers clap their hands and the hills ring
6. God will rule the world with justice and the

                            All:

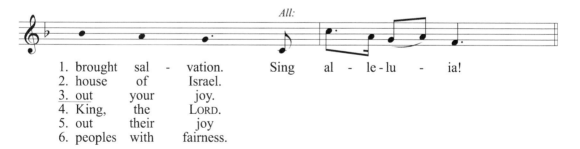

1. brought sal - vation.   Sing al - le - lu - ia!
2. house of Israel.
3. out your joy.
4. King, the Lord.
5. out their joy
6. peoples with fairness.

Performance Notes

Verses 1–3 are the Lectionary selections for the Immaculate Conception.

Sing to the Lord

Antiphon / Melody ♩. = 58

Sing to the Lord, sing to the Lord,

Descant

Sing to the Lord, sing to the

co - vered in glo - ry: O sing to the Lord.

Lord, O sing to the Lord.

Verses *Exodus 15:1-6, 17-18*

1. I will sing to the LORD, glo - rious his triumph!
2. The LORD is a warrior! The LORD is his name.
3. Your right hand, LORD, glorious in its power,
4. You will lead your people and plant them on your mountain,

1. Horse and rider he has thrown in - to the sea!
2. The chariots of Pharaoh he hurled in - to the sea,
3. your right hand, LORD, has shat - tered the enemy.
4. the place, O LORD, where you have made your home,

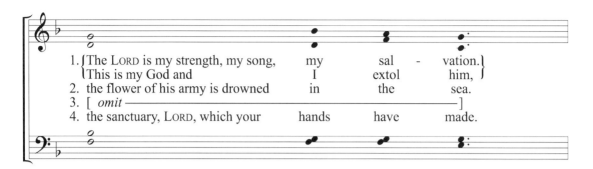

1. {The LORD is my strength, my song, my sal - vation.}
{This is my God and I extol him,}
2. the flower of his army is drowned in the sea.
3. [omit —————————————————————]
4. the sanctuary, LORD, which your hands have made.

1. my father's God and I give him praise.
2. The deeps hide them; they sank like a stone.
3. In the greatness of your glory you crushed the foe.
4. The LORD will reign for e - ver and ever.

Speak Your Word, O Lord

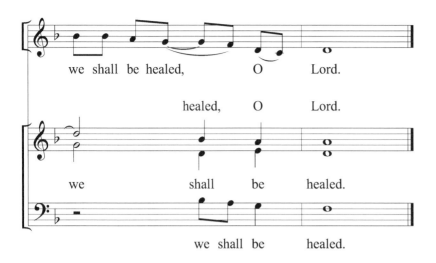

we shall be healed,   O   Lord.

healed,   O   Lord.

we   shall   be   healed.

we shall be   healed.

Verses   *Isaiah 55:1, 5, 6-7ac, 10ab, 11ab; 56:6a, 7abd, 8; Psalm 86:1-10*

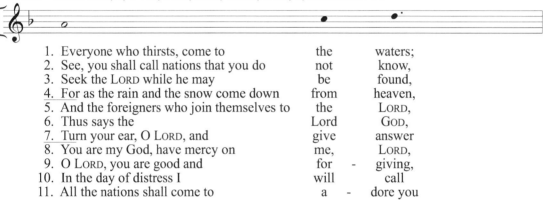

1. Everyone who thirsts, come to the waters;
2. See, you shall call nations that you do not know,
3. Seek the LORD while he may be found,
4. For as the rain and the snow come down from heaven,
5. And the foreigners who join themselves to the LORD,
6. Thus says the Lord GOD,
7. Turn your ear, O LORD, and give answer
8. You are my God, have mercy on me, LORD,
9. O LORD, you are good and for - giving,
10. In the day of distress I will call
11. All the nations shall come to a - dore you

1. and you that have no money, come, buy and eat!
2. and nations that do not know you shall run to you,
3. call upon him while he is near;
4. and do not return there until they have wa - tered the earth,
5. these I will bring to my ho - ly mountain,
6. who gathers the out - casts of Israel,
7. for I am poor and needy.
8. for I cry to you all the day long.
9. full of love to all who call.
10. and surely you will re - ply.
11. and glorify your name, O LORD,

1. Come, buy wine and milk
2. because of the LORD your God, the Holy One of Israel,
3. let the wicked for - sake their way;
4. so shall my word be that goes out from my mouth;
5. and make them joyful in my house of prayer;
6. I will gather o - thers to them
7. Preserve my life, for I am faithful;
8. Give joy to your ser - vant, O LORD,
9. Give heed, O LORD, to my prayer
10. Among the gods there is none like you, O LORD,
11. for you are great and do mar - ve - lous deeds,

1. without money and with - out price.
2. for he has glo - ri - fied you.
3. let them return to the LORD, that he may have mer - cy on them.
4. it shall not return to me empty.
5. for my house shall be called a house of prayer for all peoples.
6. besides those al - rea - dy gathered.
7. save the servant who trusts in you.
8. for to you I lift up my soul.
9. and attend to the sound of my voice.
10. nor work to com - pare with yours.
11. you who a - lone are God.

Performance Notes

Verses 7–11 are used only when necessary for reasons of time.

Take Hold of Eternal Life

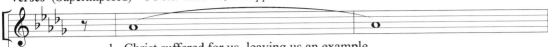

Verses (Superimposed)   *1 Peter 2:21-24; Philippians 2:6-11*

1. Christ suffered for us, leaving us an example,
   so that we should follow in his steps.
2. "He commited no sin, and no deceit was found in his mouth."
3. When he was abused, he did not return abuse;
   when he suffered, he did not threaten.
4. Christ entrusted himself to the one who judges justly.
5. He himself bore our sins in his body on the cross,
   so that, free from sins, we might live for righteousness.
6. By his wounds we have been healed.
7. Though he was in the form of God, Christ Jesus did not regard
   equality with God as something to be exploited.
8. He emptied himself, taking the form of a slave;
   being born in human likeness, he humbled himself.
9. Christ became obedient to the point of death—even death on a cross.
10. Therefore God also highly exalted him
    and gave him the name that is above every name,
11. so that at the name of Jesus every knee should bend,
    in heaven and on earth and under the earth,
12. and every tongue confess that Jesus Christ is Lord,
    to the glory of God the Father.

Antiphon ♪ = 69-72

Take hold of e-ter-nal life, you were called to e-ter-nal life; un-

til the day of Christ take hold of e-ter-nal life.

Performance Notes

The superimposed verses should be sung in free speech rhythm on the monotone indicated during the first half of the antiphon. The voice parts could be vocalized to 'oo' when the verses are being sung, coming back in with the text in the second half of the antiphon.

The metronome marking indicates the solemn tread needed by this piece.

Take Your Place at the Table

Antiphon / Melody ♩. = 54

Take your place at the ta-ble; serve one an-o-ther in

Tenor / Alto Descant

Take your place at the ta - ble;

just - ice; do this and you shall live.

serve each o - ther; do this and you shall live.

Verses *Psalm 112:1-9*

Cantor:

1. Happy are those who fear the LORD, who take delight in all God's com-mands.
2. Their descendants shall be powerful on earth; the children of the up - right are blessed.
3. Wealth and riches are in their homes, their justice stands firm for ever.
4. They are lights in the darkness for the upright; they are generous, merci - ful and just.
5. Good people take pity and lend, they conduct their af - fairs with honor.
6. The just will ne - ver waver, they will be remem - bered for ever.
7. They have no fear of e - vil news; with firm hearts they trust in the LORD.
8. With steadfast hearts they will not fear; they will see the downfall of their foes.
9. O - pen-handed they give to the poor.
10. Their justice stands firm for ever. Their heads will be raised in glory.

All / Melody:

Do this and you shall live.

Descant:

Teach Me Your Path

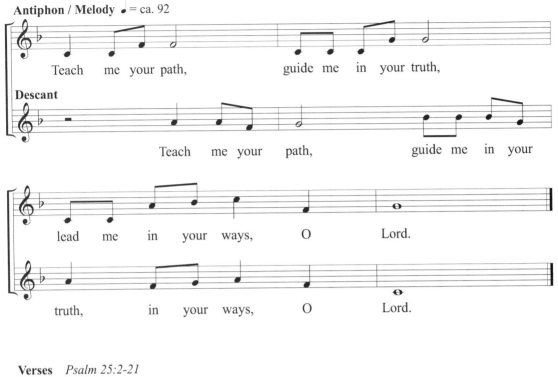

Antiphon / Melody ♩ = ca. 92

Teach me your path, guide me in your truth,

Descant

Teach me your path, guide me in your

lead me in your ways, O Lord.

truth, in your ways, O Lord.

Verses *Psalm 25:2-21*

[A] [B]

1. {My God, I trust in you,
   let me not be disap} - pointed; do not let my enemies triumph.
2. LORD, make me know your ways. LORD, teach me your paths.
3. In you I hope all the day long because of your goodness, O LORD.
4. The LORD is good and upright, showing the path to those who stray,
5. God's ways are steadfastness and truth for those faithful to the covenant de - crees.
6. Those who revere the LORD will be shown the path they should choose.
7. My eyes are always on the LORD, who will rescue my feet from the snare.
8. Relieve the anguish of my heart and set me free from my dis - tress.
9. See how many are my foes, how violent their hatred for me.

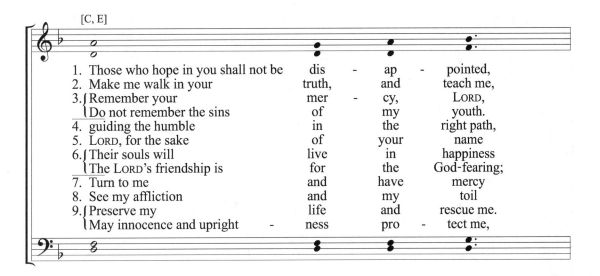

[C, E]

1. Those who hope in you shall not be	dis	- ap -	pointed,
2. Make me walk in your	truth,	and	teach me,
3. { Remember your	mer -	cy,	LORD,
Do not remember the sins	of	my	youth.
4. guiding the humble	in	the	right path,
5. LORD, for the sake	of	your	name
6. { Their souls will	live	in	happiness
The LORD's friendship is	for	the	God-fearing;
7. Turn to me	and	have	mercy
8. See my affliction	and	my	toil
9. { Preserve my	life	and	rescue me.
May innocence and upright -	ness	pro -	tect me,

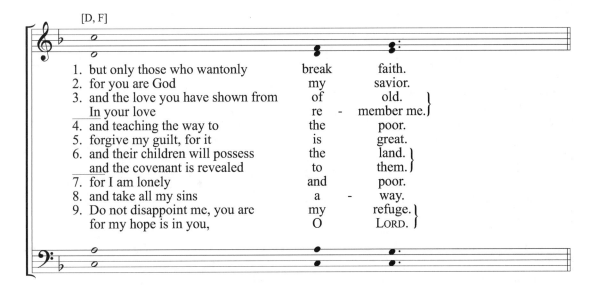

[D, F]

1. but only those who wantonly	break	faith.	
2. for you are God	my	savior.	
3. and the love you have shown from	of	old.	}
In your love	re -	member me.	
4. and teaching the way to	the	poor.	
5. forgive my guilt, for it	is	great.	
6. and their children will possess	the	land.	}
and the covenant is revealed	to	them.	
7. for I am lonely	and	poor.	
8. and take all my sins	a -	way.	
9. Do not disappoint me, you are	my	refuge.	}
for my hope is in you,	O	LORD.	

Performance Notes

Verses 2, 3bcdf, and 4 are the Lectionary selections for the First Sunday of Lent, Year B, and the Third Sunday in Ordinary Time, Year B.

The Days Are Coming, Surely Coming

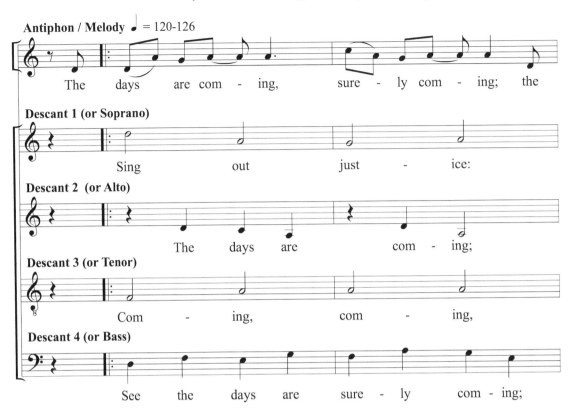

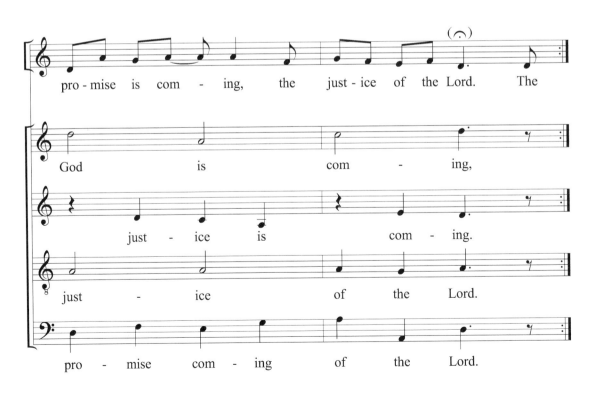

Verses (*Option A)   *Jeremiah 31:10-14*

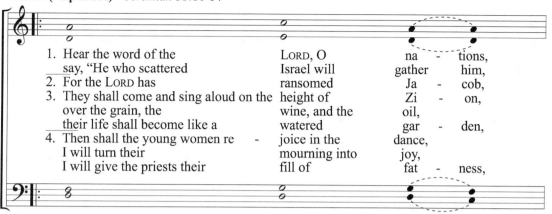

1. Hear the word of the   LORD, O   na - tions,
   ___ say, "He who scattered   Israel will   gather   him,
2. For the LORD has   ransomed   Ja - cob,
3. They shall come and sing aloud on the   height of   Zi - on,
   over the grain, the   wine, and the   oil,
   ___ their life shall become like a   watered   gar - den,
4. Then shall the young women re - joice in the   dance,
   I will turn their   mourning into   joy,
   I will give the priests their   fill of   fat - ness,

1. and declare it in the coastlands   far   a - way;
   ___ and will keep him as a shep -   herd   a   flock."
2. and has redeemed him from   hands   too   strong for him.
3. and they shall be radiant over the goodness   of   the   LORD,
   and over the young of the flock   and   the   herd;
   ___ and they shall never lan -   guish   a - gain.
4. and the young men and the old   shall   be   merry.
   I will comfort them and give them glad -   ness   for   sorrow.
   and my people shall be satisfied with my bounty,   says   the   LORD.

Verses (*Option B)   *Psalm 98:5-9*

1. Sing psalms to the   LORD with the   harp   with the   sound   of   music.
   With trumpets and the   sound of the   horn   acclaim the   King,   the   LORD.
2. Let the sea and all with - in it,   thunder;   the world and   all   its   peoples.
   [Let the rivers clap their]
   [hands and the hills ring]   out their   joy   at the presence   of   the   LORD.
3. The LORD comes,   comes to rule the   earth.   [God will rule the]
   [world with justice]
   and the peo]- ples   with   fairness.

Performance Notes

**Option A* verses are used on the First Sunday of Advent, Year C. Option B verses are used on the Thirty-third Sunday in Ordinary Time, Year C.*
The antiphon is sung twice through each time. The verse tone is repeated as necessary.
The descants may be sung by any voice; the voice indications are only suggestions.

217 The Earth Is Full of the Goodness of God

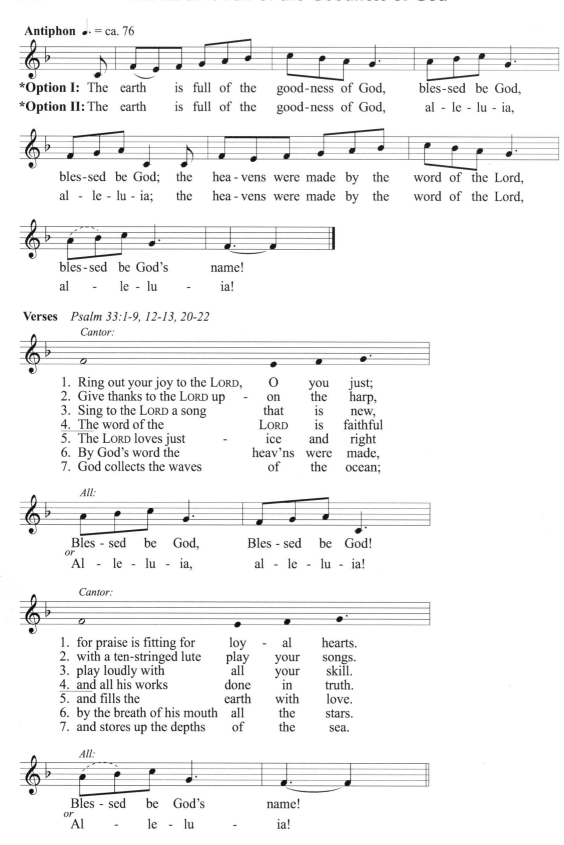

Antiphon ♩. = ca. 76

*Option I: The earth is full of the good-ness of God, bles-sed be God,
*Option II: The earth is full of the good-ness of God, al - le - lu - ia,

bles-sed be God; the hea-vens were made by the word of the Lord,
al - le - lu - ia; the hea-vens were made by the word of the Lord,

bles-sed be God's name!
al - le - lu - ia!

Verses *Psalm 33:1-9, 12-13, 20-22*

Cantor:

1. Ring out your joy to the LORD, O you just;
2. Give thanks to the LORD up - on the harp,
3. Sing to the LORD a song that is new,
4. The word of the LORD is faithful
5. The LORD loves just - ice and right
6. By God's word the heav'ns were made,
7. God collects the waves of the ocean;

All:

Bles - sed be God, Bles - sed be God!
or
Al - le - lu - ia, al - le - lu - ia!

Cantor:

1. for praise is fitting for loy - al hearts.
2. with a ten-stringed lute play your songs.
3. play loudly with all your skill.
4. and all his works done in truth.
5. and fills the earth with love.
6. by the breath of his mouth all the stars.
7. and stores up the depths of the sea.

All:

Bles - sed be God's name!
or
Al - le - lu - ia!

Verses (continued)

Cantor:

8.	Let all the earth	fear	the	LORD,
9.	For God spoke; it	came	to	be.
10.	They are happy whose God	is	the	LORD,
11.	From the heavens the	LORD	looks	forth
12.	Our soul is waiting	for	the	LORD.
13.	Our hearts find joy	in	the	LORD.
14.	May your love be upon	us,	O	LORD,

All:

Bles - sed   be   God,   Bles - sed   be   God!
or
Al - le - lu - ia,   al - le - lu - ia!

Cantor:

8.	all who live in the world	stand	in	awe.
9.	God commanded; it sprang	in - to	being.	
10.	the people who are chosen	as	his	own.
11.	and sees all the peoples	of	the	earth.
12.	The LORD is our help	and	our	shield.
13.	We trust in God's	ho - ly	name.	
14.	as we place all our	hope	in	you.

All:

Bles - sed   be   God's   name!
or
Al - le - lu - ia!

Performance Notes

Option I antiphon is used at the Easter Vigil, Song for the Word: Reading Ib Response; Verses 4–7, 10–12, and 14 are the Lectionary selections for the Easter Vigil.
Option II antiphon is used as the Song for the Week on the Fourth Sunday of Easter, Years A, B, and C.
The antiphon is preferably sung only after every two or three verses.

The Goodness of the Lord

Antiphon ♩ = ca. 88

The good - ness of the Lord: come, taste and see.

Verses   *Psalm 34:2-23*

Cantor / Choir:

1. I will bless the LORD	at	all	times,	God's praise always
2. In the LORD my soul shall	make	its	boast;	the humble shall hear
3. Glorify the	LORD	with	me.	Together let us
4. I sought the LORD	and	was	heard;	from all my ter -
5. Look towards God	and	be	radiant;	let your faces not
6. When the poor cry out	the	LORD hears them		and rescues them from all
7. The angel of the LORD	is	en - camped		around those who fear
8. Taste and see that the	LORD	is	good.	They are happy who seek re -
9. Revere the LORD,	you	his	saints.	They lack nothing, who re -
10. Strong lions suffer want	and	go	hungry	but those who seek the LORD

All:

Come, taste and see.

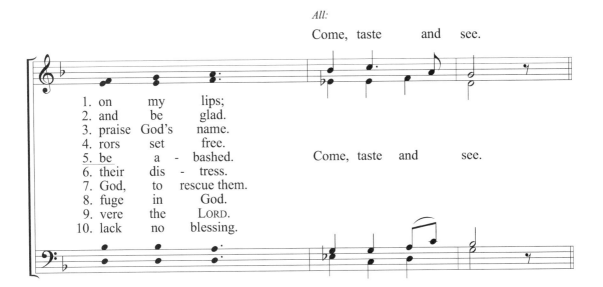

1. on	my	lips;
2. and	be	glad.
3. praise	God's	name.
4. rors	set	free.
5. be	a - bashed.
6. their	dis - tress.
7. God,	to	rescue them.
8. fuge	in	God.
9. vere	the	LORD.
10. lack	no	blessing.

Come, taste and see.

Verses (continued)

Cantor / Choir:

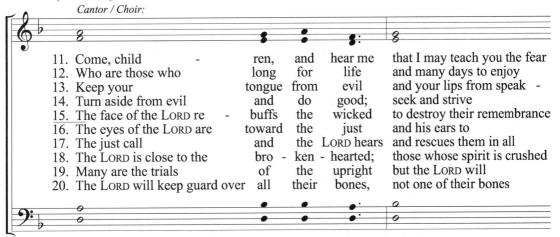

11. Come, child - ren, and hear me   that I may teach you the fear
12. Who are those who   long for life   and many days to enjoy
13. Keep your   tongue from evil   and your lips from speak -
14. Turn aside from evil   and do good;   seek and strive
15. The face of the Lord re - buffs the wicked   to destroy their remembrance
16. The eyes of the Lord are   toward the just   and his ears to
17. The just call   and the Lord hears   and rescues them in all
18. The Lord is close to the   bro - ken - hearted;   those whose spirit is crushed
19. Many are the trials   of the upright   but the Lord will
20. The Lord will keep guard over all   their bones,   not one of their bones

All:

Come, taste and see.

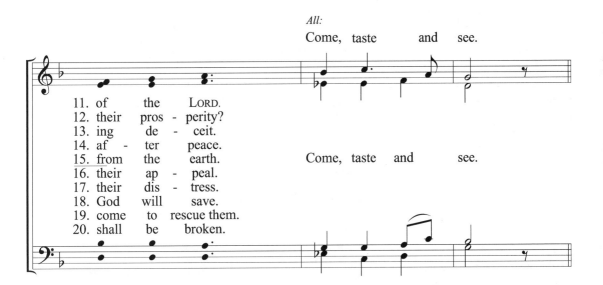

11. of the Lord.
12. their pros - perity?
13. ing de - ceit.
14. af - ter peace.
15. from the earth.   Come, taste and see.
16. their ap - peal.
17. their dis - tress.
18. God will save.
19. come to rescue them.
20. shall be broken.

Performance Notes

Verses 1–8 are the Lectionary selections for the Nineteenth Sunday in Ordinary Time, Year B.
Verses 9–14 are the Lectionary selections for the Twentieth Sunday in Ordinary Time, Year B (NB: the U.S. Lectionary erroneously repeats verses 1–6 on this day).
Verses 1–2 and 15–20 are the Lectionary selections for the Twenty-first Sunday in Ordinary Time, Year B.
Verses 1–6 are the Lectionary selections for the Fourth Sunday of Lent, Year C.

The Greatest Among You

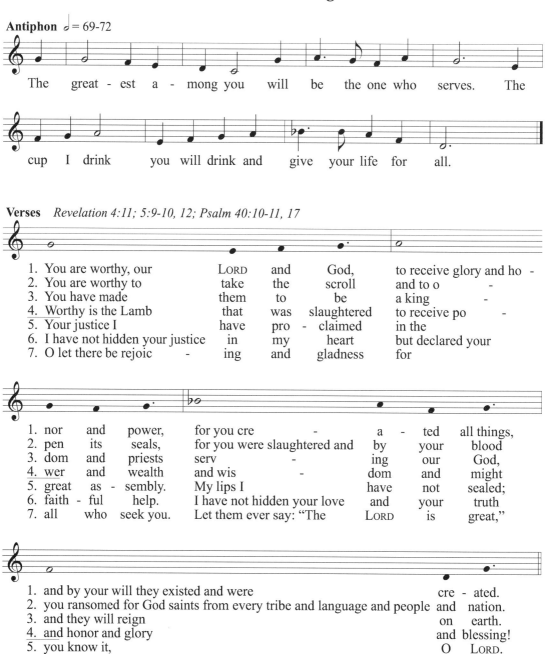

Antiphon ♩ = 69-72

The great-est a - mong you will be the one who serves. The cup I drink you will drink and give your life for all.

Verses *Revelation 4:11; 5:9-10, 12; Psalm 40:10-11, 17*

1. You are worthy, our LORD and God, to receive glory and ho -
2. You are worthy to take the scroll and to o -
3. You have made them to be a king -
4. Worthy is the Lamb that was slaughtered to receive po -
5. Your justice I have pro - claimed in the
6. I have not hidden your justice in my heart but declared your
7. O let there be rejoic - ing and gladness for

1. nor and power, for you cre - a - ted all things,
2. pen its seals, for you were slaughtered and by your blood
3. dom and priests serv - ing our God,
4. wer and wealth and wis - dom and might
5. great as - sembly. My lips I have not sealed;
6. faith - ful help. I have not hidden your love and your truth
7. all who seek you. Let them ever say: "The LORD is great,"

1. and by your will they existed and were cre - ated.
2. you ransomed for God saints from every tribe and language and people and nation.
3. and they will reign on earth.
4. and honor and glory and blessing!
5. you know it, O LORD.
6. from the great as - sembly.
7. who love your sav - ing help.

Verses *Ephesians 4:25-27, 29–5:2, 8-17, 18b-20; Philippians 2:1-5*

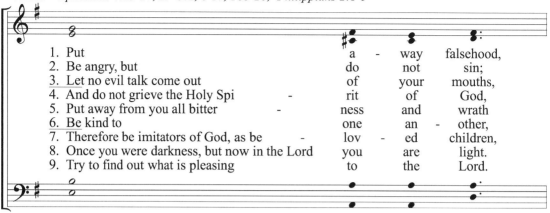

1. Put a - way falsehood,
2. Be angry, but do not sin;
3. Let no evil talk come out of your mouths,
4. And do not grieve the Holy Spi - rit of God,
5. Put away from you all bitter - ness and wrath
6. Be kind to one an - other,
7. Therefore be imitators of God, as be - lov - ed children,
8. Once you were darkness, but now in the Lord you are light.
9. Try to find out what is pleasing to the Lord.

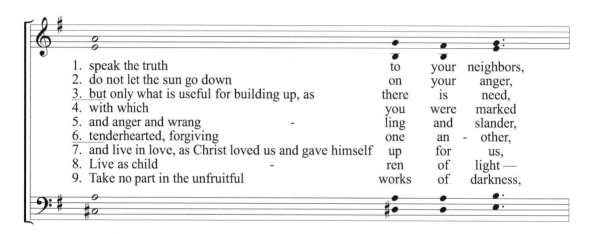

1. speak the truth to your neighbors,
2. do not let the sun go down on your anger,
3. but only what is useful for building up, as there is need,
4. with which you were marked
5. and anger and wrang - ling and slander,
6. tenderhearted, forgiving one an - other,
7. and live in love, as Christ loved us and gave himself up for us,
8. Live as child - ren of light —
9. Take no part in the unfruitful works of darkness,

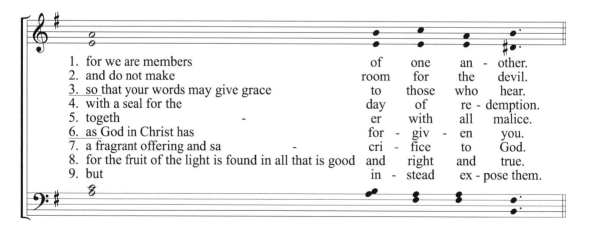

1. for we are members of one an - other.
2. and do not make room for the devil.
3. so that your words may give grace to those who hear.
4. with a seal for the day of re - demption.
5. togeth - er with all malice.
6. as God in Christ has for - giv - en you.
7. a fragrant offering and sa - cri - fice to God.
8. for the fruit of the light is found in all that is good and right and true.
9. but in - stead ex - pose them.

Verses (continued)

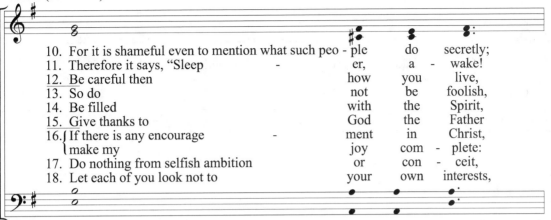

10. For it is shameful even to mention what such peo - ple do secretly;
11. Therefore it says, "Sleep - er, a - wake!
12. Be careful then how you live,
13. So do not be foolish,
14. Be filled with the Spirit,
15. Give thanks to God the Father
16. { If there is any encourage - ment in Christ,
    { make my joy com - plete:
17. Do nothing from selfish ambition or con - ceit,
18. Let each of you look not to your own interests,

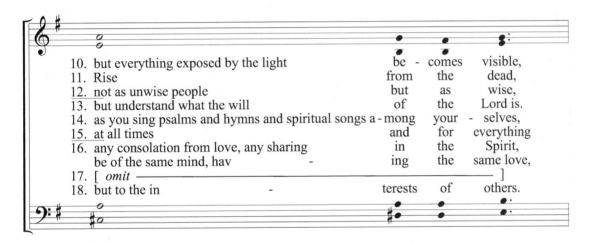

10. but everything exposed by the light be - comes visible,
11. Rise from the dead,
12. not as unwise people but as wise,
13. but understand what the will of the Lord is.
14. as you sing psalms and hymns and spiritual songs a - mong your - selves,
15. at all times and for everything
16. any consolation from love, any sharing in the Spirit,
    be of the same mind, hav - ing the same love,
17. [*omit*]
18. but to the in - terests of others.

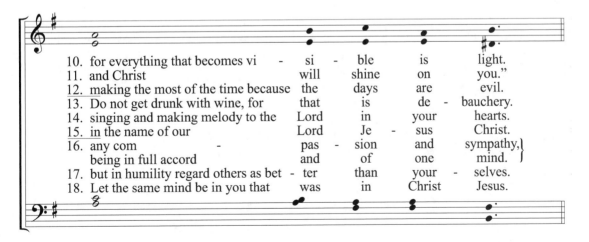

10. for everything that becomes vi - si - ble is light.
11. and Christ will shine on you."
12. making the most of the time because the days are evil.
13. Do not get drunk with wine, for that is de - bauchery.
14. singing and making melody to the Lord in your hearts.
15. in the name of our Lord Je - sus Christ.
16. any com - pas - sion and sympathy, }
    being in full accord and of one mind. }
17. but in humility regard others as bet - ter than your - selves.
18. Let the same mind be in you that was in Christ Jesus.

The Lord Is King (I)

Antiphon / Melody ♩. = 63

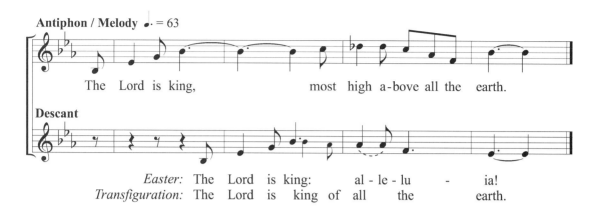

The Lord is king, most high a-bove all the earth.

Descant

Easter: The Lord is king: al - le - lu - ia!
Transfiguration: The Lord is king of all the earth.

Verses *Psalm 97:1-6, 7c, 9*

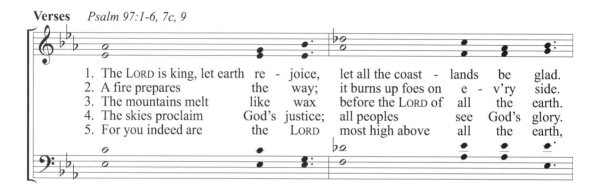

1. The LORD is king, let earth re - joice, let all the coast - lands be glad.
2. A fire prepares the way; it burns up foes on e - v'ry side.
3. The mountains melt like wax before the LORD of all the earth.
4. The skies proclaim God's justice; all peoples see God's glory.
5. For you indeed are the LORD most high above all the earth,

1. Surrounded by cloud and darkness; justice and right, God's throne.
2. God's lightnings light up the world, the earth trembles at the sight.
3. The skies proclaim God's justice; all peoples see God's glory.
4. [*omit* ———————] All you spirits, wor - ship the LORD.
5. [*omit* ———————] exalted far a - bove all spirits.

Performance Notes

Verses 1, 4, and 5 are the Lectionary selections for the Seventh Sunday of Easter, Year C.
Verses 1, 3, and 5 are the Lectionary selections for the Transfiguration of the Lord.

The Lord Is King (II)

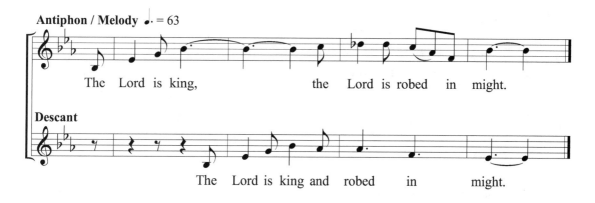

Antiphon / Melody ♩. = 63

The Lord is king, the Lord is robed in might.

Descant

The Lord is king and robed in might.

Verses *Psalm 93*

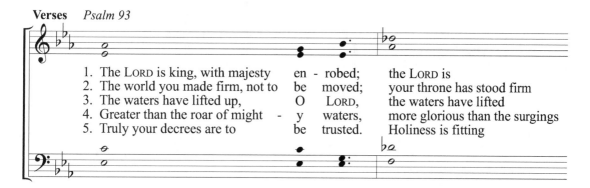

1. The LORD is king, with majesty en - robed; the LORD is
2. The world you made firm, not to be moved; your throne has stood firm
3. The waters have lifted up, O LORD, the waters have lifted
4. Greater than the roar of might - y waters, more glorious than the surgings
5. Truly your decrees are to be trusted. Holiness is fitting

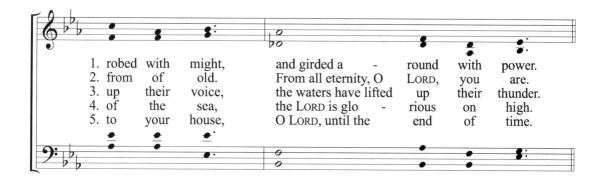

1. robed with might, and girded a - round with power.
2. from of old. From all eternity, O LORD, you are.
3. up their voice, the waters have lifted up their thunder.
4. of the sea, the LORD is glo - rious on high.
5. to your house, O LORD, until the end of time.

Performance Notes

Verses 1, 2, and 5 are the Lectionary selections for the solemnity of Christ the King, Year B.

The Lord Is My Light

Antiphon ♩ = 72

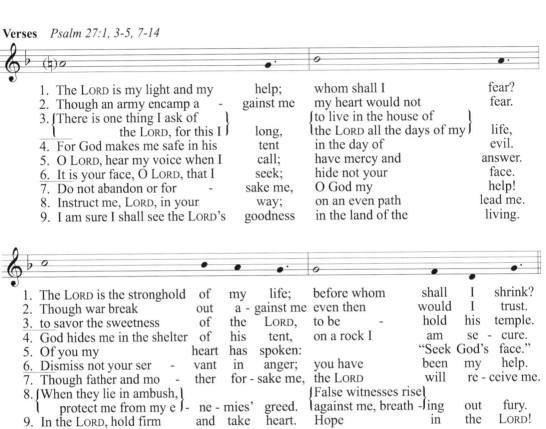

The Lord is my light, the Lord is my help: of whom shall I be a-fraid?

Verses *Psalm 27:1, 3-5, 7-14*

1. The LORD is my light and my help; whom shall I fear?
2. Though an army encamp a - gainst me my heart would not fear.
3. {There is one thing I ask of / the LORD, for this I} long, {to live in the house of / the LORD all the days of my} life,
4. For God makes me safe in his tent in the day of evil.
5. O LORD, hear my voice when I call; have mercy and answer.
6. It is your face, O LORD, that I seek; hide not your face.
7. Do not abandon or for - sake me, O God my help!
8. Instruct me, LORD, in your way; on an even path lead me.
9. I am sure I shall see the LORD's goodness in the land of the living.

1. The LORD is the stronghold of my life; before whom shall I shrink?
2. Though war break out a - gainst me even then would I trust.
3. to savor the sweetness of the LORD, to be - hold his temple.
4. God hides me in the shelter of his tent, on a rock I am se - cure.
5. Of you my heart has spoken: "Seek God's face."
6. Dismiss not your ser - vant in anger; you have been my help.
7. Though father and mo - ther for - sake me, the LORD will re - ceive me.
8. {When they lie in ambush, / protect me from my e}- ne - mies' greed. {False witnesses rise / against me, breath -}ing out fury.
9. In the LORD, hold firm and take heart. Hope in the LORD!

Performance Notes

Verses 1, 3, and 9 are the Lectionary selections for the Third Sunday in Ordinary Time, Year A.
Verses 1, 5, 6, and 9 are the Lectionary selections for the Second Sunday of Lent, Year C.

The Lord Will Bless His People

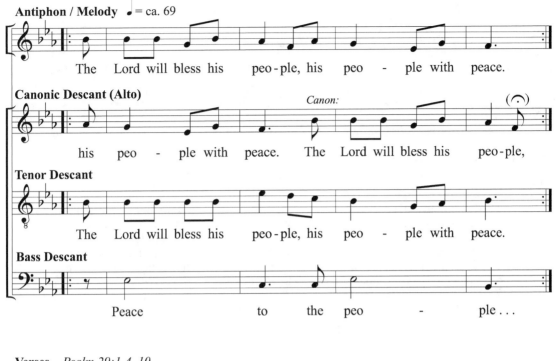

Antiphon / Melody ♩ = ca. 69

The Lord will bless his peo-ple, his peo - ple with peace.

Canonic Descant (Alto) *Canon:*

his peo - ple with peace. The Lord will bless his peo-ple,

Tenor Descant

The Lord will bless his peo-ple, his peo - ple with peace.

Bass Descant

Peace to the peo - ple . . .

Verses *Psalm 29:1-4, 10*

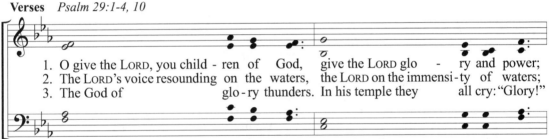

1. O give the LORD, you child - ren of God, give the LORD glo - ry and power;
2. The LORD's voice resounding on the waters, the LORD on the immensi-ty of waters;
3. The God of glo - ry thunders. In his temple they all cry: "Glory!"

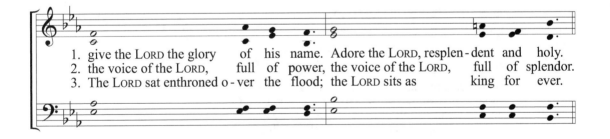

1. give the LORD the glory of his name. Adore the LORD, resplen-dent and holy.
2. the voice of the LORD, full of power, the voice of the LORD, full of splendor.
3. The LORD sat enthroned o - ver the flood; the LORD sits as king for ever.

Performance Notes

The antiphon is sung twice each time. The alto canon may give rise to the temptation to sing the antiphon more than twice, a temptation which should be resisted except perhaps after the final psalm verse!

The Love of God

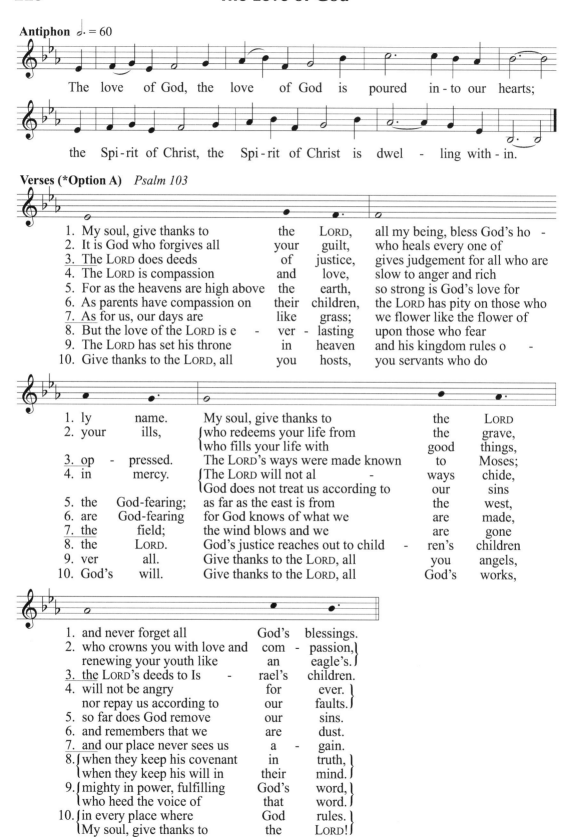

Antiphon ♩. = 60

The love of God, the love of God is poured in-to our hearts;

the Spi-rit of Christ, the Spi-rit of Christ is dwel - ling with-in.

Verses (*Option A)   *Psalm 103*

1. My soul, give thanks to the LORD, all my being, bless God's ho -
2. It is God who forgives all your guilt, who heals every one of
3. The LORD does deeds of justice, gives judgement for all who are
4. The LORD is compassion and love, slow to anger and rich
5. For as the heavens are high above the earth, so strong is God's love for
6. As parents have compassion on their children, the LORD has pity on those who
7. As for us, our days are like grass; we flower like the flower of
8. But the love of the LORD is e - ver - lasting upon those who fear
9. The LORD has set his throne in heaven and his kingdom rules o -
10. Give thanks to the LORD, all you hosts, you servants who do

1. ly name. My soul, give thanks to the LORD
2. your ills, {who redeems your life from the grave,
   {who fills your life with good things,
3. op - pressed. The LORD's ways were made known to Moses;
4. in mercy. {The LORD will not al - ways chide,
   {God does not treat us according to our sins
5. the God-fearing; as far as the east is from the west,
6. are God-fearing for God knows of what we are made,
7. the field; the wind blows and we are gone
8. the LORD. God's justice reaches out to child - ren's children
9. ver all. Give thanks to the LORD, all you angels,
10. God's will. Give thanks to the LORD, all God's works,

1. and never forget all God's blessings.
2. who crowns you with love and com - passion,}
   renewing your youth like an eagle's.}
3. the LORD's deeds to Is - rael's children.
4. will not be angry for ever. }
   nor repay us according to our faults.}
5. so far does God remove our sins.
6. and remembers that we are dust.
7. and our place never sees us a - gain.
8. {when they keep his covenant in truth, }
   {when they keep his will in their mind.}
9. {mighty in power, fulfilling God's word, }
   {who heed the voice of that word.}
10. {in every place where God rules. }
    {My soul, give thanks to the LORD!}

Verses (*Option B) *Ephesians 1:3-14*

1. Blessed be the God and Father of our Lord   Jesus   Christ,
2. He destined us for adoption as his children through Je   -   sus   Christ,
3. In him we have redemption through   his   blood,
4. With all wisdom and insight he has made known to us the mystery of his   will,
5. In Christ we have also obtained an   in - heritance,
6. {In him you also, when you had heard the word of truth,
   { the gospel of your salvation, and had believed }   in   him,

1. who has blessed us in Christ with every spiritual blessing in the heaven - ly   places,
2. according to the good pleasure of   his   will,
3. the forgiveness of   our   trespasses,
4. according to his good pleasure that he set forth   in   Christ,
5. {having been destined according to the purpose of him
   { who accomplishes all things according to his counsel }   and   will,
6. were marked with the seal of the promised Ho   -   ly   Spirit;

1. just as he chose us in Christ before the foundation of   the   world
2. to the praise of his glo   -   rious   grace
3. according to the riches of   his   grace
4. as a plan for the fullness   of   time,
5. so that we, who were the first to set our hope   on   Christ,
6. this is the pledge of our inheritance toward redemption as God's own   people,

1. to be holy and blameless before him   in   love.
2. that he freely bestowed on us in the   Be -   loved.
3. that he lavished   on   us.
4. to gather up all things in him, things in heaven and things on   earth.
5. might live for the praise of   his   glory.
6. to the praise of   his   glory.

Performance Notes
Option A verses are used on Pentecost Sunday and Option B verses are used on Trinity Sunday.

The Mercy of God Is for All

Antiphon / Melody ♩. = 63

The mer-cy of God is for all, the mer-cy of God is for all, the

Descants

The mer-cy of God is for all, the mer-cy of God is for all, the

mer-cy of God, mer-cy of God, the mer-cy of God is for all.

mer-cy of God, mer-cy of God, the mer-cy of God is for all.

Verses *Psalms 130:1-6b, 7b-8; 103:1-4, 8, 10-14, 17-18*

Cantor:

1. Out of the depths I cry to you, O LORD; LORD, hear my voice!
2. If you, O LORD, should mark our guilt, LORD, who would sur - vive?
3. My soul is waiting for the LORD, I count on God's word.
4. Because with the LORD there is mercy and fullness of re - demption,
5. My soul, give thanks to the LORD, all my being, bless God's ho - ly name.
6. It is God who forgives all your guilt, who heals every one of your ills,
7. The LORD is compassion and love, slow to anger and rich in mercy.
8. For as the heavens are high above the earth so strong is God's love for the God-fearing.
9. As parents have compassion on their children, the LORD has pity on those who are God-fearing
10. The love of the LORD is everlasting upon those who fear the LORD.

All / Melody:

The mer-cy of God is for all.

Descants:

The mer-cy of God is for all.

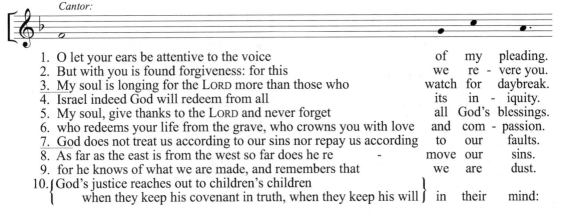

Cantor:

1. O let your ears be attentive to the voice of my pleading.
2. But with you is found forgiveness: for this we re - vere you.
3. My soul is longing for the LORD more than those who watch for daybreak.
4. Israel indeed God will redeem from all its in - iquity.
5. My soul, give thanks to the LORD and never forget all God's blessings.
6. who redeems your life from the grave, who crowns you with love and com - passion.
7. God does not treat us according to our sins nor repay us according to our faults.
8. As far as the east is from the west so far does he re - move our sins.
9. for he knows of what we are made, and remembers that we are dust.
10. { God's justice reaches out to children's children
   when they keep his covenant in truth, when they keep his will } in their mind:

All / Melody:

The mer-cy of God is for all.

Descants:

The mer-cy of God is for all.

The Message Goes Forth

Antiphon *(marziale)* ♩ = 120

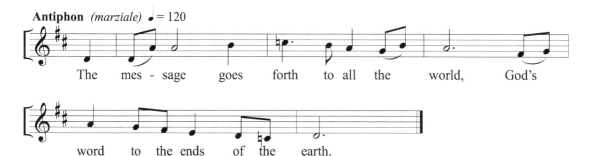

The mes - sage goes forth to all the world, God's word to the ends of the earth.

Verses *Psalm 19:2-14*

1. The heavens proclaim the glory of God, and the firmament shows forth the work
2. No speech, no word, no voice is heard yet their span extends through
3. There God has placed a tent for the sun; it comes forth like a bridegroom coming
4. At the end of the sky is the rising of the sun; to the furthest end of the sky
5. The law of the LORD is perfect, it re -
6. The precepts of the LORD are right, they glad -
7. The fear of the LORD is holy, abid -
8. They are more to be desired than gold, than the pur -
9. So in them your servant finds in-struction; great reward is
10. From presumption restrain your servant and let

1. of God's hands. Day unto day takes up the story
2. all the earth, [*omit* ————————————]
3. from his tent, [*omit* ————————————]
4. is its course. [*omit* ————————————]
5. vives the soul. The rule of the LORD is to be trusted,
6. den the heart. The command of the LORD is clear,
7. ing for ever. The decrees of the LORD are truth
8. est of gold and sweeter are they than honey,
9. in their keeping. But can we discern all our errors?
10. it not rule me. Then shall I be blameless,

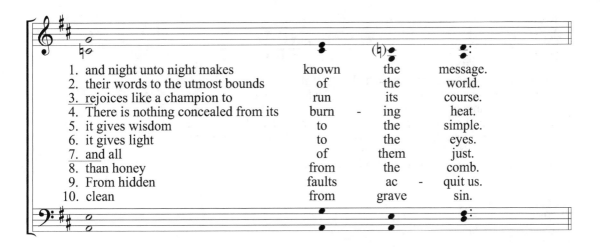

1. and night unto night makes   known   the   message.
2. their words to the utmost bounds   of   the   world.
3. rejoices like a champion to   run   its   course.
4. There is nothing concealed from its   burn - ing   heat.
5. it gives wisdom   to   the   simple.
6. it gives light   to   the   eyes.
7. and all   of   them   just.
8. than honey   from   the   comb.
9. From hidden   faults   ac - quit us.
10. clean   from   grave   sin.

Performance Notes

Verses 5, 7, 9, and 10 are the Lectionary selections for the Twenty-sixth Sunday in Ordinary Time, Year B.

The People of God Are the Vineyard   228

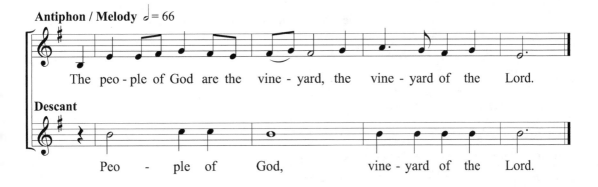

Antiphon / Melody ♩ = 66

The peo - ple of God are the vine - yard, the vine - yard of the Lord.

Descant

Peo - ple of God, vine - yard of the Lord.

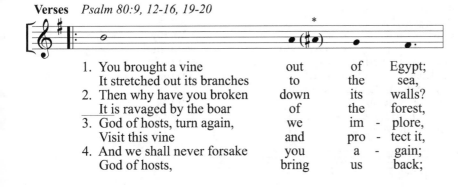

Verses   *Psalm 80:9, 12-16, 19-20*

1. You brought a vine   out   of   Egypt;
     It stretched out its branches   to   the   sea,
2. Then why have you broken   down   its   walls?
     It is ravaged by the boar   of   the   forest,
3. God of hosts, turn again,   we   im - plore,
     Visit this vine   and   pro - tect it,
4. And we shall never forsake   you   a - gain;
     God of hosts,   bring   us   back;

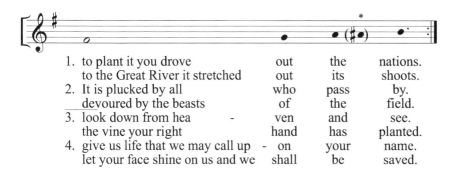

1. to plant it you drove   out   the   nations.
   to the Great River it stretched   out   its   shoots.
2. It is plucked by all   who   pass   by.
   devoured by the beasts   of   the   field.
3. look down from hea   -   ven   and   see.
   the vine your right   hand   has   planted.
4. give us life that we may call up - on   your   name.
   let your face shine on us and we shall   be   saved.

Performance Notes

For an increased Yiddish feel, sing an A sharp (but retain G natural).

229 The Prayer of Our Hearts

Antiphon ♩. = ca. 42

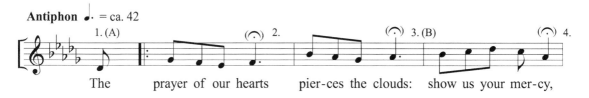

The   prayer of our hearts   pier-ces the clouds: show us your mer-cy,

show us your love.   The

Verses *Psalms 123; 141:1-4, 8-9; 143:1-2, 7-8, 10*

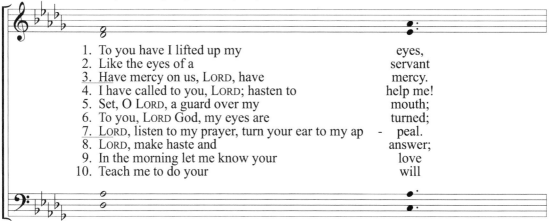

1. To you have I lifted up my   eyes,
2. Like the eyes of a   servant
3. Have mercy on us, LORD, have   mercy.
4. I have called to you, LORD; hasten to   help me!
5. Set, O LORD, a guard over my   mouth;
6. To you, LORD God, my eyes are   turned;
7. LORD, listen to my prayer, turn your ear to my ap - peal.
8. LORD, make haste and   answer;
9. In the morning let me know your   love
10. Teach me to do your   will

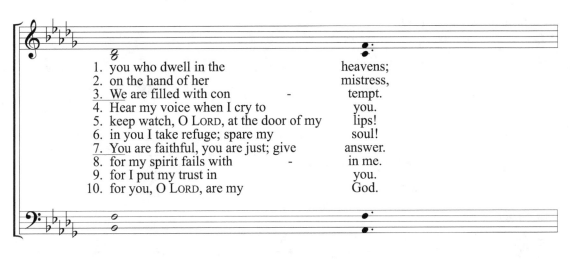

1. you who dwell in the · heavens;
2. on the hand of her · mistress,
3. We are filled with con - tempt.
4. Hear my voice when I cry to · you.
5. keep watch, O LORD, at the door of my · lips!
6. in you I take refuge; spare my · soul!
7. You are faithful, you are just; give · answer.
8. for my spirit fails with - in me.
9. for I put my trust in · you.
10. for you, O LORD, are my · God.

1. my eyes, like the · eyes · of · slaves
2. so our eyes are on the · LORD · our · God
3. Indeed all too full · is · our · soul
4. Let my prayer rise before · you · like · incense,
5. Do not turn my heart to things · that · are · wrong,
6. From the trap they have laid for me · keep · me · safe;
7. Do not call your ser - vant · to · judgement
8. Do not · hide · your · face
9. Make me know the way · I · should · walk;
10. Let your good · spi - rit · guide me

1. on the hand · of · their · lords.
2. till we · are · shown · mercy.
3. with the scorn of the rich, the disdain · of · the · proud.
4. the raising of my hands like an even - ing · ob - lation.
5. to evil deeds with those · who · are · sinners.
6. keep me from the snares of those · who · do · evil.
7. for no one is just · in · your · sight.
8. lest I become like those · in · the · grave.
9. to you I lift · up · my · soul.
10. in ways that are le - vel · and · smooth.

Performance Notes

As indicated, the antiphon may be sung as a two-part round (A and B), the second part entering halfway through, or as a four-part round (1–4).

The Seed That Falls on the Good Ground

Antiphon / Melody ♩ = ca. 76

The seed that falls on the good ground will bear a-bun-dant

Antiphon / Melody

fruit, will bear a-bun-dant fruit.

Soprano Descant

fruit, will bear a-bun-dant fruit.

Alto Descant

fruit, will bear a-bun-dant fruit.

Tenor Descant

fruit, will bear a-bun-dant fruit.

Verses *Psalm 65:10-14*

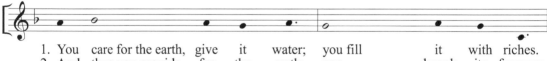

1. You care for the earth, give it water; you fill it with riches.
2. And thus you provide for the earth; you drench its furrows;
3. You crown the year with your goodness. [*omit* —————————————]
4. The hills are gird - ed with joy, the meadows co - vered with flocks,

1. Your river in hea - ven brims over to provide its grain.
2. you level it, soften it with showers; you bless its growth.
3. A - bundance flows in your steps; in the pastures of the wilderness it flows.
4. the valleys are decked with wheat. They shout for joy, yes, they sing.

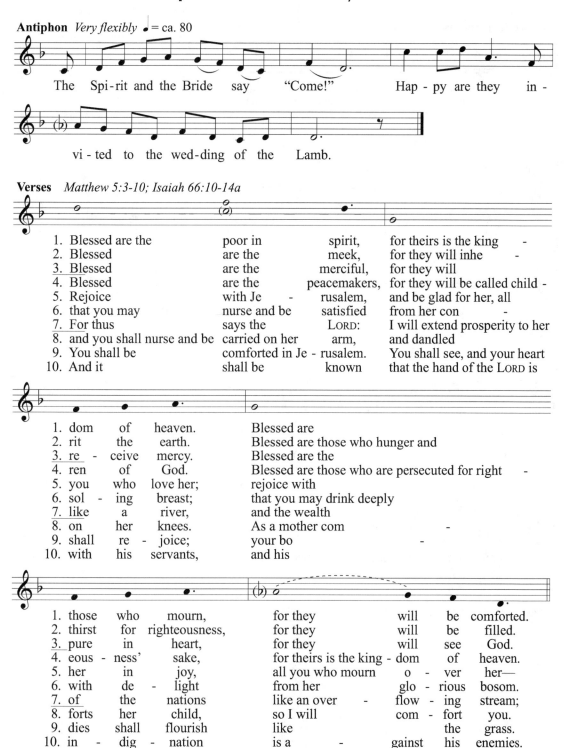

Antiphon *Very flexibly* ♩ = ca. 80

The Spi-rit and the Bride say "Come!" Hap-py are they in-vi-ted to the wed-ding of the Lamb.

Verses *Matthew 5:3-10; Isaiah 66:10-14a*

1. Blessed are the poor in spirit, for theirs is the king-
2. Blessed are the meek, for they will inhe-
3. Blessed are the merciful, for they will
4. Blessed are the peacemakers, for they will be called child-
5. Rejoice with Je - rusalem, and be glad for her, all
6. that you may nurse and be satisfied from her con-
7. For thus says the LORD: I will extend prosperity to her
8. and you shall nurse and be carried on her arm, and dandled
9. You shall be comforted in Je - rusalem. You shall see, and your heart
10. And it shall be known that the hand of the LORD is

1. dom of heaven. Blessed are
2. rit the earth. Blessed are those who hunger and
3. re - ceive mercy. Blessed are the
4. ren of God. Blessed are those who are persecuted for right-
5. you who love her; rejoice with
6. sol - ing breast; that you may drink deeply
7. like a river, and the wealth
8. on her knees. As a mother com-
9. shall re - joice; your bo-
10. with his servants, and his

1. those who mourn, for they will be comforted.
2. thirst for righteousness, for they will be filled.
3. pure in heart, for they will see God.
4. eous - ness' sake, for theirs is the king - dom of heaven.
5. her in joy, all you who mourn o - ver her—
6. with de - light from her glo - rious bosom.
7. of the nations like an over - flow - ing stream;
8. forts her child, so I will com - fort you.
9. dies shall flourish like the grass.
10. in - dig - nation is a - gainst his enemies.

Performance Notes

In both antiphon and tone, the A-naturals with flats in parentheses indicate optional "blue notes."
In measure one of the verse tone, sing either the F or C.

232 The Stone Which the Builders Rejected

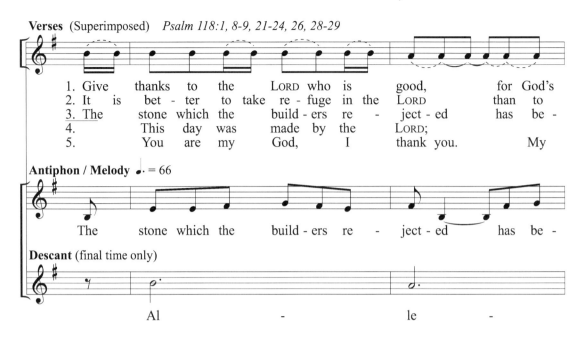

Verses (Superimposed) *Psalm 118:1, 8-9, 21-24, 26, 28-29*

1. Give thanks to the LORD who is good, for God's
2. It is bet - ter to take re - fuge in the LORD than to
3. The stone which the build - ers re - ject - ed has be -
4. This day was made by the LORD;
5. You are my God, I thank you. My

Antiphon / Melody ♩. = 66

The stone which the build - ers re - ject - ed has be -

Descant (final time only)

Al - le -

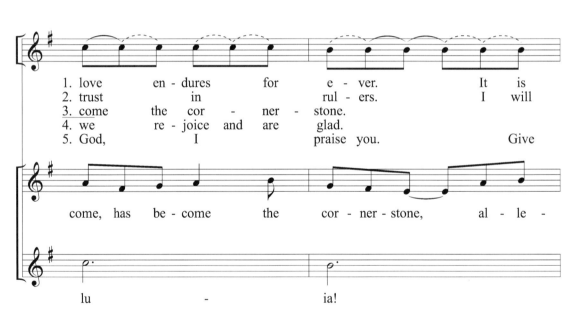

1. love en - dures for e - ver. It is
2. trust in rul - ers. I will
3. come the cor - ner - stone.
4. we re - joice and are glad.
5. God, I praise you. Give

come, has be - come the cor - ner - stone, al - le -

lu - ia!

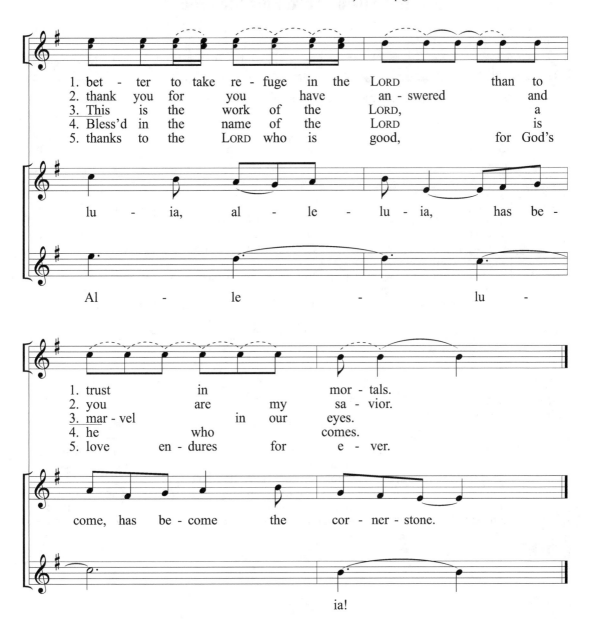

1. bet - ter   to   take   re - fuge   in   the   LORD   than   to
2. thank   you   for   you   have   an - swered   and
3. This   is   the   work   of   the   LORD,   a
4. Bless'd   in   the   name   of   the   LORD   is
5. thanks   to   the   LORD   who   is   good,   for   God's

lu - ia,   al - le - lu - ia,   has   be -

Al - le - lu -

1. trust   in   mor - tals.
2. you   are   my   sa - vior.
3. mar - vel   in   our   eyes.
4. he   who   comes.
5. love   en - dures   for   e - ver.

come,   has   be - come   the   cor - ner - stone.

ia!

The Strong Lord Sets Me Free

Antiphon ♩ = 80

The strong Lord sets me free, in his love de-lights in me.

Verses *Psalm 18*

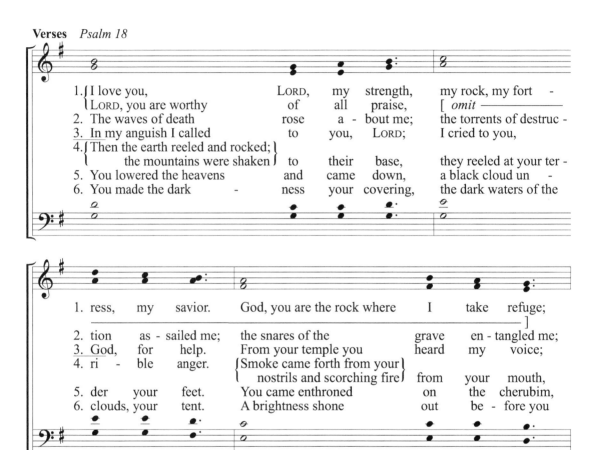

1. {I love you, LORD, my strength, my rock, my fort -
   {LORD, you are worthy of all praise, [*omit* ————
2. The waves of death rose a - bout me; the torrents of destruc -
3. In my anguish I called to you, LORD; I cried to you,
4. {Then the earth reeled and rocked;}
   {   the mountains were shaken} to their base, they reeled at your ter -
5. You lowered the heavens and came down, a black cloud un -
6. You made the dark - ness your covering, the dark waters of the

1. ress, my savior. God, you are the rock where I take refuge;
2. tion as - sailed me; the snares of the grave en - tangled me;]
3. God, for help. From your temple you heard my voice;
4. ri - ble anger. {Smoke came forth from your}
   {   nostrils and scorching fire} from your mouth,
5. der your feet. You came enthroned on the cherubim,
6. clouds, your tent. A brightness shone out be - fore you

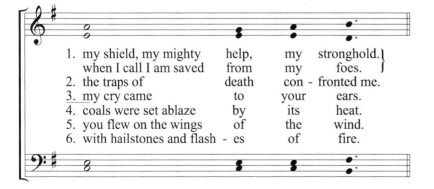

1. my shield, my mighty help, my stronghold.}
   when I call I am saved from my foes. }
2. the traps of death con - fronted me.
3. my cry came to your ears.
4. coals were set ablaze by its heat.
5. you flew on the wings of the wind.
6. with hailstones and flash - es of fire.

Verses (continued)

7. LORD, you thundered in the heavens, Most High, you let your
8. The bed of the ocean was re - vealed; the foundations of the world
9. From on high you reached down and seized me; you drew me out of the
10. They assailed me in the day of my mis - fortune, but you, LORD, were
11. You rewarded me because I was just, repaid me, for my
12. Your judgements are all be - fore me; I have never neglected
13. You repaid me because I was just and my hands were clean
14. With the sincere you show your - self sin - cere, but the cunning you out -
15. You, O LORD, are my lamp, my God who light -
16. Your ways, O God, are perfect; your word, O LORD, is
17. For who is God but you, LORD? Who is a rock but

7. voice be heard. You shot your arrows, scat - tered the foe,
8. were laid bare at the thunder of your threat, O LORD,
9. might - y waters. You snatched me from my pow - er - ful foe,
10. my sup - port. You brought me forth in - to freedom,
11. hands were clean, for I have kept your way, O LORD,
12. your com - mands. I have always been up - right be - fore you;
13. in your eyes. You are loving with those who love you,
14. do in cunning. For you save a hum - ble people
15. ens my darkness. With you I can break through a - ny barrier,
16. pur - est gold. You indeed are the shield
17. you, my God? You who gird me with strength

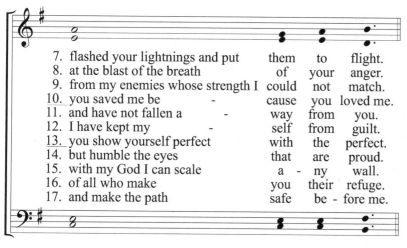

7. flashed your lightnings and put them to flight.
8. at the blast of the breath of your anger.
9. from my enemies whose strength I could not match.
10. you saved me be - cause you loved me.
11. and have not fallen a - way from you.
12. I have kept my - self from guilt.
13. you show yourself perfect with the perfect.
14. but humble the eyes that are proud.
15. with my God I can scale a - ny wall.
16. of all who make you their refuge.
17. and make the path safe be - fore me.

Verses (continued)

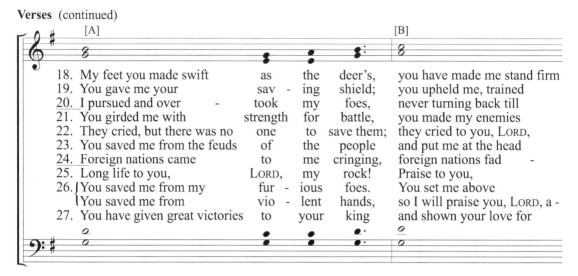

[A] ... [B]

18. My feet you made swift   as   the   deer's,   you have made me stand firm
19. You gave me your   sav - ing   shield;   you upheld me, trained
20. I pursued and over - took   my   foes,   never turning back till
21. You girded me with   strength   for   battle,   you made my enemies
22. They cried, but there was no   one   to   save them;   they cried to you, LORD,
23. You saved me from the feuds   of   the   people   and put me at the head
24. Foreign nations came   to   me   cringing,   foreign nations fad -
25. Long life to you,   LORD,   my   rock!   Praise to you,
26. { You saved me from my   fur - ious   foes.   You set me above
  { You saved me from   vio - lent   hands,   so I will praise you, LORD, a -
27. You have given great victories   to   your   king   and shown your love for

[C]

18. on   the   heights.   You have trained my   hands   for   battle
19. me   with   care.   You gave me freedom   for   my   steps;
20. they   were   slain.   I smote them so they   could   not   rise;
21. fall   be - neath me,   you made my   foes   take   flight;
22. but   in   vain.   I crushed them fine as dust be - fore   the   wind;
23. of   the   nations.   People unknown   to   me   served me;
24. ed   a - way.   [omit ————————————]
25. God,   who   saves me,   the God who gives   me   re - dress
26. my   as - sailants. }   [omit ————————————]
   mong   the   nations; }
27. your   a - nointed,   [omit ————————————]

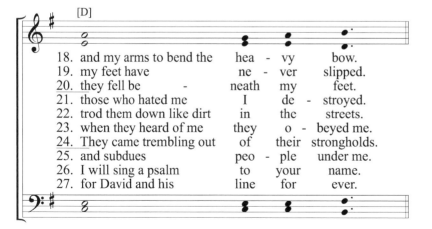

[D]

18. and my arms to bend the   hea - vy   bow.
19. my feet have   ne - ver   slipped.
20. they fell be - neath   my   feet.
21. those who hated me   I   de - stroyed.
22. trod them down like dirt   in   the   streets.
23. when they heard of me   they   o - beyed me.
24. They came trembling out   of   their   strongholds.
25. and subdues   peo - ple   under me.
26. I will sing a psalm   to   your   name.
27. for David and his   line   for   ever.

Performance Notes

Verses 1, 25ab, and 27ab are the Lectionary selections for the Thirty-first Sunday in Ordinary Time, Year B.

The Word of God at Work in Us

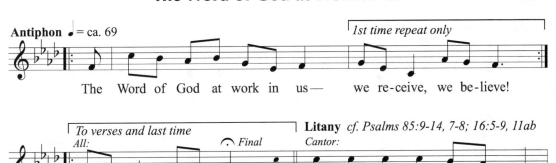

Antiphon ♩= ca. 69 — *1st time repeat only*

The Word of God at work in us— we re-ceive, we be-lieve!

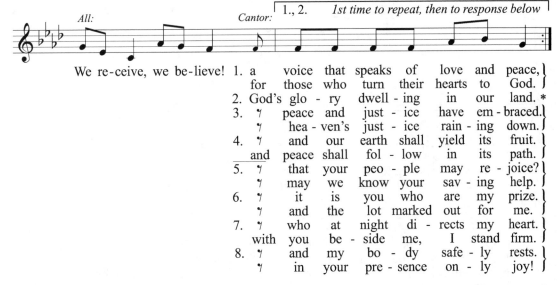

To verses and last time — **Litany** *cf. Psalms 85:9-14, 7-8; 16:5-9, 11ab*

All: / Final / Cantor:

we re-ceive, we be-lieve!

1. We lis-ten to the Word of God,
   for all God's peo-ple and God's friends,
2. God's sav-ing time is draw-ing near,
3. ᛞ Faith-ful-ness and mer-cy meet,
   ᛞ Faith is spring-ing from the earth,
4. Our God will pros-per all we do,
   ᛞ Right-eous-ness will lead the way,
5. ᛞ Will you not re-store our life
   ᛞ Let us see your mer-cy, Lord;
6. ᛞ Lord, my por-tion and my cup—
   Your he-ri-tage is my de-light,
7. I bless the Lord who coun-sels me,
   ᛞ Lord, I keep you in my sight—
8. My heart and soul re-joice in you
   ᛞ You have shown the path of life,

All: / Cantor: / 1., 2. *1st time to repeat, then to response below*

We re-ceive, we be-lieve!

1. a voice that speaks of love and peace,⟩
   for those who turn their hearts to God.⟩
2. God's glo-ry dwell-ing in our land. *
3. ᛞ peace and just-ice have em-braced.⟩
   ᛞ hea-ven's just-ice rain-ing down.⟩
4. ᛞ and our earth shall yield its fruit.⟩
   and peace shall fol-low in its path.⟩
5. ᛞ that your peo-ple may re-joice?⟩
   ᛞ may we know your sav-ing help.⟩
6. ᛞ it is you who are my prize.⟩
   ᛞ and the lot marked out for me.⟩
7. ᛞ who at night di-rects my heart.⟩
   with you be-side me, I stand firm.⟩
8. ᛞ and my bo-dy safe-ly rests.⟩
   ᛞ in your pre-sence on-ly joy!⟩

*Repeat omitted

All: / *To antiphon*

We re-ceive, we be-lieve!

There Is Mercy in the Lord

Antiphon / Melody ♩ = 84

1. (A)   2.   3. (B)   4.

There is mer-cy in the Lord, there is full-ness of re-

Optional Bass

In the Lord, in the

demp-tion. There is mer-cy in the Lord, there is full-ness

Lord, in the Lord, in the Lord, in the Lord,

of re-demp-tion. There is mer-cy in the Lord.

in the Lord, in the Lord, in the Lord.

Verses   *Psalm 130:1-6b, 7b-8*

1. Out of the depths I cry to you, O LORD, LORD, hear my voice!
2. If you, O LORD, should mark our guilt, LORD, who would sur - vive?
3. My soul is waiting for the LORD, I count on God's word.
4. Because with the LORD there is mercy and fullness of re - demption,

1. O let your ears be at - tentive to the voice of my pleading.
2. But with you is found for - giveness: for this we re - vere you.
3. My soul is longing for the LORD more than those who watch for daybreak.
4. Israel indeed God will re - deem from all its i - niquity.

Performance Notes

The antiphon may be sung in a two-part (A and B) or four-part (1–4) round as indicated. After the final stanza, the round may continue as long as desired.
The Optional Bass part is only used once the four-part round is firmly established.

They Shall Adore You

236

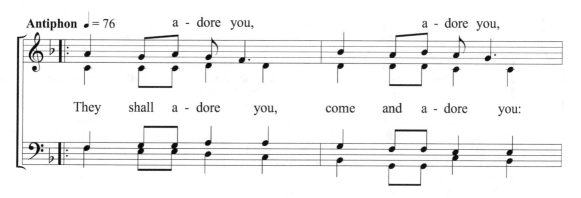

Antiphon ♩ = 76

a - dore you,   a - dore you,

They shall a - dore you,   come and a - dore you:

come.

Lord, e - v'ry na - tion shall come, shall come.

come.

Verses   *Psalm 72*

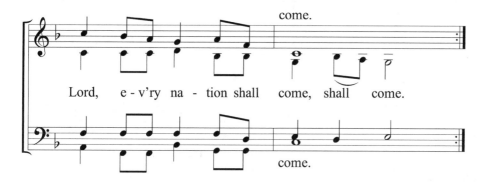

[A]   [B]

1. O God, give your judgement   to   the   king,   to a king's
2. May the mountains bring forth peace   for   the   people   and
3. He shall endure like the sun   and   the   moon   from
4. In his days just   -   ice   shall   flourish   and peace
5. Before him his ene   -   mies   shall   fall,   his foes
6. The kings of She   -   ba   and   Seba   shall
7. For he shall save the poor   when   they   cry,   and the needy
8. From oppression he will res   -   cue   their   lives,   to him their
9. May corn be abundant   in   the   land   to the peaks
10. May his name be   blessed   for   ever   and endure
11. Blessed be the LORD, the   God   of   Israel,   who a   -

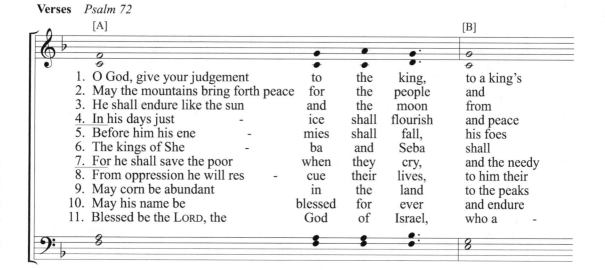

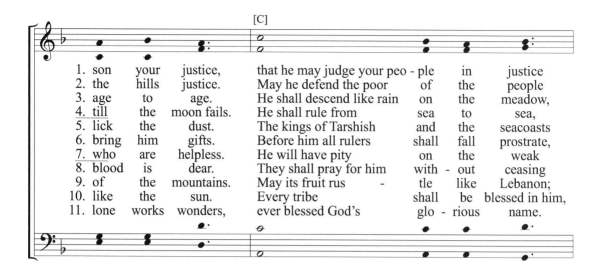

[C]

1. son	your	justice,	that he may judge your peo - ple	in	justice
2. the	hills	justice.	May he defend the poor	of	the	people
3. age	to	age.	He shall descend like rain	on	the	meadow,
4. till	the	moon fails.	He shall rule from	sea	to	sea,
5. lick	the	dust.	The kings of Tarshish	and	the	seacoasts
6. bring	him	gifts.	Before him all rulers	shall	fall	prostrate,
7. who	are	helpless.	He will have pity	on	the	weak
8. blood	is	dear.	They shall pray for him	with - out	ceasing
9. of	the	mountains.	May its fruit rus - tle	like	Lebanon;
10. like	the	sun.	Every tribe	shall	be	blessed in him,
11. lone	works	wonders,	ever blessed God's	glo - rious	name.

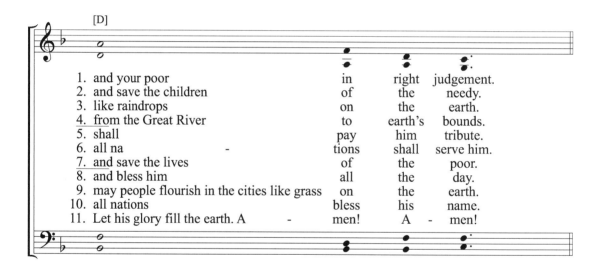

[D]

1. and your poor	in	right	judgement.
2. and save the children	of	the	needy.
3. like raindrops	on	the	earth.
4. from the Great River	to	earth's	bounds.
5. shall	pay	him	tribute.
6. all na - tions	shall	serve him.
7. and save the lives	of	the	poor.
8. and bless him	all	the	day.
9. may people flourish in the cities like grass	on	the	earth.
10. all nations	bless	his	name.
11. Let his glory fill the earth. A - men!	A -	men!

Performance Notes

Verses 1, 4, 5cd, 6, and 7 are the Lectionary selections for Epiphany.

Verses *Psalm 81:2-11, 14, 16cd*

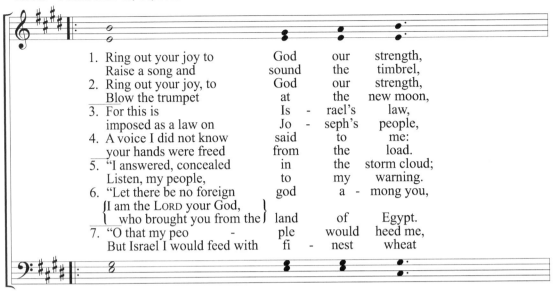

1. Ring out your joy to God our strength,
   Raise a song and sound the timbrel,
2. Ring out your joy, to God our strength,
   Blow the trumpet at the new moon,
3. For this is Is - rael's law,
   imposed as a law on Jo - seph's people,
4. A voice I did not know said to me:
   your hands were freed from the load.
5. "I answered, concealed in the storm cloud;
   Listen, my people, to my warning.
6. "Let there be no foreign god a - mong you,
   {I am the LORD your God,
   { who brought you from the } land of Egypt.
7. "O that my peo - ple would heed me,
   But Israel I would feed with fi - nest wheat

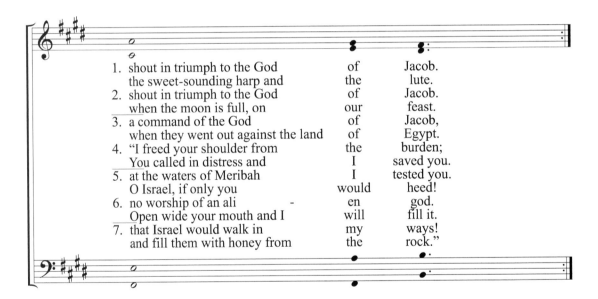

1. shout in triumph to the God of Jacob.
   the sweet-sounding harp and the lute.
2. shout in triumph to the God of Jacob.
   when the moon is full, on our feast.
3. a command of the God of Jacob,
   when they went out against the land of Egypt.
4. "I freed your shoulder from the burden;
   You called in distress and I saved you.
5. at the waters of Meribah I tested you.
   O Israel, if only you would heed!
6. no worship of an ali - en god.
   Open wide your mouth and I will fill it.
7. that Israel would walk in my ways!
   and fill them with honey from the rock."

Performance Notes

The antiphon is sung twice through each time. It also works by itself as a two-part round, the second part entering at "(the) joy of the Lord . . . ."

This Is My Body

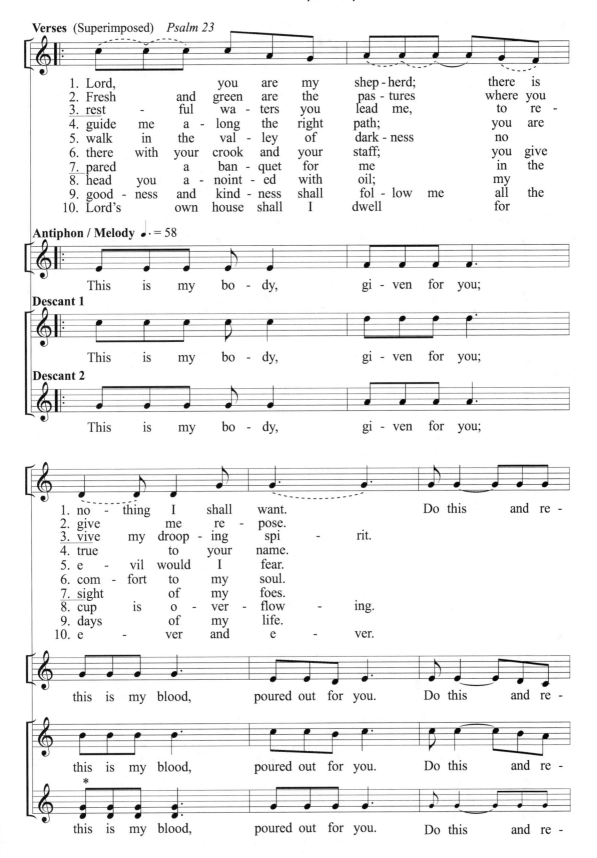

mem-ber me; do this and re - mem-ber me.

3. Near
4. You
5. If I
6. You are
7. You have pre -
8. My
9. Sure-ly
10. In the

mem-ber me; do this and re - mem-ber me.

mem-ber me; do this and re - mem-ber me.

mem-ber me; do this and re - mem-ber me.

Performance Notes

In measure three of Descant 2, sing D in antiphon, G when verse is superimposed.
The first four measures of the descants and antiphon are vocalized (perhaps to 'oo') or hummed when a verse is superimposed.

239   This Is the Bread

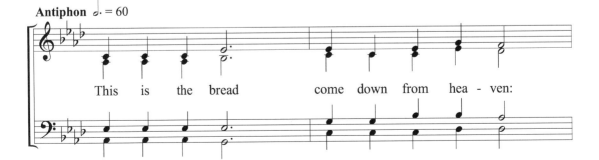

Antiphon ♩. = 60

This is the bread come down from hea-ven:

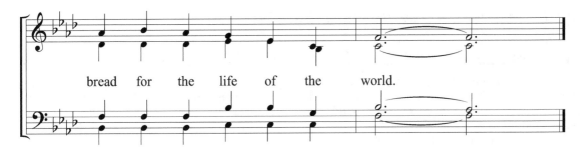

bread   for   the   life   of   the   world.

Verses   *Psalm 78:3, 4cd, 23-25, 27-29, 35, 54-55*

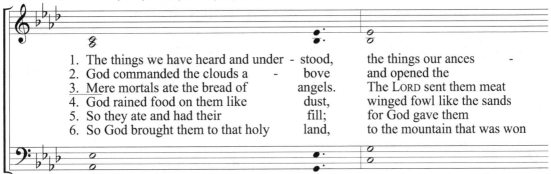

1. The things we have heard and under - stood,   the things our ances -
2. God commanded the clouds a - bove   and opened the
3. Mere mortals ate the bread of   angels.   The LORD sent them meat
4. God rained food on them like   dust,   winged fowl like the sands
5. So they ate and had their   fill;   for God gave them
6. So God brought them to that holy   land,   to the mountain that was won

1. tors have told us; the glories and the might of the LORD
2. gates of heaven; rained down manna for their food,
3. in a - bundance. So God brought them to that ho - ly land,
4. of the sea; let it fall in the midst of their camp
5. all they craved. They remembered that God was their rock,
6. by his hand; drove our the na - tions be - fore them,

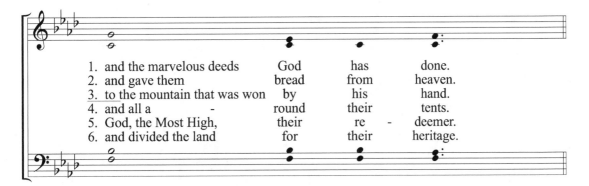

1. and the marvelous deeds God has done.
2. and gave them bread from heaven.
3. to the mountain that was won by his hand.
4. and all a - round their tents.
5. God, the Most High, their re - deemer.
6. and divided the land for their heritage.

Performance Notes

Verses 1–3 are the Lectionary selections for the Eighteenth Sunday in Ordinary Time, Year B.

This Is the Day

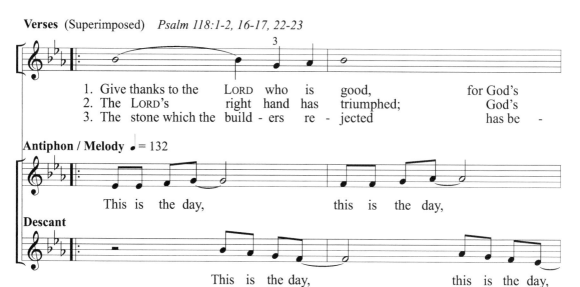

Verses (Superimposed) *Psalm 118:1-2, 16-17, 22-23*

1. Give thanks to the LORD who is good, for God's
2. The LORD's right hand has triumphed; God's
3. The stone which the build - ers re - jected has be -

Antiphon / Melody ♩ = 132

This is the day, this is the day,

Descant

This is the day, this is the day,

1. love endures for e - ver. Let the
2. right hand raised me up.
3. come the cor - ner - stone.

this is the day the Lord has made;

this is the day, let us re - joice,

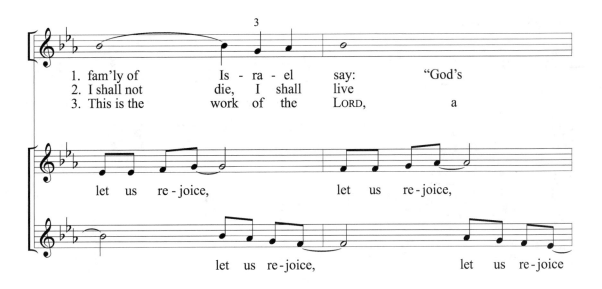

1. fam'ly of   Is - ra - el   say: "God's
2. I shall not   die, I shall   live
3. This is the   work of the   Lord,   a

let us re - joice,   let us re - joice,

let us re-joice,   let us re - joice

1. love endures for   e - ver."
2. and recount   God's   deeds.
3. marvel in   our   eyes.

let us re - joice   and be   glad.

and be   glad.

Those Who Do Justice

Antiphon ♩ = 86

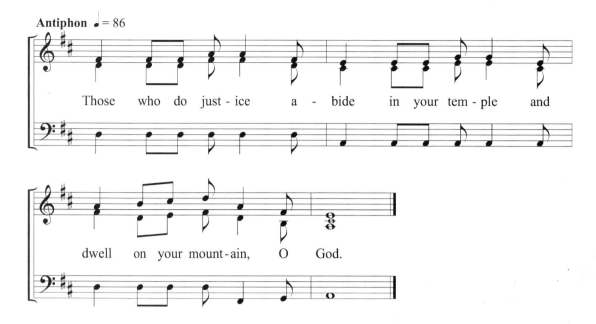

Those who do just-ice a - bide in your tem - ple and

dwell on your mount-ain, O God.

Verses *Psalms 15:2-5b; 112:1bc, 4-5, 7, 9ab; 119:1-3*

Cantor / Choir:

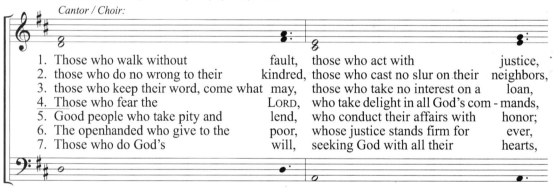

1. Those who walk without   fault,   those who act with   justice,
2. those who do no wrong to their   kindred,   those who cast no slur on their   neighbors,
3. those who keep their word, come what   may,   those who take no interest on a   loan,
4. Those who fear the   LORD,   who take delight in all God's com - mands,
5. Good people who take pity and   lend,   who conduct their affairs with   honor;
6. The openhanded who give to the   poor,   whose justice stands firm for   ever,
7. Those who do God's   will,   seeking God with all their   hearts,

All:

Shall dwell on your mount-ain, O God.

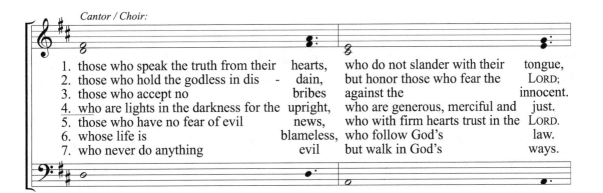

Cantor / Choir:

1. those who speak the truth from their hearts, who do not slander with their tongue,
2. those who hold the godless in dis - dain, but honor those who fear the LORD;
3. those who accept no bribes against the innocent.
4. who are lights in the darkness for the upright, who are generous, merciful and just.
5. those who have no fear of evil news, who with firm hearts trust in the LORD.
6. whose life is blameless, who follow God's law.
7. who never do anything evil but walk in God's ways.

All:

Shall dwell on your mount-ain, O God.

Performance Notes

Verses 1–3 are the Lectionary selections for the Twenty-second Sunday in Ordinary Time, Year B, and the Sixteenth Sunday in Ordinary Time, Year C.

Those Who Do the Will of God

Antiphon / Melody ♩ = 92-96

Those who do the will of God are my sis - ters, and my

Descant

Those who do the will of God are my sis - ters and my

bro - thers and my mo - thers.

bro - thers and my mo - thers.

Verses *1 John 4:7-21*

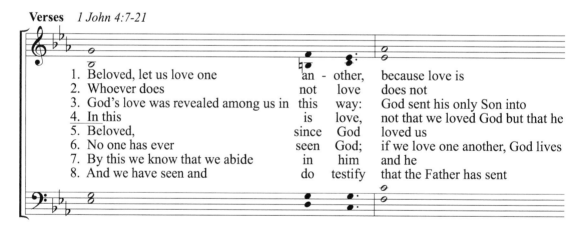

1. Beloved, let us love one an - other, because love is
2. Whoever does not love does not
3. God's love was revealed among us in this way: God sent his only Son into
4. In this is love, not that we loved God but that he
5. Beloved, since God loved us
6. No one has ever seen God; if we love one another, God lives
7. By this we know that we abide in him and he
8. And we have seen and do testify that the Father has sent

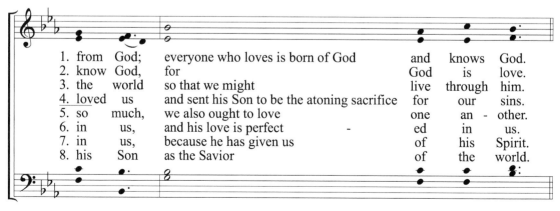

1. from God; everyone who loves is born of God and knows God.
2. know God, for God is love.
3. the world so that we might live through him.
4. loved us and sent his Son to be the atoning sacrifice for our sins.
5. so much, we also ought to love one an - other.
6. in us, and his love is perfect - ed in us.
7. in us, because he has given us of his Spirit.
8. his Son as the Savior of the world.

Verses (continued)

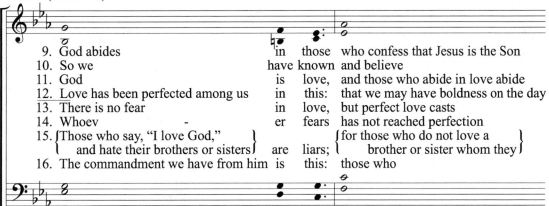

9. God abides in those who confess that Jesus is the Son
10. So we have known and believe
11. God is love, and those who abide in love abide
12. Love has been perfected among us in this: that we may have boldness on the day
13. There is no fear in love, but perfect love casts
14. Whoev - er fears has not reached perfection
15. {Those who say, "I love God," and hate their brothers or sisters} are liars; {for those who do not love a brother or sister whom they}
16. The commandment we have from him is this: those who

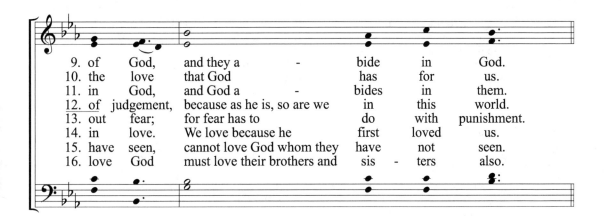

9. of God, and they a - bide in God.
10. the love that God has for us.
11. in God, and God a - bides in them.
12. of judgement, because as he is, so are we in this world.
13. out fear; for fear has to do with punishment.
14. in love. We love because he first loved us.
15. have seen, cannot love God whom they have not seen.
16. love God must love their brothers and sis - ters also.

Performance Notes

The descant can be sung at pitch by altos and/or tenors.

Those Who Fear the Lord

Antiphon ♩ = ca. 76

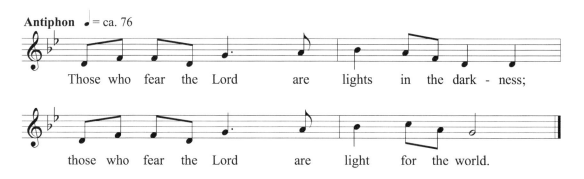

Those who fear the Lord are lights in the dark - ness;

those who fear the Lord are light for the world.

Verses *Psalm 112:4-8a, 9*

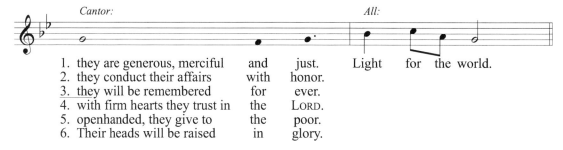

Cantor: *All:*

1. They are lights in the darkness for the upright;   Lights in the dark - ness;
2. Good people take pity and lend,
3. The just will ne - ver waver,
4. They have no fear of e - vil news;
5. With steadfast hearts they will not fear;
6. Their justice stands firm for ever.

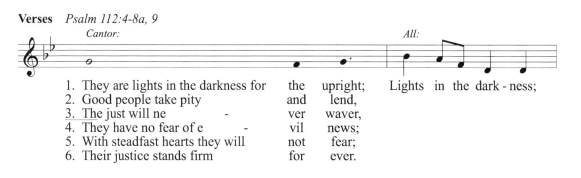

Cantor: *All:*

1. they are generous, merciful and just.   Light for the world.
2. they conduct their affairs with honor.
3. they will be remembered for ever.
4. with firm hearts they trust in the LORD.
5. openhanded, they give to the poor.
6. Their heads will be raised in glory.

Those Who Love Me, I Will Deliver

Verses *Psalm 91; Isaiah 58:8, 9c-10, 11c-12, 14*

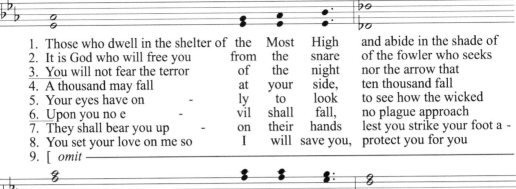

1. Those who dwell in the shelter of the Most High and abide in the shade of
2. It is God who will free you from the snare of the fowler who seeks
3. You will not fear the terror of the night nor the arrow that
4. A thousand may fall at your side, ten thousand fall
5. Your eyes have on - ly to look to see how the wicked
6. Upon you no e - vil shall fall, no plague approach
7. They shall bear you up - on their hands lest you strike your foot a -
8. You set your love on me so I will save you, protect you for you
9. [omit ————————————————

1. the Al - mighty say to the LORD: "My re - fuge, my stronghold,
2. to de - stroy you; God will conceal you with his pinions,
3. flies by day, nor the plague that prowls in the darkness
4. at your right, you, it will ne - ver ap - proach;
5. are re - paid, you who have said: "LORD, my refuge!"
6. where you dwell. For you God has command - ed the angels
7. gainst a stone. On the lion and the viper you will tread
8. know my name. When you call I shall answer: "I am with you,"
9. ————————] With length of days I will con - tent you;

1. the God in whom I trust."
2. and under his wings you will find refuge.
3. nor the scourge that lays waste at noon.
4. God's faithfulness is buck - ler and shield.
5. and have made the Most High your dwelling.
6. to keep you in all your ways.
7. and trample the young lion and the dragon.
8. I will save you in distress and give you glory.
9. I shall let you see my sav - ing power.

Verses (continued)

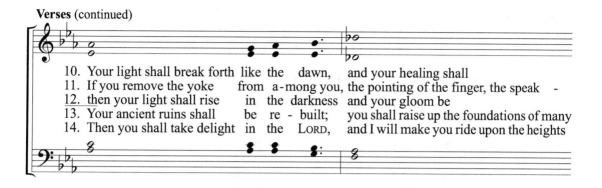

10. Your light shall break forth like the dawn, and your healing shall
11. If you remove the yoke from a-mong you, the pointing of the finger, the speak -
12. then your light shall rise in the darkness and your gloom be
13. Your ancient ruins shall be re - built; you shall raise up the foundations of many
14. Then you shall take delight in the LORD, and I will make you ride upon the heights

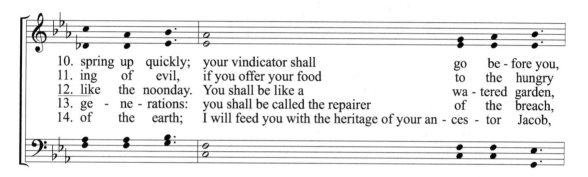

10. spring up quickly; your vindicator shall go be - fore you,
11. ing of evil, if you offer your food to the hungry
12. like the noonday. You shall be like a wa - tered garden,
13. ge - ne - rations: you shall be called the repairer of the breach,
14. of the earth; I will feed you with the heritage of your an - ces - tor Jacob,

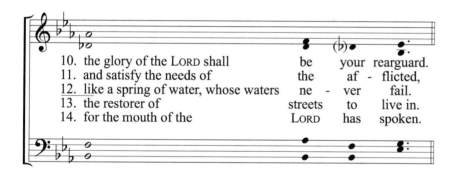

10. the glory of the LORD shall be your rearguard.
11. and satisfy the needs of the af - flicted,
12. like a spring of water, whose waters ne - ver fail.
13. the restorer of streets to live in.
14. for the mouth of the LORD has spoken.

Verse (Superimposed)   *Psalm 17*

1. LORD, hear a cause that is just, pay
2. Turn your ear to my prayer, no de
3. you may my judgement come forth. Your
4. search my heart, you
5. test me and you find in me no wrong. My
6. violence because of your word,   [I
7. there was no faltering
8. [here and I call, you will hear me, O God. Turn your
9. play your great love, whose right hand saves your
10. [Guard me as the apple of your eye.
11. violent attack of the wicked. My foes en
12. hearts tight shut, their mouths speak proudly. They ad
13. Their eyes are watching to
14. lions ready to claw, or some young
15. rise, confront them, strike them down! Let your
16. hand, O LORD, rescue me from
17. in this present life. You
18. joice in abundance of offspring and
19. As for me, in my justice,
20. filled, when I awake, with the

Antiphon / Melody ♩ = ca. 63

To   gaze   on   your   glo - ry   will

Canonic Descant   *Canon*

be   my   de - light.   To

Bass Descant

To   gaze   on   your   glo - ry   will

Alternate Bass Descant *

see   your   glo - ry

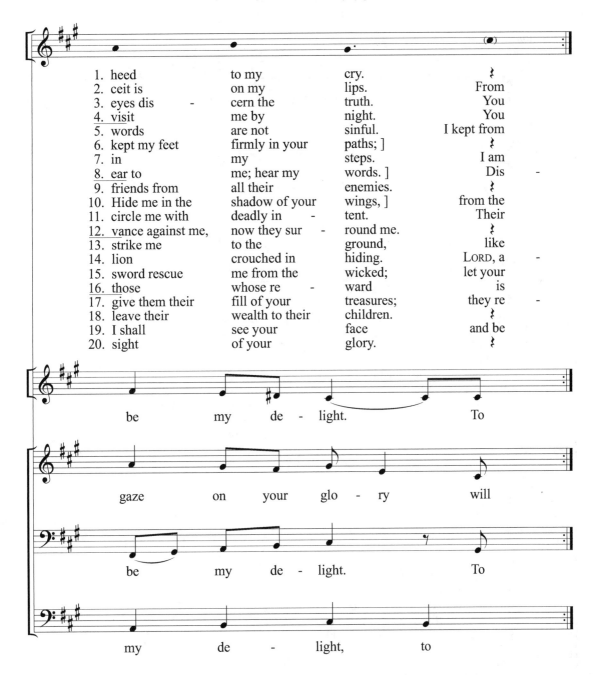

1. heed	to my	cry.	𝄾
2. ceit is	on my	lips.	From
3. eyes dis -	cern the	truth.	You
4. visit	me by	night.	You
5. words	are not	sinful.	I kept from
6. kept my feet	firmly in your	paths;]	𝄾
7. in	my	steps.	I am
8. ear to	me; hear my	words.]	Dis -
9. friends from	all their	enemies.	𝄾
10. Hide me in the	shadow of your	wings,]	from the
11. circle me with	deadly in -	tent.	Their
12. vance against me,	now they sur -	round me.	𝄾
13. strike me	to the	ground,	like
14. lion	crouched in	hiding.	LORD, a -
15. sword rescue	me from the	wicked;	let your
16. those	whose re -	ward	is
17. give them their	fill of your	treasures;	they re -
18. leave their	wealth to their	children.	𝄾
19. I shall	see your	face	and be
20. sight	of your	glory.	𝄾

be   my   de - light.   To

gaze   on   your   glo - ry   will

be   my   de - light.   To

my   de - light,   to

Performance Notes

The Alternate Bass Descant cannot be used simultaneously with the main bass descant; it can be used only when the chant is sung unaccompanied.

Verses 1, 2, 6–8, 10, and 19–20 are the Lectionary selections for the Thirty-second Sunday in Ordinary Time, Year C. Note that in verses 6, 8, and 10, brackets indicate the Lectionary selection portion.

To You, O Lord, I Lift My Soul

Antiphon / Melody ♩ = 69

To you, O Lord, I lift my soul; I trust in you, my God.

Descant

To you, O Lord; I trust in you, my God.

Verses *Psalm 25:2-21*

[A]

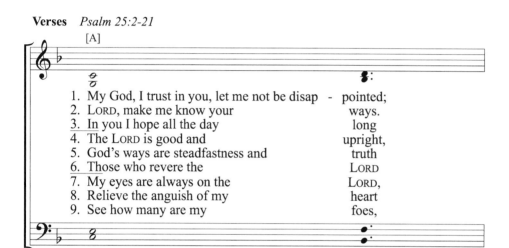

1. My God, I trust in you, let me not be disap - pointed;
2. LORD, make me know your ways.
3. In you I hope all the day long
4. The LORD is good and upright,
5. God's ways are steadfastness and truth
6. Those who revere the LORD
7. My eyes are always on the LORD,
8. Relieve the anguish of my heart
9. See how many are my foes,

[B]

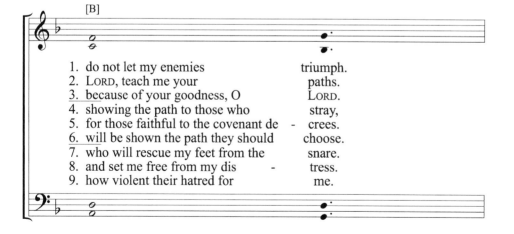

1. do not let my enemies triumph.
2. LORD, teach me your paths.
3. because of your goodness, O LORD.
4. showing the path to those who stray,
5. for those faithful to the covenant de - crees.
6. will be shown the path they should choose.
7. who will rescue my feet from the snare.
8. and set me free from my dis - tress.
9. how violent their hatred for me.

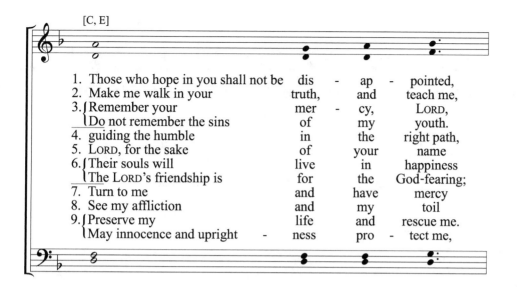

1. Those who hope in you shall not be dis - ap - pointed,
2. Make me walk in your truth, and teach me,
3. ⌠Remember your mer - cy, LORD,
   ⌊Do not remember the sins of my youth.
4. guiding the humble in the right path,
5. LORD, for the sake of your name
6. ⌠Their souls will live in happiness
   ⌊The LORD's friendship is for the God-fearing;
7. Turn to me and have mercy
8. See my affliction and my toil
9. ⌠Preserve my life and rescue me.
   ⌊May innocence and upright - ness pro - tect me,

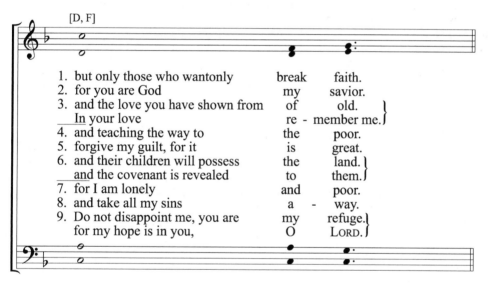

1. but only those who wantonly break faith.
2. for you are God my savior.
3. and the love you have shown from of old. ⌉
   In your love re - member me. ⌟
4. and teaching the way to the poor.
5. forgive my guilt, for it is great.
6. and their children will possess the land. ⌉
   and the covenant is revealed to them. ⌟
7. for I am lonely and poor.
8. and take all my sins a - way.
9. Do not disappoint me, you are my refuge. ⌉
   for my hope is in you, O LORD. ⌟

Performance Notes

Verses 2, 4, 5ab, and 6ef are the Lectionary selections for the First Sunday of Advent, Year C.

Touch Me and See

Antiphon / Melody ♩ = 69

Touch me and see, come here and eat: I am your bread, al-le-lu-ia.

Descant

Touch me, come, see: I am your bread, al-le-lu-ia.

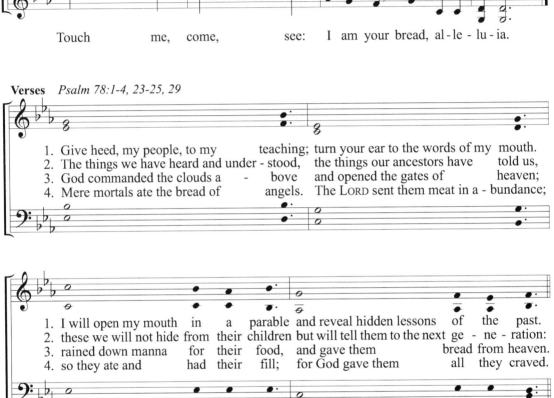

Verses *Psalm 78:1-4, 23-25, 29*

1. Give heed, my people, to my teaching; turn your ear to the words of my mouth.
2. The things we have heard and under-stood, the things our ancestors have told us,
3. God commanded the clouds a - bove and opened the gates of heaven;
4. Mere mortals ate the bread of angels. The LORD sent them meat in a-bundance;

1. I will open my mouth in a parable and reveal hidden lessons of the past.
2. these we will not hide from their children but will tell them to the next ge - ne - ration:
3. rained down manna for their food, and gave them bread from heaven.
4. so they ate and had their fill; for God gave them all they craved.

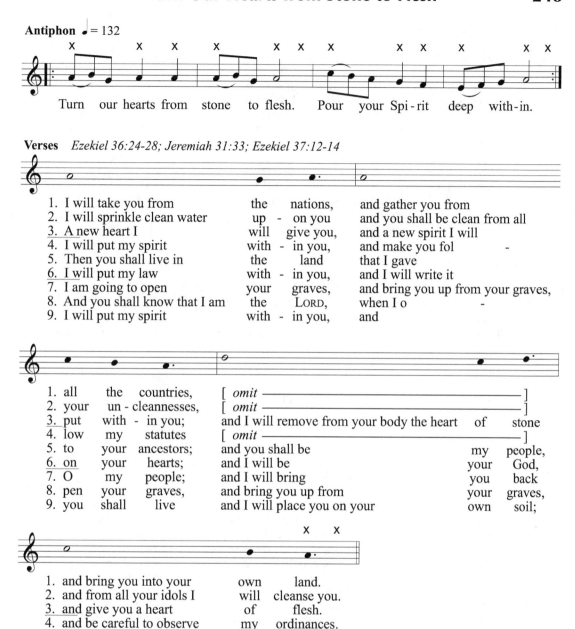

Performance Notes

Percussion or handclaps may be added, as indicated by X's, both during the antiphon and at the end of the psalm verses to lead back into the antiphon.

The antiphon should be repeated every time it is sung.

Turn to Me, Answer Me

Verses (Superimposed)   *Psalm 86*

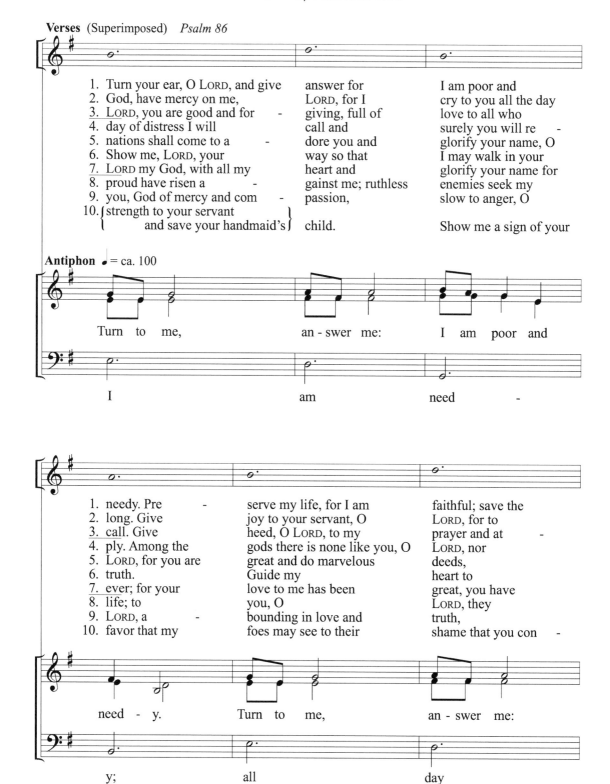

1. Turn your ear, O LORD, and give answer for I am poor and
2. God, have mercy on me, LORD, for I cry to you all the day
3. LORD, you are good and for - giving, full of love to all who
4. day of distress I will call and surely you will re -
5. nations shall come to a - dore you and glorify your name, O
6. Show me, LORD, your way so that I may walk in your
7. LORD my God, with all my heart and glorify your name for
8. proud have risen a - gainst me; ruthless enemies seek my
9. you, God of mercy and com - passion, slow to anger, O
10. { strength to your servant
     { and save your handmaid's } child. Show me a sign of your

Antiphon ♩ = ca. 100

Turn to me,   an - swer me: I am poor and

I   am   need   -

1. needy. Pre - serve my life, for I am faithful; save the
2. long. Give joy to your servant, O LORD, for to
3. call. Give heed, O LORD, to my prayer and at -
4. ply. Among the gods there is none like you, O LORD, nor
5. LORD, for you are great and do marvelous deeds,
6. truth. Guide my heart to
7. ever; for your love to me has been great, you have
8. life; to you, O LORD, they
9. LORD, a - bounding in love and truth,
10. favor that my foes may see to their shame that you con -

need - y.   Turn to me,   an - swer me:

y;   all   day

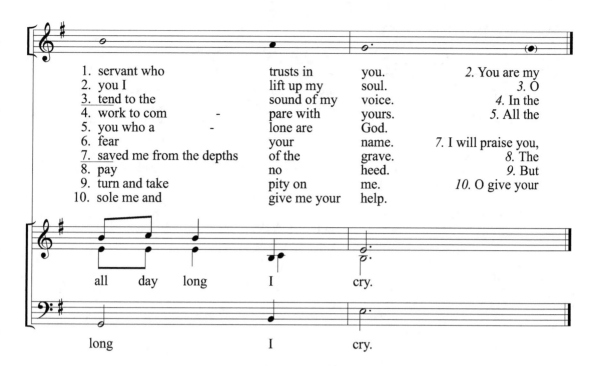

1. servant who	trusts in	you.
2. you I	lift up my	soul.
3. tend to the	sound of my	voice.
4. work to com -	pare with	yours.
5. you who a -	lone are	God.
6. fear	your	name.
7. saved me from the depths	of the	grave.
8. pay	no	heed.
9. turn and take	pity on	me.
10. sole me and	give me your	help.

2. You are my
3. O
4. In the
5. All the

7. I will praise you,
8. The
9. But
10. O give your

all   day   long   I   cry.

long   I   cry.

250 Turn to the Lord

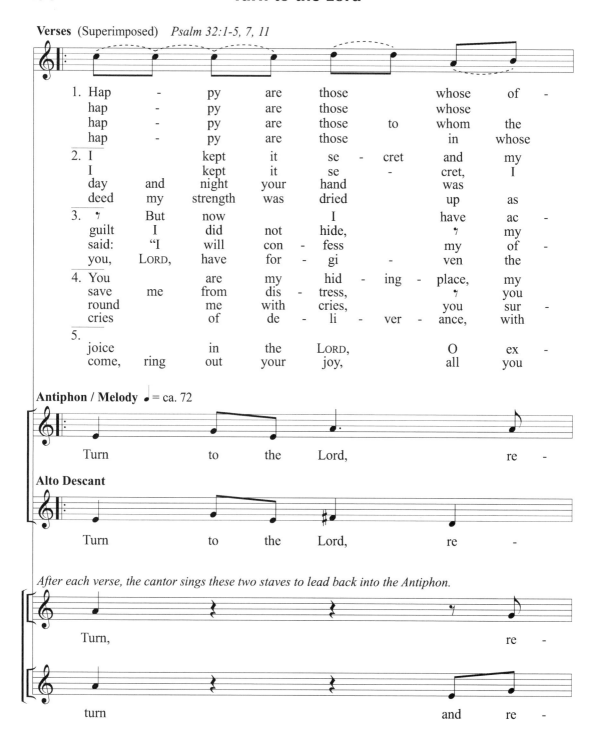

Verses (Superimposed) *Psalm 32:1-5, 7, 11*

1. Hap - py are those whose of -
   hap - py are those whose
   hap - py are those to whom the
   hap - py are those in whose

2. I kept it se - cret and my
   I kept it se - cret, I
   day and night your hand was
   deed my strength was dried up as

3. ⁷ But now I have ac -
   guilt I did not hide, ⁷ my
   said: "I will con - fess my of -
   you, LORD, have for - gi - ven the

4. You are my hid - ing - place, my
   save me from dis - tress, ⁷ you
   round me with cries, you sur -
   cries of de - li - ver - ance, with

5. joice in the LORD, O ex -
   come, ring out your joy, all you

Antiphon / Melody ♩ = ca. 72

Turn to the Lord, re -

Alto Descant

Turn to the Lord, re -

After each verse, the cantor sings these two staves to lead back into the Antiphon.

Turn, re -

turn and re -

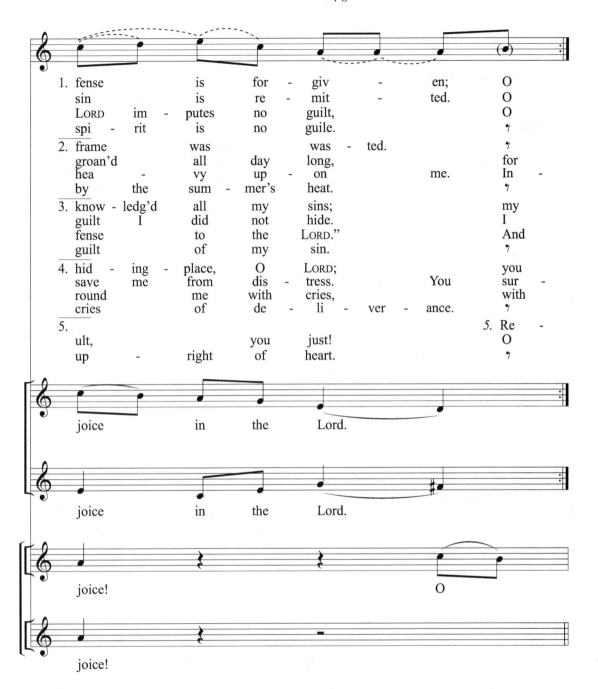

1. fense   is   for - giv - en;   O
   sin   is   re - mit - ted.   O
   LORD im - putes no   guilt,   O
   spi - rit   is   no   guile.   ,

2. frame   was   was - ted.   ,
   groan'd   all   day   long,   for
   hea - vy   up -   on   me.   In -
   by   the   sum - mer's heat.   ,

3. know - ledg'd all   my   sins;   my
   guilt   I   did   not   hide.   I
   fense   to   the   LORD."   And
   guilt   of   my   sin.   ,

4. hid - ing - place,   O   LORD;   you
   save   me   from   dis - tress.   You   sur -
   round   me   with   cries,   with
   cries   of   de -   li - ver - ance. ,

5.
   ult,   you   just!   O
   up - right   of   heart.   ,

joice   in   the   Lord.

joice   in   the   Lord.

joice!   O

joice!

Performance Notes

Verses 1–3 and 5 are the Lectionary selections for the Sixth Sunday in Ordinary Time, Year B.
Verses 1 and 3–5 are the Lectionary selections for the Eleventh Sunday in Ordinary Time, Year C.

251   Unless a Grain of Wheat

Antiphon / Melody ♩ = 72–76

Un - less a grain of wheat falls to the ground and dies, it re-

Alto Descant

Un - less a grain of wheat falls to the ground and dies, it re-

mains a sin - gle grain, it re - mains a sin - gle grain.

mains a sin - gle grain, it re - mains a sin - gle grain.

Verses   *Psalm 126*

1. When the LORD delivered Zi - on from bondage, it seemed like a dream.
2. The heathens themselves said: "What marvels the LORD worked for them!"
3. Deliver us, O LORD, from our bondage as streams in dry land.
4. They go out, they go out, full of tears, carrying seed for the sowing;

1. Then was our mouth filled with laughter, on our lips there were songs.
2. What marvels the LORD worked for us! Indeed we were glad.
3. Those who are sow - ing in tears will sing when they reap.
4. they come back, they come back, full of song, carry - ing their sheaves.

Venite, Adoremus

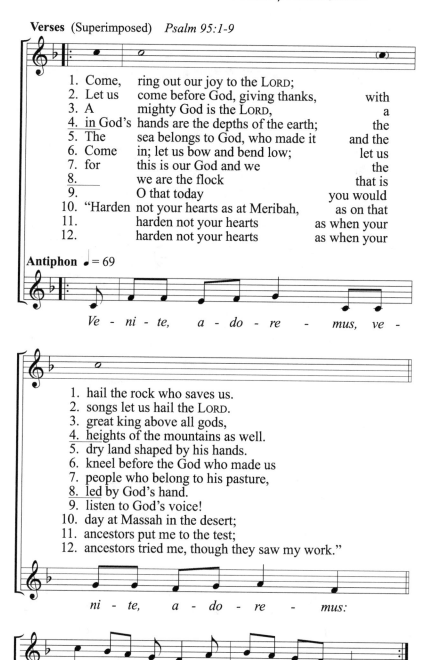

Verses (Superimposed)   *Psalm 95:1-9*

1. Come,   ring out our joy to the Lord;
2. Let us   come before God, giving thanks,   with
3. A   mighty God is the Lord,   a
4. in God's hands are the depths of the earth;   the
5. The   sea belongs to God, who made it   and the
6. Come   in; let us bow and bend low;   let us
7. for   this is our God and we   the
8.   we are the flock   that is
9.   O that today   you would
10. "Harden not your hearts as at Meribah,   as on that
11.   harden not your hearts   as when your
12.   harden not your hearts   as when your

Antiphon ♩ = 69

Ve - ni - te,   a - do - re - mus,   ve -

1. hail the rock who saves us.
2. songs let us hail the Lord.
3. great king above all gods,
4. heights of the mountains as well.
5. dry land shaped by his hands.
6. kneel before the God who made us
7. people who belong to his pasture,
8. led by God's hand.
9. listen to God's voice!
10. day at Massah in the desert;
11. ancestors put me to the test;
12. ancestors tried me, though they saw my work."

ni - te,   a - do - re - mus:

come, let us wor-ship and   bow be-fore the Lord.

Performance Notes

Verses 1–8 are the Lectionary selections for the Anniversary of the Dedication of a Church.
The antiphon can be used as an ostinato chant, or with psalm verses. When using the psalm, the antiphon should be established before the cantor begins to chant the psalm verses. As the verses are chanted, the first half of the antiphon can be sung quietly underneath with its text, or simply hummed. The second half of the antiphon (with its text) then becomes a refrain at the end of each verse.

Walk in My Ways

Verses (*Option A*)   *Psalm 96*

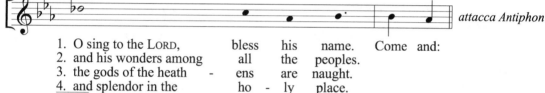

1. O sing a new song to the Lord, sing to the Lord all | the | earth.
2. Proclaim God's help day by day, tell among the nations | his | glory
3. The Lord is great and worthy of praise, to be feared above | all | gods;
4. It was the Lord who made the heavens. His are majesty and honor | and | power
5. Give the Lord, you families of peoples, give the Lord glory | and | power;
6. Bring an offering and enter God's courts, worship the Lord in | the | temple.
7. Proclaim to the nations: "God is king." The world was made firm in | its | place;
8. Let the heavens rejoice and earth | be | glad,
9. let the land and all it bears | re - | joice,
10. at the presence of the Lord | who | comes,
11. who comes with justice to rule | the | world,

attacca Antiphon

1. O sing to the Lord, | bless | his | name. Come and:
2. and his wonders among | all | the | peoples.
3. the gods of the heath - | ens | are | naught.
4. and splendor in the | ho - ly | place.
5. give the Lord the glory | of | his | name.
6. O earth, stand in fear | of | the | Lord.
7. God will judge the peo - | ple | in | fairness.
8. let the sea and all within it | thun - der | praise,
9. all the trees of the wood | shout | for | joy
10. who comes to | rule | the | earth,
11. and to judge the peo - | ples | with | truth.

Verses (*Option B*)   *Psalm 119:105-112*

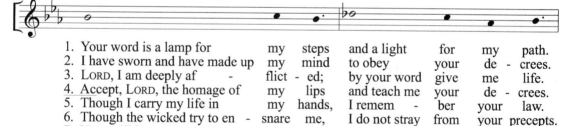

1. Your word is a lamp for | my | steps | and a light | for | my | path.
2. I have sworn and have made up | my | mind | to obey | your | de - crees.
3. Lord, I am deeply af - | flict - ed; | by your word | give | me | life.
4. Accept, Lord, the homage of | my | lips | and teach me | your | de - crees.
5. Though I carry my life in | my | hands, | I remem - ber | your | law.
6. Though the wicked try to en - snare | me, | I do not stray | from | your precepts.
7. Your will is my heritage for | e - ver, | the joy | of | my | heart.
8. I set myself to carry out your | sta - tutes | in full - ness | for | ever.

attacca Antiphon

Come and:

Performance Notes

**Option A verses are used on the Third Sunday in Ordinary Time, Year B. Option B verses are used on the First
Sunday of Lent, Year B.*
As indicated, the antiphon may be sung as a 2-part round.

We Have Sinned, Lord

Verses (Superimposed) *Psalm 51:3-6b, 12-14, 17*

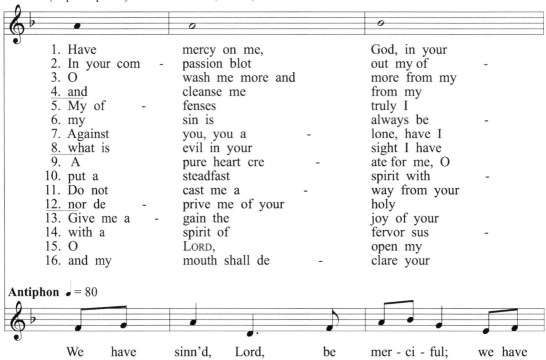

1. Have mercy on me, God, in your
2. In your com - passion blot out my of -
3. O wash me more and more from my
4. and cleanse me from my
5. My of - fenses truly I
6. my sin is always be -
7. Against you, you a - lone, have I
8. what is evil in your sight I have
9. A pure heart cre - ate for me, O
10. put a steadfast spirit with -
11. Do not cast me a - way from your
12. nor de - prive me of your holy
13. Give me a - gain the joy of your
14. with a spirit of fervor sus -
15. O LORD, open my
16. and my mouth shall de - clare your

Antiphon ♩ = 80

We have sinn'd, Lord, be mer - ci - ful; we have

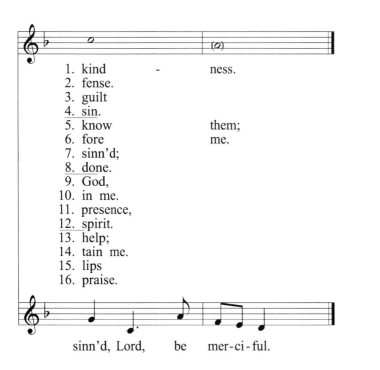

1. kind - ness.
2. fense.
3. guilt
4. sin.
5. know them;
6. fore me.
7. sinn'd;
8. done.
9. God,
10. in me.
11. presence,
12. spirit.
13. help;
14. tain me.
15. lips
16. praise.

sinn'd, Lord, be mer-ci-ful.

We Look to You, O Lord

Verses *Psalm 123*

1. To you have I lifted up my eyes,
2. my eyes, like the eyes of slaves
3. Like the eyes of a servant on the hand of her mistress,
4. Have mercy on us, LORD, have mercy.
5. Indeed all too full is our soul with the scorn of the rich,

1. you who dwell in the heavens; Have mer-cy, mer-cy.
2. on the hand of their lords.
3. {so our eyes are on the / LORD our God till we are} shown mercy.
4. We are filled with con - tempt.
5. the disdain of the proud.

We Receive from Your Fullness

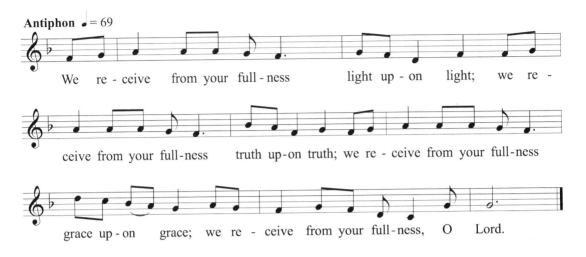

Antiphon ♩ = 69

We re-ceive from your full-ness light up-on light; we re-ceive from your full-ness truth up-on truth; we re-ceive from your full-ness grace up-on grace; we re-ceive from your full-ness, O Lord.

Verses *1 John 1:5-7; Isaiah 35:1-4*

1. This is the message we have heard from him and proclaim to you,
2. If we say that we have fellowship with him while we are walking in darkness,
3. but if we walk in the light as he himself is the light,
4. The wilderness and the dry land shall be glad, the desert shall rejoice and blossom;
5. The glory of Lebanon shall be given to it, the majesty of Carmel and Sharon.
6. Strengthen the weak hands, and make firm the feeble knees.
7. Here is your God. He will come with vengeance, with terrible recompense.

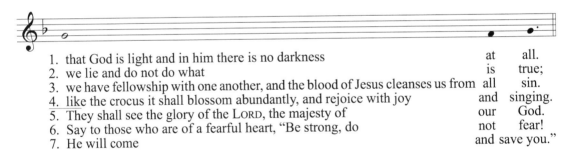

1. that God is light and in him there is no darkness at all.
2. we lie and do not do what is true;
3. we have fellowship with one another, and the blood of Jesus cleanses us from all sin.
4. like the crocus it shall blossom abundantly, and rejoice with joy and singing.
5. They shall see the glory of the LORD, the majesty of our God.
6. Say to those who are of a fearful heart, "Be strong, do not fear!
7. He will come and save you."

We Shall Be Like You

Verses (Superimposed)   *Psalm 27:1, 4, 7-14*

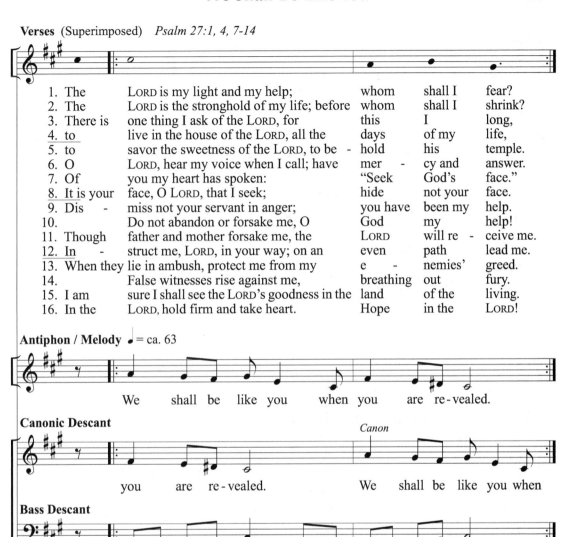

1. The   LORD is my light and my help;   whom   shall I   fear?
2. The   LORD is the stronghold of my life; before   whom   shall I   shrink?
3. There is   one thing I ask of the LORD, for   this   I   long,
4. to   live in the house of the LORD, all the   days   of my   life,
5. to   savor the sweetness of the LORD, to be - hold   his   temple.
6. O   LORD, hear my voice when I call; have   mer - cy and   answer.
7. Of   you my heart has spoken: "Seek   God's   face."
8. It is your   face, O LORD, that I seek;   hide   not your   face.
9. Dis - miss not your servant in anger;   you have   been my   help.
10.   Do not abandon or forsake me, O   God   my   help!
11. Though   father and mother forsake me, the   LORD   will re - ceive me.
12. In - struct me, LORD, in your way; on an   even   path   lead me.
13. When they lie in ambush, protect me from my   e - nemies'   greed.
14.   False witnesses rise against me,   breathing   out   fury.
15. I am   sure I shall see the LORD's goodness in the   land   of the   living.
16. In the   LORD, hold firm and take heart.   Hope   in the   LORD!

Antiphon / Melody ♩ = ca. 63

We shall be like you when you are re-vealed.

Canonic Descant

Canon

you are re-vealed.   We shall be like you when

Bass Descant

We shall be like you when you are re-vealed.

We Will Follow You, Lord

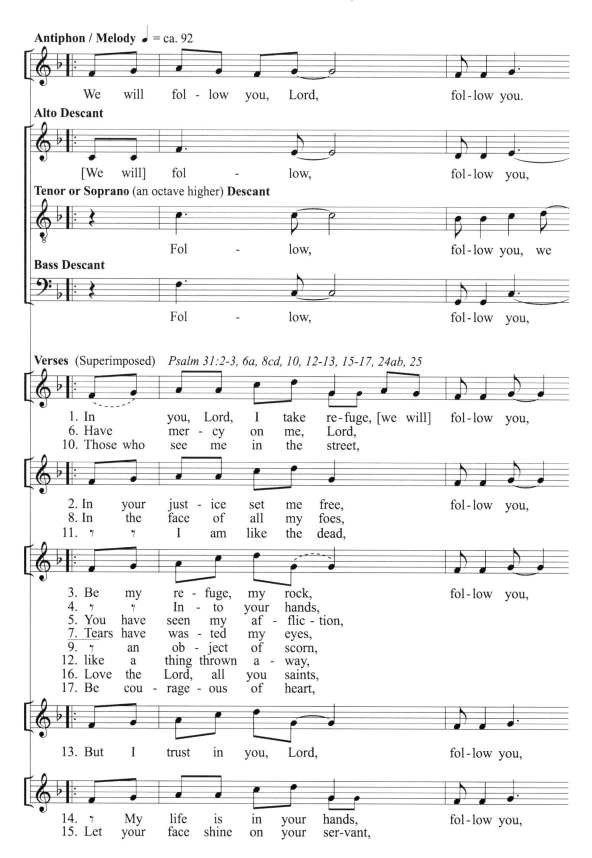

Antiphon / Melody ♩ = ca. 92

We will fol-low you, Lord, fol-low you.

Alto Descant

[We will] fol - low, fol-low you,

Tenor or Soprano (an octave higher) **Descant**

Fol - low, fol-low you, we

Bass Descant

Fol - low, fol-low you,

Verses (Superimposed) *Psalm 31:2-3, 6a, 8cd, 10, 12-13, 15-17, 24ab, 25*

1. In you, Lord, I take re-fuge, [we will] fol-low you,
6. Have mer - cy on me, Lord,
10. Those who see me in the street,

2. In your just - ice set me free, fol-low you,
8. In the face of all my foes,
11. ⁊ ⁊ I am like the dead,

3. Be my re-fuge, my rock, fol-low you,
4. ⁊ ⁊ In - to your hands,
5. You have seen my af - flic - tion,
7. Tears have was - ted my eyes,
9. ⁊ an ob - ject of scorn,
12. like a thing thrown a - way,
16. Love the Lord, all you saints,
17. Be cou - rage - ous of heart,

13. But I trust in you, Lord, fol-low you,

14. ⁊ My life is in your hands, fol-low you,
15. Let your face shine on your ser-vant,

We will fol-low you, Lord, fol-low you.

fol - low, fol-low you.

will fol - low, fol-low you.

fol - low, fol-low you.

1. let me not be put to shame, [we will] fol-low you.
6. ℣ for I am in dis - tress,
10. ℣ run far a - way from me,

2. swift-ly hear me and save me, fol-low you.
8. I am a re - proach,
11. ℣ for - got - ten by all,

3. might-y strong-hold to save me, fol-low you.
4. I com - mend my spi - rit,
5. the dis - tress of my soul,
7. ℣ my throat and my heart,
9. and of fear to my friends,
12. yes, a thing thrown a - way,
16. for the Lord guards the faith - ful,
17. all who hope in the Lord,

13. I say: "You are my God," fol-low you.

14. ℣ de - li - ver me from ha - tred, fol-low you.
15. ℟ save me in your love,

When the Poor Cry Out

Antiphon / Melody ♩ = 88

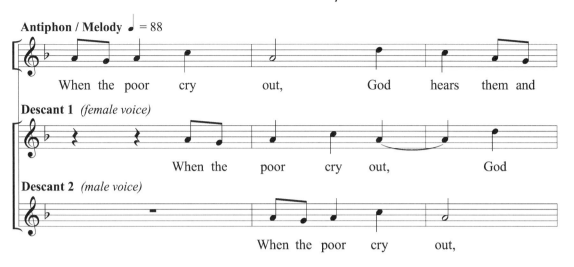

When the poor cry out, God hears them and

Descant 1 *(female voice)*

When the poor cry out, God

Descant 2 *(male voice)*

When the poor cry out,

saves them.

hears them.

God hears . . .

Verses *Psalm 34:2-3, 17-19, 23*

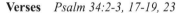

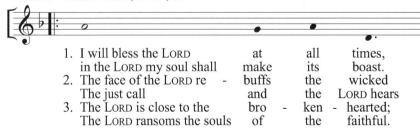

1. I will bless the LORD   at   all   times,
   in the LORD my soul shall   make   its   boast.
2. The face of the LORD re - buffs   the   wicked
   The just call   and   the   LORD hears
3. The LORD is close to the   bro - ken - hearted;
   The LORD ransoms the souls   of   the   faithful.

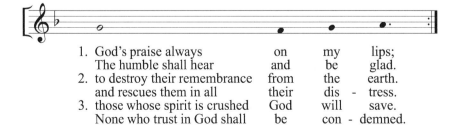

1. God's praise always   on   my   lips;
   The humble shall hear   and   be   glad.
2. to destroy their remembrance   from   the   earth.
   and rescues them in all   their   dis - tress.
3. those whose spirit is crushed   God   will   save.
   None who trust in God shall   be   con - demned.

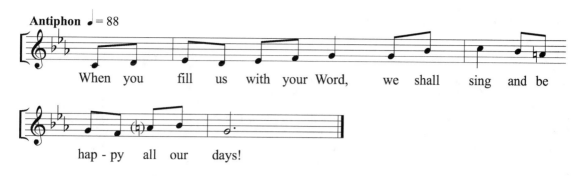

Antiphon ♩ = 88

When you fill us with your Word, we shall sing and be

hap - py all our days!

Verses (*Option A) *Psalm 90:3-6, 12-17*

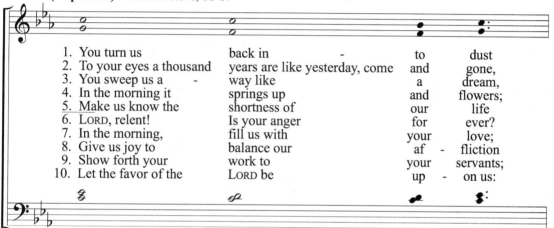

1. You turn us   back in -   to   dust
2. To your eyes a thousand   years are like yesterday, come   and   gone,
3. You sweep us a -   way like   a   dream,
4. In the morning it   springs up   and   flowers;
5. Make us know the   shortness of   our   life
6. LORD, relent!   Is your anger   for   ever?
7. In the morning,   fill us with   your   love;
8. Give us joy to   balance our   af -   fliction
9. Show forth your   work to   your   servants;
10. Let the favor of the   LORD be   up -   on us:

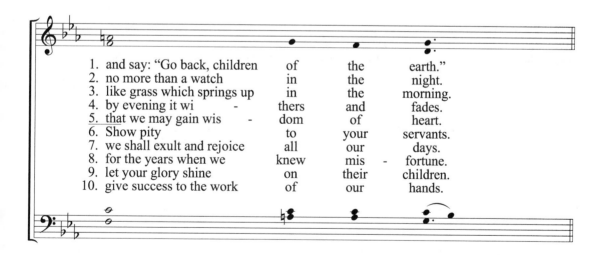

1. and say: "Go back, children   of   the   earth."
2. no more than a watch   in   the   night.
3. like grass which springs up   in   the   morning.
4. by evening it wi -   thers   and   fades.
5. that we may gain wis -   dom   of   heart.
6. Show pity   to   your   servants.
7. we shall exult and rejoice   all   our   days.
8. for the years when we   knew   mis -   fortune.
9. let your glory shine   on   their   children.
10. give success to the work   of   our   hands.

Verses (*Option B) *Psalm 95:1-2, 6-9*

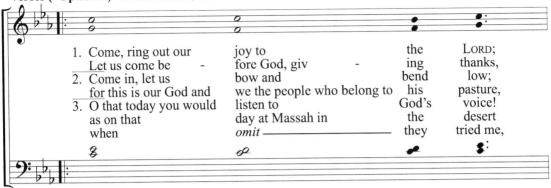

1. Come, ring out our joy to the LORD;
   Let us come be - fore God, giv - ing thanks,
2. Come in, let us bow and bend low;
   for this is our God and we the people who belong to his pasture,
3. O that today you would listen to God's voice!
   as on that day at Massah in the desert
   when *omit* ———————— they tried me,

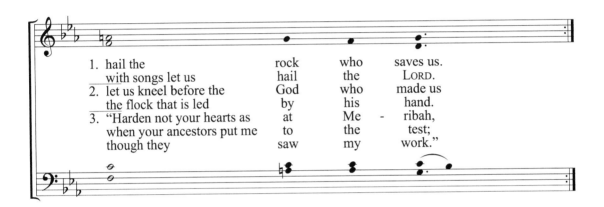

1. hail the rock who saves us.
   with songs let us hail the LORD.
2. let us kneel before the God who made us
   the flock that is led by his hand.
3. "Harden not your hearts as at Me - ribah,
   when your ancestors put me to the test;
   though they saw my work."

Performance Notes

Option A verses 5–10 are used on the Twenty-eighth Sunday in Ordinary Time, Year B. Option B verses are alternate verses for the Eighteenth Sunday in Ordinary Time, Year C.

Option A verses 1–7 and 10 are used on the Eighteenth Sunday in Ordinary Time, Year C; the antiphon should be sung only after every two verses.

Where Two or Three Are Gathered

Antiphon / Melody ♩ = ca. 65

Where two or three are ga-thered, ga-thered in my name, there am

Descants

Where two or three are ga-thered, ga-thered in my name, there am

I, there am I in the midst of them.

I, there am I in the midst of them.

Verses *Romans 12:1-2, 4-5, 9-17, 20ab, 21; 13:8, 9a, 9g-10; 14:8-9; 15:5-7*

1. I appeal to you, brothers	and	sisters,
2. Do not be conformed to	this	world,
3. For as in one body we have ma -	ny	members,
4. Let love be genuine; hate what	is	evil,
5. Do not lag	in	zeal,
6. Bless those	who	persecute you;
7. Live in harmony with one	an -	other;
8. If your enemies are hun -	gry,	feed them;
9. Owe no	one	anything,
10. The commandments are summed up in	this	word:
11. If we live, we live to	the	Lord,
12. May the God of steadfastness and	en -	couragement
13. [*omit* ————————————————————		

1. by the mercies   of   God,
2. but be transformed by the renewing of   your   minds,
3. and not all the members have the   same   function,
4. hold fast to what   is   good;
5. be ardent in spirit, serve   the   Lord.
6. bless and do   not   curse them.
7. do not   be   haughty,
8. if they are thirsty, give them something   to   drink.
9. except to love one   an - other;
10. "Love your neighbor as   your - self."
11. and if we die, we die to   the   Lord;
12. grant you to live in harmony with one   an - other,
13. ——————————————————]

1. to present your bodies as a liv - ing   sacrifice,
2. so that you may discern what is the will   of   God,
3. so we, who are many, are one body   in   Christ,
4. love one another with mutual   af - fection:
5. { Rejoice in hope, be patient   in   suffering,
    Contribute to the needs of   the   saints;
6. Rejoice with those who   re - joice,
7. { but associate with   the   lowly;
    Do not repay anyone evil   for   evil,
8. Do not be overcome   by   evil,
9. for the one who loves   an - other
10. Love does no wrong to   a   neighbor;
11. { so then, whether we live or whether   we   die,
    To this end Christ died and lived   a - gain,
12. in accordance with   Christ   Jesus,
13. Welcome one another, therefore, just as Christ   has   welcomed you,

1. holy and accept - a - ble   to   God.
2. what is good and accept - a - ble   and   perfect.
3. and individually we are members   of   one   an - other.
4. outdo one another   in   show - ing   honor.
5. per - se - vere   in   prayer. }
    extend hospita - li - ty   to   strangers. }
6. weep   with   those   who   weep.
7. do not claim to be wis - er   than   you   are. }
    but take thought for what is noble in   the   sight   of   all. }
8. but overcome   e - vil   with   good.
9. has   ful - filled   the   law.
10. therefore, love is the fulfill - ing   of   the   law.
11. we   are—————   the   Lord's. }
    so that he might be Lord of both the   dead   and   the   living. }
12. { so that together with one voice you may }
     glorify the God and Father of our }   Lord   Je - sus   Christ.
13. for the   glo - ry   of   God.

Who Can This Be

Antiphon ♩. = 60

Who can this be, who can this be, that the wind and the

sea o - bey him?

Verses *Psalm 27:1, 3-5, 7-14*

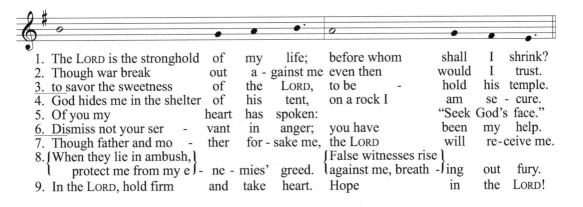

1. The LORD is my light   and   my   help;   whom   shall   I   fear?
2. Though an army en - camp a - gainst me my heart   would not   fear.
3. {There is one thing I   {to live in the house of
       ask of the LORD, for} this   I   long, the LORD all the days} of   my   life,
4. For God makes me safe   in   his   tent   in the   day   of   evil.
5. O LORD, hear my voice when   I   call;   have mer - cy   and answer.
6. It is your face, O LORD, that   I   seek;   hide   not   your face.
7. Do not abandon   or   for - sake me, O   God   my   help!
8. Instruct me, LORD,   in   your   way;   on an e - ven   path lead me.
9. I am sure I shall see   the LORD's goodness in the land   of   the   living.

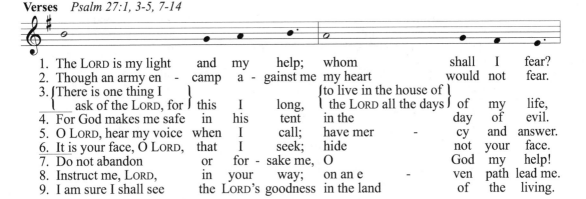

1. The LORD is the stronghold   of   my   life;   before whom   shall   I   shrink?
2. Though war break   out   a - gainst me even then   would   I   trust.
3. to savor the sweetness   of   the   LORD,   to be -   hold   his   temple.
4. God hides me in the shelter   of   his   tent,   on a rock I   am   se - cure.
5. Of you my   heart   has   spoken: "Seek God's face."
6. Dismiss not your ser - vant   in   anger;   you have   been   my   help.
7. Though father and mo - ther   for - sake me,   the LORD   will   re-ceive me.
8. {When they lie in ambush,   {False witnesses rise
   protect me from my e} - ne - mies'   greed. against me, breath -}ing   out   fury.
9. In the LORD, hold firm   and   take   heart. Hope   in   the   LORD!

Why Stare into the Sky?

Verses (Superimposed) *Psalm 68:2-6, 19-22, 33-36*

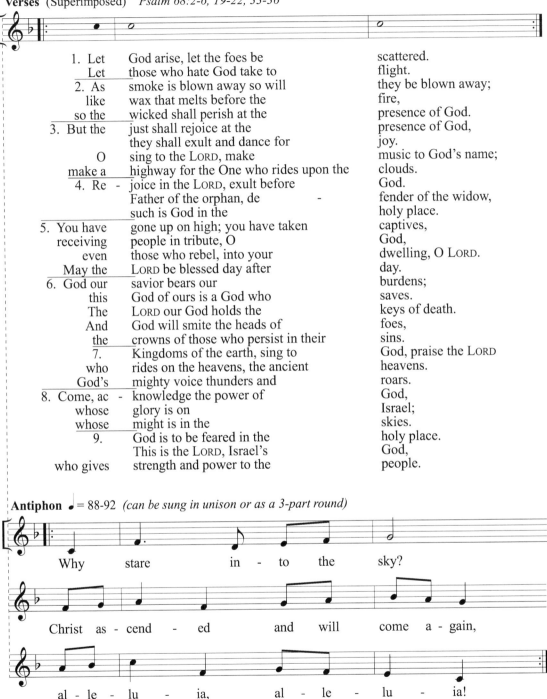

1. Let	God arise, let the foes be	scattered.
Let	those who hate God take to	flight.
2. As	smoke is blown away so will	they be blown away;
like	wax that melts before the	fire,
so the	wicked shall perish at the	presence of God.
3. But the	just shall rejoice at the	presence of God,
	they shall exult and dance for	joy.
O	sing to the LORD, make	music to God's name;
make a	highway for the One who rides upon the	clouds.
4. Re -	joice in the LORD, exult before	God.
	Father of the orphan, de -	fender of the widow,
	such is God in the	holy place.
5. You have	gone up on high; you have taken	captives,
receiving	people in tribute, O	God,
even	those who rebel, into your	dwelling, O LORD.
May the	LORD be blessed day after	day.
6. God our	savior bears our	burdens;
this	God of ours is a God who	saves.
The	LORD our God holds the	keys of death.
And	God will smite the heads of	foes,
the	crowns of those who persist in their	sins.
7.	Kingdoms of the earth, sing to	God, praise the LORD
who	rides on the heavens, the ancient	heavens.
God's	mighty voice thunders and	roars.
8. Come, ac -	knowledge the power of	God,
whose	glory is on	Israel;
whose	might is in the	skies.
9.	God is to be feared in the	holy place.
	This is the LORD, Israel's	God,
who gives	strength and power to the	people.

Antiphon ♩ = 88-92 *(can be sung in unison or as a 3-part round)*

Why stare in - to the sky?

Christ as - cend - ed and will come a - gain,

al - le - lu - ia, al - le - lu - ia!

Antiphon ♩ = ca. 80

With all my heart I cry: an-swer me, O Lord;

an - swer me, O Lord.

Verses *Psalm 119:145-152*

Cantor: *All:*

1. I call with all my heart; Lord,   hear me,   An-swer me, O Lord;
2. I call upon you,   save me
3. I rise before dawn and cry for   help,
4. My eyes watch through the   night
5. In your love hear my voice, O   Lord;
6. Those who harm me unjustly draw   near;
7. But you, O Lord, are   close,
8. Long have I known that your   will

Cantor: *All:*

1. I will keep your   statutes.   An-swer me, O Lord.
2. and I will do your   will.
3. I hope in your   word.
4. to ponder your   promise.
5. give me life by your de -   crees.
6. they are far from your   law.
7. your commands are   truth.
8. is established for   ever.

With All My Heart I Cry (II)

Antiphon ♩ = ca. 80

With all my heart I cry: how I love your law,

how I love your law.

Verses *Psalm 119:57, 72, 76-77, 127-130*

Cantor: *All:*

1. My part, I have resolved, O   LORD,
2. The law from your mouth means   more to me
3. Let your love be ready to con - sole me
4. Let your love come and I shall   live
5. That is why I love your com - mands
6. why I rule my life by your   precepts,
7. Your will is wonderful in - deed;
8. The unfolding of your word gives   light

How I love your law;

Cantor: *All:*

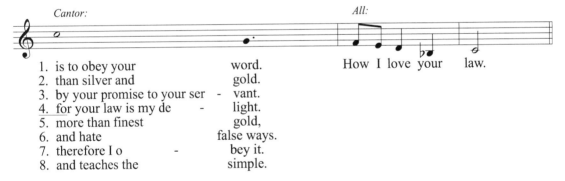

1. is to obey your   word.
2. than silver and   gold.
3. by your promise to your ser - vant.
4. for your law is my de - light.
5. more than finest   gold,
6. and hate   false ways.
7. therefore I o - bey it.
8. and teaches the   simple.

How I love your law.

Performance Notes

The verses may be sung in pairs, the antiphon only occurring after the even-numbered verses.

Antiphon ♩ = 92

With all my heart I praise you, tell - ing all your won - ders,

sing a joy - ful song to you.

Verses *Psalm 9:1-21*

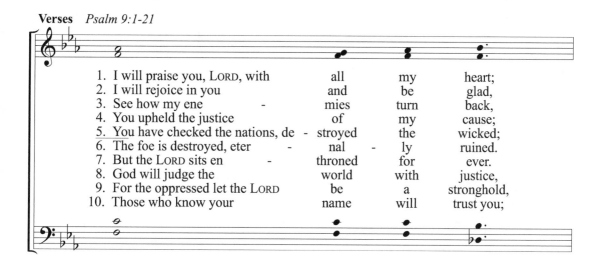

1. I will praise you, LORD, with all my heart;
2. I will rejoice in you and be glad,
3. See how my ene - mies turn back,
4. You upheld the justice of my cause;
5. You have checked the nations, de - stroyed the wicked;
6. The foe is destroyed, eter - nal - ly ruined.
7. But the LORD sits en - throned for ever.
8. God will judge the world with justice,
9. For the oppressed let the LORD be a stronghold,
10. Those who know your name will trust you;

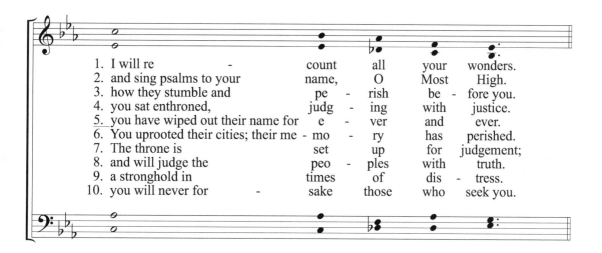

1. I will re - count all your wonders.
2. and sing psalms to your name, O Most High.
3. how they stumble and pe - rish be - fore you.
4. you sat enthroned, judg - ing with justice.
5. you have wiped out their name for e - ver and ever.
6. You uprooted their cities; their me - mo - ry has perished.
7. The throne is set up for judgement;
8. and will judge the peo - ples with truth.
9. a stronghold in times of dis - tress.
10. you will never for - sake those who seek you.

Verses (continued)

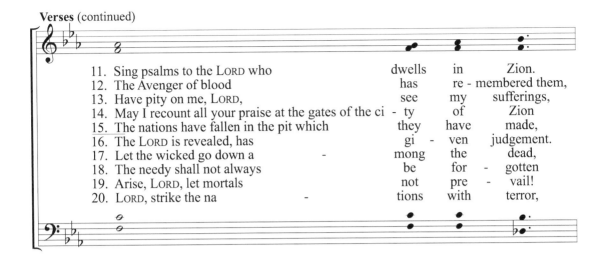

11. Sing psalms to the LORD who   dwells   in   Zion.
12. The Avenger of blood   has   re - membered them,
13. Have pity on me, LORD,   see   my   sufferings,
14. May I recount all your praise at the gates of the ci - ty   of   Zion
15. The nations have fallen in the pit which   they   have   made,
16. The LORD is revealed, has   gi - ven   judgement.
17. Let the wicked go down a   -   mong   the   dead,
18. The needy shall not always   be   for - gotten
19. Arise, LORD, let mortals   not   pre - vail!
20. LORD, strike the na   -   tions   with   terror,

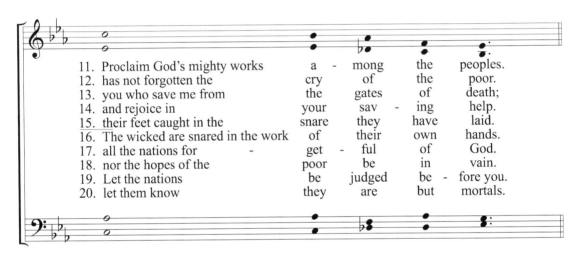

11. Proclaim God's mighty works   a - mong   the   peoples.
12. has not forgotten the   cry   of   the   poor.
13. you who save me from   the   gates   of   death;
14. and rejoice in   your   sav - ing   help.
15. their feet caught in the   snare   they   have   laid.
16. The wicked are snared in the work   of   their   own   hands.
17. all the nations for   -   get - ful   of   God.
18. nor the hopes of the   poor   be   in   vain.
19. Let the nations   be   judged   be - fore you.
20. let them know   they   are   but   mortals.

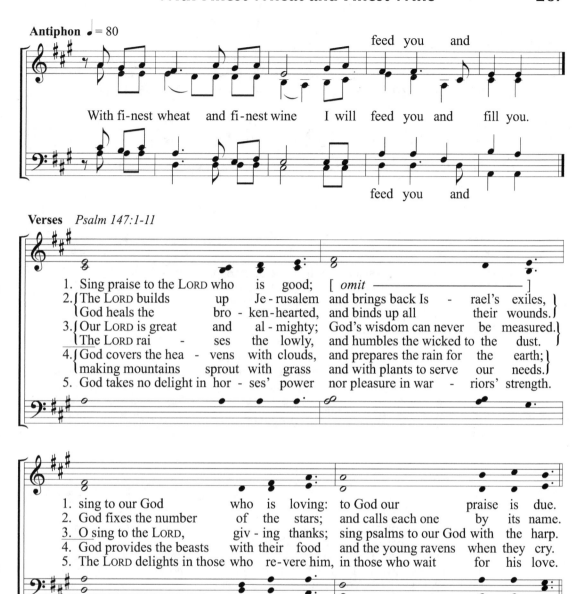

Antiphon ♩ = 80

feed you and

With fi-nest wheat and fi-nest wine I will feed you and fill you.

feed you and

Verses *Psalm 147:1-11*

1. Sing praise to the LORD who is good; [*omit* —————————————————]
2. ʃ The LORD builds up Je-rusalem and brings back Is - rael's exiles, ⎱
   ⎰ God heals the bro - ken-hearted, and binds up all their wounds. ⎰
3. ʃ Our LORD is great and al - mighty; God's wisdom can never be measured. ⎱
   ⎰ The LORD rai - ses the lowly, and humbles the wicked to the dust. ⎰
4. ʃ God covers the hea - vens with clouds, and prepares the rain for the earth; ⎱
   ⎰ making mountains sprout with grass and with plants to serve our needs. ⎰
5. God takes no delight in hor - ses' power nor pleasure in war - riors' strength.

1. sing to our God who is loving: to God our praise is due.
2. God fixes the number of the stars; and calls each one by its name.
3. O sing to the LORD, giv - ing thanks; sing psalms to our God with the harp.
4. God provides the beasts with their food and the young ravens when they cry.
5. The LORD delights in those who re-vere him, in those who wait for his love.

Within Your Temple

Antiphon ♩ = 76

With - in your tem - ple, your ho - ly dwel - ling, we re - call your lov - ing - kind - ness, O Lord our God.

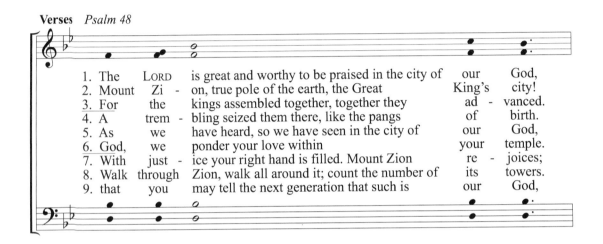

Verses *Psalm 48*

1. The LORD is great and worthy to be praised in the city of our God,
2. Mount Zi - on, true pole of the earth, the Great King's city!
3. For the kings assembled together, together they ad - vanced.
4. A trem - bling seized them there, like the pangs of birth.
5. As we have heard, so we have seen in the city of our God,
6. God, we ponder your love within your temple.
7. With just - ice your right hand is filled. Mount Zion re - joices;
8. Walk through Zion, walk all around it; count the number of its towers.
9. that you may tell the next generation that such is our God,

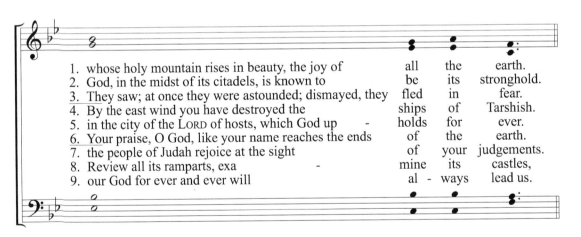

1. whose holy mountain rises in beauty, the joy of all the earth.
2. God, in the midst of its citadels, is known to be its stronghold.
3. They saw; at once they were astounded; dismayed, they fled in fear.
4. By the east wind you have destroyed the ships of Tarshish.
5. in the city of the LORD of hosts, which God up - holds for ever.
6. Your praise, O God, like your name reaches the ends of the earth.
7. the people of Judah rejoice at the sight of your judgements.
8. Review all its ramparts, exa - mine its castles,
9. our God for ever and ever will al - ways lead us.

Worthy Is the Lamb Who Was Slain

Antiphon / Melody ♩. = ca. 72

Worth - y is the Lamb who was slain, worth-y of power,

Descant

Worth - y is the Lamb, worth - y,

worth-y of glo - ry. Worth - y is the Lamb who was slain,

worth-y of glo - ry. Worth - y is the Lamb,

worth - y of wis - dom and might.

worth - y of wis - dom and might.

Verses *Psalms 24:7; 72:5-6, 8, 18-19*

Cantor: *All / Melody:*

1. Lift your heads, O an - cient doors: worth-y of pow'r, worth-y of glo-ry.
2. May he live as long as the sun:
3. May he be like rain on the grass:
4. May he rule from sea to sea:
5. Bless the God of Is - ra - el:
6. Bles - sed be God's glo - ri - ous name:

Descant:

Worth - y, worth-y of glo - ry.

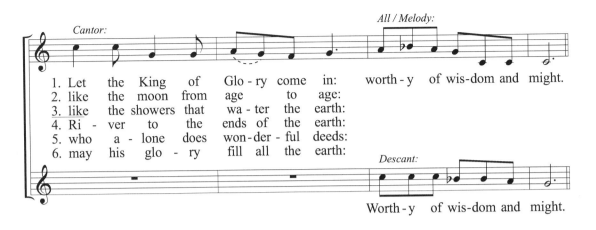

Cantor: / *All / Melody:*

1. Let the King of Glo-ry come in: worth-y of wis-dom and might.
2. like the moon from age to age:
3. like the showers that wa-ter the earth:
4. Ri-ver to the ends of the earth:
5. who a-lone does won-der-ful deeds:
6. may his glo-ry fill all the earth:

Descant:

Worth-y of wis-dom and might.

Verses (continued) *Psalm 72:1, 9-12, 14, 15bc, 17*

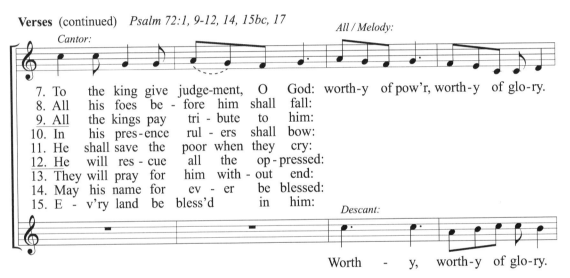

Cantor: / *All / Melody:*

7. To the king give judge-ment, O God: worth-y of pow'r, worth-y of glo-ry.
8. All his foes be-fore him shall fall:
9. All the kings pay tri-bute to him:
10. In his pres-ence rul-ers shall bow:
11. He shall save the poor when they cry:
12. He will res-cue all the op-pressed:
13. They will pray for him with-out end:
14. May his name for ev-er be blessed:
15. E-v'ry land be bless'd in him:

Descant:

Worth — y, worth-y of glo-ry.

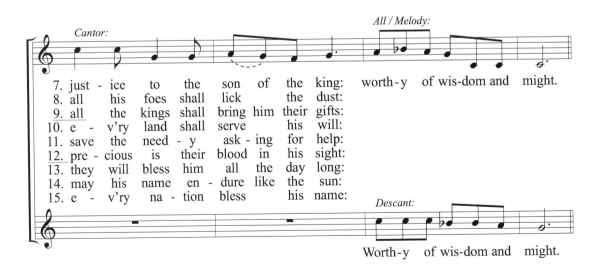

Cantor: / *All / Melody:*

7. just-ice to the son of the king: worth-y of wis-dom and might.
8. all his foes shall lick the dust:
9. all the kings shall bring him their gifts:
10. e-v'ry land shall serve his will:
11. save the need-y ask-ing for help:
12. pre-cious is their blood in his sight:
13. they will bless him all the day long:
14. may his name en-dure like the sun:
15. e-v'ry na-tion bless his name:

Descant:

Worth-y of wis-dom and might.

Antiphon / Melody ♩ = ca. 76

You a-lone are Lord, there is no o-ther; we be-long to you, cho-sen in love.

Verses / Melody *Psalm 33:10-22*

1. The LORD foils the de - signs of the nations, and defeats the plans of the peoples.
2. They are happy, whose God is the LORD, the people who are chosen as his own.
3. From the heavenly dwelling God gazes on all the dwellers on the earth;
4. A king is not saved by his army, nor a warrior preserved by his strength.
5. The LORD looks on those who fear him, on those who hope in his love,
6. Our soul is waiting for the LORD. The LORD is our help and our shield.
7. [*omit*]

1. The counsel of the LORD stands for ever, the plans of God's heart from age to age.
2. From the heavens the LORD looks forth and sees all the peoples of the earth.
3. God who shapes the hearts of them all and considers all their deeds.
4. A vain hope for safety is the horse; despite its power it can - not save.
5. to rescue their souls from death, to keep them alive in famine.
6. Our hearts find joy in the LORD. We trust in God's ho - ly name.
7. May your love be up - on us, O LORD, as we place all our hope in you.

271   You Alone Are My Help

Antiphon ♩. = ca. 60

You a-lone are my help: O Lord, up-hold my life.

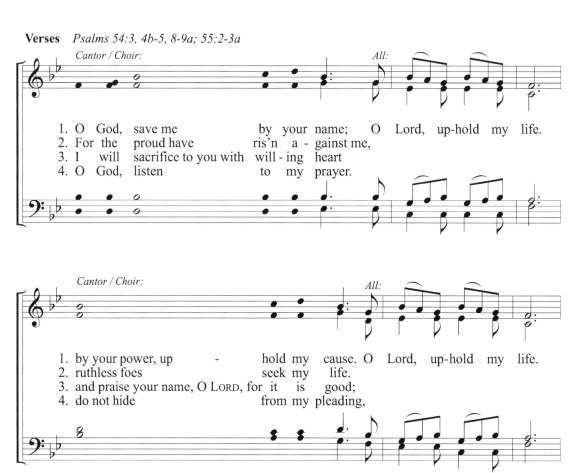

Verses   *Psalms 54:3, 4b-5, 8-9a; 55:2-3a*

Cantor / Choir: *All:*

1. O God, save me   by your name; O Lord, up-hold my life.
2. For the proud have   ris'n a - gainst me,
3. I will sacrifice to you with will-ing heart
4. O God, listen   to my prayer.

Cantor / Choir: *All:*

1. by your power, up - hold my cause. O Lord, up-hold my life.
2. ruthless foes   seek my life.
3. and praise your name, O LORD, for it is good;
4. do not hide   from my pleading,

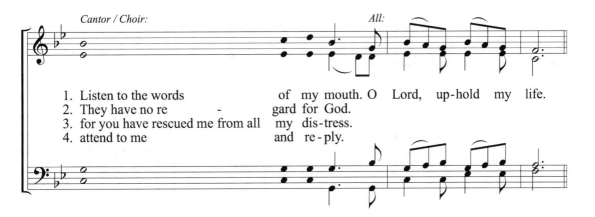

Cantor / Choir:

All:

1. Listen to the words   of my mouth. O Lord, up-hold my life.
2. They have no re   -   gard for God.
3. for you have rescued me from all   my dis-tress.
4. attend to me   and re-ply.

Performance Notes

Verses 1–3 are the Lectionary selections for the Twenty-fifth Sunday in Ordinary Time, Year B.

You Are a Priest For Ever

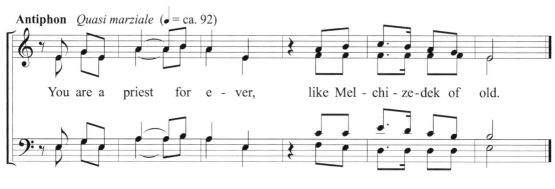

Antiphon *Quasi marziale* (♩ = ca. 92)

You are a priest for e - ver, like Mel - chi - ze - dek of old.

Verses *Psalm 110:1-4*

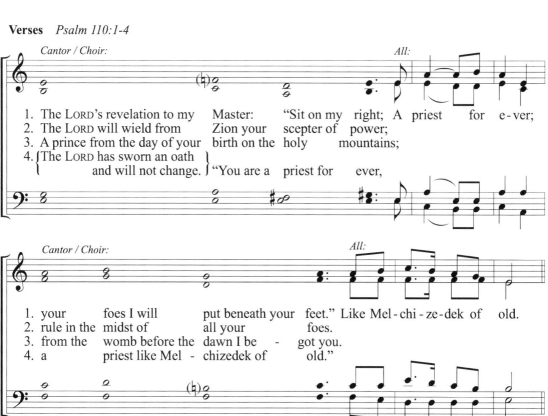

Cantor / Choir: *All:*

1. The LORD's revelation to my   Master: "Sit on my   right; A priest   for e - ver;
2. The LORD will wield from   Zion your   scepter of   power;
3. A prince from the day of your   birth on the   holy   mountains;
4. {The LORD has sworn an oath   and will not change. } "You are a   priest for   ever,

Cantor / Choir: *All:*

1. your   foes I will   put beneath your   feet." Like Mel - chi - ze - dek of   old.
2. rule in the   midst of   all your   foes.
3. from the   womb before the   dawn I be - got you.
4. a   priest like Mel - chizedek of   old."

You Are God's Temple

Verses (Superimposed) *Psalms 133; 134; and 135:1-2*

1. How good and how pleasant it is, when
2. It is like precious oil upon the head,
3. running down upon Aaron's beard, up -
4. It is like the dew of Hermon which
5. For there the LORD gives bles - sing,
6. O come, bless the LORD, all
7. who stand in the house of the LORD, in the
8. Lift up your hands to the holy place and
9. May the LORD bless you from Zi - on,
10. Praise the name of the LORD,
11. who stand in the house of the LORD, in the

Antiphon ♩. = 46

You are God's tem - ple, the Spi - rit with - in you; God's
You are God's tem - ple, God's
You are ho - ly,

1. people live in uni - ty.
2. running down up - on the beard,
3. on the collar of his robes.
4. falls on the heights of Zion.
5. life for e - ver.
6. you who serve the LORD,
7. courts of the house of our God.
8. bless the LORD through the night.
9. God who made both heaven and earth.
10. praise, you servants of the LORD,
11. courts of the house of our God.

tem - ple is ho - ly, that tem - ple is you.

you are ho - ly.

Performance Notes

The tenor descant (bass clef) should only be sung when the antiphon is sung independently of the verses.

You Are Good and Forgiving

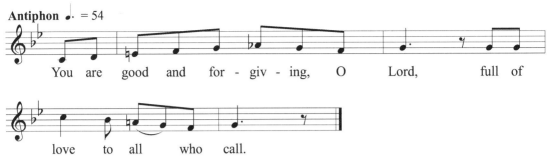

Antiphon ♩. = 54

You are good and for-giv-ing, O Lord, full of

love to all who call.

Verses *Psalm 86:5-6, 9-10, 15-16*

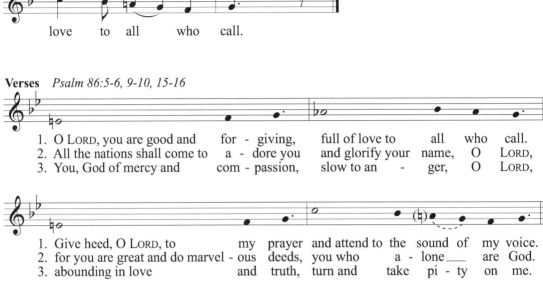

1. O LORD, you are good and for - giving, full of love to all who call.
2. All the nations shall come to a - dore you and glorify your name, O LORD,
3. You, God of mercy and com - passion, slow to an - ger, O LORD,

1. Give heed, O LORD, to my prayer and attend to the sound of my voice.
2. for you are great and do marvel - ous deeds, you who a - lone are God.
3. abounding in love and truth, turn and take pi - ty on me.

You Are Light in the Lord

Antiphon / Melody ♩ = 76

You are light in the Lord: live no long - er in

Descant 1

You are light:

Tenor Descant

You are light, no long - er in

dark-ness but walk in the light.

live and walk in the light.

dark - ness: walk in the light.

Verses *Isaiah 58:8-12; 60:1-5, 19-22*

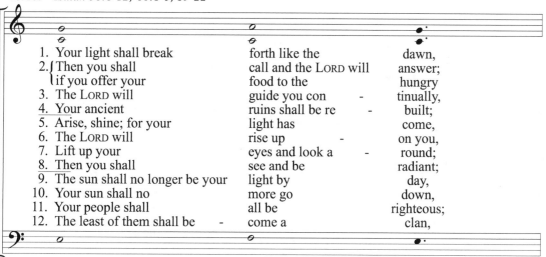

1. Your light shall break forth like the dawn,
2. Then you shall call and the LORD will answer;
  if you offer your food to the hungry
3. The LORD will guide you con - tinually,
4. Your ancient ruins shall be re - built;
5. Arise, shine; for your light has come,
6. The LORD will rise up - on you,
7. Lift up your eyes and look a - round;
8. Then you shall see and be radiant;
9. The sun shall no longer be your light by day,
10. Your sun shall no more go down,
11. Your people shall all be righteous;
12. The least of them shall be - come a clan,

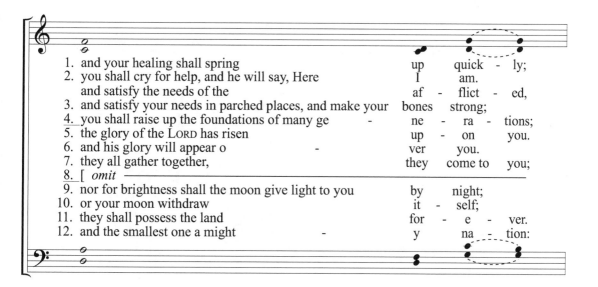

1. and your healing shall spring up quick - ly;
2. you shall cry for help, and he will say, Here I am.
  and satisfy the needs of the af - flict - ed,
3. and satisfy your needs in parched places, and make your bones strong;
4. you shall raise up the foundations of many ge - ne - ra - tions;
5. the glory of the LORD has risen up - on you.
6. and his glory will appear o - ver you.
7. they all gather together, they come to you;
8. [omit ————
9. nor for brightness shall the moon give light to you by night;
10. or your moon withdraw it - self;
11. they shall possess the land for - e - ver.
12. and the smallest one a might - y na - tion:

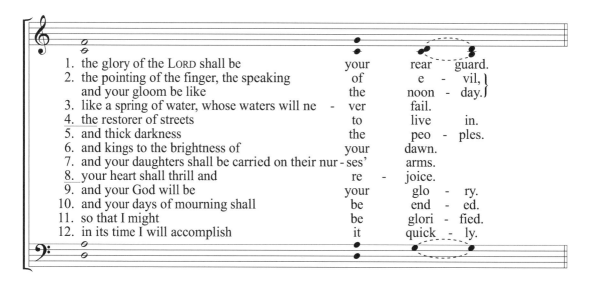

1. your vindicator shall go be - fore you,
2. If you remove the yoke from a - mong you,
   then your light shall rise in the dark - ness
3. and you shall be like a wa - tered gar - den,
4. you shall be called the repairer of the breach,
5. For darkness shall co - ver the earth,
6. Nations shall come to your light,
7. your sons shall come from far a - way,
8. ————————————————————————]
9. but the LORD will be your ever - last - ing light,
10. for the LORD will be your ever - last - ing light,
11. They are the shoot that I planted, the work of my hands,
12. I am the LORD;

1. the glory of the LORD shall be your rear guard.
2. the pointing of the finger, the speaking of e - vil,⎤
   and your gloom be like the noon - day.⎦
3. like a spring of water, whose waters will ne - ver fail.
4. the restorer of streets to live in.
5. and thick darkness the peo - ples.
6. and kings to the brightness of your dawn.
7. and your daughters shall be carried on their nur - ses' arms.
8. your heart shall thrill and re - joice.
9. and your God will be your glo - ry.
10. and your days of mourning shall be end - ed.
11. so that I might be glori - fied.
12. in its time I will accomplish it quick - ly.

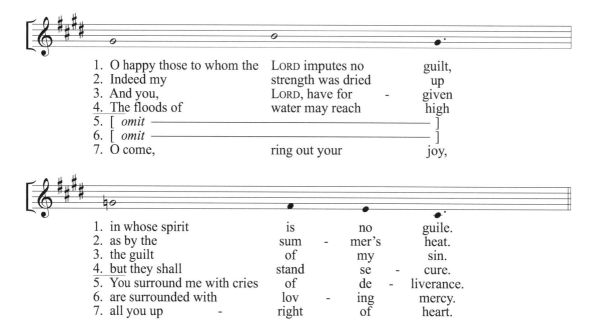

1. O happy those to whom the   LORD imputes no   guilt,
2. Indeed my   strength was dried   up
3. And you,   LORD, have for   -   given
4. The floods of   water may reach   high
5. [*omit* —————————————————]
6. [*omit* —————————————————]
7. O come,   ring out your   joy,

1. in whose spirit   is   no   guile.
2. as by the   sum - mer's   heat.
3. the guilt   of   my   sin.
4. but they shall   stand   se - cure.
5. You surround me with cries   of   de - liverance.
6. are surrounded with   lov - ing   mercy.
7. all you up   -   right   of   heart.

You Are My Praise

Verses *Psalm 22:26b-32*

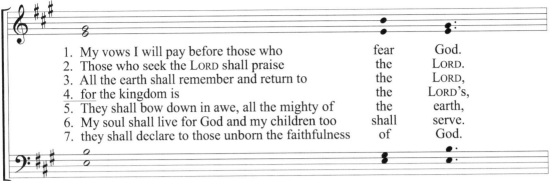

1. My vows I will pay before those who   fear   God.
2. Those who seek the LORD shall praise   the   LORD.
3. All the earth shall remember and return to   the   LORD,
4. for the kingdom is   the   LORD's,
5. They shall bow down in awe, all the mighty of   the   earth,
6. My soul shall live for God and my children too   shall   serve.
7. they shall declare to those unborn the faithfulness   of   God.

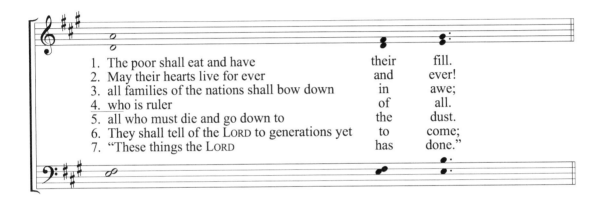

1. The poor shall eat and have   their   fill.
2. May their hearts live for ever   and   ever!
3. all families of the nations shall bow down   in   awe;
4. who is ruler   of   all.
5. all who must die and go down to   the   dust.
6. They shall tell of the LORD to generations yet   to   come;
7. "These things the LORD   has   done."

Performance Notes

Verses 1–3 and 5–7 are the Lectionary selections for the Fifth Sunday of Easter, Year B.

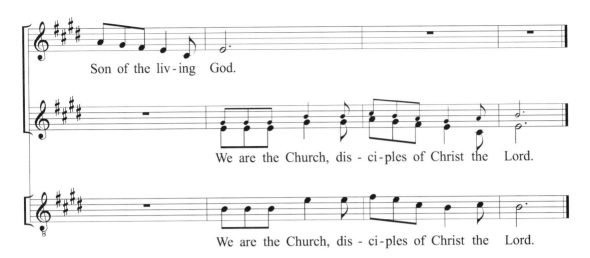

Son of the liv-ing God.

We are the Church, dis-ci-ples of Christ the Lord.

We are the Church, dis-ci-ples of Christ the Lord.

Verses *Psalm 116:10-19*

1. I trusted, even when I said: "I am sorely af - flicted,"
2. How can I repay the LORD for his goodness to me?
3. My vows to the LORD I will ful - fill before all the people.
4. Your servant, LORD, your servant am I; you have loosened my bonds.
5. My vows to the LORD I will ful - fill before all the people,

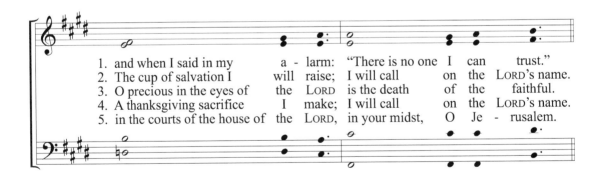

1. and when I said in my a - larm: "There is no one I can trust."
2. The cup of salvation I will raise; I will call on the LORD's name.
3. O precious in the eyes of the LORD is the death of the faithful.
4. A thanksgiving sacrifice I make; I will call on the LORD's name.
5. in the courts of the house of the LORD, in your midst, O Je - rusalem.

Performance Notes

In the antiphon, the assembly sings the full-size notes, imitating the cantor's melody, while choir members may add the descant part in cue-size notes. If by chance the assembly becomes confused and sings the descant part instead of the main melody at any point, this does not matter: a built-in congregational mistake that still fits! It would even be possible for the assembly to sing all their sections of the antiphon to the same melody.

Antiphon ♩ = 80

You are rich in mer-cy, mer-cy, O Lord our God.

Verses (*Option A)   *Isaiah 61:10–62:5*

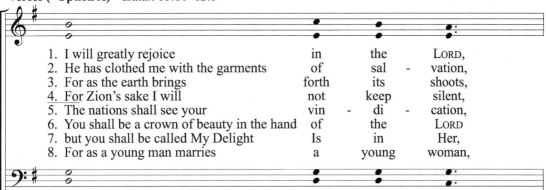

1. I will greatly rejoice in the LORD,
2. He has clothed me with the garments of sal - vation,
3. For as the earth brings forth its shoots,
4. For Zion's sake I will not keep silent,
5. The nations shall see your vin - di - cation,
6. You shall be a crown of beauty in the hand of the LORD
7. but you shall be called My Delight Is in Her,
8. For as a young man marries a young woman,

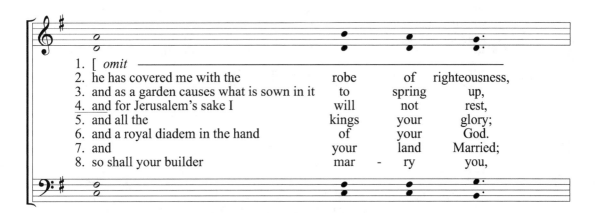

1. [*omit* ────────────────────────
2. he has covered me with the robe of righteousness,
3. and as a garden causes what is sown in it to spring up,
4. and for Jerusalem's sake I will not rest,
5. and all the kings your glory;
6. and a royal diadem in the hand of your God.
7. and your land Married;
8. so shall your builder mar - ry you,

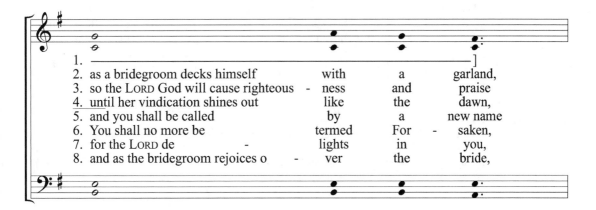

1. ──────────────────────────]
2. as a bridegroom decks himself with a garland,
3. so the LORD God will cause righteous - ness and praise
4. until her vindication shines out like the dawn,
5. and you shall be called by a new name
6. You shall no more be termed For - saken,
7. for the LORD de - lights in you,
8. and as the bridegroom rejoices o - ver the bride,

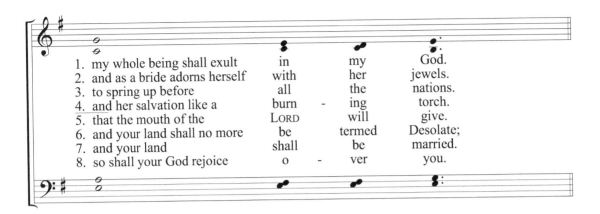

1. my whole being shall exult — in — my — God.
2. and as a bride adorns herself — with — her — jewels.
3. to spring up before — all — the — nations.
4. and her salvation like a — burn - ing — torch.
5. that the mouth of the — LORD — will — give.
6. and your land shall no more — be — termed — Desolate;
7. and your land — shall — be — married.
8. so shall your God rejoice — o - ver — you.

Verses (*Option B) *Isaiah 66:10-14*

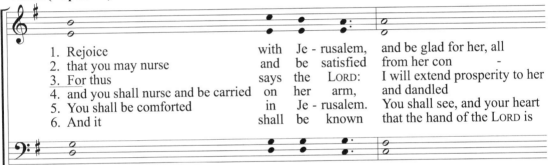

1. Rejoice — with — Je - rusalem, — and be glad for her, all
2. that you may nurse — and — be — satisfied — from her con -
3. For thus — says — the — LORD: — I will extend prosperity to her
4. and you shall nurse and be carried — on — her — arm, — and dandled
5. You shall be comforted — in — Je - rusalem. — You shall see, and your heart
6. And it — shall — be — known — that the hand of the LORD is

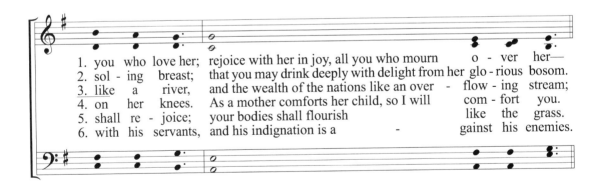

1. you who love her; — rejoice with her in joy, all you who mourn — o - ver — her—
2. sol - ing — breast; — that you may drink deeply with delight from her glo - rious — bosom.
3. like a — river, — and the wealth of the nations like an over - flow - ing — stream;
4. on her — knees. — As a mother comforts her child, so I will — com - fort — you.
5. shall re - joice; — your bodies shall flourish — like — the — grass.
6. with his — servants, — and his indignation is a - — gainst — his — enemies.

Performance Notes

The antiphon may be sung twice each time. If desired, the repetition could overlap on the final note, with "You are" being sung at the same time as "God."

*Option A verses are used on the Twenty-eighth Sunday in Ordinary Time, Year A. Option B verses are used on the Fourth Sunday of Lent, Year B, and the Second Sunday of Easter, Year A.

Antiphon ♩ = 80

You are rich in mer-cy, mer-cy, O Lord our God.

Verses (*Option A)   *Psalm 130:1-6b, 7b-8*

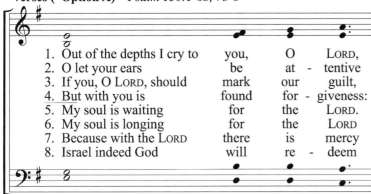

1. Out of the depths I cry to you, O LORD,
2. O let your ears be at - tentive
3. If you, O LORD, should mark our guilt,
4. But with you is found for - giveness:
5. My soul is waiting for the LORD.
6. My soul is longing for the LORD
7. Because with the LORD there is mercy
8. Israel indeed God will re - deem

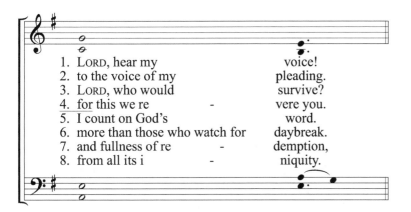

1. LORD, hear my voice!
2. to the voice of my pleading.
3. LORD, who would survive?
4. for this we re - vere you.
5. I count on God's word.
6. more than those who watch for daybreak.
7. and fullness of re - demption,
8. from all its i - niquity.

Verses (*Option B)   *Wisdom 11:21–12:2*

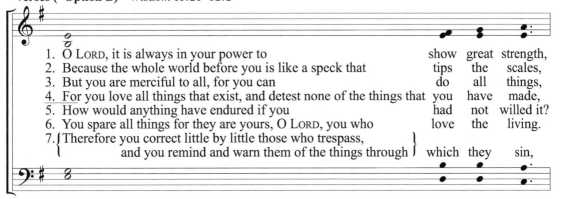

1. O LORD, it is always in your power to show great strength,
2. Because the whole world before you is like a speck that tips the scales,
3. But you are merciful to all, for you can do all things,
4. For you love all things that exist, and detest none of the things that you have made,
5. How would anything have endured if you had not willed it?
6. You spare all things for they are yours, O LORD, you who love the living.
7. {Therefore you correct little by little those who trespass,
   and you remind and warn them of the things through} which they sin,

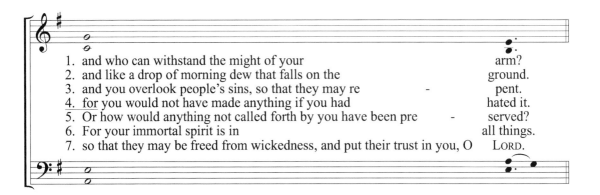

1. and who can withstand the might of your — arm?
2. and like a drop of morning dew that falls on the — ground.
3. and you overlook people's sins, so that they may re - pent.
4. for you would not have made anything if you had — hated it.
5. Or how would anything not called forth by you have been pre - served?
6. For your immortal spirit is in — all things.
7. so that they may be freed from wickedness, and put their trust in you, O LORD.

Performance Notes

The antiphon may be sung twice each time. If desired, the repetition could overlap on the final note, with "You are" being sung at the same time as "God."

*Option A verses are used on the Twenty-eighth Sunday in Ordinary Time, Years B and C. Option B verses are used on Ash Wednesday.

You Are the Shepherd

Verses *Psalms 78:52-55, 70-72; 80:2-4, 18-19*

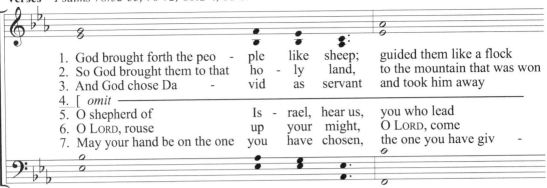

1. God brought forth the peo - ple like sheep; guided them like a flock
2. So God brought them to that ho - ly land, to the mountain that was won
3. And God chose Da - vid as servant and took him away
4. [*omit* ————————————————
5. O shepherd of Is - rael, hear us, you who lead
6. O LORD, rouse up your might, O LORD, come
7. May your hand be on the one you have chosen, the one you have giv -

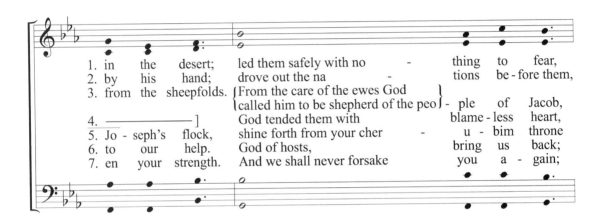

1. in the desert; led them safely with no - thing to fear,
2. by his hand; drove out the na - tions be - fore them,
3. from the sheepfolds. {From the care of the ewes God called him to be shepherd of the peo} - ple of Jacob,
4. —————————————] God tended them with blame - less heart,
5. Jo - seph's flock, shine forth from your cher - u - bim throne
6. to our help. God of hosts, bring us back;
7. en your strength. And we shall never forsake you a - gain;

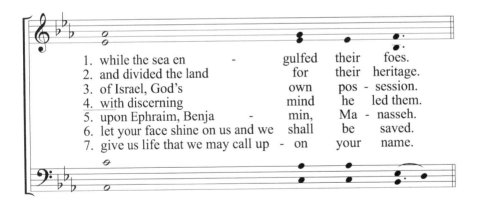

1. while the sea en - gulfed their foes.
2. and divided the land for their heritage.
3. of Israel, God's own pos - session.
4. with discerning mind he led them.
5. upon Ephraim, Benja - min, Ma - nasseh.
6. let your face shine on us and we shall be saved.
7. give us life that we may call up - on your name.

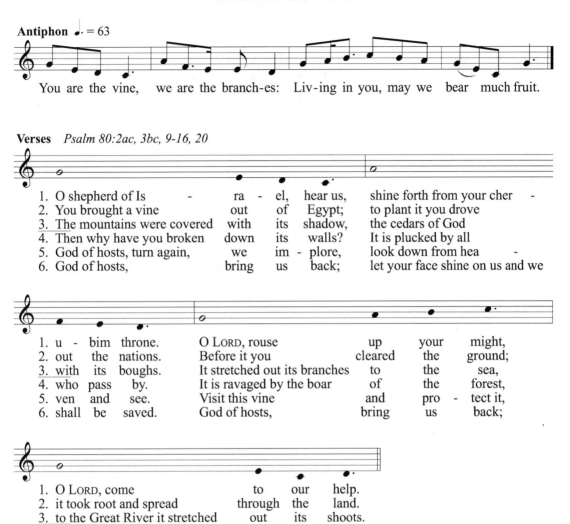

Antiphon ♩. = 63

You are the vine, we are the branch-es: Liv-ing in you, may we bear much fruit.

Verses *Psalm 80:2ac, 3bc, 9-16, 20*

1. O shepherd of Is - ra - el, hear us, shine forth from your cher -
2. You brought a vine out of Egypt; to plant it you drove
3. The mountains were covered with its shadow, the cedars of God
4. Then why have you broken down its walls? It is plucked by all
5. God of hosts, turn again, we im - plore, look down from hea -
6. God of hosts, bring us back; let your face shine on us and we

1. u - bim throne. O Lord, rouse up your might,
2. out the nations. Before it you cleared the ground;
3. with its boughs. It stretched out its branches to the sea,
4. who pass by. It is ravaged by the boar of the forest,
5. ven and see. Visit this vine and pro - tect it,
6. shall be saved. God of hosts, bring us back;

1. O Lord, come to our help.
2. it took root and spread through the land.
3. to the Great River it stretched out its shoots.
4. devoured by the beasts of the field.
5. the vine your right hand has planted.
6. let your face shine on us and we shall be saved.

You Have Given Everything Its Place

Antiphon ♩ = c. 92

You have gi-ven e-v'ry-thing its place in the world, the
hea-vens, the earth and the stars.

Verses *Psalm 8:2, 4-10*

Cantor / Choir:

All: You are Lord of all.

1. {How great is your name, O LORD
   our God, through all} the earth! You are Lord of all.
2. When I see the heavens, the work of your hands,
3. what are we that you should keep us in mind,
4. Yet you have made us little less than gods;
5. You gave us power over the work of your hands,
6. All of them, sheep and cattle,
7. birds of the air, and fish
8. How great is your name, O LORD our God,

Cantor / Choir:

All: You are Lord of all.

1. Your majesty is praised above the heavens. You are Lord of all.
2. the moon and the stars which you ar - ranged,
3. mere mortals that you care for us?
4. and crowned us with glory and honor.
5. put all things under our feet.
6. yes, even the sa - vage beasts,
7. that make their way through the waters.
8. through all the earth!

Performance Notes
The antiphon may be sung as a two-part round as indicated.

You Have Shown You Love Us

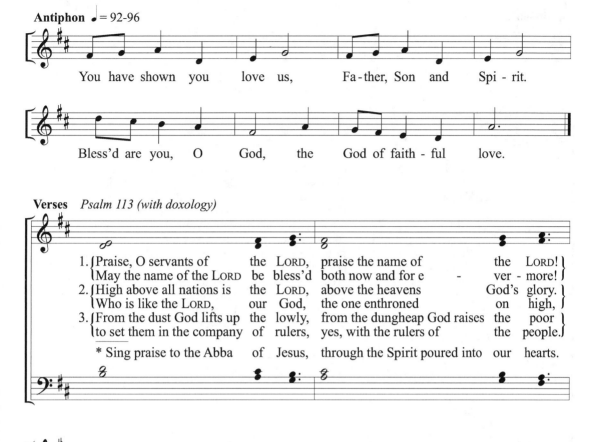

Antiphon ♩ = 92-96

You have shown you love us, Fa-ther, Son and Spi - rit.

Bless'd are you, O God, the God of faith - ful love.

Verses *Psalm 113 (with doxology)*

1. {Praise, O servants of the LORD, praise the name of the LORD!
   {May the name of the LORD be bless'd both now and for e - ver - more!
2. {High above all nations is the LORD, above the heavens God's glory.
   {Who is like the LORD, our God, the one enthroned on high,
3. {From the dust God lifts up the lowly, from the dungheap God raises the poor
   {to set them in the company of rulers, yes, with the rulers of the people.

* Sing praise to the Abba of Jesus, through the Spirit poured into our hearts.

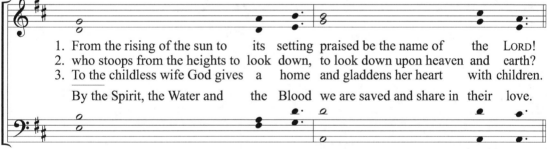

1. From the rising of the sun to its setting praised be the name of the LORD!
2. who stoops from the heights to look down, to look down upon heaven and earth?
3. To the childless wife God gives a home and gladdens her heart with children.

By the Spirit, the Water and the Blood we are saved and share in their love.

Performance Notes

*Trinitarian doxology for use on Trinity Sunday.

You Open Your Hand

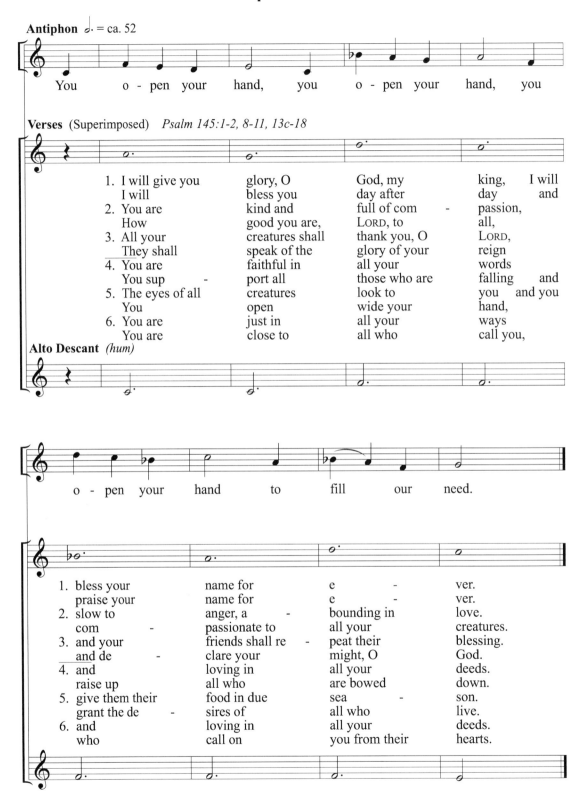

Antiphon ♩. = ca. 52

You o - pen your hand, you o - pen your hand, you

Verses (Superimposed) *Psalm 145:1-2, 8-11, 13c-18*

1. I will give you glory, O God, my king, I will
   I will bless you day after day and
2. You are kind and full of com - passion,
   How good you are, LORD, to all,
3. All your creatures shall thank you, O LORD,
   They shall speak of the glory of your reign
4. You are faithful in all your words
   You sup - port all those who are falling and
5. The eyes of all creatures look to you and you
   You open wide your hand,
6. You are just in all your ways
   You are close to all who call you,

Alto Descant *(hum)*

o - pen your hand to fill our need.

1. bless your name for e - ver.
   praise your name for e - ver.
2. slow to anger, a - bounding in love.
   com - passionate to all your creatures.
3. and your friends shall re - peat their blessing.
   and de - clare your might, O God.
4. and loving in all your deeds.
   raise up all who are bowed down.
5. give them their food in due sea - son.
   grant the de - sires of all who live.
6. and loving in all your deeds.
   who call on you from their hearts.

Verses (alternate setting)   *Psalm 145:1-2, 8-11, 13c-18*

1. I will give you glory, O God my king, I will bless your
2. You are kind and full of com - passion, slow to anger, abound -
3. All your creatures shall thank you, O LORD, and your friends shall re -
4. You are faithful in all your words and loving in
5. The eyes of all creatures look to you and you give them their food
6. You are just in all your ways and loving in

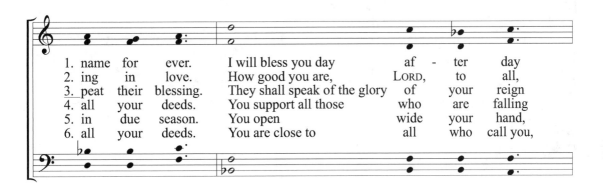

1. name for ever. I will bless you day af - ter day
2. ing in love. How good you are, LORD, to all,
3. peat their blessing. They shall speak of the glory of your reign
4. all your deeds. You support all those who are falling
5. in due season. You open wide your hand,
6. all your deeds. You are close to all who call you,

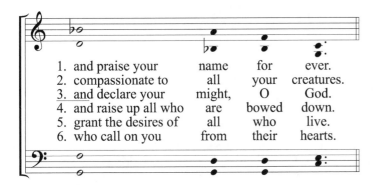

1. and praise your name for ever.
2. compassionate to all your creatures.
3. and declare your might, O God.
4. and raise up all who are bowed down.
5. grant the desires of all who live.
6. who call on you from their hearts.

Performance Notes
Verses 2, 5, and 6 are the Lectionary selections for the Eighteenth Sunday in Ordinary Time, Year A.
Verses 3, 5, and 6 are the Lectionary selections for the Seventeenth Sunday in Ordinary Time, Year B.
The psalm verses are pointed separately for use by either the superimposed tone or the alternate verse tone.
If the alternate verses are used, the superimposed tone could be hummed as a tenor descant during the antiphon.

You Shall Be a Royal Priesthood

Antiphon ♩ = ca. 76

You shall be a roy-al priest-hood, ho-ly na-tion that I keep. Go, pro-claim the com-ing king-dom; tend my lost and scat-tered sheep.

Verses *Revelation 4:11; 5:9-10, 12b-d, 13b-d; 4:8c; Romans 5:6, 8-12*

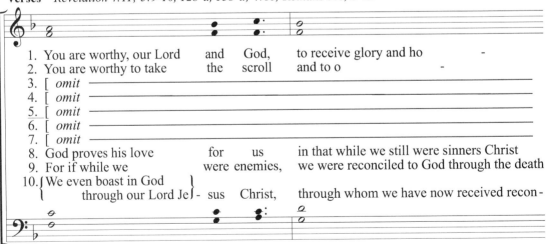

1. You are worthy, our Lord and God, to receive glory and ho -
2. You are worthy to take the scroll and to o -
3. [*omit*
4. [*omit*
5. [*omit*
6. [*omit*
7. [*omit*
8. God proves his love for us in that while we still were sinners Christ
9. For if while we were enemies, we were reconciled to God through the death
10. {We even boast in God
    { through our Lord Je}- sus Christ, through whom we have now received recon-

1. nor and power, for you crea - ted all things,
2. pen its seals, for you were slaughtered and by your blood
3. ———————] you have made them to be a kingdom and priests
4. ———————] Worthy is the Lamb that was slaughtered
5. ———————] To the one seated on the throne and to the Lamb
6. ———————] Holy, ho - ly, holy,
7. ———————] While we were still weak,
8. died for us. Much more sure - ly then,
9. of his Son, much more surely, having been reconciled,
10. cil - i - ation. Just as sin came into the world through one man,

1. and by your will they ex - isted
2. you ran - somed for God
3. serv - ing our God,
4. to receive power and wealth and wis - dom and might
5. be blessing and honor and glo - ry and might
6. the Lord God the Al - mighty,
7. at the right time,
8. now that we have been justified by his blood,
9. [omit ——————————————————————]
10. and death came through sin,

1. and were cre - ated.
2. saints from every tribe and language and peo - ple and nation;
3. and they will reign on earth.
4. and honor and glo - ry and blessing.
5. for e - ver and ever.
6. who was and is and is to come.
7. Christ died for the un - godly.
8. will we be saved through him from the wrath of God.
9. will we be saved by his life.
10. so death spread to all because all have sinned.

Performance Notes

The antiphon is the hymn tune STUTTGART. *It would perhaps be preferable to perform this in chant style, unaccompanied, at half-note = ca. 80.*

You Will Show Us (Me) the Path of Life

Antiphon ♩. = 65

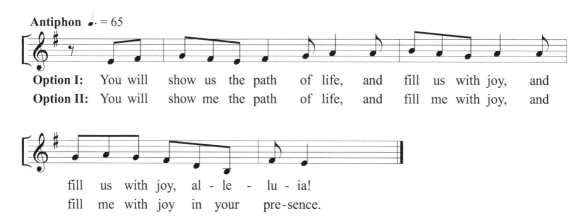

Option I: You will show us the path of life, and fill us with joy, and

Option II: You will show me the path of life, and fill me with joy, and

fill us with joy, al - le - lu - ia!

fill me with joy in your pre-sence.

Verses *Psalm 16:1-2, 5-11*

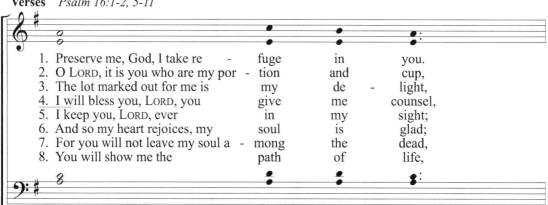

1. Preserve me, God, I take re - fuge in you.
2. O Lᴏʀᴅ, it is you who are my por - tion and cup,
3. The lot marked out for me is my de - light,
4. I will bless you, Lᴏʀᴅ, you give me counsel,
5. I keep you, Lᴏʀᴅ, ever in my sight;
6. And so my heart rejoices, my soul is glad;
7. For you will not leave my soul a - mong the dead,
8. You will show me the path of life,

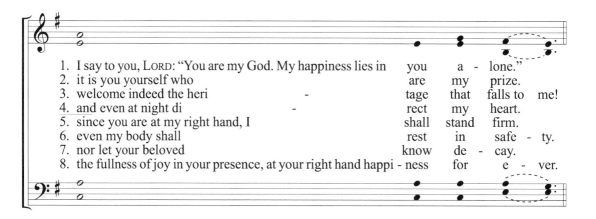

1. I say to you, Lᴏʀᴅ: "You are my God. My happiness lies in you a - lone."
2. it is you yourself who are my prize.
3. welcome indeed the heri - tage that falls to me!
4. and even at night di - rect my heart.
5. since you are at my right hand, I shall stand firm.
6. even my body shall rest in safe - ty.
7. nor let your beloved know de - cay.
8. the fullness of joy in your presence, at your right hand happi - ness for e - ver.

Performance Notes

Option I antiphon is used on the Third Sunday of Easter, Year A. Option II antiphon is used on the Thirty-first Sunday in Ordinary Time, Year B.

Verses 1–2, 4–5, 6–7, and 8 are the Lectionary selections for the Third Sunday of Easter, Year A.

This psalm tone is derived from the old Gregorian chant tonus peregrinus.

Your Mercy Is My Hope

Antiphon ♩ = ca. 76

Your mer-cy is my hope, your pro-mise is my song: my

heart re-joi-ces in your pow'r to save.

Verses *Psalm 13*

Flex measure for verses 2 and 4

2. How long must I bear grief in my soul,

4. As for   me,

1. How long, O Lord, will you
    this sorrow in my heart day

3. {Look at me, answer me, Lord
   {lest my enemy say: "I have
    I trust in your merci   -

5. Let me sing to you, Lord, for your goodness

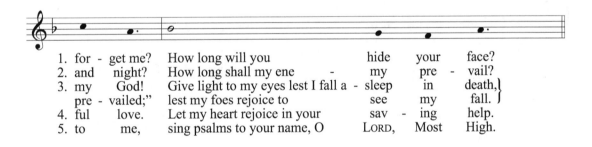

1. for - get me?	How long will you		hide	your	face?
2. and night?	How long shall my ene -		my	pre -	vail?
3. my God!	Give light to my eyes lest I fall a -	sleep	in	death,}
pre - vailed;"	lest my foes rejoice to		see	my	fall. }
4. ful love.	Let my heart rejoice in your		sav -	ing	help.
5. to me,	sing psalms to your name, O		Lord,	Most	High.

Psalm text: The Grail (England), © 1963, 1986, 1993, 2000, The Grail, GIA Publications, Inc., agent. All rights reserved. Used with permission.
Music and antiphon text: © 2005, The Collegeville Composers Group. Published and administered by Liturgical Press, Collegeville, MN 56321. All rights reserved.

289   Your Word Is Life, Lord

Antiphon ♩ = 63-66

Your word is life, Lord, life with-out end.

Verses (*Option A)   *Psalm 19:8-11, 15*

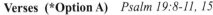

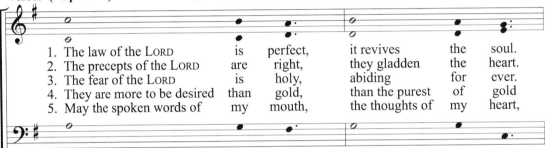

1. The law of the LORD   is   perfect,   it revives   the   soul.
2. The precepts of the LORD   are   right,   they gladden   the   heart.
3. The fear of the LORD   is   holy,   abiding   for   ever.
4. They are more to be desired   than   gold,   than the purest   of   gold
5. May the spoken words of   my   mouth,   the thoughts of   my   heart,

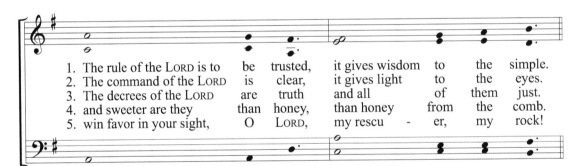

1. The rule of the LORD is to   be   trusted,   it gives wisdom   to   the   simple.
2. The command of the LORD   is   clear,   it gives light   to   the   eyes.
3. The decrees of the LORD   are   truth   and all   of   them   just.
4. and sweeter are they   than   honey,   than honey   from   the   comb.
5. win favor in your sight,   O   LORD,   my rescu - er,   my   rock!

Verses (*Option B)   *John 6:35, 37-40, 48-51, 53-58, 63*

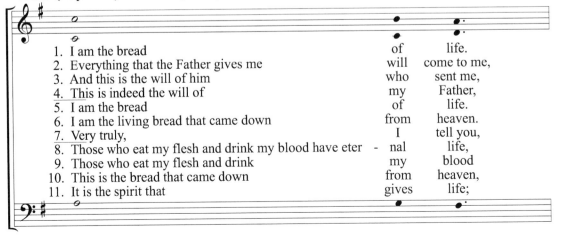

1. I am the bread   of   life.
2. Everything that the Father gives me   will   come to me,
3. And this is the will of him   who   sent me,
4. This is indeed the will of   my   Father,
5. I am the bread   of   life.
6. I am the living bread that came down   from   heaven.
7. Very truly,   I   tell you,
8. Those who eat my flesh and drink my blood have eter - nal   life,
9. Those who eat my flesh and drink   my   blood
10. This is the bread that came down   from   heaven,
11. It is the spirit that   gives   life;

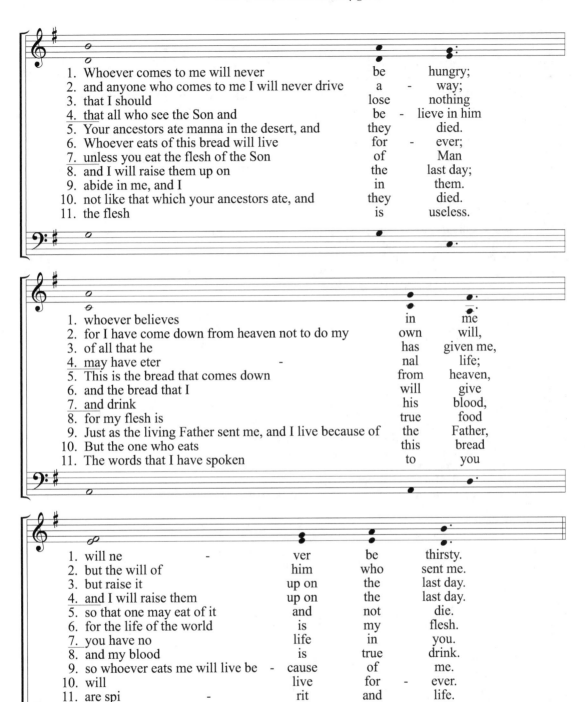

1. Whoever comes to me will never be hungry;
2. and anyone who comes to me I will never drive a - way;
3. that I should lose nothing
4. that all who see the Son and be - lieve in him
5. Your ancestors ate manna in the desert, and they died.
6. Whoever eats of this bread will live for - ever;
7. unless you eat the flesh of the Son of Man
8. and I will raise them up on the last day;
9. abide in me, and I in them.
10. not like that which your ancestors ate, and they died.
11. the flesh is useless.

1. whoever believes in me
2. for I have come down from heaven not to do my own will,
3. of all that he has given me,
4. may have eter - nal life;
5. This is the bread that comes down from heaven,
6. and the bread that I will give
7. and drink his blood,
8. for my flesh is true food
9. Just as the living Father sent me, and I live because of the Father,
10. But the one who eats this bread
11. The words that I have spoken to you

1. will ne - ver be thirsty.
2. but the will of him who sent me.
3. but raise it up on the last day.
4. and I will raise them up on the last day.
5. so that one may eat of it and not die.
6. for the life of the world is my flesh.
7. you have no life in you.
8. and my blood is true drink.
9. so whoever eats me will live be - cause of me.
10. will live for - ever.
11. are spi - rit and life.

Performance Notes

Option A verses 1–4 are used on the Third Sunday of Lent, Year B, at the Easter Vigil, and on the Fifteenth Sunday in Ordinary Time, Year C; verses 1–3 and 5 are used on the Third Sunday in Ordinary Time, Year C.
Option B verses are used on the Twenty-first Sunday in Ordinary Time, Year B.

Yours Is the Day

Antiphon ♩. = ca. 54

Yours is the day, yours is the night, yours are the poor and the low - ly.

Verses *Psalms 74:12, 15-17, 19-21; 80:9-12*

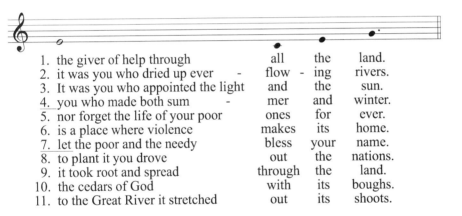

1. God is our king from time past,
2. It was you who opened springs and torrents;
3. Yours is the day and yours is the night.
4. It was you who fixed the bounds of the earth;
5. Do not give Israel, your dove, to the hawk
6. Remember your covenant; every cave in the land
7. Do not let the oppressed return dis - ap - pointed;
8. You brought a vine out of Egypt;
9. Before it you cleared the ground;
10. The mountains were covered with its shadow,
11. It stretched out its branches to the sea,

1. the giver of help through all the land.
2. it was you who dried up ever - flow - ing rivers.
3. It was you who appointed the light and the sun.
4. you who made both sum - mer and winter.
5. nor forget the life of your poor ones for ever.
6. is a place where violence makes its home.
7. let the poor and the needy bless your name.
8. to plant it you drove out the nations.
9. it took root and spread through the land.
10. the cedars of God with its boughs.
11. to the Great River it stretched out its shoots.

The letter A, B, or C preceding the number refers to the accompaniment edition, and c/c refers to the Cantor/Choir edition.

A

A Light Will Shine on Us This Day – A13, B13, C13, C20, c/c1

A New Commandment I Give to You – A49, B55, C55, c/c2

A River Flows – A238, B237, C239, c/c3

A Woman Clothed with the Sun – A223, B222, C224, c/c4

All That Is True – A175, c/c5

All the Ends of the Earth – A14, B14, B87, C14, C179, c/c6

All Things Are from the Lord – A156, c/c7

All Who Labor, Come to Me – A133, B204, C206, c/c8

All You Nations – A128, B131, C131, c/c9

All Your Sins Have Been Forgiven – C127, c/c10

Alleluia, Alleluia, Alleluia! (I) – B75, C75, c/c11

Alleluia, Alleluia, Alleluia! (II) – A62, B68, C68, c/c11

Alleluia, Send Out Your Spirit – A93, B96, C96, c/c12

Arise, Jerusalem, Look to the East – A23, B23, C23, c/c13

Arise, Jerusalem, Stand on the Height – A4, B6, C4, c/c13

As a Bridegroom Rejoices – A240, B239, C100, c/c14

As One Body in Your Spirit – C103, c/c15

As Seed for the Sowing – A136, A139, c/c16–17

Ask and Receive (I) – A143, c/c18

Ask and Receive (II) – A239, B238, C146, C240, c/c19

At Your Word Our Hearts Are Burning – A75, c/c20

B

Be Patient, Beloved – A9, c/c21

Be Strong, Our God Has Come to Save Us (I) – B9, C9, c/c22

Be Strong, Our God Has Come to Save Us (II) – B164, c/c22

Because You Are Filled with the Spirit – B173, c/c23

Behold, the Bridegroom Is Here (I) – B118, c/c24

Behold, the Bridegroom Is Here (II) – A192, B3, c/c25

Behold the Lamb of God! – A97, B100, c/c26

Bless the Lord, My Soul – C27, c/c27

Blessed Are You, Lord – A169, B171, c/c28

Blest Are the Poor in Spirit – A102, A103, c/c29

Blest Are You Who Weep – C112, c/c30

C

Cast Out into the Deep – C109, c/c31

Change Your Heart and Mind – A171, c/c32

Chosen in Christ, Blessed in Christ – B139, c/c33

Christ Is the Light – A211, A213, B210, B212, C212, C214, c/c34

Christ Laid Down His Life for Us – A172, B170, c/c35

Christ, Our Pasch – A67, B70, C70, c/c36

Christ the Lord Is Risen Again – A65, B71, C71, c/c37

Clothed in Christ, One in Christ – A28, B28, B69, C69, c/c38

Come, All You Good and Faithful Servants – A195, c/c39

Come, Come to the Banquet – A146, C43, c/c40

Come, Lord, and Save Us – A8, c/c41

Come, My Children – B176, c/c42

"Come," Says My Heart – B92, C92, c/c43

Come to Me and Drink – A94, B97, C97, c/c44

Come to Me and You Shall Never Hunger – A147, B148, c/c45

Courage! Get Up! – B185, c/c46

D

Do Not Abandon Me, Lord! – B186, C188, c/c47

Do Not Store Up Earthly Treasures – C149, C171, c/c48

Don't Be Afraid – A150, B133, C152, C196, c/c49

E

Eat My Flesh and Drink My Blood – A236, B235, C237, c/c50

Everlasting Is Your Love – A155, c/c51

Every Valley Shall Be Filled – C6, c/c52

F

Father, into Your Hands – A51, B57, C57, c/c53

Finest Food! Choicest Wine! – A178, c/c54

For Ever, For Ever, We Praise You For Ever – A200, c/c55

For You My Soul Is Thirsting – A158, C129, c/c56

Forgive, and You Will Be Forgiven – C115, c/c57

From the East and West, from the North and South – A186, C158, c/c58

From the Fullness of Our Hearts – C118, c/c59

G

Give Peace to Those Who Wait – A163, B165, C166, c/c60

Give Thanks to the Lord, Alleluia (I) – A70, c/c61

Give Thanks to the Lord, Alleluia (II) – B129, c/c62

Give the Lord Power – A180, c/c63

Give Us Living Water – A37, B39, C39, c/c64

Give: Your Father Sees – A210, B209, C211, c/c65

Go to the Ends of the Earth – C120, c/c66

God, Come to My Aid (I) – C154, c/c67

God, Come to My Aid (II) – A144, B146, C147, c/c68

God Feeds Us, God Saves Us – A115, C183, c/c69

God Goes Up with Shouts of Joy – A87, B90, C90, c/c70

God Heals the Broken – B109, C173, c/c71

God, Let All the Peoples Praise You – A152, C87, c/c72

God of Hosts, Bring Us Back – B2, C11, c/c73

God of Life, God of Hope – C193, c/c74

God Remembers His Covenant For Ever – B18, c/c75

God, Who Raised Jesus from the Dead – A232, B231, C233, c/c76

God's Love Is Revealed to Us – A15, B15, C28, c/c77

God's Tender Mercy – A6, B215, C217, c/c78

Great In Our Midst Is the Holy One – C8, c/c79

Guard Me as the Apple of Your Eye! – B180, C181, c/c80

H

Happy Are They Who Dwell in Your House – A244, B38, C18, c/c81

Happy Are They Who Follow – A108, c/c82

Happy Are They Whose God Is the Lord – B199, C151, c/c83

Heal Me in Your Mercy – B112, c/c84

Heal My Soul – B114, c/c85

Heaven and Earth Will Fade Away – A109, B194, c/c86

Here I Am – A96, B99, C107, c/c87

Here in Your Presence – B121, c/c88

Here Is My Servant, Here Is My Son – A34, B26, B34, C26, c/c89

Home for the Lonely – B143, C144, C161, c/c90

Hosanna, Hosanna, Hosanna in the Highest – A44, B50, C50, c/c91

How Happy Are You – A194, B175, c/c92

How I Thirst for You – A235, B234, C236, c/c93

How Wonderful Your Name, O Lord – C201, c/c94

The letter A, B, or C preceding the number refers to the accompaniment edition, and c/c refers to the Cantor/Choir edition.

The letter A, B, or C preceding the number refers to the accompaniment edition, and c/c refers to the Cantor/Choir edition.

40:8a	Here I Am – A96, B99, C107, c/c87	85:7	Show Us, Lord, Your Kindness – A149, B5, c/c208
41:5b	Heal My Soul – B114, c/c85	86:5a	You Are Good and Forgiving – A138, c/c274
42:2	Like a Deer That Longs for Running Streams – A59, B65, C65, c/c141	88:1-2	Let My Prayer Come Before You, Lord – A189, B189, C191, c/c134
42:3	How I Thirst for You – A235, B234, C236, c/c93	89:1	I Will Sing For Ever of Your Love – A129, B11, c/c112
43:1	My God, My Strength, Defend My Cause – A41, B45, C45, c/c161	90:1	In Every Age, O Lord, You Have Been Our Refuge – C164, c/c118
46:5	A River Flows – A238, B237, C239, c/c3	90:14	When You Fill Us with Your Word – B178, C148, c/c260
47:1	All You Nations – A128, B131, C131, c/c9	91:14-15	Those Who Love Me, I Will Deliver – A29, B29, C29, C38, c/c244
47:6	God Goes Up with Shouts of Joy – A87, B90, C90, c/c70	91:15	I Am With You – C30, c/c97
48:10	Within Your Temple – A131, B134, C134, c/c268	92:1	It Is Good to Give You Thanks, O Lord – B126, C117, c/c122
50:23b	I Will Show God's Salvation – A120, c/c111	93:1a	The Lord Is King (II) – B196, c/c222
51:3	We Have Sinned, Lord – A30, B208, C167, c/c254	95:6	Venite, Adoremus – A245, B107, C246, c/c252
51:10	Lord, Cleanse My Heart – A61, B46, C67, c/c149	96:7b, 4a	Give the Lord Power – A180, c/c63
54:4	You Alone Are My Help – A137, B140, C141, c/c271	95:7b-8a	Listen! Listen! Open Your Hearts! – A36, B37, C37, c/c144
62:6a	In God Alone Is My Soul at Rest – A114, c/c119	97:1a, 9a	The Lord Is King (I) – A221, B220, C93, c/c221
63:2	For You My Soul Is Thirsting – A158, C129, c/c56	98:1-2	Sing to God a New Song – A79, B83, C83, c/c210
66:1-2	Let All the Earth Cry Out Your Praises – A73, B77, C77, c/c133	98:3c	All the Ends of the Earth – A14, B14, B87, C14, C179, c/c6
66:4	Let All the Earth Adore and Praise You – A73, B98, C77, c/c133	100:3c	People of God, Flock of the Lord – A123, C81, c/c182
67:2a	May God Bless Us in Mercy – A21, B21, C21, c/c157	103:3b	Heal Me in Your Mercy – B112, c/c84
67:4	God, Let All the Peoples Praise You – A152, C87, c/c72	103:3b	If You Will Love Each Other – A165, c/c117
67:7	Our God Has Blessed Us – A249, B248, C250, c/c179	103:8	Merciful and Tender – A111, A164, B117, C36, C114, C187, c/c159
68:6-7, 35	Home for the Lonely – B143, C144, C161, c/c90	104:1-2	Bless the Lord, My Soul – C27, c/c27
69:14c	In Your Abundant Love – A126, c/c121	104:28b	You Open Your Hand – A127, B144, c/c285
70:2, 6	God, Come to My Aid (II) – A144, B146, C147, c/c68	104:30	Send Out Your Spirit – A52, B58, C58, c/c203
72:7	Justice Shall Flourish – A5, c/c127	104:30	Alleluia, Send Out Your Spirit – A93, B96, C96, c/c12
72:11	They Shall Adore You – A24, B24, C24, c/c236	105:4	Seek the Lord! Long for the Lord! – A32, A101, A182, B32, C32, c/c202
74:16, 19, 21	Yours Is the Day – B149, C150, c/c290	105:7a, 8a	God Remembers His Covenant For Ever – B18, c/c75
78a, c	Rise Up and Tell All Your Children – A227, B226, C228, c/c195	107:1b	Give Thanks to the Lord, Alleluia (II) – B129, c/c62
80:19	God of Hosts, Bring Us Back – B2, C11, c/c73	109:26	Heal Me in Your Mercy – B112, c/c84
81:1-2	Ring Out Your Joy – B120, c/c194	110:4b	You Are a Priest For Ever – C204, c/c272
81:17	With Finest Wheat and Finest Wine – A202, B201, C203, c/c267	112:4a	Those Who Fear the Lord – A105, c/c243
84:4	Happy Are They Who Dwell in Your House – A244, B38, C18, c/c81	113:1, 7b	Praise to God Who Lifts Up the Poor – C170, c/c185
85:1-3	Turn to Me, Answer Me – A154, B156, C156, c/c249		

Colossians

3:1	Do Not Store Up Earthly Treasures – C149, C171, c/c48
3:16	Let the Word Make a Home in Your Heart – A19, B161, c/c136

1 Thessalonians

1:4	You Alone Are Lord – A181, c/c270
2:13	The Word of God at Work in Us – A188, c/c234

2 Thessalonians

3:5	God of Life, God of Hope – C193, c/c74

1 Timothy

6:12, 14	Take Hold of Eternal Life – C174, c/c213

Hebrews

2:4	Take Your Place at the Table – C177, c/c214
12:2	Set the Earth on Fire – C155, c/c204
13:8	Jesus Christ, the Same Today, Yesterday and Evermore – A22, B22, C22, c/c123

James

1:21	Let the Word Make a Home in Your Heart – A19, B161, c/c136
5:7a, 8b	Be Patient, Beloved – A9, c/c21

1 Peter

2:2	Like Newborn Children – A69, B74, C74, c/c142

1 John

3:2	We Shall Be Like You – A222, B221, C223, c/c257
3:16	Christ Laid Down His Life for Us – A172, B170, c/c35
4:9	God's Love Is Revealed to Us – A15, B15, C28, c/c77

Revelation

1:6	Worthy Is the Lamb Who Was Slain – A196, B195, C197, c/c269
1:8	Listen, Listen to the Voice of Jesus – A198, B197, c/c145
3:20	Listen, Listen to the Voice of Jesus – A198, B197, c/c145
3:20	Listen: I Stand at the Door and Knock – A140, C143, c/c143
5:12	Worthy Is the Lamb Who Was Slain – A196, B195, C197, c/c269
12:1	A Woman Clothed with the Sun – A223, B222, C224, c/c4
19:9	The Spirit and the Bride Say "Come!" – A231, B230, C232, c/c231
21:3b	I Will Dwell with You – A237, B236, C238, c/c105
21:23	Our City Has No Need of Sun or Moon – A25, B25, C25, c/c176
22:17	The Spirit and the Bride Say "Come!" – A231, B230, C232, c/c231

The letter A, B, or C preceding the number refers to the accompaniment edition, and c/c refers to the Cantor/Choir edition.

Christ Laid Down His Life for Us – A172, B170, c/c35
Our Cup of Blessing – A48, B54, C54, c/c177
Our Glory and Pride Is the Cross of Jesus Christ – A47, B53, C53, C227, c/c178
This Is My Body – A50, B56, C56, c/c238
With Finest Wheat and Finest Wine – A202, B201, C203, c/c267

Good Friday

Christ Laid Down His Life for Us – A172, B170, c/c35
Father, into Your Hands – A51, B57, C57, c/c53

Easter

A New Commandment I Give to You – A49, B55, C55, c/c2
All the Ends of the Earth – A14, B14, B87, C14, C179, c/c6
Alleluia, Alleluia, Alleluia! (I) – B75, C75, c/c11
Alleluia, Alleluia, Alleluia! (II) – A62, B68, C68, c/c11
Alleluia, Send Out Your Spirit – A93, B96, C96, c/c12
At Your Word Our Hearts Are Burning – A75, c/c20
Christ the Lord Is Risen Again – A65, B71, C71, c/c37
Christ, Our Pasch – A67, B70, C70, c/c36
Clothed in Christ, One in Christ – A28, B69, C69, c/c38
"Come," Says My Heart – B92, C92, c/c43
Give Thanks to the Lord, Alleluia (I) – A70, c/c61
God, Let All the Peoples Praise You – C87, c/c72
I Am the Way: Follow Me – A81, c/c96
I Know I Shall See the Goodness of the Lord – A90, c/c100
I Will Praise You, Lord – A56, B62, C62, C78, c/c107
I Will Praise Your Name For Ever (I) – C84, c/c108
I Will See You Again – A88, B91, C91, c/c110
If You Love Me, Feed My Lambs (I) – C79, c/c115
Joyfully You Will Draw Water – A57, B27, B205, C63, c/c126
Keep Us in Your Name – C94, c/c130
Let All the Earth Cry Out Your Praises – A73, B77, C77, c/c133
Let Your Love Be Upon Us, O Lord – A80, c/c138
Like a Deer That Longs for Running Streams – A59, B65, C65, c/c141
Like Newborn Children – A69, B74, C74, c/c142
Live on in My Love – A85, A91, B88, B94, C88, c/c147
Lord, Cleanse My Heart – A61, B46, C67, c/c149
My Portion and My Cup – A54, B60, B193, C60, c/c165
My Sheep I Will Pasture – C208, c/c166
My Shepherd Is the Lord – A39, A233, B42, B82, B141, B191, B232, C82, C207, C234, c/c167
People of God, Flock of the Lord – C81, c/c182
Put Your Hand Here, Thomas – A72, B76, C76, c/c187
Send Out Your Spirit – A52, B58, C58, c/c203
Shine Your Face on Us, Lord – B78, c/c206
Shout to the Ends of the Earth – B86, C86, c/c207
Sing to God a New Song – A79, B83, C83, c/c210
Sing to the Lord – A55, B61, C61, c/c211
The Earth Is Full of the Goodness of God (I) – A76, B80, C80, c/c217
The Earth Is Full of the Goodness of God (II) – A53, B59, C59, c/c217
The Lord Is King (I) – C93, c/c221
The Stone Which the Builders Rejected – B81, c/c232
This Is the Day – A66, B72, C72, c/c240
Touch Me and See – A71, B79, c/c247
You Are My Praise – B84, c/c277

You Are Rich in Mercy – A68, A176, c/c279
You Are the Shepherd – A78, c/c281
You Are the Vine – A82, B85, c/c282
You Will Show Us the Path of Life – A74, c/c287
Your Word Is Life, Lord – B36, c/c289

Ascension

God Goes Up with Shouts of Joy – A87, B90, C90, c/c70
I Will See You Again – A88, B91, C91, c/c110
Shout to the Ends of the Earth – A89, c/c207
The Lord Is King (I) – C93, c/c221
Why Stare into the Sky? – A86, B89, C89, c/c263

Pentecost

Alleluia, Send Out Your Spirit – A93, B96, C96, c/c12
Come to Me and Drink – A94, B97, C97, c/c44
Send Out Your Spirit – A52, B58, C58, c/c203
The Love of God – A92, B95, B200, C95, c/c225

Christ the King

Alleluia, Send Out Your Spirit – A93, B96, C96, c/c12
Christ Laid Down His Life for Us – A172, B170, c/c35
Keep Us in Your Name – C94, c/c130
Let Us Go Rejoicing – C198, c/c137
Listen, Listen to the Voice of Jesus – A198, B197, c/c145
Take Hold of Eternal Life – C174, c/c213
The Lord Is King (I) – C93, c/c221
The Lord Is King (II) – B196, c/c222
Worthy Is the Lamb Who Was Slain – A196, B195, C197, c/c269

Holy Trinity

For Ever, For Ever, We Praise You For Ever – A200, c/c55
Happy Are They Whose God Is the Lord – B199, C151, c/c83
How Wonderful Your Name, O Lord – C201, c/c94
The Love of God – A92, B200, C95, c/c225
You Have Shown You Love Us – A199, B198, C200, c/c284

Body and Blood of Christ

A New Commandment I Give to You – A49, B55, C55, c/c2
At Your Word Our Hearts Are Burning – A75, c/c20
Come, Come to the Banquet – C43, c/c40
Eat My Flesh and Drink My Blood – A236, B235, C237, c/c50
Finest Food! Choicest Wine! – A178, c/c54
Not on Bread Alone Are We Nourished – A31, C31, c/c169
Raise the Cup of Salvation – B202, c/c188
This Is My Body – A50, B56, C56, c/c238
With Finest Wheat and Finest Wine – A202, B201, C203, c/c267
You Are a Priest For Ever – C204, c/c272

Sacred Heart

A New Commandment I Give to You – A49, B55, C55, c/c2
All Who Labor, Come to Me – B204, C206, c/c8
Christ Laid Down His Life for Us – A172, B170, c/c35
Come to Me and Drink – A94, B97, C97, c/c44
Joyfully You Will Draw Water – B27, B205, c/c126
My Sheep I Will Pasture – C208, c/c166
My Shepherd Is the Lord – A39, A233, B42, B82, B141, B191, B232, C82, C207, C234, c/c167
Your Word Is Life, Lord – A58, B64, C64, c/c289

Christian Initiation / Baptism

A New Commandment I Give to You – A49, B55, C55, c/c2
A River Flows – A238, B237, C239, c/c3
As Seed for the Sowing – A136, A139, c/c16–17
Ask and Receive (I) – A143, c/c18
Ask and Receive (II) – A239, B238, C240, c/c19
At Your Word Our Hearts Are Burning – A75, c/c20
Because You Are Filled with the Spirit – B173, c/c23
Bless the Lord, My Soul – C27, c/c27
Chosen in Christ, Blessed in Christ – B139, c/c33
Christ Laid Down His Life for Us – A172, B170, c/c35
Clothed in Christ, One in Christ – A28, B28, B69, C69, c/c38
Come to Me and Drink – A94, B97, C97, c/c44
Come, All You Good and Faithful Servants – A195, c/c39
Come, Come to the Banquet – A146, C43, c/c40
Come, My Children – B176, c/c42
"Come," Says My Heart – B92, C92, c/c43
Do Not Abandon Me, Lord! – B186, C188, c/c47
Do Not Store Up Earthly Treasures – C149, C171, c/c48
Finest Food! Choicest Wine! – A178, c/c54
For You My Soul Is Thirsting – A158, C129, c/c56
From the East and West, from the North and South – A186, C158, c/c58
Give Us Living Water – A37, B39, C39, c/c64
Go to the Ends of the Earth – C120, c/c66
God Feeds Us, God Saves Us – A115, C183, c/c69
Happy Are They Who Follow – A108, c/c82
Happy Are They Whose God Is the Lord – B199, C151, c/c83
Heaven and Earth Will Fade Away – A109, B194, c/c86
How I Thirst for You – A235, B234, C236, c/c93
I Am the Way: Follow Me – A81, c/c96
I Will Dwell with You – A237, B236, C238, c/c105
I Will Praise You, I Will Thank You – A215, B214, C216, c/c106
If You Love Me, Feed My Lambs (I) – C79, c/c115
If You Love Me, Feed My Lambs (II) – A219, B218, C220, c/c116
Joyfully You Will Draw Water – A57, B27, B205, C63, c/c126
Keep These Words in Your Heart and Soul – A118, c/c129
Let the Word Make a Home in Your Heart – A19, B161, c/c136
Light of the World – A100, A106, c/c140
Like Newborn Children – A69, B74, C74, c/c142
Listen, Listen to the Words of Jesus – A148, c/c146
Listen: I Stand at the Door and Knock – A140, c/c143
Live on in My Love – A85, A91, B88, B94, C88, c/c147
Lord, This Is the People – A230, B229, C231, c/c151
Lose Your Life and Save It – B167, B227, C130, c/c153
Love Bears All Things – C106, c/c154
Love Is My Desire – A121, c/c155
My Shepherd Is the Lord – A39, A233, B42, B82, B141, B191, B232, C82, C207, C234, c/c167
Not on Bread Alone Are We Nourished – A31, C31, c/c169
Our Cup of Blessing – A48, B54, C54, c/c177
People of God, Flock of the Lord – A123, C81, c/c182
Speak Your Word, O Lord – C121, c/c212
Take Hold of Eternal Life – C174, c/c213
Take Your Place at the Table – C177, c/c214
The Greatest Among You – B182, c/c219
The Last Shall Be First – A168, c/c220
The Love of God – A92, B95, B200, C95, c/c225
The Seed That Falls on the Good Ground – A135, c/c230

The Word of God at Work in Us – A188, c/c234
This Is My Body – A50, B56, C56, c/c238
Those Who Do the Will of God – B124, c/c242
Walk in My Ways – B31, B103, c/c253
We Will Follow You, Lord – C133, c/c258
When You Fill Us with Your Word – B178, C148, c/c260
With All My Heart I Cry (II) – A142, c/c265
You Are God's Temple – A247, A246, A248, c/c273
You Are Light in the Lord – A40, B44, C44, c/c275
You Are the Shepherd – A78, c/c281
You Shall Be a Royal Priesthood – A124, c/c286
Your Word Is Life, Lord – A58, B36, B64, C64, c/c289

Confirmation

A New Commandment I Give to You – A49, B55, C55, c/c2
Alleluia, Send Out Your Spirit – A93, B96, C96, c/c12
As One Body in Your Spirit – C103, c/c15
Because You Are Filled with the Spirit – B173, c/c23
Bless the Lord, My Soul – C27, c/c27
Chosen in Christ, Blessed in Christ – B139, c/c33
Christ Laid Down His Life for Us – A172, B170, c/c35
Come, All You Good and Faithful Servants – A195, c/c39
Give Us Living Water – A37, B39, C39, c/c64
Go to the Ends of the Earth – C120, c/c66
I Loved Wisdom More Than Health or Beauty – B179, C163, c/c102
I Will Praise You, I Will Thank You – A215, B214, C216, c/c106
If You Love Me, Feed My Lambs (II) – A219, B218, C220, c/c116
Light of the World – A100, A106, c/c140
Live on in My Love – A85, A91, B88, B94, C88, c/c147
Lord, This Is the People – A230, B229, C231, c/c151
Lose Your Life and Save It – A228, B167, B227, C130, c/c153
Love Bears All Things – C106, c/c154
People of God, Flock of the Lord – A123, C81, c/c182
Send Out Your Spirit – A52, B58, C58, c/c203
Set the Earth on Fire – C155, c/c204
The Love of God – A92, B95, B200, C95, c/c225
Walk in My Ways – B103, c/c253
We Will Follow You, Lord – C133, c/c258
You Are God's Temple – A247, A246, A248, c/c273

Marriage

A New Commandment I Give to You – A49, B55, C55, c/c2
All That Is True – A175, c/c5
All Things Are from the Lord – A156, c/c7
As a Bridegroom Rejoices – A240, B239, C100, c/c14
At Your Word Our Hearts Are Burning – A75, c/c20
Because You Are Filled with the Spirit – B173, c/c23
Behold, the Bridegroom Is Here (I) – B118, c/c24
Finest Food! Choicest Wine! – A178, c/c54
God Remembers His Covenant For Ever – B18, c/c75
God's Love Is Revealed to Us – A15, B15, C28, c/c77
Here I Am – A96, B99, C107, c/c87
How Happy Are You – A194, B175, c/c92
How Wonderful Your Name, O Lord – C201, c/c94
I Will Dwell with You – A237, B236, C238, c/c105
Jesus Christ, the Same Today, Yesterday and Evermore – A22, B22, C22, c/c123
Keep Us in Your Name – B127, c/c130

Let the Word Make a Home in Your Heart – A19, c/c136
Let Us Go Rejoicing – A2, B245, C198, c/c137
Light of the World – A100, A106, c/c140
Live on in My Love – A85, A91, B88, B94, C88, c/c147
Love Bears All Things – C106, c/c154
Love the Lord Your God – A112, A185, C140, c/c156
May God Bless Us in Mercy – A21, B21, C21, c/c157
May God Grant Us Joy of Heart – A250, B249, C251, c/c158
Merciful and Tender – A111, A164, B117, C36, C114, C187, c/c159
My Soul Rejoices in God – A225, B8, B224, C12, C226, c/c168
Our God Has Blessed Us – A249, B248, C250, c/c179
The Earth Is Full of the Goodness of God (I) – A76, B80, C80, c/c217
The Earth Is Full of the Goodness of God (II) – A53, B59, C59, c/c217
The Goodness of the Lord – B150, C41, c/c218
The Spirit and the Bride Say "Come!" – A231, B230, C232, c/c231
Those Who Do the Will of God – B124, c/c242
Those Who Fear the Lord – A105, c/c243
Walk in My Ways – B103, c/c253
You Are God's Temple – A247, B246, C248, c/c273
You Are Rich in Mercy – A176, c/c279
You Have Given Everything Its Place – A179, B174, C175, c/c283

Holy Orders / Religious Profession
A New Commandment I Give to You – A49, B55, C55, c/c2
All Who Labor, Come to Me – A133, C206, c/c8
Ask and Receive (I) – A143, c/c18
At Your Word Our Hearts Are Burning – A75, c/c20
Because You Are Filled with the Spirit – B173, c/c23
Behold, the Bridegroom Is Here (I) – B118, c/c24
Blest Are the Poor in Spirit – A103, c/c29
Cast Out into the Deep – C109, c/c31
Chosen in Christ, Blessed in Christ – B139, c/c33
Christ Laid Down His Life for Us – A172, B170, c/c35
Come, All You Good and Faithful Servants – A195, c/c39
Do Not Store Up Earthly Treasures – C149, C171, c/c48
Don't Be Afraid – A150, C152, C196, c/c49
Go to the Ends of the Earth – C120, c/c66
God, Come to My Aid – A144, B146, C147, C154, c/c67–68
Happy Are They Who Dwell in Your House – A244, B38, C18, c/c81
Here I Am – A96, B99, C107, c/c87
How I Thirst for You – A235, B234, C236, c/c93
I Am the Resurrection – A43, B49, C49, c/c95
I Am the Way: Follow Me – A81, c/c96
I Know I Shall See the Goodness of the Lord – A90, c/c100
I Loved Wisdom More Than Health or Beauty – B179, C163, c/c102
I Shall Dwell in the House of the Lord – A177, c/c103
I Will Sing For Ever of Your Love – A129, B11, c/c112
If You Love Me, Feed My Lambs (I) – C79, c/c115
If You Love Me, Feed My Lambs (II) – A219, B218, C220, c/c116
Let the Word Make a Home in Your Heart – A19, B161, c/c136
Light of the World – A100, A106, c/c140

Like a Deer That Longs for Running Streams – A59, B65, C65, c/c141
Listen, Listen to the Words of Jesus – A148, c/c146
Live on in My Love – A85, A91, B88, B94, C88, c/c147
Lord, This Is the People – A230, B229, C231, c/c151
Lose Your Life and Save It – A228, B167, B227, C130, c/c153
Love Bears All Things – C106, c/c154
Love Is My Desire – A121, c/c155
Love the Lord Your God – A112, A185, C140, c/c156
May God Bless Us in Mercy – A21, B21, C21, c/c157
My Portion and My Cup – A54, B60, B193, C60, C132, c/c165
My Soul Rejoices in God – A225, B8, B224, C12, C226, c/c168
Not on Bread Alone Are We Nourished – A31, C31, c/c169
One Thing I Seek – A122, B125, C125, c/c173
Our Cup of Blessing – A48, B54, C54, c/c177
People of God, Flock of the Lord – A123, C81, c/c182
Praise to God Who Lifts Up the Poor – C170, c/c185
Raise the Cup of Salvation – B202, c/c188
Salvation Has Come to This House – C190, c/c197
Seek the Lord! Long for the Lord! – A101, A182, c/c202
Set the Earth on Fire – C155, c/c204
Take Hold of Eternal Life – C174, c/c213
Take Your Place at the Table – C177, c/c214
The Greatest Among You – B182, c/c219
The Last Shall Be First – A168, c/c220
Those Who Do Justice – A151, B160, C142, c/c241
Those Who Do the Will of God – B124, c/c242
Walk in My Ways – B31, B103, c/c253
We Will Follow You, Lord – C133, c/c258
You Are a Priest For Ever – C204, c/c272
You Are God's Temple – A247, B246, C248, c/c273
You Are My Praise – B84, c/c277
You Are the Shepherd – A78, c/c281
You Shall Be a Royal Priesthood – A124, c/c286
You Will Show Me the Path of Life – B188, c/c287
You Will Show Us the Path of Life – A74, c/c287

Reconciliation / Penance
A River Flows – A238, B237, C239, c/c3
All Who Labor, Come to Me – A133, B204, C206, c/c8
All Your Sins Have Been Forgiven – C127, c/c10
Change Your Heart and Mind – A171, c/c32
Come to Me and Drink – A94, B97, C97, c/c44
Do Not Abandon Me, Lord! – B186, C188, c/c47
Don't Be Afraid – A150, B133, c/c49
Everlasting Is Your Love – A155, c/c51
Every Valley Shall Be Filled – C6, c/c52
For You My Soul Is Thirsting – A158, C129, c/c56
Forgive, and You Will Be Forgiven – C115, c/c57
From the Fullness of Our Hearts – C118, c/c59
Give Peace to Those Who Wait – A163, B165, C166, c/c60
Give: Your Father Sees – A210, B209, C211, c/c65
God of Hosts, Bring Us Back – B2, C11, c/c73
Happy Are They Who Follow – A108, c/c82
Heal Me in Your Mercy – B112, c/c84
Heal My Soul – B114, c/c85
How I Thirst for You – A235, B234, C236, c/c93
I Am With You – C30, c/c97
I Called in My Distress – A218, B217, C219, c/c99
I Know I Shall See the Goodness of the Lord – A90, c/c100

I Shall Dwell in the House of the Lord – A177, c/c103
I Thank You, Lord, with All My Heart – C180, c/c104
I Will Dwell with You – A237, B236, C238, c/c105
If You Will Love Each Other – A165, c/c117
Jesus, Mighty Lord, Come Save Us – A12, c/c124
Keep My Soul in Peace – A187, c/c128
Keep These Words in Your Heart and Soul – A118, c/c129
Like a Deer That Longs for Running Streams – A59, B65, C65, c/c141
Listen! Listen! Open Your Hearts! – A36, B37, C37, c/c144
Look on My Toil – A116, B119, C119, c/c148
Lord, Cleanse My Heart – A61, B46, C67, c/c149
Lord, You Are Close – A167, c/c152
Lose Your Life and Save It – A228, B167, B227, C130, c/c153
Love Is My Desire – A121, c/c155
Love the Lord Your God – A112, A185, C140, c/c156
May God Bless Us in Mercy – A21, B21, C21, c/c157
May God Grant Us Joy of Heart – A250, B249, C251, c/c158
Merciful and Tender – A111, A164, B117, C36, C114, C187, c/c159
My Grace Is Enough – B136, c/c162
My Plans for You Are Peace – A193, B192, C194, c/c164
My Sheep I Will Pasture – C208, c/c166
My Shepherd Is the Lord – A39, A233, B42, B82, B141, B191, B232, C82, C207, C234, c/c167
Open Your Hand, Lord – B145, c/c175
Remember, Lord – A170, c/c193
Save Us, Lord – A125, C128, c/c199–200
Seek the Lord! Long for the Lord! – A32, A101, A182, B32, C32, c/c202
Show Us, Lord, Your Kindness – A149, B5, c/c208
Speak Your Word, O Lord – C121, c/c212
Teach Me Your Path – B30, c/c215
The Last Shall Be First – A168, c/c220
The Mercy of God Is for All – A153, c/c226
The Prayer of Our Hearts – C186, c/c229
There Is Mercy in the Lord – A42, B47, C47, c/c235
Those Who Fear the Lord – A105, c/c243
Those Who Love Me, I Will Deliver – A29, C29, C38, c/c244
Turn Our Hearts from Stone to Flesh – A35, B35, C35, c/c248
Turn to the Lord – B111, C126, c/c250
We Have Sinned, Lord – A30, B208, C167, c/c254
We Look to You, O Lord – B135, c/c255
When the Poor Cry Out – C185, c/c259
Where Two or Three Are Gathered – A162, c/c261
With All My Heart I Cry (I) – A160, c/c264
You Are Good and Forgiving – A138, c/c274
You Are My Hiding-Place, O Lord – C48, c/c276
You Are Rich in Mercy – A68, A208, A176, B207, B43, B177, C178, C209, c/c279–280
Your Mercy Is My Hope – A110, B113, C113, c/c288

Pastoral Care of the Sick

A River Flows – A238, B237, C239, c/c3
All Who Labor, Come to Me – A133, B204, C206, c/c8
Be Patient, Beloved – A9, c/c21
Be Strong, Our God Has Come to Save Us (I) – B9, C9, c/c22
Be Strong, Our God Has Come to Save Us (II) – B164, c/c22
Cast Out into the Deep – C109, c/c31
"Come," Says My Heart – B92, C92, c/c43
Don't Be Afraid – A150, B133, C152, C196, c/c49

Everlasting Is Your Love – A155, c/c51
Every Valley Shall Be Filled – C6, c/c52
Give Peace to Those Who Wait – A163, B165, C166, c/c60
God Heals the Broken – B109, C173, c/c71
God of Life, God of Hope – C193, c/c74
Guard Me as the Apple of Your Eye! – B180, C181, c/c80
Heal Me in Your Mercy – B112, c/c84
Heaven and Earth Will Fade Away – A109, B194, c/c86
Home for the Lonely – C161, c/c90
I Am With You – C30, c/c97
I Am Your Savior, My People – A166, A168, C169, c/c98
I Called in My Distress – A218, B217, C219, c/c99
I Know I Shall See the Goodness of the Lord – A90, c/c100
I Shall Dwell in the House of the Lord – A177, c/c103
I Thank You, Lord, with All My Heart – C180, c/c104
I Will Dwell with You – A237, B236, C238, c/c105
I Will Praise You, Lord – A56, B62, C62, C78, c/c107
If I Must Drink This Cup – A46, B52, C52, c/c114
In God Alone Is My Soul at Rest – A114, c/c119
In the Presence of the Angels – C108, c/c120
In Your Abundant Love – A126, c/c121
Jesus Christ, the Same Today, Yesterday and Evermore – A22, B22, C22, c/c123
Lead Me, Guide Me – B110, C110, c/c132
Let Your Love Be Upon Us, O Lord – A33, A80, B181, c/c138
Like a Deer That Longs for Running Streams – A59, B65, C65, c/c141
Lord, You Are Close – A167, c/c152
Love Bears All Things – C106, c/c154
Merciful and Tender – A164, c/c159
My Plans for You Are Peace – A193, B192, C194, c/c164
My Shepherd Is the Lord – A39, A233, B42, B82, B141, B191, B232, C82, C207, C234, c/c167
Our Help Shall Come from the Lord – A182, c/c180
Remember, Lord – A170, c/c193
Save Me, O Lord – A117, c/c198
Shine Out, O Lord; You Are My God – B106, c/c205
Shine Your Face on Us, Lord – B78, c/c206
Speak Your Word, O Lord – C121, c/c212
The Lord Is My Light – A99, B122, C33, c/c223
The Mercy of God Is for All – A153, c/c226
The Prayer of Our Hearts – C186, c/c229
This Is My Body – A50, B56, C56, c/c238
Those Who Love Me, I Will Deliver – A29, B29, C29, C38, c/c244
To You, O Lord, I Lift My Soul – A1, B1, C2, c/c246
When the Poor Cry Out – C185, c/c259
Where Two or Three Are Gathered – A162, c/c261
You Alone Are My Help – A137, B140, C141, c/c271
You Are My Hiding-Place, O Lord – C48, c/c276
You Are the Shepherd – A78, c/c281
Your Mercy Is My Hope – A110, B113, C113, c/c288

Funerals

All That Is True – A175, c/c5
All Who Labor, Come to Me – A133, B204, C206, c/c8
Be Patient, Beloved – A9, c/c21
"Come," Says My Heart – B92, C92, c/c43
Come to Me and Drink – A94, B97, C97, c/c44
Eat My Flesh and Drink My Blood – A236, B235, C237, c/c50
Everlasting Is Your Love – A155, c/c51

For You My Soul Is Thirsting – A158, C129, c/c56

God, Who Raised Jesus from the Dead – A232, B231, B233, c/c76

How I Thirst for You – A235, B234, C236, c/c93

I Am the Resurrection – A43, B49, C49, c/c95

I Am the Way: Follow Me – A81, c/c96

I Know I Shall See the Goodness of the Lord – A90, c/c100

I Shall Dwell in the House of the Lord – A177, c/c103

I Will Dwell with You – A237, B236, C238, c/c105

I Will See You Again – A88, B91, C91, c/c110

I Will Walk in the Presence of the Lord – B33, B166, c/c113

In God Alone Is My Soul at Rest – A114, c/c119

Jesus Christ, the Same Today, Yesterday and Evermore – A22, B22, C22, c/c123

Let Us Go Rejoicing – A2, B245, c/c137

Live on in My Love – A85, A91, B88, B94, C88, c/c147

Lord, Listen to My Prayer – A234, B233, C235, c/c150

Lord, You Are Close – A167, c/c152

Merciful and Tender – A111, A164, B117, C36, C114, C187, c/c159

My Portion and My Cup – A54, B60, B193, C60, C132, c/c165

My Shepherd Is the Lord – A39, A233, B42, B82, B141, B191, B232, C82, C207, C234, c/c167

One Thing I Seek – A122, B125, C125, c/c173

Our Glory and Pride Is the Cross of Jesus Christ – A47, B53, C53, C227, c/c178

Rejoice, Your Names Are Written in Heaven – C136, c/c192

The Lord Is My Light – A99, B122, C33, c/c223

This Is My Body – A50, B56, C56, c/c238

Those Who Love Me, I Will Deliver – A29, B29, C29, C38, c/c244

To You, O Lord, I Lift My Soul – A1, B1, C2, c/c246

Unless a Grain of Wheat – B48, c/c251

You Will Show Me the Path of Life – B188, c/c287

You Will Show Us the Path of Life – A74, c/c287

Your Word Is Life, Lord – A58, B36, B64, B158, C64, c/c289

Blessed Virgin Mary

A Woman Clothed with the Sun – A223, B222, C224, c/c4

As a Bridegroom Rejoices – A240, B239, C100, c/c14

My Soul Rejoices in God – A225, B8, B224, C12, C226, c/c168

Rise Up, O Lord – A224, B223, C225, c/c196

Sing to God a New Song – A79, B83, C83, c/c210

The Spirit and the Bride Say "Come!" – A231, B230, C232, c/c231

Saints

Come, All You Good and Faithful Servants – A195, c/c39

Give: Your Father Sees – A210, B209, C211, c/c65

God's Tender Mercy – A6, B215, C217, c/c78

I Called in My Distress – A218, B217, C219, c/c99

I Will Praise You, I Will Thank You – A215, B214, C216, c/c106

If You Love Me, Feed My Lambs (II) – A219, B218, C220, c/c116

John Was Sent from God – A214, B213, C215, c/c125

Lord, This Is the People – A230, B229, C231, c/c151

Rejoice in the Lord on This Feast of the Saints – A229, B228, C230, c/c190

Rejoice, Your Names Are Written in Heaven – C136, c/c192

Take Hold of Eternal Life – C174, c/c213

Take Your Place at the Table – C177, c/c214

The Message Goes Forth – A98, B101, c/c227

The Spirit and the Bride Say "Come!" – A231, B230, C232, c/c231

You Are Peter – A217, B216, C218, c/c278

Eucharistic Devotion

As Seed for the Sowing – A136, c/c16

At Your Word Our Hearts Are Burning – A75, c/c20

Behold the Lamb of God! – A97, B100, c/c26

Behold, the Bridegroom Is Here (I) – B118, c/c24

Christ Laid Down His Life for Us – A172, B170, c/c35

Come to Me and Drink – A94, B97, C97, c/c44

Come to Me and You Shall Never Hunger – A147, B148, c/c45

Come, Come to the Banquet – A146, c/c40

Eat My Flesh and Drink My Blood – A236, B235, C237, c/c50

Finest Food! Choicest Wine! – A178, c/c54

For You My Soul Is Thirsting – A158, C129, c/c56

Give Us Living Water – A37, B39, C39, c/c64

God Feeds Us, God Saves Us – A115, c/c69

God Heals the Broken – B109, C173, c/c71

Here in Your Presence – B121, c/c88

How I Thirst for You – A235, B234, C236, c/c93

I Am the Resurrection – A43, B49, C49, c/c95

Like a Deer That Longs for Running Streams – A59, B65, C65, c/c141

Live on in My Love – A85, A91, B88, B94, C88, c/c147

My Portion and My Cup – A54, B60, B193, C60, C132, c/c165

O Praise the Lord, Jerusalem – A203, B151, c/c172

The Goodness of the Lord – B150, C41, c/c218

This Is My Body – A50, B56, C56, c/c238

This Is the Bread – B147, B155, c/c239

Touch Me and See – A71, B79, c/c247

Venite, Adoremus – A245, B107, C246, c/c252

With Finest Wheat and Finest Wine – A202, B201, C203, c/c267

You Are the Shepherd – A78, c/c281

You Are the Vine – A82, c/c282

You Open Your Hand – A127, c/c285

Your Word Is Life, Lord – B158, c/c289

The letter A, B, or C preceding the number refers to the accompaniment edition, and c/c refers to the Cantor/Choir edition.

You Are God's Temple – A247, B246, C248, c/c273
You Are Peter – A217, B216, C218, c/c278

Comfort and Consolation
All Who Labor, Come to Me – A133, B204, C206, c/c8
Arise, Jerusalem, Look to the East – A23, B23, C23, c/c13
Arise, Jerusalem, Stand on the Height – A4, B6, C4, c/c13
Be Patient, Beloved – A9, c/c21
Be Strong, Our God Has Come to Save Us (I) – B9, C9, c/c22
Blest Are the Poor in Spirit – A102, c/c29
"Come," Says My Heart – B92, C92, c/c43
Every Valley Shall Be Filled – C6, c/c52
God Heals the Broken – B109, C173, c/c71
I Am With You – C30, c/c97
I Am Your Savior, My People – A166, B168, C169, c/c98
I Know I Shall See the Goodness of the Lord – A90, c/c100
I Will Praise You, Lord – A56, B62, C62, C78, c/c107
I Will See You Again – A88, B91, C91, c/c110
Keep My Soul in Peace – A187, c/c128
Look on My Toil – A116, B119, C119, c/c148
Lord, You Are Close – A167, c/c152
My Shepherd Is the Lord – A39, A233, B42, B82, B141, B191, B232, C82, C207, C234, c/c167
One Thing I Seek – A122, B125, C125, c/c173
Rejoice, Rejoice, All You Who Love Jerusalem! – A38, B40, C40, c/c191
The Lord Is My Light – A99, B122, C33, C122, c/c223
The Mercy of God Is for All – A153, c/c226
The Spirit and the Bride Say "Come!" – A231, B230, C232, c/c231
This Is My Body – A50, B56, C56, c/c238
You Are My Hiding-Place, O Lord – C48, c/c276
You Are Rich in Mercy – A68, A176, B43, c/c279
You Will Show Me the Path of Life – B188, c/c287
You Will Show Us the Path of Life – A74, c/c287
Your Mercy Is My Hope – A110, B113, C113, c/c288

Compassion
Heal Me in Your Mercy – B112, c/c84
I Will Praise Your Name For Ever (I) – C84, c/c108
If You Love Me, Feed My Lambs (I) – C79, c/c115
In Your Abundant Love – A126, c/c121
Light of the World – A106, c/c140
Lord, You Are Close – A167, c/c152
Merciful and Tender – A111, A164, B117, C36, C114, C187, c/c159
Open Your Hand, Lord – B145, c/c175
Save Us, Lord – B142, c/c201
The Love of God – A92, B95, C95, c/c225
The Mercy of God Is for All – A153, c/c226
Those Who Fear the Lord – A105, c/c243
You Are Good and Forgiving – A138, c/c274
You Open Your Hand – A127, B144, c/c285

Conversion / Repentance
All Your Sins Have Been Forgiven – C127, c/c10
Behold, the Bridegroom Is Here (I) – B118, c/c24
Change Your Heart and Mind – A171, c/c32
Give Us Living Water – A37, B39, C39, c/c64
God of Hosts, Bring Us Back – B2, C11, c/c73
Heal Me in Your Mercy – B112, c/c84

Heal My Soul – B114, c/c85
Listen! Listen! Open Your Hearts! – A36, B37, C37, c/c144
Look on My Toil – A116, B119, C119, c/c148
Lord, Cleanse My Heart – A61, B46, C67, c/c149
Lose Your Life and Save It – A228, B227, B167, C130, C165, c/c153
Love Is My Desire – A121, c/c155
Merciful and Tender – A111, A164, B117, C36, C114, C187, c/c159
My Grace Is Enough – B136, c/c162
Remember, Lord – A170, c/c193
Set the Earth on Fire – C155, c/c204
Shine Out, O Lord; You Are My God – B106, c/c205
The Last Shall Be First – A168, c/c220
The Prayer of Our Hearts – C186, c/c229
There Is Mercy in the Lord – A42, B47, C47, c/c235
Turn Our Hearts from Stone to Flesh – A35, B35, C35, c/c248
Turn to the Lord – B111, C126, c/c250
We Look to You, O Lord – B135, c/c255
You Are Light in the Lord – A40, B44, C44, c/c275
You Are Rich in Mercy – A208, B207, B177, C178, C209, c/c280
You Are the Vine – A82, B85, c/c282

Courage and Strength
All Who Labor, Come to Me – A133, B204, C206, c/c8
Be Patient, Beloved – A9, c/c21
Be Strong, Our God Has Come to Save Us (I) – B9, C9, c/c22
Be Strong, Our God Has Come to Save Us (II) – B164, c/c22
Come, My Children – B176, c/c42
Courage! Get Up! – B185, c/c46
Don't Be Afraid – A150, B133, C152, C196, c/c49
Give Thanks to the Lord, Alleluia (I) – A70, c/c61
God Heals the Broken – B109, C173, c/c71
God of Life, God of Hope – C193, c/c74
I Love You, Lord – A183, c/c101
I Shall Dwell in the House of the Lord – A177, c/c103
In Every Age, O Lord, You Have Been Our Refuge – C164, c/c118
In God Alone Is My Soul at Rest – A114, c/c119
Lead Me, Guide Me – A107, B110, C110, c/c132
Let Your Love Be Upon Us, O Lord – A33, A80, B181, c/c138
Lift Up Your Heads, Stand and Believe – C3, c/c139
One Thing I Seek – A122, B125, C125, c/c173
Salvation Has Come to This House – C190, c/c197
Save Us, Lord – A125, B128, C128, c/c199–200
The Lord Is My Light – A99, B122, C33, C122, c/c223
The Strong Lord Sets Me Free – A184, B116, C116, c/c233
Those Who Love Me, I Will Deliver – A29, B29, C38, C29, c/c244
Who Can This Be – B130, c/c262
You Will Show Me the Path of Life – B188, c/c287
You Will Show Us the Path of Life – A74, c/c287

Covenant
A Light Will Shine on Us This Day – A13, B13, C13, C20, c/c1
All Things Are from the Lord – A156, c/c7
As a Bridegroom Rejoices – A240, B239, C100, c/c14
As Seed for the Sowing – A139, c/c17
Behold, the Bridegroom Is Here (I) – B118, c/c24

Exile
Be Strong, Our God Has Come to Save Us (II) – B164, c/c22
Give Peace to Those Who Wait – A163, B165, C166, c/c60
God of Life, God of Hope – C193, c/c74
Laughter Fills Our Mouths – B184, C5, c/c131
My Plans for You Are Peace – A193, B192, C194, c/c164
O Let My Tongue Cleave to My Mouth – B41, c/c171
Praise the Lord, Alleluia! – B108, c/c184

Faith
Change Your Heart and Mind – A171, c/c32
Come to Me and You Shall Never Hunger – A147, B148, c/c45
Don't Be Afraid – A150, B133, C152, C196, c/c49
Eat My Flesh and Drink My Blood – A236, B235, C237, c/c50
I Am the Resurrection – A43, B49, C49, c/c95
In God Alone Is My Soul at Rest – A114, c/c119
Lift Up Your Heads, Stand and Believe – C3, c/c139
Listen, Listen to the Words of Jesus – A148, c/c146
Love Bears All Things – C106, c/c154
Planted Like a Tree – C111, c/c183
Put Your Hand Here, Thomas – A72, B76, C76, c/c187
Take Hold of Eternal Life – C174, c/c213
The Word of God at Work in Us – A188, c/c234
Unless a Grain of Wheat – B48, c/c251
Who Can This Be – B130, c/c262
With All My Heart I Cry (II) – A142, c/c265

Faithfulness of God
All Things Are from the Lord – A156, c/c7
As a Bridegroom Rejoices – A240, B239, C100, c/c14
As One Body in Your Spirit – C103, c/c15
As Seed for the Sowing – A136, c/c16
Ask and Receive (I) – A143, c/c18
Ask and Receive (II) – C146, c/c19
Be Strong, Our God Has Come to Save Us (II) – B164, c/c22
Behold, the Bridegroom Is Here (I) – B118, c/c24
Blessed Are You, Lord – A169, B171, c/c28
Blest Are the Poor in Spirit – A102, c/c29
Cast Out into the Deep – C109, c/c31
Christ Is the Light – A211, A213, B210, B212, C212, C214, c/c34
Come, All You Good and Faithful Servants – A195, c/c39
Come, Come to the Banquet – A146, C43, c/c40
Come, Lord, and Save Us – A8, c/c41
Come, My Children – B176, c/c42
Do Not Store Up Earthly Treasures – C171, c/c48
Don't Be Afraid – A150, B133, C152, C196, c/c49
Everlasting Is Your Love – A155, c/c51
From the Fullness of Our Hearts – C118, c/c59
Go to the Ends of the Earth – C120, c/c66
God Feeds Us, God Saves Us – A115, C183, c/c69
God Heals the Broken – B109, C173, c/c71
God of Life, God of Hope – C193, c/c74
God Remembers His Covenant For Ever – B18, c/c75
Happy Are They Whose God Is the Lord – B199, c/c83
Heal Me in Your Mercy – B112, c/c84
Heaven and Earth Will Fade Away – A109, B194, c/c86
Here in Your Presence – B121, c/c88
Home for the Lonely – B143, C144, C161, c/c90
I Am With You – C30, c/c97
I Called in My Distress – A218, B217, C219, c/c99

I Know I Shall See the Goodness of the Lord – A90, c/c100
I Shall Dwell in the House of the Lord – A177, c/c103
I Thank You, Lord, with All My Heart – C180, c/c104
I Will Praise Your Name For Ever (II) – A132, C189, c/c109
I Will Sing For Ever of Your Love – A129, B11, c/c112
In the Presence of the Angels – C108, c/c120
Keep Us in Your Name – B127, C94, c/c130
Let All the Earth Adore and Praise You – A73, B98, C77, c/c133
Let All the Earth Cry Out Your Praises – A73, B77, C77, c/c133
Let Your Love Be Upon Us, O Lord – A33, A80, B181, c/c138
Listen, Listen to the Words of Jesus – A148, c/c146
Lord, You Are Close – A167, c/c152
May God Grant Us Joy of Heart – A250, B249, C251, c/c158
Merciful and Tender – A111, A164, B117, C36, C114, C187, c/c159
My Grace Is Enough – B136, c/c162
My Lips Will Tell of Your Justice – C105, c/c163
My Sheep I Will Pasture – C208, c/c166
Open Your Hand, Lord – B145, c/c175
Our Help Shall Come from the Lord – C182, c/c180
Our Shelter and Our Help – C124, c/c181
People of God, Flock of the Lord – A123, C81, c/c182
Praise the Lord, Alleluia! – B108, c/c184
Rejoice in the Lord, Again Rejoice! – A7, B7, C7, c/c189
Save Us, Lord – B142, c/c201
Sing and Make Music – A248, B247, C249, c/c209
Speak Your Word, O Lord – C121, c/c212
The Mercy of God Is for All – A153, c/c226
Those Who Love Me, I Will Deliver – C29, c/c244
Who Can This Be – B130, c/c262
You Alone Are Lord – A181, c/c270
You Are My Praise – B84, c/c277
You Are Rich in Mercy – A68, A176, B43, c/c279
You Have Shown You Love Us – A199, B198, C200, c/c284
You Open Your Hand – A127, B144, c/c285
Yours Is the Day – B149, C150, c/c290

Family Life / Parenthood
How Happy Are You – A194, B175, c/c92
Let the Word Make a Home in Your Heart – A19, B161, c/c136
Those Who Fear the Lord – A105, c/c243
You Are God's Temple – A247, B246, C248, c/c273

Food / Hunger
As Seed for the Sowing – A136, c/c16
Blest Are You Who Weep – C112, c/c30
Come to Me and You Shall Never Hunger – A147, B148, c/c45
Come, Come to the Banquet – A146, C43, c/c40
Finest Food! Choicest Wine! – A178, c/c54
Give: Your Father Sees – A210, B209, C211, c/c65
God Feeds Us, God Saves Us – A115, C183, c/c69
If You Love Me, Feed My Lambs (I) – C79, c/c115
Not on Bread Alone Are We Nourished – A31, C31, c/c169
Save Us, Lord – B142, c/c201
This Is the Bread – B147, B155, c/c239
With Finest Wheat and Finest Wine – A202, B201, C203, c/c267

Forgiveness / Reconciliation
All Who Labor, Come to Me – A133, B204, C206, c/c8
All Your Sins Have Been Forgiven – C127, c/c10

Worthy Is the Lamb Who Was Slain – A196, B195, C197, c/c269

You Are My Praise – B84, c/c277

You Have Given Everything Its Place – A179, B174, C175, c/c283

You Have Shown You Love Us – A199, B198, C200, c/c284

Yours Is the Day – B149, C150, c/c290

God the Father (Creator)

Everlasting Is Your Love – A155, c/c51

I Will Praise You, I Will Thank You – A215, B214, C216, c/c106

Let All the Earth Adore and Praise You – A73, B98, C77, c/c133

Let All the Earth Cry Out Your Praises – A73, B77, C77, c/c133

Shout to the Ends of the Earth – A89, B86, C86, c/c207

The Lord Will Bless His People – A27, c/c224

You Have Shown You Love Us – A199, B198, C200, c/c284

Grace

All Your Sins Have Been Forgiven – C127, c/c10

Because You Are Filled with the Spirit – B173, c/c23

"Come," Says My Heart – B92, C92, c/c43

Courage! Get Up! – B185, c/c46

Do Not Abandon Me, Lord! – B186, C188, c/c47

Don't Be Afraid – A150, B133, C152, C196, c/c49

From the Fullness of Our Hearts – C118, c/c59

Give Thanks to the Lord, Alleluia (I) – A70, c/c61

God's Love Is Revealed to Us – A15, B15, C28, c/c77

God's Tender Mercy – B215, C217, c/c78

Happy Are They Who Follow – A108, c/c82

Heal Me in Your Mercy – B112, c/c84

I Am Your Savior, My People – A166, B168, C169, c/c98

I Shall Dwell in the House of the Lord – A177, c/c103

I Will Walk in the Presence of the Lord – B33, B166, c/c113

In the Presence of the Angels – C108, c/c120

Lose Your Life and Save It – A228, B227, B167, C130, c/c153

Love Is My Desire – A121, c/c155

Merciful and Tender – A111, A164, B117, C36, C114, C187, c/c159

My Grace Is Enough – B136, c/c162

My Sheep I Will Pasture – C208, c/c166

Our Glory and Pride Is the Cross of Jesus Christ – A47, B53, C53, C227, c/c178

Praise to God Who Lifts Up the Poor – C170, c/c185

Remember, Lord – A170, c/c193

Shine Out, O Lord; You Are My God – B106, c/c205

Speak Your Word, O Lord – C121, c/c212

The Last Shall Be First – A168, c/c220

The Love of God – A92, B95, C95, c/c225

The Mercy of God Is for All – A153, c/c226

The Strong Lord Sets Me Free – A184, B116, C116, c/c233

Turn Our Hearts from Stone to Flesh – A35, B35, C35, c/c248

Turn to the Lord – B111, C126, c/c250

We Receive from Your Fullness – A16, B16, C16, c/c256

When the Poor Cry Out – C185, c/c259

You Alone Are My Help – A137, B140, C141, c/c271

You Are Good and Forgiving – A138, c/c274

You Are Light in the Lord – A40, B44, C44, c/c275

You Are My Hiding-Place, O Lord – C48, c/c276

You Are Rich in Mercy – A68, A176, A208, B43, B177, B207, C178, C209, c/c279–280

Grieving / Mourning

Do Not Abandon Me, Lord! – B186, C188, c/c47

How I Thirst for You – A235, B234, C236, c/c93

Let My Prayer Come Before You, Lord – A189, B189, C191, c/c134

Lord, Listen to My Prayer – A234, B233, C235, c/c150

My God, My God – A45, B51, C51, c/c160

My Shepherd Is the Lord – A39, A233, B42, B82, B141, B191, B232, C82, C207, C234, c/c167

O Let My Tongue Cleave to My Mouth – B41, c/c171

Guidance

Ask and Receive (I) – A143, c/c18

Cast Out into the Deep – C109, c/c31

Change Your Heart and Mind – A171, c/c32

"Come," Says My Heart – B92, C92, c/c43

Do Not Store Up Earthly Treasures – C171, c/c48

Don't Be Afraid – A150, B133, C152, C196, c/c49

God of Life, God of Hope – C193, c/c74

Heaven and Earth Will Fade Away – A109, B194, c/c86

I Am the Way: Follow Me – A81, c/c96

I Loved Wisdom More Than Health or Beauty – A141, B179, C163, c/c102

If You Will Love Each Other – A165, c/c117

In Every Age, O Lord, You Have Been Our Refuge – C164, c/c118

Keep These Words in Your Heart and Soul – A118, c/c129

Lead Me, Guide Me – A107, B110, C110, c/c132

Light of the World – A100, A106, c/c140

Listen, Listen to the Words of Jesus – A148, c/c146

Listen: I Stand at the Door and Knock – A140, C143, c/c143

Look on My Toil – A116, B119, C119, c/c148

Lose Your Life and Save It – C165, c/c153

Love the Lord Your God – A112, A185, C140, c/c156

My Grace Is Enough – B136, c/c162

My Sheep I Will Pasture – C208, c/c166

My Shepherd Is the Lord – A39, A233, B42, B82, B141, B191, B232, C82, C207, C234, c/c167

Not on Bread Alone Are We Nourished – A31, C31, c/c169

One Thing I Seek – A122, B125, C125, c/c173

Remember, Lord – A170, c/c193

Rise Up and Tell All Your Children – A227, B226, C228, c/c195

Save Me, O Lord – A117, c/c198

Speak Your Word, O Lord – C121, c/c212

Teach Me Your Path – B30, c/c215

The Lord Is My Light – A99, B122, C33, C122, c/c223

The Prayer of Our Hearts – C186, c/c229

The Word of God at Work in Us – A188, c/c234

Those Who Do Justice – A151, B160, C142, c/c241

To You, O Lord, I Lift My Soul – A1, B1, C2, c/c246

Turn Our Hearts from Stone to Flesh – A35, B35, C35, c/c248

Turn to Me, Answer Me – A154, B156, C156, c/c249

Walk in My Ways – B31, B103, c/c253

We Will Follow You, Lord – C133, c/c258

When You Fill Us with Your Word – B178, C148, c/c260

Where Two or Three Are Gathered – A162, c/c261

With All My Heart I Cry (II) – A142, c/c265

You Are Light in the Lord – A40, B44, C44, c/c275
You Will Show Me the Path of Life – B188, c/c287
You Will Show Us the Path of Life – A74, c/c287
Your Word Is Life, Lord – A58, B36, B64, C64, c/c289

Healing

All Who Labor, Come to Me – A133, B204, C206, c/c8
All Your Sins Have Been Forgiven – C127, c/c10
Be Patient, Beloved – A9, c/c21
Be Strong, Our God Has Come to Save Us (I) – B9, C9, c/c22
Be Strong, Our God Has Come to Save Us (II) – B164, c/c22
Change Your Heart and Mind – A171, c/c32
Courage! Get Up! – B185, c/c46
Don't Be Afraid – A150, B133, C152, C196, c/c49
Give Peace to Those Who Wait – A163, B165, C166, c/c60
God Heals the Broken – B109, C173, c/c71
Guard Me as the Apple of Your Eye! – B180, C181, c/c80
Heal Me in Your Mercy – B112, c/c84
Heal My Soul – B114, c/c85
I Called in My Distress – A218, B217, C219, c/c99
I Will Dwell with You – A237, B236, C238, c/c105
Let Your Love Be Upon Us, O Lord – A33, A80, B181, c/c138
Like a Deer That Longs for Running Streams – A59, B65, C65, c/c141
Lord, Cleanse My Heart – A61, B46, C67, c/c149
Lord, You Are Close – A167, c/c152
My Sheep I Will Pasture – C208, c/c166
Praise the Lord, Alleluia! – B108, c/c184
Shine Out, O Lord; You Are My God – B106, c/c205
The Last Shall Be First – A168, c/c220
The Mercy of God Is for All – A153, c/c226
Turn to the Lord – B111, C126, c/c250
We Have Sinned, Lord – A30, B208, C167, c/c254
You Alone Are My Help – A137, B140, C141, c/c271
You Are Light in the Lord – A40, B44, C44, c/c275
You Are Rich in Mercy – B177, C178, c/c280

Heaven

I Shall Dwell in the House of the Lord – A177, c/c103
I Will Dwell with You – A237, B236, C238, c/c105
My Portion and My Cup – A54, B60, B193, C60, C132, c/c165
Rejoice, Your Names Are Written in Heaven – C136, c/c192
The Spirit and the Bride Say "Come!" – A231, B230, C232, c/c231
We Shall Be Like You – A222, B221, C223, c/c257

Holy Spirit

Alleluia, Send Out Your Spirit – A93, B96, C96, c/c12
As One Body in Your Spirit – C103, c/c15
Because You Are Filled with the Spirit – B173, c/c23
Chosen in Christ, Blessed in Christ – B139, c/c33
Clothed in Christ, One in Christ – A28, B28, B69, C69, c/c38
Give Us Living Water – A37, B39, C39, c/c64
God, Who Raised Jesus from the Dead – A232, B231, C233, c/c76
I Loved Wisdom More Than Health or Beauty – A141, B179, C163, c/c102
I Will See You Again – A88, B91, C91, c/c110
Send Out Your Spirit – A52, B58, C58, c/c203
The Love of God – A92, B95, B200, C95, c/c225

The Spirit and the Bride Say "Come!" – A231, B230, C232, c/c231
You Are God's Temple – A247, B246, C248, c/c273
You Have Shown You Love Us – A199, B198, C200, c/c284

Hope and Trust

A River Flows – A238, B237, C239, c/c3
All Who Labor, Come to Me – A133, B204, C206, c/c8
Be Patient, Beloved – A9, c/c21
Be Strong, Our God Has Come to Save Us (I) – B9, C9, c/c22
Cast Out into the Deep – C109, c/c31
Come to Me and You Shall Never Hunger – A147, B148, c/c45
Come, All You Good and Faithful Servants – A195, c/c39
"Come," Says My Heart – B92, C92, c/c43
Courage! Get Up! – B185, c/c46
Do Not Store Up Earthly Treasures – C171, c/c48
Don't Be Afraid – A150, B133, C152, C196, c/c49
Every Valley Shall Be Filled – C6, c/c52
Father, into Your Hands – A51, B57, C57, c/c53
Give Us Living Water – A37, B39, C39, c/c64
God Heals the Broken – B109, C173, c/c71
God of Life, God of Hope – C193, c/c74
God, Who Raised Jesus from the Dead – A232, B231, C233, c/c76
Great In Our Midst Is the Holy One – C8, c/c79
I Am Your Savior, My People – A166, B168, C169, c/c98
I Called in My Distress – A218, B217, C219, c/c99
I Will See You Again – A88, B91, C91, c/c110
I Will Walk in the Presence of the Lord – B33, B166, c/c113
In Every Age, O Lord, You Have Been Our Refuge – C164, c/c118
In God Alone Is My Soul at Rest – A114, c/c119
Joyfully You Will Draw Water – A57, B27, B205, C63, c/c126
Keep My Soul in Peace – A187, c/c128
Lead Me, Guide Me – A107, B110, C110, c/c132
Let Your Love Be Upon Us, O Lord – A33, A80, B181, c/c138
Lift Up Your Heads, Stand and Believe – C3, c/c139
Look on My Toil – A116, B119, C119, c/c148
Lord, You Are Close – A167, c/c152
Love Bears All Things – C106, c/c154
Merciful and Tender – A111, A164, B117, C36, C114, C187, c/c159
My Grace Is Enough – B136, c/c162
My Lips Will Tell of Your Justice – C105, c/c163
My Portion and My Cup – A54, B60, B193, C60, C132, c/c165
My Sheep I Will Pasture – C208, c/c166
My Shepherd Is the Lord – A39, A233, B42, B82, B141, B191, B232, C82, C207, C234, c/c167
One Thing I Seek – A122, B125, C125, c/c173
Our Help Shall Come from the Lord – C182, c/c180
Our Shelter and Our Help – C124, c/c181
Planted Like a Tree – C111, c/c183
Rejoice, Your Names Are Written in Heaven – C136, c/c192
Seek the Lord! Long for the Lord! – A32, A101, A182, B32, C32, c/c202
Shine Your Face on Us, Lord – B78, c/c206
Show Us, Lord, Your Kindness – A149, B5, c/c208
Teach Me Your Path – B30, c/c215
The Days Are Coming, Surely Coming – C1, c/c216
The Lord Is My Light – A99, B122, C33, C122, c/c223
The Love of God – A92, B95, C95, c/c225

The Mercy of God Is for All – A153, c/c226
The Strong Lord Sets Me Free – A184, B116, C116, c/c233
The Word of God at Work in Us – A188, c/c234
Those Who Love Me, I Will Deliver – A29, B29, C38, C29, c/c244
To Gaze on Your Glory – A134, B137, C137, c/c245
To You, O Lord, I Lift My Soul – A1, B1, C2, c/c246
Turn to the Lord – B111, C126, c/c250
We Will Follow You, Lord – C133, c/c258
Who Can This Be – B130, c/c262
You Alone Are Lord – A181, c/c270
You Are My Hiding-Place, O Lord – C48, c/c276
You Are Rich in Mercy – B177, C178, c/c280
You Open Your Hand – A127, B144, c/c285
You Will Show Me the Path of Life – B188, c/c287
You Will Show Us the Path of Life – A74, c/c287
Your Mercy Is My Hope – A110, B113, C113, c/c288

Humility

A New Commandment I Give to You – A49, B55, C55, c/c2
Christ Laid Down His Life for Us – A172, B170, c/c35
Here I Am – A96, B99, C107, c/c87
If I Must Drink This Cup – A46, B52, C52, c/c114
Keep My Soul in Peace – A187, c/c128
Lord, Cleanse My Heart – A61, B46, C67, c/c149
My Soul Rejoices in God – A225, B8, B224, C12, C226, c/c168
Take Hold of Eternal Life – C174, c/c213
Take Your Place at the Table – C177, c/c214
The Greatest Among You – B182, c/c219
The Last Shall Be First – A168, c/c220
The Prayer of Our Hearts – C186, c/c229
To You, O Lord, I Lift My Soul – A1, B1, C2, c/c246
We Look to You, O Lord – B135, c/c255
You Are My Hiding-Place, O Lord – C48, c/c276

Jesus Christ

All Things Are from the Lord – A156, c/c7
At Your Word Our Hearts Are Burning – A75, c/c20
Because You Are Filled with the Spirit – B173, c/c23
Behold the Lamb of God! – A97, B100, c/c26
Chosen in Christ, Blessed in Christ – B139, c/c33
Christ Is the Light – A211, A213, B210, B212, C212, C214, c/c34
Christ Laid Down His Life for Us – A172, B170, c/c35
Christ the Lord Is Risen Again – A65, B71, C71, c/c37
Clothed in Christ, One in Christ – A28, B28, B69, C69, c/c38
Here Is My Servant, Here Is My Son – A34, B26, B34, C26, c/c89
I Am the Resurrection – A43, B49, C49, c/c95
I Am the Way: Follow Me – A81, c/c96
I Will See You Again – A88, B91, C91, c/c110
Jesus Christ, the Same Today, Yesterday and Evermore – A22, B22, C22, c/c123
Jesus, Mighty Lord, Come Save Us – A12, c/c124
Let the King of Glory Come In – A11, B211, C213, c/c135
Light of the World – A100, A106, c/c140
Listen, Listen to the Voice of Jesus – A198, B197, c/c145
Listen, Listen to the Words of Jesus – A148, c/c146
Live on in My Love – A85, A91, B88, B94, C88, c/c147
Lose Your Life and Save It – C165, c/c153

Our Glory and Pride Is the Cross of Jesus Christ – A47, B53, C53, C227, c/c178
Take Hold of Eternal Life – C174, c/c213
The Love of God – A92, B95, B200, C95, c/c225
The Stone Which the Builders Rejected – B81, c/c232
Worthy Is the Lamb Who Was Slain – A196, B195, C197, c/c269
You Are the Shepherd – A78, c/c281
You Shall Be a Royal Priesthood – A124, c/c286

Journey / Pilgrimage

All That Is True – A175, c/c5
Be Strong, Our God Has Come to Save Us (I) – B9, C9, c/c22
Be Strong, Our God Has Come to Save Us (II) – B164, c/c22
Cast Out into the Deep – C109, c/c31
Come, All You Good and Faithful Servants – A195, c/c39
Do Not Store Up Earthly Treasures – C149, c/c48
God of Life, God of Hope – C193, c/c74
Home for the Lonely – B143, C144, C161, c/c90
How I Thirst for You – A235, B234, C236, c/c93
I Am the Way: Follow Me – A81, c/c96
I Know I Shall See the Goodness of the Lord – A90, c/c100
I Shall Dwell in the House of the Lord – A177, c/c103
Let Us Go Rejoicing – A2, B245, C198, c/c137
Lord, This Is the People – A230, B229, C231, c/c151
Lose Your Life and Save It – A228, B227, B167, C130, c/c153
My Sheep I Will Pasture – C208, c/c166
Now Is the Hour – A3, c/c170
One Thing I Seek – A122, B125, C125, c/c173
Our City Has No Need of Sun or Moon – A25, B25, C25, c/c176
Rejoice, Rejoice, All You Who Love Jerusalem! – A38, B40, C40, c/c191
Take Hold of Eternal Life – C174, c/c213
Teach Me Your Path – B30, c/c215
Unless a Grain of Wheat – B48, c/c251
Walk in My Ways – B31, B103, c/c253
We Will Follow You, Lord – C133, c/c258
You Are Light in the Lord – A40, B44, C44, c/c275

Joy / Gladness / Delight

A River Flows – A238, B237, C239, c/c3
All That Is True – A175, c/c5
All Things Are from the Lord – A156, c/c7
All You Nations – A128, B131, C131, c/c9
As a Bridegroom Rejoices – A240, B239, C100, c/c14
Come to Me and You Shall Never Hunger – A147, B148, c/c45
Come, All You Good and Faithful Servants – A195, c/c39
For Ever, For Ever, We Praise You For Ever – A200, c/c55
From the East and West, from the North and South – A186, C158, c/c58
God's Love Is Revealed to Us – A15, B15, C28, c/c77
Great In Our Midst Is the Holy One – C8, c/c79
Happy Are They Whose God Is the Lord – C151, c/c83
How Wonderful Your Name, O Lord – C201, c/c94
I Will See You Again – A88, B91, C91, c/c110
In the Presence of the Angels – C108, c/c120
It Is Good to Give You Thanks, O Lord – B126, C117, c/c122
Joyfully You Will Draw Water – A57, B27, B205, C63, c/c126
Laughter Fills Our Mouths – B184, C5, c/c131
Let Us Go Rejoicing – A2, B245, C198, c/c137

Like Newborn Children – A69, B74, C74, c/c142
Listen: I Stand at the Door and Knock – A140, C143, c/c143
May God Grant Us Joy of Heart – A250, B249, C251, c/c158
My Portion and My Cup – A54, B60, B193, C60, C132, c/c165
People of God, Flock of the Lord – A123, C81, c/c182
Rejoice in the Lord, Again Rejoice! – A7, B7, C7, c/c189
Rejoice, Rejoice, All You Who Love Jerusalem! – A38, B40, C40, c/c191
Rejoice, Your Names Are Written in Heaven – C136, c/c192
Ring Out Your Joy – B120, c/c194
Shout to the Ends of the Earth – A89, B86, C86, c/c207
Sing to the Lord – A55, B61, C61, c/c211
The Earth Is Full of the Goodness of God (I) – A76, B80, C80, c/c217
The Earth Is Full of the Goodness of God (II) – A53, B59, C59, c/c217
This Day Is Holy to the Lord Our God – C101, c/c237
This Is the Day – A66, B72, C72, c/c240
Turn to the Lord – B111, C126, c/c250
Venite, Adoremus – A245, B107, C246, c/c252
With All My Heart I Praise You – B115, c/c266
You Are Rich in Mercy – A68, A176, B43, c/c279
You Have Given Everything Its Place – A179, B174, C175, c/c283
You Will Show Me the Path of Life – B188, c/c287
You Will Show Us the Path of Life – A74, c/c287

Kin(g)dom / Kin(g)ship / Reign of God
All You Nations – A128, B131, C131, c/c9
At Your Word Our Hearts Are Burning – A75, c/c20
Be Patient, Beloved – A9, c/c21
Be Strong, Our God Has Come to Save Us (I) – B9, C9, c/c22
Be Strong, Our God Has Come to Save Us (II) – B164, c/c22
Behold, the Bridegroom Is Here (II) – A192, B3, c/c25
Blest Are the Poor in Spirit – A102, A103, c/c29
Blest Are You Who Weep – C112, c/c30
Come, Lord, and Save Us – A8, c/c41
Do Not Store Up Earthly Treasures – C149, c/c48
Give: Your Father Sees – A210, B209, C211, c/c65
God's Tender Mercy – A6, c/c78
I Will Dwell with You – A237, B236, C238, c/c105
I Will Praise Your Name For Ever (I) – C84, c/c108
I Will Praise Your Name For Ever (II) – A132, C189, c/c109
Jesus Christ, the Same Today, Yesterday and Evermore – A22, B22, C22, c/c123
Justice Shall Flourish – A5, c/c127
Let the King of Glory Come In – A11, B211, C213, c/c135
Lift Up Your Heads, Stand and Believe – C3, c/c139
Open, You Skies: Rain Down the Just One – A10, B10, C10, c/c174
Our City Has No Need of Sun or Moon – A25, B25, C25, c/c176
Praise to God Who Lifts Up the Poor – C170, c/c185
Proclaim the Wonders God Has Done – C99, c/c186
Rejoice in the Lord, Again Rejoice! – A7, B7, C7, c/c189
Rejoice, Your Names Are Written in Heaven – C136, c/c192
Take Hold of Eternal Life – C174, c/c213
The Days Are Coming, Surely Coming – C1, c/c216
The Last Shall Be First – A168, c/c220
The Lord Is King (I) – A221, B220, C93, c/c221
The Spirit and the Bride Say "Come!" – A231, B230, C232, c/c231

They Shall Adore You – A24, B24, C24, c/c236
Those Who Do Justice – A151, B160, C142, c/c241
Walk in My Ways – B31, B103, c/c253
You Are My Praise – B84, c/c277
You Shall Be a Royal Priesthood – A124, c/c286

Lament / Suffering
Do Not Abandon Me, Lord! – B186, C188, c/c47
God, Come to My Aid (II) – A144, B146, C147, c/c68
How I Thirst for You – A235, B234, C236, c/c93
I Am Your Savior, My People – A166, B168, C169, c/c98
In Your Abundant Love – A126, c/c121
Let My Prayer Come Before You, Lord – A189, B189, C191, c/c134
Look on My Toil – A116, B119, C119, c/c148
Lose Your Life and Save It – A228, B227, B167, C130, c/c153
My God, My God – A45, B51, C51, c/c160
My God, My Strength, Defend My Cause – A41, B45, C45, c/c161
O Let My Tongue Cleave to My Mouth – B41, c/c171
Remember, Lord – A170, c/c193
Save Us, Lord – A125, c/c199
Shine Out, O Lord; You Are My God – B106, c/c205
The Mercy of God Is for All – A153, c/c226
The People of God Are the Vineyard – A174, c/c228
Turn to Me, Answer Me – A154, B156, C156, c/c249
We Have Sinned, Lord – A30, B208, C167, c/c254
You Are Rich in Mercy – B177, B178, c/c280
Your Mercy Is My Hope – A110, B113, C113, c/c288

Life
Eat My Flesh and Drink My Blood – A236, B235, C237, c/c50
God of Life, God of Hope – C193, c/c74
God's Love Is Revealed to Us – A15, B15, C28, c/c77
God, Who Raised Jesus from the Dead – A232, B231, C233, c/c76
I Am the Way: Follow Me – A81, c/c96
I Will Praise You, I Will Thank You – A215, B214, C216, c/c106
In Every Age, O Lord, You Have Been Our Refuge – C164, c/c118
Let the Word Make a Home in Your Heart – A19, B161, c/c136
Love the Lord Your God – A112, A185, C140, c/c156
This Is the Bread – B147, B155, c/c239
Your Word Is Life, Lord – B158, c/c289

Light
A Light Will Shine on Us This Day – A13, B13, C13, C20, c/c1
Christ Is the Light – A211, A213, B210, B212, C212, C214, c/c34
Light of the World – A100, A106, c/c140
Our City Has No Need of Sun or Moon – A25, B25, C25, c/c176
Shine Your Face on Us, Lord – B78, c/c206
The Lord Is My Light – A99, B122, C33, C122, c/c223
Those Who Fear the Lord – A105, c/c243
We Receive from Your Fullness – A16, B16, C16, c/c256
We Shall Be Like You – A222, B221, C223, c/c257
You Are Light in the Lord – A40, B44, C44, c/c275

Loneliness
Do Not Abandon Me, Lord! – B186, C188, c/c47
Heaven and Earth Will Fade Away – A109, B194, c/c86
In Your Abundant Love – A126, c/c121
Let My Prayer Come Before You, Lord – A189, B189, C191, c/c134
Lord, You Are Close – A167, c/c152

Longing / Seeking / Thirsting
All Who Labor, Come to Me – A133, C204, C206, c/c8
All Your Sins Have Been Forgiven – C127, c/c10
Ask and Receive (I) – A143, c/c18
Ask and Receive (II) – C146, c/c19
Be Patient, Beloved – A9, c/c21
"Come," Says My Heart – B92, C92, c/c43
Come to Me and Drink – A94, B97, C97, c/c44
Come to Me and You Shall Never Hunger – A147, B148, c/c45
Do Not Abandon Me, Lord! – B186, C188, c/c47
Do Not Store Up Earthly Treasures – C149, C171, c/c48
Eat My Flesh and Drink My Blood – A236, B235, C237, c/c50
For You My Soul Is Thirsting – A158, C129, c/c56
Give Peace to Those Who Wait – A163, B165, C166, c/c60
Give Us Living Water – A37, B39, C39, c/c64
God, Come to My Aid (I) – C154, c/c67
God, Come to My Aid (II) – A144, B146, C147, c/c68
Happy Are They Who Dwell in Your House – A244, B38, C18, c/c81
How I Thirst for You – A235, B234, C236, c/c93
I Know I Shall See the Goodness of the Lord – A90, c/c100
In Your Abundant Love – A126, c/c121
Keep My Soul in Peace – A187, c/c128
Let My Prayer Come Before You, Lord – A189, B189, C191, c/c134
Let Your Love Be Upon Us, O Lord – A33, A80, B181, c/c138
Light of the World – A100, c/c140
Like a Deer That Longs for Running Streams – A59, B65, C65, c/c141
Like Newborn Children – A69, B74, C74, c/c142
Lord, Cleanse My Heart – A61, B46, C67, c/c149
Lord, Listen to My Prayer – A234, B233, C235, c/c150
Lord, This Is the People – A230, B229, C231, c/c151
My God, My Strength, Defend My Cause – A41, B45, C45, c/c161
One Thing I Seek – A122, B125, C125, c/c173
Open Your Hand, Lord – B145, c/c175
Remember, Lord – A170, c/c193
Save Me, O Lord – A117, c/c198
Save Us, Lord – B142, c/c201
Seek the Lord! Long for the Lord! – A32, A101, A182, B32, C32, c/c202
Shine Out, O Lord; You Are My God – B106, c/c205
Shine Your Face on Us, Lord – B78, c/c206
Speak Your Word, O Lord – C121, c/c212
The Lord Is My Light – A99, B122, C33, C122, c/c223
The Mercy of God Is for All – A153, c/c226
The Prayer of Our Hearts – C186, c/c229
To Gaze on Your Glory – A134, B137, C137, c/c245
Turn to Me, Answer Me – A154, B156, C156, c/c249
We Have Sinned, Lord – A30, B208, C167, c/c254

We Look to You, O Lord – B135, c/c255
We Shall Be Like You – A222, B221, C223, c/c257
With All My Heart I Cry (I) – A160, B162, c/c264
You Are Rich in Mercy – B177, C178, c/c280
You Will Show Me the Path of Life – B188, c/c287
You Will Show Us the Path of Life – A74, c/c287

Loss
Do Not Abandon Me, Lord! – B186, C188, c/c47
How I Thirst for You – A235, B234, C236, c/c93
In Your Abundant Love – A126, c/c121
Look on My Toil – A116, B119, C119, c/c148
Lord, Listen to My Prayer – A234, B233, C235, c/c150
My God, My God – A45, B51, C51, c/c160
O Let My Tongue Cleave to My Mouth – B41, c/c171
Turn to Me, Answer Me – A154, B156, C156, c/c249

Love for God
A New Commandment I Give to You – A49, B55, C55, c/c2
Ask and Receive (I) – A143, c/c18
Don't Be Afraid – A150, B133, C152, C196, c/c49
For Ever, For Ever, We Praise You For Ever – A200, c/c55
For You My Soul Is Thirsting – A158, C129, c/c56
I Love You, Lord – A183, c/c101
I Will Praise Your Name For Ever (I) – C84, c/c108
I Will Praise Your Name For Ever (II) – A132, C189, c/c109
I Will Sing For Ever of Your Love – A129, B11, c/c112
In God Alone Is My Soul at Rest – A114, c/c119
In the Presence of the Angels – C108, c/c120
Love Bears All Things – C106, c/c154
Love the Lord Your God – A112, A185, C140, c/c156
Proclaim the Wonders God Has Done – C99, c/c186
Those Who Do the Will of God – B124, c/c242
Those Who Love Me, I Will Deliver – C29, c/c244
To You, O Lord, I Lift My Soul – A1, B1, C2, c/c246
With All My Heart I Cry (II) – A142, c/c265
With All My Heart I Praise You – B115, c/c266
You Alone Are Lord – A181, c/c270

Love for Others
A New Commandment I Give to You – A49, B55, C55, c/c2
All That Is True – A175, c/c5
Ask and Receive (II) – A239, B238, C240, c/c19
Christ Laid Down His Life for Us – A172, B170, c/c35
Forgive, and You Will Be Forgiven – C115, c/c57
If You Love Me, Feed My Lambs (I) – C79, c/c115
If You Love Me, Feed My Lambs (II) – A219, B218, C220, c/c116
If You Will Love Each Other – A165, c/c117
Light of the World – A106, c/c140
Live on in My Love – A85, A91, B88, B94, C88, c/c147
Love Bears All Things – C106, c/c154
Love Is My Desire – A121, c/c155
Love the Lord Your God – A112, A185, C140, c/c156
Take Your Place at the Table – C177, c/c214
The Last Shall Be First – A168, c/c220
Those Who Do the Will of God – B124, c/c242
Those Who Fear the Lord – A105, c/c243
Where Two or Three Are Gathered – A162, c/c261
You Are God's Temple – A247, B246, C248, c/c273
You Are Light in the Lord – A40, B44, C44, c/c275

Love of God for Us

All Who Labor, Come to Me – A133, B204, C206, c/c8
All Your Sins Have Been Forgiven – C127, c/c10
As a Bridegroom Rejoices – A240, B239, C100, c/c14
Ask and Receive (I) – A143, c/c18
Behold, the Bridegroom Is Here (I) – B118, c/c24
Blest Are You Who Weep – C112, c/c30
Chosen in Christ, Blessed in Christ – B139, c/c33
Come to Me and You Shall Never Hunger – A147, B148, c/c45
Come, All You Good and Faithful Servants – A195, c/c39
Come, Lord, and Save Us – A8, c/c41
Come, My Children – B176, c/c42
Do Not Store Up Earthly Treasures – C171, c/c48
Don't Be Afraid – A150, B133, C152, C196, c/c49
Everlasting Is Your Love – A155, c/c51
Forgive, and You Will Be Forgiven – C115, c/c57
Go to the Ends of the Earth – C120, c/c66
God Feeds Us, God Saves Us – A115, C183, c/c69
God Heals the Broken – B109, C173, c/c71
God of Life, God of Hope – C193, c/c74
God's Love Is Revealed to Us – A15, B15, C28, c/c77
Heal Me in Your Mercy – B112, c/c84
Home for the Lonely – B143, C144, C161, c/c90
I Am the Way: Follow Me – A81, c/c96
I Am With You – C30, c/c97
I Shall Dwell in the House of the Lord – A177, c/c103
I Thank You, Lord, with All My Heart – C180, c/c104
I Will Praise Your Name For Ever (II) – A132, C189, c/c109
I Will Sing For Ever of Your Love – A129, B11, c/c112
If You Will Love Each Other – A165, c/c117
In the Presence of the Angels – C108, c/c120
In Your Abundant Love – A126, c/c121
Let All the Earth Adore and Praise You – A73, B98, C77, c/c133
Let All the Earth Cry Out Your Praises – A73, B77, C77, c/c133
Let Your Love Be Upon Us, O Lord – A33, A80, B181, c/c138
Like Newborn Children – A69, B74, C74, c/c142
Live on in My Love – A85, A91, B88, B94, C88, c/c147
Lord, You Are Close – A167, c/c152
Love Is My Desire – A121, c/c155
May God Grant Us Joy of Heart – A250, B249, C251, c/c158
Merciful and Tender – A111, A164, B117, C36, C114, C187, c/c159
My Lips Will Tell of Your Justice – C105, c/c163
My Sheep I Will Pasture – C208, c/c166
My Shepherd Is the Lord – A39, A233, B42, B82, B141, B191, B232, C82, C207, C234, c/c167
Open Your Hand, Lord – B145, c/c175
Our Help Shall Come from the Lord – C182, c/c180
Praise the Lord, Alleluia! – B108, c/c184
Praise to God Who Lifts Up the Poor – C170, c/c185
Remember, Lord – A170, c/c193
The Love of God – A92, B95, B200, C95, c/c225
The Mercy of God Is for All – A153, c/c226
The Strong Lord Sets Me Free – A184, B116, C116, c/c233
The Word of God at Work in Us – A188, c/c234
Those Who Do the Will of God – B124, c/c242
Those Who Love Me, I Will Deliver – C29, c/c244
When the Poor Cry Out – C185, c/c259
Where Two or Three Are Gathered – A162, c/c261
Within Your Temple – A131, B134, C134, c/c268
You Alone Are Lord – A181, c/c270

You Are Good and Forgiving – A138, c/c274
You Are Rich in Mercy – A68, A176, B43, c/c279
You Are the Shepherd – A78, c/c281
You Have Given Everything Its Place – A179, B174, C175, c/c283
You Have Shown You Love Us – A199, B198, C200, c/c284

Majesty / Power of God

All the Ends of the Earth – A14, B14, B87, C14, C179, c/c6
All Things Are from the Lord – A156, c/c7
All You Nations – A128, B131, C131, c/c9
At Your Word Our Hearts Are Burning – A75, c/c20
Bless the Lord, My Soul – C27, c/c27
Blessed Are You, Lord – A169, B171, c/c28
Cast Out into the Deep – C109, c/c31
Give Thanks to the Lord, Alleluia (II) – B129, c/c62
Give the Lord Power – A180, c/c63
God Feeds Us, God Saves Us – A115, C183, c/c69
God Goes Up with Shouts of Joy – A87, B90, C90, c/c70
Great In Our Midst Is the Holy One – C8, c/c79
How Wonderful Your Name, O Lord – C201, c/c94
I Love You, Lord – A183, c/c101
I Thank You, Lord, with All My Heart – C180, c/c104
I Will Praise Your Name For Ever (I) – C84, c/c108
I Will Praise Your Name For Ever (II) – A132, C189, c/c109
In Every Age, O Lord, You Have Been Our Refuge – C164, c/c118
Let All the Earth Adore and Praise You – A73, B98, C77, c/c133
Let All the Earth Cry Out Your Praises – A73, B77, C77, c/c133
Let the King of Glory Come In – A11, B211, B213, c/c135
Listen! Listen! Open Your Hearts! – A36, B37, C37, c/c144
O Praise the Lord, Jerusalem – A203, B151, c/c172
Praise the Lord, Alleluia! – B108, c/c184
Praise to God Who Lifts Up the Poor – C170, c/c185
Proclaim the Wonders God Has Done – C99, c/c186
Rejoice in the Lord, Again Rejoice! – A7, B7, C7, c/c189
Save Us, Lord – B128, C128, c/c200
Send Out Your Spirit – A52, B58, C58, c/c203
Shout to the Ends of the Earth – A89, B86, C86, c/c207
The Earth Is Full of the Goodness of God (I) – A76, B80, C80, c/c217
The Earth Is Full of the Goodness of God (II) – A53, B59, C59, c/c217
The Lord Is King (I) – A221, B220, C93, c/c221
The Lord Will Bless His People – A27, c/c224
This Is the Day – A66, B72, C72, c/c240
To Gaze on Your Glory – A134, B137, C137, c/c245
Walk in My Ways – B103, c/c253
Within Your Temple – A131, B134, C134, c/c268
You Alone Are Lord – A181, c/c270
You Are My Praise – B84, c/c277
You Have Given Everything Its Place – A179, B174, C175, c/c283
Yours Is the Day – B149, C150, c/c290

Mercy / Pity

All Your Sins Have Been Forgiven – C127, c/c10
Blest Are the Poor in Spirit – A102, A103, c/c29
From the Fullness of Our Hearts – C118, c/c59

Give Peace to Those Who Wait – A163, B165, C166, c/c60
God's Tender Mercy – B215, C217, c/c78
I Am Your Savior, My People – A166, B168, C169, c/c98
I Called in My Distress – A218, B217, C219, c/c99
Light of the World – A106, c/c140
Lord, Cleanse My Heart – A61, B46, C67, c/c149
Lord, You Are Close – A167, c/c152
May God Grant Us Joy of Heart – A250, B249, C251, c/c158
Merciful and Tender – A111, A164, B117, C36, C114, C187, c/c159
My Grace Is Enough – B136, c/c162
My Sheep I Will Pasture – C208, c/c166
Remember, Lord – A170, c/c193
Shine Out, O Lord; You Are My God – B106, c/c205
Shine Your Face on Us, Lord – B78, c/c206
Show Us, Lord, Your Kindness – A149, B5, c/c208
The Love of God – A92, B95, C95, c/c225
The Mercy of God Is for All – A153, c/c226
The Prayer of Our Hearts – C186, c/c229
There Is Mercy in the Lord – A42, B47, C47, c/c235
We Have Sinned, Lord – A30, B208, C167, c/c254
We Look to You, O Lord – B135, c/c255
You Are Good and Forgiving – A138, c/c274
You Are Rich in Mercy – A68, A176, A208, B43, B177, B207, C178, C209, c/c279–280
Your Mercy Is My Hope – A110, B113, C113, c/c288

Mission / Ministry

A New Commandment I Give to You – A49, B55, C55, c/c2
As One Body in Your Spirit – C103, c/c15
Because You Are Filled with the Spirit – B173, c/c23
Cast Out into the Deep – C109, c/c31
Chosen in Christ, Blessed in Christ – B139, c/c33
Christ Laid Down His Life for Us – A172, B170, c/c35
Give: Your Father Sees – A210, B209, C211, c/c65
Go to the Ends of the Earth – C120, c/c66
If You Love Me, Feed My Lambs (I) – C79, c/c115
If You Love Me, Feed My Lambs (II) – A219, B218, C220, c/c116
If You Will Love Each Other – A165, c/c117
Light of the World – A100, A106, c/c140
Live on in My Love – A85, A91, B88, B94, C88, c/c147
Love Bears All Things – C106, c/c154
Proclaim the Wonders God Has Done – C99, c/c186
The Greatest Among You – B182, c/c219
The Message Goes Forth – A98, B101, c/c227
Those Who Do Justice – A151, B160, C142, c/c241
Those Who Fear the Lord – A105, c/c243
Unless a Grain of Wheat – B48, c/c251
Where Two or Three Are Gathered – A162, c/c261
You Are Light in the Lord – A40, B44, C44, c/c275
You Are the Vine – A82, B85, c/c282
You Shall Be a Royal Priesthood – A124, c/c286

Morning / Evening / Night

All That Is True – A175, c/c5
All Things Are from the Lord – A156, c/c7
Arise, Jerusalem, Look to the East – A23, B23, C23, c/c13
Arise, Jerusalem, Stand on the Height – A4, B6, C4, c/c13
Christ Is the Light – A211, B210, C212, c/c34
Clothed in Christ, One in Christ – A28, B28, B69, C69, c/c38

Come, All You Good and Faithful Servants – A195, c/c39
Everlasting Is Your Love – A155, c/c51
For Ever, For Ever, We Praise You For Ever – A200, c/c55
Give Peace to Those Who Wait – A163, B165, C166, c/c60
Give Us Living Water – A37, B39, C39, c/c64
God's Tender Mercy – B215, C217, c/c78
How Wonderful Your Name, O Lord – C201, c/c94
I Am Your Savior, My People – A166, B168, C169, c/c98
If You Will Love Each Other – A165, c/c117
In Every Age, O Lord, You Have Been Our Refuge – C164, c/c118
It Is Good to Give You Thanks, O Lord – B126, C117, c/c122
Jesus, Mighty Lord, Come Save Us – A12, c/c124
Keep My Soul in Peace – A187, c/c128
Let My Prayer Come Before You, Lord – A189, B189, C191, c/c134
Listen! Listen! Open Your Hearts! – A36, B37, C37, c/c144
Listen, Listen to the Words of Jesus – A148, c/c146
May God Bless Us in Mercy – A21, B21, C21, c/c157
One Thing I Seek – A122, B125, C125, c/c173
Our City Has No Need of Sun or Moon – A25, B25, C25, c/c176
Our Help Shall Come from the Lord – A182, c/c180
Shine Your Face on Us, Lord – B78, c/c206
The Lord Is My Light – A99, B122, C33, C122, c/c223
This Day Is Holy to the Lord Our God – C101, c/c237
Those Who Love Me, I Will Deliver – A29, B29, C38, C29, c/c244
To You, O Lord, I Lift My Soul – A1, B1, C2, c/c246
Venite, Adoremus – A245, B107, C246, c/c252
When You Fill Us with Your Word – B178, C148, c/c260
Where Two or Three Are Gathered – A162, c/c261
With All My Heart I Cry (I) – A160, B162, c/c264
With All My Heart I Praise You – B115, c/c266
You Have Given Everything Its Place – A179, B174, C175, c/c283
Your Word Is Life, Lord – A58, B36, B64, C64, c/c289
Yours Is the Day – B149, C150, c/c290

Music

All the Ends of the Earth – A14, B14, B87, C14, C179, c/c6
All You Nations – A128, B131, C131, c/c9
From the Fullness of Our Hearts – C118, c/c59
God's Love Is Revealed to Us – A15, B15, C28, c/c77
It Is Good to Give You Thanks, O Lord – B126, C117, c/c122
Let All the Earth Adore and Praise You – A73, B98, C77, c/c133
Let the Word Make a Home in Your Heart – A19, B161, c/c136
People of God, Flock of the Lord – A123, C81, c/c182
Ring Out Your Joy – B120, c/c194
Sing and Make Music – A248, B247, C249, c/c209
Sing to God a New Song – A79, B83, C83, c/c210
The Earth Is Full of the Goodness of God (I) – A76, B80, C80, c/c217
The Earth Is Full of the Goodness of God (II) – A53, B59, C59, c/c217
When You Fill Us with Your Word – B178, C148, c/c260
With All My Heart I Praise You – B115, c/c266

Mystery of God

Because You Are Filled with the Spirit – B173, c/c23

Praise to God Who Lifts Up the Poor – C170, c/c185
Save Me, O Lord – A117, c/c198
Save Us, Lord – A125, B128, B142, C128, c/c199–201
Shine Out, O Lord; You Are My God – B106, c/c205
Shine Your Face on Us, Lord – B78, c/c206
Shout to the Ends of the Earth – A89, B86, C86, c/c207
Show Us, Lord, Your Kindness – A149, B5, c/c208
Sing and Make Music – A248, B247, C249, c/c209
The Goodness of the Lord – B150, C41, c/c218
The Lord Is My Light – A99, B122, C33, C122, c/c223
The Lord Will Bless His People – A27, c/c224
The Love of God – A92, B95, B200, C95, c/c225
The Strong Lord Sets Me Free – A184, B116, C116, c/c233
Those Who Love Me, I Will Deliver – A29, B29, C38, C29, c/c244
To Gaze on Your Glory – A134, B137, C137, c/c245
To You, O Lord, I Lift My Soul – A1, B1, C2, c/c246
When the Poor Cry Out – C185, c/c259
Who Can This Be – B130, c/c262
With All My Heart I Praise You – B115, c/c266
You Alone Are Lord – A181, c/c270
You Alone Are My Help – A137, B140, C141, c/c271
You Are Rich in Mercy – A68, B43, c/c279
You Are the Shepherd – A78, c/c281
You Open Your Hand – A127, B144, c/c285
Your Mercy Is My Hope – A110, B113, C113, c/c288
Yours Is the Day – B149, C150, c/c290

Redemption

All Your Sins Have Been Forgiven – C127, c/c10
Be Strong, Our God Has Come to Save Us (I) – B9, C9, c/c22
Be Strong, Our God Has Come to Save Us (II) – B164, c/c22
Behold, the Bridegroom Is Here (I) – B118, c/c24
Blest Are the Poor in Spirit – A102, c/c29
Blest Are You Who Weep – C112, c/c30
Change Your Heart and Mind – A171, c/c32
Chosen in Christ, Blessed in Christ – B139, c/c33
Christ Laid Down His Life for Us – A172, B170, c/c35
Clothed in Christ, One in Christ – A28, B28, c/c38
Come, Lord, and Save Us – A8, c/c41
Come, My Children – B176, c/c42
Don't Be Afraid – A150, B133, C152, C196, c/c49
Every Valley Shall Be Filled – C6, c/c52
God's Tender Mercy – B215, C217, c/c78
God, Come to My Aid (II) – A144, B146, C147, c/c68
Heal Me in Your Mercy – B112, c/c84
Heal My Soul – B114, c/c85
I Am the Way: Follow Me – A81, c/c96
I Called in My Distress – A218, B217, C219, c/c99
I Will Praise You, Lord – A56, B62, C62, C78, c/c107
Keep Us in Your Name – B127, C94, c/c130
Laughter Fills Our Mouths – B184, C5, c/c131
Lead Me, Guide Me – A107, B110, C110, c/c132
Let All the Earth Adore and Praise You – A73, B98, C77, c/c133
Let All the Earth Cry Out Your Praises – A73, B77, C77, c/c133
Love Is My Desire – A121, c/c155
Merciful and Tender – A111, A164, B117, C36, C114, C187, c/c159
My Plans for You Are Peace – A193, B192, C194, c/c164

My Sheep I Will Pasture – C208, c/c166
My Soul Rejoices in God – A225, B8, B224, C12, C226, c/c168
Open Your Hand, Lord – B145, c/c175
Our Shelter and Our Help – C124, c/c181
Praise the Lord, Alleluia! – B108, c/c184
Rejoice, Your Names Are Written in Heaven – C136, c/c192
Remember, Lord – A170, c/c193
Shine Out, O Lord; You Are My God – B106, c/c205
Shout to the Ends of the Earth – A89, B86, C86, c/c207
Take Hold of Eternal Life – C174, c/c213
The Days Are Coming, Surely Coming – C1, c/c216
The Love of God – B200, c/c225
The Mercy of God Is for All – A153, c/c226
The Spirit and the Bride Say "Come!" – A231, B230, C232, c/c231
There Is Mercy in the Lord – A42, B47, C47, c/c235
Those Who Love Me, I Will Deliver – C29, c/c244
Turn Our Hearts from Stone to Flesh – A35, B35, C35, c/c248
Turn to the Lord – B111, C126, c/c250
Who Can This Be – B130, c/c262
With All My Heart I Praise You – B115, c/c266
You Alone Are My Help – A137, B140, C141, c/c271
You Are My Hiding-Place, O Lord – C48, c/c276
You Are Rich in Mercy – A176, A208, B177, B207, C178, C209, c/c279–280
You Are the Shepherd – A78, c/c281

Refuge

A River Flows – A238, B237, C239, c/c3
All Who Labor, Come to Me – A133, B204, C206, c/c8
Blest Are the Poor in Spirit – A102, c/c29
Cast Out into the Deep – C109, c/c31
"Come," Says My Heart – B92, C92, c/c43
Come to Me and You Shall Never Hunger – A147, B148, c/c45
Do Not Store Up Earthly Treasures – C149, C171, c/c48
Don't Be Afraid – A150, B133, C152, C196, c/c49
God, Come to My Aid (I) – C154, c/c67
God, Come to My Aid (II) – A144, B146, C147, c/c68
God, Who Raised Jesus from the Dead – A232, B231, C233, c/c76
Happy Are They Who Dwell in Your House – A244, B38, C18, c/c81
Home for the Lonely – B143, C144, C161, c/c90
I Am Your Savior, My People – A166, B168, C169, c/c98
I Know I Shall See the Goodness of the Lord – A90, c/c100
I Love You, Lord – A183, c/c101
I Shall Dwell in the House of the Lord – A177, c/c103
In Every Age, O Lord, You Have Been Our Refuge – C164, c/c118
In God Alone Is My Soul at Rest – A114, c/c119
Keep My Soul in Peace – A187, c/c128
Lead Me, Guide Me – A107, B110, C110, c/c132
Let Your Love Be Upon Us, O Lord – A33, A80, B181, c/c138
My Lips Will Tell of Your Justice – C105, c/c163
My Portion and My Cup – A54, B60, B193, C60, C132, c/c165
One Thing I Seek – A122, B125, C125, c/c173
Our Help Shall Come from the Lord – C182, c/c180
Our Shelter and Our Help – C124, c/c181
Save Me, O Lord – A117, c/c198
Save Us, Lord – A125, c/c199

Shine Out, O Lord; You Are My God – B106, c/c205
The Lord Is My Light – A99, B122, C33, C122, c/c223
The Strong Lord Sets Me Free – A184, B116, C116, c/c233
To Gaze on Your Glory – A134, B137, C137, c/c245
We Will Follow You, Lord – C133, c/c258
When the Poor Cry Out – C185, c/c259
Who Can This Be – B130, c/c262
You Alone Are My Help – A137, B140, C141, c/c271
You Are My Hiding-Place, O Lord – C48, c/c276
You Open Your Hand – A127, B144, c/c285
You Will Show Me the Path of Life – B188, c/c287
You Will Show Us the Path of Life – A74, c/c287

Rest
Here in Your Presence – B121, c/c88
I Shall Dwell in the House of the Lord – A177, c/c103
In God Alone Is My Soul at Rest – A114, c/c119
My Portion and My Cup – A54, B60, B193, C60, C132, c/c165
My Sheep I Will Pasture – C208, c/c166
My Shepherd Is the Lord – A39, A233, B42, B82, B141, B191,
    B232, C82, C207, C234, c/c167
Sing to the Lord – A55, B61, C61, c/c211

Salvation
All the Ends of the Earth – A14, B14, B87, C14, C179, c/c6
All Who Labor, Come to Me – A133, B204, C206, c/c8
As a Bridegroom Rejoices – A240, B239, B100, c/c14
Ask and Receive (II) – C146, c/c19
Be Patient, Beloved – A9, c/c21
Be Strong, Our God Has Come to Save Us (I) – B9, C9, c/c22
Be Strong, Our God Has Come to Save Us (II) – B164, c/c22
Behold the Lamb of God! – A97, B100, c/c26
Behold, the Bridegroom Is Here (I) – B118, c/c24
Blest Are the Poor in Spirit – A102, c/c29
Cast Out into the Deep – C109, c/c31
Chosen in Christ, Blessed in Christ – B139, c/c33
Come, All You Good and Faithful Servants – A195, c/c39
Come, Lord, and Save Us – A8, c/c41
Do Not Abandon Me, Lord! – B186, C188, c/c47
Don't Be Afraid – A150, B133, C152, C196, c/c49
Give Us Living Water – A37, B39, C39, c/c64
God Feeds Us, God Saves Us – A115, C183, c/c69
God Heals the Broken – B109, C173, c/c71
God of Hosts, Bring Us Back – B2, C11, c/c73
God of Life, God of Hope – C193, c/c74
God's Love Is Revealed to Us – A15, B15, C28, c/c77
God, Come to My Aid (II) – A144, B146, C147, c/c68
God, Who Raised Jesus from the Dead – A232, B231, C233,
    c/c76
Great In Our Midst Is the Holy One – C8, c/c79
Happy Are They Whose God Is the Lord – C151, c/c83
Heal Me in Your Mercy – B112, c/c84
Heal My Soul – B114, c/c85
Home for the Lonely – B143, C144, C161, c/c90
I Am the Way: Follow Me – A81, c/c96
I Am With You – C30, c/c97
I Am Your Savior, My People – A166, B168, B169, c/c98
I Love You, Lord – A183, c/c101
I Thank You, Lord, with All My Heart – C180, c/c104
I Will Dwell with You – A237, B236, B238, c/c105
I Will Praise You, Lord – A56, B62, C62, C78, c/c107

I Will Show God's Salvation – A120, c/c111
In the Presence of the Angels – C108, c/c120
Jesus, Mighty Lord, Come Save Us – A12, c/c124
Joyfully You Will Draw Water – A57, B27, B205, C63, c/c126
Keep My Soul in Peace – A187, c/c128
Keep Us in Your Name – B127, C94, c/c130
Laughter Fills Our Mouths – B184, C5, c/c131
Lead Me, Guide Me – A107, B110, C110, c/c132
Lose Your Life and Save It – A228, B167, B227, C130, c/c153
Love Is My Desire – A121, c/c155
May God Grant Us Joy of Heart – A250, B249, C251, c/c158
My God, My Strength, Defend My Cause – A41, B45, C45,
    c/c161
My Lips Will Tell of Your Justice – C105, c/c163
My Plans for You Are Peace – A193, B192, C194, c/c164
My Portion and My Cup – A54, B60, B193, C60, C132, c/c165
My Sheep I Will Pasture – C208, c/c166
My Shepherd Is the Lord – A39, A233, B42, B82, B141, B191,
    B232, C82, C207, C234, c/c167
Our Help Shall Come from the Lord – C182, c/c180
Praise to God Who Lifts Up the Poor – C170, c/c185
Raise the Cup of Salvation – B202, c/c188
Rise Up and Tell All Your Children – A227, B226, C228,
    c/c195
Salvation Has Come to This House – C190, c/c197
Save Me, O Lord – A117, c/c198
Save Us, Lord – A125, B128, B142, C128, c/c199–201
Shine Out, O Lord; You Are My God – B106, c/c205
Show Us, Lord, Your Kindness – A149, B5, c/c208
Sing to God a New Song – A79, B83, C83, c/c210
Speak Your Word, O Lord – C121, c/c212
Take Hold of Eternal Life – C174, c/c213
The Love of God – B200, c/c225
The Mercy of God Is for All – A153, c/c226
The Spirit and the Bride Say "Come!" – A231, B230, C232,
    c/c231
The Strong Lord Sets Me Free – A184, B116, C116, c/c233
Those Who Love Me, I Will Deliver – A29, B29, C29, C38,
    c/c244
Turn Our Hearts from Stone to Flesh – A35, B35, C35, c/c248
We Receive from Your Fullness – A16, B16, C16, c/c256
We Shall Be Like You – A222, B221, C223, c/c257
When the Poor Cry Out – C185, c/c259
You Alone Are Lord – A181, c/c270
You Alone Are My Help – A137, B140, C141, c/c271
You Are Rich in Mercy – A176, c/c279
You Will Show Me the Path of Life – B188, c/c287
You Will Show Us the Path of Life – A74, c/c287
Your Mercy Is My Hope – A110, B113, C113, c/c288

Second Coming
Arise, Jerusalem, Look to the East – A23, B23, C23, c/c13
Arise, Jerusalem, Stand on the Height – A4, B6, C4, c/c13
At Your Word Our Hearts Are Burning – A75, c/c20
Be Patient, Beloved – A9, c/c21
Be Strong, Our God Has Come to Save Us (I) – B9, C9, c/c22
Be Strong, Our God Has Come to Save Us (II) – B164, c/c22
Behold, the Bridegroom Is Here (II) – A192, B3, c/c25
Clothed in Christ, One in Christ – A28, B28, B69, C69, c/c38
Come, Lord, and Save Us – A8, c/c41
Every Valley Shall Be Filled – C6, c/c52

Heaven and Earth Will Fade Away – A109, B194, c/c86
I Am the Resurrection – A43, B49, C49, c/c95
I Will Dwell with You – A237, B236, C238, c/c105
I Will See You Again – A88, B91, C91, c/c110
Jesus, Mighty Lord, Come Save Us – A12, c/c124
Let the King of Glory Come In – A11, B211, C213, c/c135
Lift Up Your Heads, Stand and Believe – C3, c/c139
My Plans for You Are Peace – A193, B192, C194, c/c164
My Portion and My Cup – A54, B60, B193, C60, C132, c/c165
Our City Has No Need of Sun or Moon – A25, B25, C25, c/c176
Sing to the Lord – A55, B61, C61, c/c211
Take Hold of Eternal Life – C174, c/c213
The Days Are Coming, Surely Coming – C1, c/c216
They Shall Adore You – A24, B24, C24, c/c236
We Receive from Your Fullness – A16, B16, C16, c/c256
Why Stare into the Sky? – A86, B89, C89, c/c263
Worthy Is the Lamb Who Was Slain – A196, B195, C197, c/c269

Sin and Temptation
All Your Sins Have Been Forgiven – C127, c/c10
Change Your Heart and Mind – A171, c/c32
Do Not Abandon Me, Lord! – B186, C188, c/c47
Heal My Soul – B114, c/c85
Like a Deer That Longs for Running Streams – A59, B65, C65, c/c141
Lord, Cleanse My Heart – A61, B46, C67, c/c149
Remember, Lord – A170, c/c193
Those Who Love Me, I Will Deliver – A29, B29, C38, C29, c/c244
Turn Our Hearts from Stone to Flesh – A35, B35, C35, c/c248
Turn to the Lord – B111, C126, c/c250
We Have Sinned, Lord – A30, B208, C167, c/c254
You Are My Hiding-Place, O Lord – C48, c/c276
You Are Rich in Mercy – B177, C178, c/c280

Social Concern and Justice
A New Commandment I Give to You – A49, B55, C55, c/c2
Be Patient, Beloved – A9, c/c21
Blest Are the Poor in Spirit – A102, c/c29
Blest Are You Who Weep – C112, c/c30
Forgive, and You Will Be Forgiven – C115, c/c57
Give: Your Father Sees – A210, B209, C211, c/c65
God Heals the Broken – B109, C173, c/c71
Home for the Lonely – B143, C144, C161, c/c90
If You Love Me, Feed My Lambs (I) – C79, c/c115
If You Love Me, Feed My Lambs (II) – A219, B218, C220, c/c116
Justice Shall Flourish – A5, c/c127
Light of the World – A106, c/c140
Live on in My Love – A85, A91, B88, B94, C88, c/c147
My Soul Rejoices in God – A225, B8, B224, C12, C226, c/c168
Now Is the Hour – A3, c/c170
Praise to God Who Lifts Up the Poor – C170, c/c185
Take Your Place at the Table – C177, c/c214
The Days Are Coming, Surely Coming – C1, c/c216
The Greatest Among You – B182, c/c219
Those Who Do Justice – A151, B160, C142, c/c241
Those Who Do the Will of God – B124, c/c242
Those Who Fear the Lord – A105, c/c243

Those Who Love Me, I Will Deliver – C29, c/c244
When the Poor Cry Out – C185, c/c259
You Are Light in the Lord – A40, B44, C44, c/c275
Yours Is the Day – B149, C150, c/c290

Thanksgiving / Harvest
All Things Are from the Lord – A156, c/c7
All You Nations – A128, B131, C131, c/c9
Come, All You Good and Faithful Servants – A195, c/c39
Everlasting Is Your Love – A155, c/c51
Finest Food! Choicest Wine! – A178, c/c54
For Ever, For Ever, We Praise You For Ever – A200, c/c55
From the East and West, from the North and South – A186, C158, c/c58
Give Thanks to the Lord, Alleluia (I) – A70, c/c61
Give Thanks to the Lord, Alleluia (II) – B129, c/c62
How Wonderful Your Name, O Lord – C201, c/c94
I Thank You, Lord, with All My Heart – C180, c/c104
In the Presence of the Angels – C108, c/c120
It Is Good to Give You Thanks, O Lord – B126, C117, c/c122
Jesus Christ, the Same Today, Yesterday and Evermore – A22, B22, C22, c/c123
Laughter Fills Our Mouths – B184, C5, c/c131
Let All the Earth Adore and Praise You – A73, B98, C77, c/c133
Let All the Earth Cry Out Your Praises – A73, B77, C77, c/c133
May God Grant Us Joy of Heart – A250, B249, C251, c/c158
Merciful and Tender – A111, A164, B117, C36, C114, C187, c/c159
O Praise the Lord, Jerusalem – A203, B151, c/c172
Our God Has Blessed Us – A249, B248, C250, c/c179
People of God, Flock of the Lord – A123, C81, c/c182
Sing and Make Music – A248, B247, C249, c/c209
The Earth Is Full of the Goodness of God (I) – A76, B80, C80, c/c217
The Earth Is Full of the Goodness of God (II) – A53, B59, C59, c/c217
The Love of God – A92, A95, C95, c/c225
This Day Is Holy to the Lord Our God – C101, c/c237
This Is the Day – A66, B72, C72, c/c240

Truth
All That Is True – A175, c/c5
I Am the Way: Follow Me – A81, c/c96
Teach Me Your Path – B30, c/c215
We Receive from Your Fullness – A16, B16, C16, c/c256
With All My Heart I Cry (II) – A142, c/c265

Water
A River Flows – A238, B237, C239, c/c3
Come to Me and Drink – A94, B97, C97, c/c44
Come to Me and You Shall Never Hunger – A147, B148, c/c45
For You My Soul Is Thirsting – A158, C129, c/c56
Give Us Living Water – A37, B39, C39, c/c64
How I Thirst for You – A235, B234, C236, c/c93
I Will Dwell with You – A237, B236, C238, c/c105
Joyfully You Will Draw Water – A57, B27, B205, C63, c/c126
Like a Deer That Longs for Running Streams – A59, B65, C65, c/c141
Lord, Cleanse My Heart – A61, B46, C67, c/c149

Welcome / Hospitality

All That Is True – A175, c/c5

Come, All You Good and Faithful Servants – A195, c/c39

Come, Come to the Banquet – A146, C43, c/c40

From the East and West, from the North and South – A186, C158, c/c58

Home for the Lonely – B143, C144, C161, c/c90

If You Love Me, Feed My Lambs (I) – C79, c/c115

If You Will Love Each Other – A165, c/c117

Let Us Go Rejoicing – A2, B245, C198, c/c137

Light of the World – A106, c/c140

Listen: I Stand at the Door and Knock – A140, C143, c/c143

Now Is the Hour – A3, c/c170

Rejoice, Rejoice, All You Who Love Jerusalem! – A38, B40, C40, c/c191

Take Your Place at the Table – C177, c/c214

Where Two or Three Are Gathered – A162, c/c261

Wisdom

I Loved Wisdom More Than Health or Beauty – A141, B179, C163, c/c102

In Every Age, O Lord, You Have Been Our Refuge – C164, c/c118

Listen: I Stand at the Door and Knock – A140, C143, c/c143

Lose Your Life and Save It – C165, c/c153

When You Fill Us with Your Word – B178, C148, c/c260

With All My Heart I Cry (II) – A142, c/c265

Witness

Because You Are Filled with the Spirit – B173, c/c23

Christ Laid Down His Life for Us – A172, B170, c/c35

Don't Be Afraid – A150, B133, C152, C196, c/c49

Go to the Ends of the Earth – C120, c/c66

Here I Am – A96, B99, C107, c/c87

I Will Sing For Ever of Your Love – A129, B11, c/c112

Light of the World – A100, c/c140

Live on in My Love – A85, A91, B88, B94, C88, c/c147

My Lips Will Tell of Your Justice – C105, c/c163

Proclaim the Wonders God Has Done – C99, c/c186

Rejoice, Your Names Are Written in Heaven – C136, c/c192

Set the Earth on Fire – C155, c/c204

Shout to the Ends of the Earth – A89, B86, C86, c/c207

The Message Goes Forth – A98, B101, c/c227

The Word of God at Work in Us – A188, c/c234

Those Who Do Justice – A151, B160, C142, c/c241

Those Who Fear the Lord – A105, c/c243

You Are Light in the Lord – A40, B44, C44, c/c275

You Shall Be a Royal Priesthood – A124, c/c286

Word of God

As One Body in Your Spirit – C103, c/c15

As Seed for the Sowing – A136, A139, c/c16–17

At Your Word Our Hearts Are Burning – A75, c/c20

God Feeds Us, God Saves Us – A115, C183, c/c69

Happy Are They Whose God Is the Lord – B199, c/c83

Heaven and Earth Will Fade Away – A109, B194, c/c86

Let the Word Make a Home in Your Heart – A19, B161, c/c136

Listen, Listen to the Voice of Jesus – A198, B197, c/c145

Not on Bread Alone Are We Nourished – A31, C31, c/c169

Speak Your Word, O Lord – C121, c/c212

The Earth Is Full of the Goodness of God (I) – A76, B80, C80, c/c217

The Earth Is Full of the Goodness of God (II) – A53, B59, C59, c/c217

The Message Goes Forth – A98, B101, c/c227

The Seed That Falls on the Good Ground – A135, c/c230

The Word of God at Work in Us – A188, c/c234

Walk in My Ways – B31, c/c253

When You Fill Us with Your Word – B178, C148, c/c260

With All My Heart I Cry (II) – A142, c/c265

Your Word Is Life, Lord – A58, B36, B64, B158, C64, c/c289

For each Sunday and solemnity, this index designates which song is intended to serve as the Song for the Week, the Song for the Word, and the Song for the Table. The numbers given refer to the Cantor/Choir edition only.

Liturgical Day	Liturgical Year/Cycle	Song for the Week	Song for the Word	Song for the Table
First Sunday of Advent	A	246	137	170
	B	246	73	25
	C	216	246	139
Second Sunday of Advent	A	13	127	78
	B	73	208	13
	C	13	131	52
Third Sunday of Advent	A	189	41	21
	B	189	168	22
	C	189	79	22
Fourth Sunday of Advent	A	174	135	124
	B	174	112	168
	C	174	73	168
Christmas	ABC	1	6 or 77	256
Holy Family	A	77	92	136
	B	1	75	256
	C	1	81	77
Mary, Mother of God	ABC	1	157	123
Epiphany	ABC	13	236	176
Baptism of the Lord	A	89	224	38
	B	89	126	38
	C	89	27	77
First Sunday of Lent	A	244	254	169
	B	244	215	253
	C	244	97	169
Second Sunday of Lent	A	202	138	89
	B	202	113	89
	C	202	223	89
Third Sunday of Lent	A	248	144	64
	B	248	289 or 144	81 or 64
	C	248	159 or 144	244 or 64
Fourth Sunday of Lent	A	191	167	275
	B	191	171 or 167	279 or 275
	C	191	218 or 167	40 or 275
Fifth Sunday of Lent	A	161	235	95
	B	161	149 or 235	251 or 95
	C	161	131 or 235	276 or 95
Palm Sunday of the Lord's Passion	ABC	91	160	114

The Sacred Triduum

Liturgical Day	Place / Use	Number
Holy Thursday	Entrance Song	178
	Song for the Word	177
	Song for the Washing of Feet	2
	Song for the Table	238
Good Friday	Song for the Word	53
Easter Vigil	Response I	203 or 217
	Response II	165
	Response III	211
	Response IV	107
	Response V	126
	Response VI	289
	Response VII	141 or 126 or 149
	Epistle Response	11
	Baptismal Acclamation	38
	Song for the Table	36
Easter Sunday	Song for the Week	37
	Song for the Word	240
	Song for the Table	36

Liturgical Day	Liturgical Year/Cycle	Song for the Week	Song for the Word	Song for the Table
Second Sunday of Easter	A	279 or 142	61	247 or 187
	B	142	11	187
	C	142	11	187
Third Sunday of Easter	A	133	287	20
	B	133	206	247
	C	133	107	115
Fourth Sunday of Easter	A	217	167	281
	B	217	232	167
	C	217	182	167
Fifth Sunday of Easter	A	210	138	96 or 282
	B	210	277	282
	C	210	108	2
Sixth Sunday of Easter	A	207	133	147
	B	207	6	147
	C	207	72	147
The Ascension of the Lord	ABC	263	70	110
Seventh Sunday of Easter	A	207	100	147
	B	43	110	147
	C	43	221	130
Pentecost Sunday	ABC	225	12	44

Liturgical Day	Liturgical Year/Cycle	Song for the Week	Song for the Word	Song for the Table
Second Sunday in Ordinary Time	A	133	87	26
	B	133	87	26
	C	133	186	14
Third Sunday in Ordinary Time	A	227	223	140
	B	227	215	253
	C	237	289	15
Fourth Sunday in Ordinary Time	A	202	29	29
	B	202	144	205
	C	244	163	154
Fifth Sunday in Ordinary Time	A	252	243	140
	B	252	184	71
	C	87	120	31
Sixth Sunday in Ordinary Time	A	132	82	86
	B	132	250	84
	C	132	183	30
Seventh Sunday in Ordinary Time	A	288	159	156
	B	288	85	266
	C	288	159	57
Eighth Sunday in Ordinary Time	A	233	119	69
	B	233	159	24
	C	233	122	59
Ninth Sunday in Ordinary Time	A	148	198	129
	B	148	194	88
	C	148	66	212
Tenth Sunday in Ordinary Time	A	223	111	155
	B	223	235	242
	C	223	107	181
Eleventh Sunday in Ordinary Time	A	173	182	286
	B	173	122	130
	C	173	250	10
Twelfth Sunday in Ordinary Time	A	199	121	285
	B	200	62	262
	C	200	56	153
Thirteenth Sunday in Ordinary Time	A	9	112	153
	B	9	107	49
	C	9	165	258
Fourteenth Sunday in Ordinary Time	A	268	109	8
	B	268	255	162
	C	268	133	192
Fifteenth Sunday in Ordinary Time	A	245	230	16
	B	245	208	33
	C	245 or 123	289	156
Sixteenth Sunday in Ordinary Time	A	271	274	17 or 143
	B	271	167	201
	C	271	241	143
Seventeenth Sunday in Ordinary Time	A	102	265	19
	B	90	285	175
	C	90	120	19
Eighteenth Sunday in Ordinary Time	A	68	285	40 or 45
	B	68	239	45
	C	68	260	48

Liturgical Day	Liturgical Year/Cycle	Song for the Week	Song for the Word	Song for the Table
Nineteenth Sunday in Ordinary Time	A	146	208	49
	B	290	218	172
	C	290	83	49
Twentieth Sunday in Ordinary Time	A	241	72	226
	B	81	218	235 or 239
	C	288	67	204
Twenty-first Sunday in Ordinary Time	A	249	51	7
	B	249	218	289
	C	249	66	58
Twenty-second Sunday in Ordinary Time	A	249	56	153
	B	249	241	136
	C	9 or 249	90	58
Twenty-third Sunday in Ordinary Time	A	264	144	261
	B	264	172	22
	C	102	118	153
Twenty-fourth Sunday in Ordinary Time	A	60	159	117
	B	60	113	153
	C	60	254	40
Twenty-fifth Sunday in Ordinary Time	A	98	152	220
	B	98	271	35
	C	98	185	48
Twenty-sixth Sunday in Ordinary Time	A	28	193	32 or 35
	B	28	227	23
	C	202	71	213
Twenty-seventh Sunday in Ordinary Time	A	283	228	5
	B	283	92	42
	C	283	144	214
Twenty-eighth Sunday in Ordinary Time	A	279	103	54
	B	280	260	102
	C	280	6	104
Twenty-ninth Sunday in Ordinary Time	A	283	63	270
	B	80	138	219
	C	80	180	69
Thirtieth Sunday in Ordinary Time	A	202	101	233 or 156
	B	202	131	46
	C	202	259	229
Thirty-first Sunday in Ordinary Time	A	58	128	234
	B	47	233	287
	C	159 or 47	109	197
Thirty-second Sunday in Ordinary Time	A	134 or 102	56	25
	B	134	184 or 172	167
	C	134	245	74
Thirty-third Sunday in Ordinary Time	A	164	92	39
	B	164	165	86
	C	164	216	49
Christ the King	A	269	167	145
	B	269	222	145
	C	269	137	123

Solemnities and Feasts of the Lord and the Saints	Liturgical Year/Cycle	Song for the Day	Song for the Word	Song for the Table
The Most Holy Trinity	A	284	55	225
	B	284	83	225
	C	284	94	225
The Most Holy Body and Blood of Christ	A	267	172	238
	B	267	188	238
	C	267	272	238
The Most Sacred Heart of Jesus	A	2	159	8
	B	8	126	44
	C	8	167	166
Presentation of the Lord (February 2)	ABC	34	135	34
The Nativity of Saint John the Baptist (June 24)	ABC	125	106	78
Saints Peter and Paul, Apostles (June 29)	ABC	278	99	116
The Transfiguration of the Lord (August 6)	ABC	89	221	257
Assumption of the Blessed Virgin Mary (August 15)	ABC	4	196	168
Exaltation of the Holy Cross (September 14)	ABC	178	195	153
All Saints (November 1)	ABC	190	151	231
All Souls (November 2)	ABC	76	167 or 150 or 93	50
Dedication of the Lateran Basilica (November 9)	ABC	105	3	19
The Immaculate Conception of the Blessed Virgin Mary (December 8)	ABC	14	210	168
Other Liturgies				
Ash Wednesday	ABC	280	254	65
Anniversary of the Dedication of a Church	ABC	268	81 or 252 or 137	273
Thanksgiving Day	ABC	209	179	158